T0291152

Transforming Government Organizations

Fresh Ideas and Examples From the Field

A Volume in
Contemporary Human Resources Management
Issues, Challenges and Opportunities

Series Editor
Ronald R. Sims, *College of William and Mary*

Contemporary Human Resources Management Issues, Challenges and Opportunities

Ronald R. Sims, Series Editor

Transforming Government Organizations

Fresh Ideas and Examples From the Field

Edited by

Ronald R. Sims
College of William and Mary

William I. Sauser, Jr.
Harbert College of Business
Auburn University

Sheri Bias
Saint Leo University

INFORMATION AGE PUBLISHING, INC.
Charlotte, NC • www.infoagepub.com

Library of Congress Cataloging-in-Publication Data

Record for this book is available from the Library of Congress
http://www.loc.gov

ISBN: 978-1-68123-455-7 (Paperback)
       978-1-68123-456-4 (Hardcover)
       978-1-68123-457-1 (ebook)

Printed in the United States of America

CONTENTS

LISTS OF TABLES
AND FIGURES

TABLES

Transforming Government Organizations:
Fresh Ideas and Examples From the Field, pp. vii–ix
Copyright © 2016 by Information Age Publishing

FIGURES

ACKNOWLEDGMENTS

We are indebted to George F. Johnson at Information Age Publishing, who once again has provided the collective outlet for our ideas. A most deserved thank you and acknowledgment goes to our top-notch group of contributors. Without their collective professional and personal efforts, based upon their own experiences with local, state and federal agencies in government organizations as practitioners, academics, and researchers the transformation challenge issues, opportunities, and learnings discussed in this book would not be available for the readers. We believe that when reading through the impressive content of their chapters you will wholeheartedly agree that they have made a significant contribution to the overall government transformation field. We are indebted to them all as colleagues and friends.

Ronald R. Sims Acknowledgment

A very special thanks goes to my coeditor Sheri Bias and a very, very special thanks goes to my colleague, friend and coeditor, William I. Sauser, Jr. This book marks a little more than 30 years of our working together and of my being able to count Bill as one of my true and inspiring friends. Bill thanks for your warmth, positive outlook, and hard work—you have always made working with you a joy. I also want to thank Herrington Bryce who continues to serve as my colleague, mentor and valued friend. The

Transforming Government Organizations:
Fresh Ideas and Examples From the Field, pp. xi–xii
Copyright © 2016 by Information Age Publishing
All rights of reproduction in any form reserved.

administrative support of the Raymond A. Mason School of Business at the College of William and Mary is also acknowledged.

Thanks and appreciation goes to my children who have always been my source of motivation.

William I. Sauser, Jr. Acknowledgment

It is always a pleasure to work with my friend Ron Sims in editing these professional reference volumes, and I am delighted that we invited Sheri Bias to join us in the present endeavor. Sheri's work added considerably to the quality of this volume. I am grateful for the fine work of our colleagues as they prepared the chapters contained herein. It is our sincere hope that the ideas we share in this volume aid others to lead successful efforts to change/transform public sector organizations. Encouragement from George Johnson throughout this project and the skill of the professional staff of Information Age Publishing in assembling the final product is greatly appreciated. I am indebted to my many colleagues at Auburn University for their friendship and support throughout my long and happy career as a professor and administrator there; War Eagle! To my amazing wife Lane I give my thanks for her continuous encouragement, support, and love.

My work on this volume is dedicated to Dr. Ronald R. Sims, a man whose life and work has really made a positive difference in this world.

Sheri Bias Acknowledgment

A big thank you goes to Information Age Publishing for allowing us the creative outlet for our efforts in this text as without them, none of this would have been possible. I am also grateful for my coeditors William Sauser and Ronald Sims for their valued mentoring during this project. It has been amazing to work with Ron as a colleague in the realm of human resources for so many years. I would also like to acknowledge the support of the Donald R. Tapia School of Business at Saint Leo University. This book is dedicated to my husband, Jim, and son Justin.

CHAPTER 1

AN INTRODUCTION TO TRANSFORMING GOVERNMENT ORGANIZATIONS

Fresh Ideas and Examples From the Field

Ronald R. Sims, William I. Sauser, Jr., and Sheri Bias

INTRODUCTION

In 2010 Information Age Publishing, released *Change (Transformation) in Government Organizations*, edited by Ronald R. Sims. This well-received volume described how organizational change methods can be used successfully to make government organizations more effective and efficient and better equipped to serve a demanding citizenry. The 2010 book brought together contributions by managers, practitioners, academics, and consultants in the study of international, federal, state, and local government efforts to respond to increased calls for change (transformation) in public sector organizations.

Since the release of the 2010 volume, calls for government transformation have continued and intensified, and a number of fresh ideas and

Transforming Government Organizations:
Fresh Ideas and Examples From the Field, pp. 1–30
Copyright © 2016 by Information Age Publishing

examples have been generated from the field. The time is now ripe for a follow-up volume laying out innovative, successful ideas for transforming government. *Transforming Government Organizations: Fresh Ideas and Examples From the Field* is that follow-up volume. It is our belief that the collection of fresh contributions such as those included in this book will add to the growing knowledge base of what does—and what does *not*—work when transformation efforts are attempted in government organizations.

The purpose of this chapter is to assist public sector managers and leaders in preparing for, initiating and implementing change efforts by highlighting the uniqueness of public sector organizations to include discussing some of the differences between public and private sector organizations. By identifying and understanding change and change measurement in public-sector organizations, public sector change leaders will increase the likelihood of successfully analyzing and adjusting their strategies and processes accordingly and to navigate the perilous change course. However, we believe that there is an increased likelihood of successful reform, change or transformation in the public sector by answering the question: What is the difference between public and private sector organizations? And this is especially important as there are continued efforts and demands for turning to the private sector as a benchmark for addressing many of the so called "ills or inefficiencies" in public sector organizations.

Change, transformation, or reform initiatives at the national, state, and local levels continue to sweep through governments in the United States and other countries, again and again. The reality is, public sector organizational change is inevitable. One need only consider the numerous efforts under Presidents Bill Clinton, George W. Bush and Barack Obama to reinvent, transform, or reform government in the U.S. over the past 3 decades. For example, under President Clinton, reinvention of government efforts were driven by a series of U.S. federal legislation action—most notably the Government Performance and Reform Act of 1993 (GPRA; Public Law 103-62). The executive branch, in the recommendations from the National Performance Review (NPR), initiated a new era of efforts to bring about change in government. Under the leadership of Vice President Gore the NPR called for national agencies to transform themselves into high-quality low-cost service, and outlined 384 recommendations for improvement providers (Cummings & Worley, 2001). These recommendations for change in government called for national agencies to transform themselves into more effective, high-quality, customer-focused service providers (Fullan, 2003). The report outlined recommendations for improvements that have resulted in a $108 billion saving for the period FY 1995–1999 (Cummings & Worley, 2009).

The No Child Left Behind Act (NCLB), which passed Congress in 2001 and was signed into law on January 8, 2002, is an example of government reform under President George W. Bush. The NCLB was the name for the most recent update to the Elementary and Secondary Education Act of 1965. The NCLB law—which grew out of concern that the American education system was no longer internationally competitive—significantly increased the federal role in holding schools responsible for the academic progress of all students (Klein, 2015). And it put a special focus on ensuring that states and schools boost the performance of certain groups of students, such as English-language learners, students in special education, and poor and minority children, whose achievement, on average, trails their peers. States did not have to comply with the new requirements, but if they didn't, they risked losing federal Title I money. While healthcare reform has gotten the most attention under the Obama administration, in January 2011, President Obama outlined his plan to create a 21st century regulatory system—one that protects public health and welfare while promoting economic growth, innovation, competitiveness, and job creation. Among other things, his executive order on regulation said the following: Always consider costs and reduce burdens for American businesses and consumers when developing rules; expand opportunities for public participation and public comment; simplify rules; promote freedom of choice; and ensure that regulations are driven by real science (White House, 2011).

The Institute of Leadership and Management (2010) and Chemengich (2013) have noted similar changes in other countries and have noted specifically that public sector organizations worldwide have been and continue to be under pressure to increase efficiency while delivering improved and integrated services. Consider the fact that public-sector reform has been at the heart of the U.K. government's agenda since 1997 as a concerted wave of reforms significantly changed the way the whole sector works. According to Bouvard, Dohrmann, and Lovegrove (2009) the country's tradition of public-sector reform dates back to the 19th century, and such reforms have been a focus for successive governments over the past 30 years. Similarly, under the prime ministership of Göran Persson, Sweden's government responded to its mid-1990s budget crisis by shaving 11% from operational budgets, with no apparent damage to performance, and then maintained tight control over future spending (Levy & Lovegrove, 2009). In 2004, Tony Blair announced the "Gershon targets"—led by Peter Gershon, then head of the Office of Government Commerce—which generated £26.5 billion a year in improved efficiencies. In November 2008, the U.K. government announced plans to save an additional £35 billion a year (Bhatia, 2009). Similarly, the integrated transformation program of Nicolas Sarkozy's government in France aimed to cut costs by €7.7 billion as of 2012. It is important to note that the adoption and implementation of these efficiency targets have gone hand in hand with reforms focused on significant improvements in outcomes, such as higher test scores in schools and reduced waiting times in hospitals. Additionally, the outcomes prize from government reform is so large that it more than justifies the enormous effort required (Bouvard, Labaye, & Tadjeddine, 2009).

Like the federal government, states across the U.S. are adopting reform efforts intended to reduce the cost of government and make it operate more effectively in meeting the needs of its constituencies. For example, faced with rising health care costs, states are designing and implementing payment reforms that fundamentally transform how the health care market provides and pays for services. Two states in particular, Ohio and Oregon, have developed an overarching vision to guide their multipayer payment and delivery system transformations. Along the way, these states have placed an emphasis on leadership, multidisciplinary engagement, availability of federal resources, and investment in infrastructure to realize their goals. As a result, both Ohio and Oregon are implementing initiatives based on the framework of the Triple Aim[1] and are on a path to achieving its objectives (Tabor, Shiras, & Kaye, 2015). In 2012, California Governor Jerry Brown signed public employee pension roll-back legislation aimed at reducing pension costs and discontinuing abuses such as "spiking" (California Faculty Association, 2012). The reform legislation was intended to make the state's retirement system economically sustainable. The State of Colorado introduced a new human resource management system with the goal of increasing flexibility in hiring, improving the employee compensation structure, and better rewarding employees through performance and tenure. Known as the "Talent Agenda," a goal of the legislation was to attract top talent to its workforce (Cummings & Worley, 2015; Hickenlooper, 2012).

Given the significant budget changes since 2008, as well as the increasing need of the community, the Washtenaw County, Michigan's Board of Commissioners has focused on identifying and working toward strategically investing for community impact to move Washtenaw County Government toward a policymaking and resource allocation paradigm that focuses on— and measures—improved quality of life in Washtenaw County (eWashtenaw, 2014). More specifically, the Board of Commissioners worked from the premise that identifying and committing to change one or more community conditions or populations means moving beyond understanding how much money they spend and how many units they deliver. Instead it means understanding and committing to what differences those investments and services make for Washtenaw County residents. It moves discussion beyond the "*what*" county government does toward the "*why*" we do it. Therefore, impacting a change in a community condition or population will involve deploying and coordinating multiple strategies, all focused on the same outcome. The Board of Commissioners believe that impacting community change cannot be accomplished by Washtenaw County Government alone, but county government can play a number of significant roles from catalyst, to facilitator and convener, to investor. And, that by their very nature, community outcomes and change efforts require multiple partners, each contributing to the change in community condition or population. Finally, in order to be effective, these partners need a *common agenda, shared measurements, mutually reinforcing activities, continuous communication, and adequate infrastructure to support shared efforts*. In 2014 the Board of Commissioners committed to a 4-year strategic plan for Washtenaw County that would focus on how its investments impact the community.

At the local level, city governments are also constantly confronted with the need to change, reform, reinvent, and transform to better serve its citizens. For example, Howell (2012) has suggested that the wave of baby boomers will transform the way cities look, from the way they grow and sprawl to minutiae such as curb heights and the fonts on street signs. One need only walk around Arlington, County, VA located just outside Washington, D.C., to notice some interesting design details. The sidewalks are wide—six feet in commercial areas and five in residential neighborhoods. Pedestrian "walk/don't walk" signs have been replaced with newer versions that count down to seconds left before the light changes. And buses sit lower, eliminating the need for passengers to climb up and down steps to board and exit. These are just a handful of the new elements that have been implemented in recent years as Arlington pursued a plan to prepare for its aging baby boomer population. Across the country, urban planners and transit officials are realizing the way boomer retirees will transform the way cities look, and are striving to meet the needs of the increasing baby boomer population. A recent World Health Organization report on aging communities, for example, highlights the need for things like greater numbers of public benches, safer crosswalks and plenty of public toilets to accommodate older people (World Health Organization, 2015).

Asheville, North Carolina City Manager Gary Jackson (Asheville City News, 2014) implemented a plan to bolster change within the Asheville Police Department (APD), including the formation of a team to support efforts within the department to foster an environment for success and effectiveness. Jackson introduced the concept to Asheville City Council's Public Safety Committee as part of an update on the police department's strategic plan. The team is responsible for coordinating with the hired consultant to bolster the organizational and cultural change spelled out in the APD's strategic plan and to identify additional avenues for employee feedback and communication. The coordinated effort of the facilitated team and the consultant are intended to provide perspectives from both within the organization and from third-party independent observation. In recent years, the fire department identified the need for and implemented cultural and operations changes, for which it was recognized at the state and national level.

At the local level, governments will need to continue supporting neighborhood involvement, community building and meeting the demand for certain public services 7 days a week, 24 hours a day. And this means that like federal and state governments local government agencies will need to adapt and innovate.

The types of government reform or change efforts introduced above suggest the reality of the need for ongoing government transformation —in the field. Change or transformation efforts in the public sector can be just as successful as those in the private sector. For example, the most recent recession has required that government agencies cut costs and find alternative methods to provide public services. As a result federal, state and local governments are outsourcing and privatizing the provision of many programs and services. At the same time, when necessary they are implementing hiring and pay freezes, downsizing, and laying off employees to stem the rising cost of government (Cummings & Worley, 2015). Yet others are finding ways to better engage citizens by conducting community-visioning processes, and technology and social media has become an indispensable foundation for helping governments connect with citizens and operate more efficiently and effectively. Additionally, training, performance management and compensation programs are being updated and implemented. Also, as seen in the Asheville, North Carolina example above, culture change initiatives are also finding their way into public sector change initiatives as a means to refocus agencies and strengthen a shared knowledge of the values, mission, and vision of an agency.

Those responsible for such change must constantly adapt to changing missions, new requirements or environmental forces; stay competitive with the latest innovations and technology; and identify ways to provide quality services to citizens whose expectations continue to evolve. Change is uncertain to say the least and often difficult to accomplish successfully, as a result a large number of change efforts fail. However, despite the number of change failures employees at various levels (i.e., frontline, middle managers, senior executives or leaders) of a public sector organization must be actively involved in leading, implementing, and measuring change efforts. Depending on the current state of the agency and the change needed the degree of change may vary and in some instances the change may require bringing in new leaders or others into the organization. And in some cases, the public sector organization may develop a contract with the private sector to offer guidance or coordinate and synchronize the necessary knowledge, skills, abilities, and resources to design, implement, measure, and/or evaluate change initiatives successfully. Additionally, the need to effectively communicate to all in the agency throughout the entire change process is vital to achieve buy-in and support for the change.

WHAT IS THE DIFFERENCE BETWEEN PUBLIC AND PRIVATE SECTOR ORGANIZATIONS?

A review of the literature comparing public- and private-sector organizations highlights a number of differences between the two sectors. For example, private sector organizations do not have the same kind of budget constraints as public sector organizations which do not allow for flexibility. Everybody knows that the economy changes and business conditions change. In the private sector, you have more flexibility to respond. You can often move dollars from one budget line to another. It does not work that way in government. Many budgets involve money earmarked for certain things (Miles, 2014). There is no latitude to move money from one bucket to another, even if doing so could result in efficiencies or cost savings. Additionally, private, for-profit organizations have smoother decision-making processes. Public sector organizations experience more turbulence, interruptions, recycles, and conflict (Nutt, 2006). Scholars attribute these differences to the roles that public and private organizations play in our society. Private sector organizations sell products or services to consumers in markets to create wealth for shareholders. The typical general purpose, tax-supported governmental agency, such as a state department of mental health, contracts for services and collects information about the needs of people that call for a public response. These distinct roles suggest vastly different kinds of expectations and accountability that may call for different decision-making practices. Decision-making research seldom accounts for these differences, so generalizing from one sector to another is suspect (Nutt, 2006).

According to Cummings and Worley (2015) the public sector is more bureaucratic and adheres more strongly to bureaucratic norms than does the private sector. Thus, differences between the two sectors differ along four key dimensions: values and structure, the multiplicity of decision makers, stakeholder diversity and access, and the extent of intergovernmental relationships. Further, many of the differences between the private and the public sectors may be a matter of degree, rather than kind (Cummings & Worley, 2015; Jurisch, Ikas, Wolf, & Kremar, 2013). Additionally, the public sector has multiple access by multiple decision makers which can make it difficult to know who is really at the top of the organization. Thus, Cummings and Worley suggest that reform, change or transformation interventions focus more on technostructural interventions, such as workflow design and structure, than on process-oriented interventions, such as team building or performance management.

The idea that the public and the private sectors are very different has been expressed in organization theory for many decades (Esteve & Ysa, 2011). Perry and Rainey (1988) illustrate this fact by recalling the etymological distinction between the terms public and private. In Latin, *publicus* means pertaining to the people, in contrast with the term *privatus*, which means set apart. Most of the studies of this field focus on specific variables (see for example, Nutt & Backoff, 1993; Perry & Rainey, 1988; Scott & Falcone, 1998). Esteve and Ysa's (2011) research suggests differences between the public and private sectors in three areas (i.e., organizational level, management level and employee level) as briefly discussed below.

On the organizational level one of the main characteristics of the public sector is the large number of formal processes that appear to be essential to ensure that it functions (Esteve & Ysa, 2011). Additionally, not only do these processes display more degrees of formalization, they also involve more red tape. Red tape can be defined as the "rules, regulations and procedures that remain in force and entail a compliance burden for the organization but have no efficacy for the rules' functional object" (Bozeman, 1993). According to Kurland and Egan (1999), public organizations have higher levels of red tape, because authority is divided among three main branches: executive, legislative and judicial. In order to prevent the abuse of power and to ensure the transparency of organizations "that belong to everyone," the degree of formalization of the public sector far exceeds that of the private sector.

On the managerial level one important factor that differentiates the managers of public organizations from those of private organizations is the decision-making process. For example, Schwenk (1990) analyzes the way in which managers in each sector interpret the appearance of conflict over a strategic decision. Schwenk suggests that the managers of private organizations see conflict as a negative sign, because it indicates that some members of the organization do not believe that the results of the strategic action are positive. On the other hand, for managers in the public sector conflict in a strategic decision has a positive component, since it shows that different stakeholders are participating in the process, thereby ensuring that the final decision will represent their interests, or at least take them into account (Esteve & Ysa, 2011). The ultimate goal of a public manager is to maximize the collective value. The manager of a private organization, on the other hand, prefers to adopt the theory of rational choice, in order to maximize the company's shareholders' wishes (Mort, Weerawardena, & Carnegie, 2003).

On the employees' level public sector employees place a higher value on carrying out tasks that are of use to society compared with their counterparts in the private sector (Esteve & Ysa, 2011). On the other hand, private sector employees place higher a value on the economic rewards they receive (de Graaf & van der Wal, 2008).

Table 1.1 offers another useful comparison of the differences between the public and private sector (Surbhi, 2015). More specifically, Surbhi

(2015) simply states that the public sector is run by the government but the private sector is run by private individuals or companies. Additionally, the public sector is engaged in the activities of providing government goods and services to the general public. The enterprises, agencies and bodies are fully owned, controlled and run by the government whether it is federal, state or a local government. The segment of a national economy that is owned, controlled and managed by private individuals or enterprises is known as the private sector.

Table 1.1.   Differences Between the Public and Private Sector

Basis of Comparison	Public Sector	Private Sector
Meaning	The section of a nation's economy, which is under the control of government, whether it is central, state or local, is known as the Public Sector.	The section of a nation's economy, which is owned and controlled by private individuals or companies is known as Private Sector.
Basic objective	To serve the citizens of the country.	Earning Profit.
Raises money from	Public Revenue like tax, duty, penalty, etc.	Issuing shares and debentures or by taking loans.
Areas	Police, Army, Mining, Health, Manufacturing, Electricity, Education, Transport, Telecommunication, Agriculture, Banking, Insurance, etc.	Finance, Information Technology, Mining, Transport, Education, Telecommunication, Manufacturing, Banking, Construction, Pharmaceuticals, etc.
Benefits of working	Job security, Retirement benefits, Allowances, Perquisites, etc.	Good salary package, Competitive environment, Incentives, etc.
Basis of Promotion	Seniority	Merit
Job Stability	Yes	No

Mares (2013) notes that "it's become cliché that government would be better if it were only run by private-sector managers using standard business practices" (p. 1). However, Mares argues that government and business management are not the same and offers 25 reasons to support her position. Several of these reasons are provided below:

1. The size, dollar value, and complexity of many government programs exceed that in the private sector.
2. The government has fewer measures of progress or success than the private sector, although that is changing as a result of the Government Performance Reform Act requirements. Spending on a

program is not equivalent to progress. The private sector has profit as a clear-cut measure.

3. The civil service and compensation rules of the government make it more difficult to encourage outstanding performance and discourage poor performance.

4. There is very little personal gain in the government for taking risks on policy or programs and being successful in achieving the goals more effectively. However there is potential for substantial criticism and other personal loss if the innovative attempt fails.

5. Private sector managers worry about creating added value, i.e., a product or service that can be sold competitively to the public. This requires the ability and skill to change, evolve, adapt, and improve constantly. Government is frequently quite different. Managers in the government often know what needs to be done and desire to do it but are facing restrictions of laws, regulations, and policies, often made years earlier for other circumstances, that prevent prompt action.

6. Authority in government may be ambiguous and unclear in some circumstances. In other cases it is very clear and tightly restricted through laws, regulations, policies, and directives that leave little, if any room for individual initiative.

7. In most outstanding private sector organizations there are clear, well-understood, job-by-job, top-to-bottom goals and objectives. In government, goals and objectives have been ill-formed, fuzzy and soft. The Government Performance Reform Act and individual departments are striving to change this. Goals in the government are often divergent which may lead to confusion.

As noted in the discussion to this point, a variety of schemes have been used to distinguish public and private organizations (e.g., Cummings & Worley, 2015; Golembiewski, 1985, 1989; Jurisch et al., 2013; Mares, 2013; Nutt, 2006; Nutt & Backoff, 1993). According to Nutt (2006) the most widely accepted classification (Nutt & Backoff, 1993) uses environmental, transactional, and process factors to highlight differences. Table 1.2 provides an overview or summary of comparisons between public- and private-sector organizations found in the literature (Sims, 2010).

As Table 1.2 highlights there are a variety of differences between public- and private-sector organizations that must be taken into consideration by those responsible for any transformation efforts in the public-sector. The next section offers a more in-depth look at some of these differences.

Table 1.2.   Evolution of Public HRM Systems and Values in the United States

• Purpose/values are to govern toward greater public good and demonstrate responsiveness to public wants and needs	• Key values are profitability and the creation of competitive advantage
• General strategic goal is mission effectiveness	• General strategic goal is competitiveness
• Adopt a political-administrative structure in service of their values and purposes	• Structure is flexible and adaptable – whatever works to support profitability and competitive advantage
• Government bureaucracy was a response to corrupt and spoils-based public employment.	• The private sector designed primarily for efficiency. Other features are secondary.
• Public bureaucracy consists of an open system, one subject to extensive external input.	• The private sector can adapt to new demands and eliminate unnecessary requirements. It can choose to focus on one market and not serve another.
• Are mostly managed under a larger chain of command and control	• Mostly operate in a corporate setting
• Policy decisions—the activities have a goal of sticking to what is indicated by law	• Managed under the rules of shareholders and corporate owners
• Operating environment is "fishbowl" public scrutiny	• Operating environment is autonomous
• There are often multiple and conflicting inputs (even within the constituencies: public, legislative, judicial, etc.)	• Can refocus on the market, select a direction, and change relatively quickly
• Stakeholders: taxpayers; inspectors; legislators	• Stakeholders: stockholders; owners; market
• The checks and balances of government create more than one line of authority	• Leadership is aligned or eventually replaced if not aligned
• Budget priorities defined by: legislators, leadership, planners	• Budget priorities defined by: customer demand
• Entrepreneurship is suspect	• Entrepreneurial
• Red tape/rules, policies	• Flexible
• Government bureaucracy often seeks, neutral, task-based experts	• May respond to trends, subjective information, or intuition. Good risk-taking behaviors are encouraged.
• Bureaucracy per se is undemocratic	• There are no requirements for a management model. Democratic processes are found to be effective in improving efficiency, teamwork, and decision making
• Are constrained to work within their authorized mission	Can change in any way they please
• Key success factors: growth rate; earnings; market share; uniqueness; advanced technology	Key success factors: best management practices; sameness; economies of scale; standardized technology

Differences in Public Versus Private Sector Organizations: An Elaboration

The overall dynamic in private sector companies is generally understood to be the pursuit of profit, achieved through competition in selling of products and services to (industrial and private) customers. In practice, managers of private companies vary in how they go about pursuing profits, however. Large firms are often aggressively pitted against each other to gain the largest share of the market, and continuous growth is seen as the ultimate goal; while many small businesses are run by people who simply want to make enough money to live a comfortable and secure lifestyle (Sims, 2010, p. 3). Some firms operate in turbulent markets, some are near-monopolists and some occupy relatively sheltered niches where there are few new entrants. Some sectors are technologically dynamic with high levels of innovation and strong connections to the science base: others are far more traditional. Managers are faced with different challenges, then. Their freedom of action in striving to meet these challenges can be constrained in different ways—while a small firm may have difficulties in raising funds for a new venture, for example, the senior management of a large firm may have to contend with shareholders who disagree with them about strategies.

The public sector appears on the surface to be a much more homogeneous and in many ways placid (i.e., at least on the surface) environment. Large and bureaucratic organizations appear to be long established and more or less monopolistic suppliers of services—not to "markets," but to society in general. Rather than pursuing profits, they are implementing policies that are usually presented as aiming to benefit society as a whole, not least by providing basic services for citizens that private market provision is liable to fail to provide efficiently or equitably. So, in contrast to the private sector, the overarching purpose of public sector organizations is to govern toward greater public good and demonstrate responsiveness to public wants and needs. The public good is addressed through the adoption of laws and policies and the establishment of public services and programs that support a broad array of citizen needs that must, by law, be discussed and adopted in an open public meeting. Responsiveness is reflected in demands for representation, efficiency, individual rights, and social equity (Nablandian, 1998).

The public sector political-administrative structure reflects the values and roles inherent in government organizations. In the classic theory of public administration, the political domain is led by elected representatives who pass legislation and enact statues in service of the public good. In turn, they delegate implementation of programs and statutes to administrative agencies (Frederickson, 1997). The political domain includes both elected and politically appointed officials, and the administrative group includes merit-based civil servants and certain executives, such as city managers, who are appointed on the basis or professional rather than political criteria (Cummings & Worley, 2009; Frederickson, 1997). This structure mirrors the private sector's distinction between a board of directors and management.

The purposes and values within public sector organizations, unlike their private-sector counterparts, are not shared necessarily by the political and administrative functions. For example, politicians serve at the pleasure of the public. Although private sector board members are elected representatives of the shareholders, their elections are not as open and public as are those of political officeholders. Politicians must compete to get elected, and continue to posture and compete to get reelected. As a result, political values of responsiveness, representation, social equity, and efficiency, and the ever-present political survival value are reflected in an open and public process where the particular interests and values of a diverse set of constituencies are brought together to produce a common view of the public good. Clearly, politics is the art and science of government (Appleby, 1978; Frederickson, 1997; Morris, 1981).

Along with the government's regulatory and taxation role these values have contributed to the perception of government as a bureaucracy, which simply refers to the administration of a government through bureaus staffed with nonelected officials (Cummings & Worley, 2009, 2015). Perceptions of bureaucracy are often negative, however, and include indifferent people exercising power through strict adherence to inflexible policies, rules, and procedures. In addition, government appetite for risk is extremely low resulting in a plethora of rules and regulations fostered to minimize any possibility of something going wrong.

Although private- and public-sector organizations can take on the characteristics of a bureaucracy, such as departmentalization, vertical decision-making processes, and many formal rules and procedures, the characteristics are more pronounced in public sector organizations. A critical reason for this phenomenon is that public sector organizations are legalized into existence, giving the organization or agency life until it is legislated out of existence. As a result, the public sector organization receives funding that sustains its existence regardless of performance. Although budgets at all levels of government are reviewed and adopted annually, the complete elimination of a public sector organization or agency is rare. The effect is that public sector organizations, despite their purpose, can be much less responsive to citizens and customers than private sector organizations because they aren't directly reliant on the customer for funding to sustain their existence.

The public sector operates in an environment of largely unlimited access to multiple authoritative decision makers, a phenomenon designed to ensure that "public business gets looked at from a variety of perspectives" (Frederickson, 1997, p. 164; see also Cummings & Worley, 2009). The public expects full and legitimate access to all government decision makers at every level. As a result, access to the decision-making process is broader and accountability is more dispersed than in private sector organizations, where such access is uncommon and responsibility is more clear-cut (Popovich, 1998). Further, government fragmentation complicates the public sector decision-making process, where it is common for different public agencies to be responsible for different steps in governmental processes. Such fragmentation often makes it confusing and difficult for citizens, clients, customers, and even public officials and staff to understand who is responsible for what decision and accountable for what product.

The need for the public sector to act in more or less politically legitimate ways makes for specific constraints and incentives for the management of public services. Even more than the managers of private businesses, the senior managers of public organizations do not have overall control over their own activities; their aims are defined and changed by political will. Overall control and decision making is to a greater or lesser extent placed outside of the individual public organization. The leadership is monitored closely: it is under continuous external pressure and it may be changed at the end of each election period (if not sooner, as when there is a crisis of confidence in the leadership). If the election results in a radically new political constellation, the aims of the public sector might change dramatically.

Usually, the time of elections is an outburst of change or reform ideas, political creativity, and new policy. This is not to say that there is no vitality and revitalization in the policy between elections; new ideas are initiated all the time. However, an election provides an important chance to bring forward policy ideas (and future change or reform initiatives) that can win the support of voters, enabling the proponents of these ideas to get into power and implement new policies.

Elections are not the only channels for influencing policies. As noted earlier, in the United States a number of interest groups are formally involved in the decision-making processes through various venues. The political power of some interest groups (especially corporations, sometimes also trade unions and other groups) is institutionalized in the U.S. political system. These, and other, interest groups also use more informal contacts with policymakers and methods like lobbying, and organizing demonstrations, petitions and other means of influence. For most interest groups, mass media serves as a major channel of communication, where it is possible to display and promote their ideas and perspectives to politicians and to those who might influence them. Mass media themselves also regularly play a role in framing the political agenda. They may give a voice to perspectives that are underrepresented in other political channels. They chart, as well as echo and articulate views of citizens about the government, for example with public opinion polls that are meant to show popular views of politicians and policies as one need only witness in the ongoing healthcare reform and immigration reform debates.

Decisions are shaped, then, through complex series of interactions. These can take diverse forms, depending on the policy issue concerned, and what the overall political context is; and on the actors and organizations involved, and their problems, and solutions and priorities, their resources of power and bargaining capabilities. Revenue is raised by local, state and federal entities from taxes and other means, and with this it funds public sector activity: to cover the costs of wages, communications, equipment and buildings, and so on. The national budget makes public sector activity possible, and its allocation defines the boundaries for public sector actions or activities.

In reality, public sector organizations depend on revenues that are based on political decisions rather than market performance. The link between revenues and services delivered is often obscure. Gretschmann (1991) notes that when the goals and objectives of public sector organizations are ambiguous and multiple ones, or are subject to frequent change, then it will become hard to fully specify which input relates to which output. It is therefore questionable whether the incentive structures of public sector organizations can be viewed in purely economic terms. Public sector organizations function under more formal legal conditions and typically need to respond to a diverse group of interests and users of public services.

All government agencies exist not for profit but to fulfill their charter or mission, which is an "inherently governmental function" (Averson, 1999, p. 1). Public sector organizations have authority to conduct their mission that is delegated either by congressional statute or by executive order. Moreover, in U.S. law, public sector organizations are prohibited from direct competition with the private sector in providing products and services. Hence, as noted in Table 1.2, unlike private-sector businesses that can change in any way they please, government agencies are constrained to work within their authorized mission. On the other hand, private corporations are prohibited from engaging in some activities that are authorized for the government only; these exclusions are described in the Constitution. Hence, the State Department has the authority to develop and implement foreign policy. The Department of Defense has the authority to develop weapon systems and hire personnel to operate them. The General Services Administration has the authority to develop and implement policies for management and office processes throughout the federal government.

The key metric for government (or nonprofit) performance is not financial in nature, but rather *mission effectiveness*. But mission effectiveness is not a definite and static thing. Usually, a public sector agency has a rather broad general mission, which incorporates many specific sub-missions or departmental missions within it. At any given time, some departmental missions may be more important than others for the needs of the country. The selection of the departmental mission priorities is an ongoing strategic planning responsibility.

Since each agency has its assigned mission, the metric for success of that mission will be unique to the agency. Success is thus defined specifically to the agency's mission. "Performance" in this context means, "How well is the agency doing its mission?" Metrics of performance answer the question "How do you know how well the agency is doing?" The answer may take the form of a balanced scorecard on the mission-oriented workforce.

But in addition to mission work, every public sector agency also contains a support workforce that does the same kinds of tasks: business systems such as payroll and human resources management, financial data accounting, and so on, utilities, facilities, maintenance, file management, forms processing, and other kinds of office work that are "generic"—essentially the same in all public sector agencies. These support functions are necessary but they do not relate directly to the mission of the agency—although they do play a role in its effectiveness and the viability of the public sector organization. The important difference between generic and specific (mission-related) metrics is that the *generic metrics can be benchmarked across other organizations*. This provides a way for public sector agencies to compare their processes with the best practices in the private sector, and to identify processes with exceptionally high or low efficiency. Typically the Baldrige criteria are used for such assessments, although other methods can yield the same kinds of generic performance metrics (Averson, 1999). For example, Averson suggests that the metrics *really needed* by public sector decision-makers fall into three general categories:

1. Strategic needs metrics: ways to assess the future needs related to the agency's general mission and sub-missions based on an analysis of the external situation. (SWOT analysis and gap analysis are often the approaches used here).
2. Mission effectiveness metrics: ways to assess the health and viability of those missions that are going to be needed in the future. Detailed definitions of these metrics are required by each unit's capability experts, as well as collection of appropriate data on outputs and outcomes.
3. Operational efficiency metrics: ways to assess the quality of support functions in enabling the needed missions to be accomplished for

the minimum cost and time. This requires standardized metrics, customer surveys and benchmarking to identify best and worst practices.

Governments are designed to focus both functions and power, and paradoxically, to disperse power and functions, so that no one government or agency is all powerful. As a result, "government" comprises a latticework of independent agencies or departments providing different public services to the same citizens and customers. The result is an intergovernmental relations environment where local, state and federal governments share power, responsibility, and, in some cases, resources (Bryson, 1995; Cummings & Worley, 1997; Golembiewski, 1985, 1969). And, such intergovernmental relations further complicate the issue of metrics, performance or accountability in public sector organizations that one does not find in the experience of private sector organizations. More will be said about metrics later in this chapter.

CHALLENGES, BARRIERS AND DRIVERS OF PUBLIC SECTOR CHANGE

Public sector organizations, such as local, state, and federal governments, face numerous challenges and operate in a complex environment of competing political, economic, and social forces. For example, today the U.S. federal government faces challenges on many fronts: fiscal, environmental, healthcare and security, to name a few. Many of these issues are complex and long-range in nature. There is no doubt that it is going to take a sustained effort over many years to address them. The U.S. government's ability to meet current and emerging challenges continues to be in jeopardy. According to the Center for Innovation in Public Service (2007) much of government remains overly hierarchical, myopic, and narrowly focused, clinging to outmoded organizational structures and strategies. In addition, many agencies have been slow to adopt best practices. While some departments and agencies have begun to reexamine their missions and operations, many federal policies, processes, procedures, and structures are decades out of date.

Calls for public sector agencies to become more citizen focused and to operate in a more business-like manner are common. Legislation and programs aimed at improving accountability, quality, and effectiveness of public sector organizations are constantly being introduced and adopted at all levels of government. In addition, public sector organizations face increasingly complex and significant challenges in responding to citizens, crafting public policy, and providing public services that not only meet but exceed expectations. Conflicting public policies at the local, state and federal level, coupled with unfunded mandates and restricted revenue, further complicate the environment in which public sector organizations operate. The record successfully responding and changing when necessary has been spotty at best, with public trust in government falling dramatically over the years. For example, the Gallup organization has found that "barely half of Americans, 51%, say they have a "great deal" or 'fair amount' of trust in the federal government to handle international problems. Less than half of Americans, 47% recently had a 'great deal' or a 'fair amount' of trust in the federal government to handle domestic problems. And only 32% 'think you can trust government in Washington to do what is right … just about always" or "most of the time.' In contrast, just over two-thirds express trust in their own state and local governments" (Trust-Government, 2007). In 2013 only 19% said that they trusted government, however, 62% had a positive view of federal workers (Pew Research Center, 2013). Vavreck (2015) has recently noted that trust in government has steadily deteriorated over the past several decades and continues to do so.

As alluded to earlier, the public sector is often described as "bureaucratic"—in a negative sense. It is often considered a slow moving, rigid, hierarchically organized system, with specialized departments that are directed towards concrete targets and having ambiguously defined limits of authority at the same time. This "bureaucratic" system is by some perceived as time-consuming, oversized and expensive, and a waste of taxpayers' money (Cummings & Worley, 2015).

The reality is that in some instances public sector organizations are "bureaucratic" in the negative sense of the word and this in itself poses a particular challenge for such entities. If this is the case the main problem when one considers change efforts in the public sector seems to be the structure of the organization. And structural change will then be the solution; as it may create better structures for absorbing change, learning, and continuous improvement.

Organizational structures might be understood as chosen, and change as guided by human intention. The development of a structure follows a strategy (Chandler 1962), where the major function of an organizational structure is to direct attention and action toward the accomplishment of pre-determined goals. Various structural forms are chosen on the basis of their ability to facilitate this goal-accomplishment (Child, 1972; Scott, 1992). However, is it possible to choose the best way to organize public sector organizations? And, is it possible to change or reorganize the public sector into this one "best" structure? The Workforce Performance Directorate (2015) of Western Australia has recently noted that it is possible to successfully change the structural forms of public sector organizations and have developed a framework to do so.

The hierarchical organization of the public sector is based on a democratic principle; it is ultimately ruled by a government that is constituted through elections. The political party or parties in power might have other perspectives on what is the best way to organize the public sector than the minority. Such political perspectives might have been considered in the elections, and the existing organization structures might therefore be understood as the democratic will of the population.

What one considers the best model is therefore continuously changing —partly as a result of democratic will. However, in many cases one will find that the voters and the media are not so much concerned with the *organization* of public sector organizations, but with their ability to deliver services as promised or their mission effectiveness as noted earlier. This means that it is up to the politicians and the civil servants to come up with the right model. And such an effort in itself is often challenging and requires change or reform or transformation.

Politicians and policymakers do not have perfect knowledge of the issues at hand. Moreover, the goals are conflicting and it is hard to choose the best solutions for all parties in every issue. Decisions are rather the results of negotiations, bargains and compromises—with other public organizations and civil interest groups.

These decisions are almost always influenced by competition for funding and a lack of resources. One decision is therefore normally made at the sacrifice of other interests. Who loses often depends on who has the power to negotiate, bargain and make compromises. This power does not only depend on what might be the most rational choice, but also on the number of members, influence, competences in the relevant field and on financial and human resources. What might appear as the absence of political will to change a public sector organization might just as well be the absence of bargaining power.

Also, it has been claimed that the "bureaucratic" system might be institutionalized in the "organizational way of doing things" (e.g., Halvorsen, Hauknes, Miles, & Roste, 2005; March & Olsen 1984, 1989; Olsen, 1992; Powell & DiMaggio, 1991; Zucker, 1983). And that the organizational way of doing things—that is, a specific way of running an activity—might in itself be a barrier to change.

Public sector organizations are not static, but changed and transformed through continual processes of interpretation and adaptation. Certain structures and processes evolve historically through selective experience and become the basis of self-organization. Public sector organizations develop considerable robustness against changes in the environment and explicit reform efforts through this organizational autonomy and internal dynamics. Hence, although public sector organizations are the result of human activity, they are not necessarily products of conscious design. The preferred models are rather taken for granted, assuming that "actors associate certain actions with certain situations by rules of appropriateness" (March & Olsen, 1984, p. 741) through socialization, education, on-the-job learning or acquiescence to convention (March & Olsen, 1989; Olsen, 1992; Powell & DiMaggio, 1991).

In that way the incentives for changes are rather organizational than political-rational. The participants enter the public sector agency or organization with individually shaped ideas, expectations and agendas, different values, interests and abilities. The organization absorbs some of these individual interests and establishes criteria by which people discover their preferences. If the participants do not agree in these preferences they might choose to exit the organization. In that way the public sector organization gets further institutionalized instead of radically changed.

Because of this change in the public sector is often perceived as something that is forced upon the organization from the outside. Political change is often associated with policy entrepreneurs, political interventions and technological change with change champions. However, personal incentives such as power, status, improved promotional prospects and salary might as well serve as a stimulus for such change activity within the public sector as well as in the private sector. This means that any public sector change effort must also take internal processes into consideration.

One should also keep in mind that change in the private sector is also often forced upon companies or business units from "the outside." In larger companies this "outside force" may be the top management or board of directors, for example. Moreover, all companies face a demanding market, as both customers and suppliers may force a company to resort to change to improve overall performance.

In the public sector the objectives for change are diverse, not clearly ranked and subject to modifications or the whims of those who have the most power. In the private sector objectives are diverse too, but once a decision has been made to embark on a change effort one tends to stick to the objectives until the plan has been finalized or aborted. In the public sector change objectives are more unclear and tend to be reformulated all the time—also after the decision has been made.

The procedures in both sectors are about decision making, but the processes leading to change in the public sector are often (but not always) political. For obvious reasons the main focus of public sector change is not sales and profits. And, as noted earlier, public sector organizations operate under other regulatory and social rules than companies.

Public sector organizations must act in accordance with constitutional principles of governance that define the basic standards for public activity: who can legitimately and reasonably decide what, when and how? Interestingly these principles appear as reasonable when considered in isolation, but may seem problematic and even contradictory if seen in context. These principles and their contradicting relations must therefore be considered when trying to understand (and implement) change in the public sector, and if possible be hierarchically arranged and prioritized on the basis of the change initiative.

CONCLUSION

For those responsible for reform, change or transformation efforts in the public sector it is important to understand some of the differences between public and private sector organizations. If for no other reason than to facilitate the transfer of change or transformation best practices from one sector to another. To some extent the public sector appears to be adopting practices that are often attributed to the private sector in order to achieve greater efficiency. Nevertheless, as discussed in this chapter there are differences between both sectors that must be taken into consideration prior to any public sector reform, change or transformation effort.

The literature on public-sector organizational change in the U.S. continues to evolve (see for example, Andrews & Shah, 2003; Answers.com, 2009; Battaglio & Condrey, 2006; Battalino, Beutler, & Shani, 1996; Capacity Development Group/BDP, UNDP, 2006; Chemengich, 2013; Davis, Cluter, Keenan, & Roediger, 2012; Esteve & Ysa, 2011; Public Sector Commission, 2015; Sims, 2009, 2010; van der Voet, 2015; Wodzicki, 2007; World Bank, 1999) and with that is the reality that today's public sector organizations are confronted with an often bewildering set of demands to change or transform their organizations' work processes.

In conclusion, change or transformation efforts will continue to be of vital importance to organizations in the public sector. Indeed, public sector culture almost demands a crisis of some sort to consider the need for change. The tendency to be change avoidant to the point of precipitating crises almost precludes second chances to successfully initiate organizational change. The consequences of failure in public sector change efforts often being catastrophic, the need to learn from successful public and private programs of organizational change/improvement is critical. The chapters in this book should help facilitate that process, and the lessons discussed will benefit those responsible for public sector change in their future projects. It is our hope that you will be open to our ideas presented in this chapter and other chapters in this book and accept the reality that demands for more and more change in public sector organizations are here to stay. You must be prepared to respond! But are you really ready?

THE CHAPTERS THAT FOLLOW

Here is the information you will encounter as you read the chapters that follow this introductory piece.

Chapter 2 "Human Resource Management and Civil Service Reform: Change (Transformation) in Government," Ronald R. Sims takes an in-depth look at the reforms and changes of human resource management (HRM) in the public sector culminating in a number of lessons learned from the various initiatives. The chapter first offers a historical look at civil service reform and project human resources management (PHRM) reform in the United States at the federal and state levels before then focusing on some PHRM models and frameworks identified by other researchers. Before concluding the chapter, lessons and limits to civil service reform (CSR) and public HRM reform, change management, and a number of principles applicable to reform in PHRM will be discussed in some detail.

Chapter 3, "Cybersecurity Mission and Management at the Department of Homeland Security: Toward a Model of Integrated Adaptation," Marcia A. Beck and Jonathan P. West first examine the difficulties the Department of Homeland Security (DHS) encounters in attempts to integrate and coordinate management practices that impact its cybersecurity mission. Beck and West then turn to a discussion of attempts by DHS to adapt its organizational, technological, and networking capacity to execute that mission.

Chapter 4, "Public Sector Retirement Systems: Either Change or Consider Bankruptcy?", William J. Woska notes that Detroit, Michigan, and Vallejo and Stockton, California, appear to be examples of a growing list of public agencies that file for bankruptcy. When an employee earns pension benefits, the agency creates a long-term liability. A majority of public jurisdictions have defined benefit retirement programs that are underfunded. Municipalities have found it difficult to offer new retirement plans due to the fact that retirement benefits are a mandatory source of collective bargaining and that a large number of public employees are unionized. Labor unions have been ideologically inclined toward defined benefit pension systems. For example, organized labor in Detroit fought to keep a defined benefit retirement program for new employees even as benefits were being reduced for current retirees. This chapter provides the background with respect to public employee retirement systems and the significance and impact of retirement programs that are not fully funded.

Chapter 5, "Federal Change: Difficult But Doable for the Effective Leader, "William J. Mea examines why achieving major change and transformation in the public sector is perceived as so difficult. Mea notes that while the public expects the Federal government to be able to resolve issues quickly, there are many barriers. With this as a backdrop, Mea discusses how barriers to making rapid change are woven into the fabric of the governing process. The chapter further examines factors that have emerged over time, such as the role of associations as discussed later that make it surprising the government accomplishes as much as it does. Mea argues that in contrast, there are multiple positive case examples of change that show how agencies can achieve positive transformation. The chapter also discusses some principles and lessons learned that have proved effective for achieving transformation. The chapter also offers ideas as to what can be done to make efforts in the Federal sector more effective.

Chapter 6, "Transition to a New State: Consolidating Organizational Resources at NASA Langley Research Center," Sheri Bias, Donna L. Phillips, and Kathleen Cabler discuss NASA LaRC's Office of Chief Financial Officer's adaption to change and ability overcome obstacles faced during the transition to a more efficient and effective organization. The fundamental assumptions underlying *any* change in a human system are analyzed. Two models of change management, William Bridges's (1991) *Transitions* and Salerno and Brock's (2008) *The Change Cycle*, are used as lenses for analyzing the initiative. Was this the correct timing? Bias, Phillips, and Cabler explore the timing of introduction of these models and the effectiveness of these models during the change process as compared to other change models. Could other models have been more effective? What process should be used to choose the model that "fits" your organizations' needs? The chapter also defines and discusses the principles of change and effective change management to bring the desired vision of the organization to fruition.

Chapter 7, "Drones in Domestic Law Enforcement: Ethical Issues, Implementation Practices, and Case Studies," Jonathan P. West and James S. Bowman examine and note that drone proliferation multiplies both probable benefits and risks. West and Bowman explore the ethical implications and implementation issues inherent in surveillance—the primary use of uninhabited aircraft. The chapter first briefly reviews the ubiquity and types of these domestic droids. The core of the inquiry analyzes the ethical challenges and implementation practices, as well as case studies in drone use. The chapter concludes with a discussion of guidelines for the present and future use of this technology.

In Chapter 8, "Developing an Online Job Analysis Questionnaire: The Ever Changing Process," Stacey Lange and Martinique Alber suggest that job analysis is one of the most critical processes for any agency as it is the foundation which ensures that an agency's selection and evaluation methods are valid and legally defensible. Given the reality that the job analysis process can be time consuming and cumbersome for many agencies to complete, Lange and Alber note that new innovations in this area should focus on streamlining the process. Lange and Alber discuss one such innovation, efficient and user friendly Online Job Analysis Questionnaire (OJAQ) and provide guidance for developing an OJAQ as well as discussing the advantages and challenges an agency may encounter along the way.

In Chapter 9, "Maintaining an Ethical Culture in Municipal Government through the use of a Professional Ethics Workshop for all City Employees," William I. Sauser, Jr. and Steven A. Reeves describe the City of Auburn, Alabama—home to Auburn University—efforts to maintain the city's excellent reputation for quality service to its citizens by providing professional ethics training to all employees of the city as a planned, proactive organizational intervention. Sauser and Reeves note that to date more than 650 employees (many of whom remain employed by the city) at all levels of the organization have undergone ethics training in the form of a 2-hour "hands-on" workshop. Sauser and Reeves provide a discussion on the following questions: what the workshop look like, how has it been received, and what has been the effectiveness of the workshop with respect to the expectations of the city leaders and employees? The chapter concludes with some "lessons learned" which the authors gladly share with others seeking to build a *culture of character* within their own public sector organization.

In Chapter 10, Caring for the Poor in Jefferson County, Alabama: A Model of Change in Government-Run Healthcare," Roger McCullough discusses efforts to turnaround Cooper Green Mercy Health Services located in Birmingham, Alabama. McCullough describes specific challenges and issues that were addressed in this transformation effort and how Cooper Green Mercy Health Services was successful in its turnaround efforts by focusing on its mission and through the strategic implementation of a plan to address the clinic's deficiencies. McCullough provides a look at the impressive results of the transformation effort at Cooper Green Mercy Health Services to include: In fiscal year 2015, the clinic saw over 56,000 patient visits, up 11.6% over the previous fiscal year. Primary care visits, the single most important success metric, were up 35%. Services were expanded in the areas of diabetes, hypertension, and pain management, and new service lines, such as Women's Health and Wellness and Behavioral Health, were added. McCullough also notes the importance of using a collaborative approach to the transformation effort which resulted in Cooper Green Mercy, in effect, becoming a portal to comprehensive, high quality medical services for the poorest citizens of the county. The collaboration proved to be an outstanding model for care of the county's indigent poor in terms of both mission and finances.

Chapter 11, "Building a Better Department of Revenue for the People of Alabama," William I. Sauser, Jr., Julie P. Magee, Don-Terry Veal, Julia B. Heflin, and Lisa P. Brantly offer a case example of the application of organizational change and strategic planning principles to the transformation of an important state agency, the Alabama Department of Revenue (ADOR). In discussing the case example the authors: (a) Describe the commissioner's vision for the ADOR and how she worked to transform the department by implementing that vision. (b) Discuss the role of Auburn University's Center for Governmental Services (CGS) in aiding the commissioner to work with her management team to sharpen that vision and identify specific projects that could further the shared vision of the commissioner and her management team. (c) Describe intensive work sessions conducted in 2011 and 2015. (d) Discuss the effectiveness of the projects resulting from the 2011 session as reported by Governor Bentley to the people of Alabama following the end of his first term. Sauser, Magee Veal, Heflin, and Brantly conclude the chapter with recommendations to other government leaders who wish to transform their organization using methods similar to those employed by the Alabama Department of Revenue.

Chapter 12, "Interlocal Diffusion and Difference: How Networks Are Transforming Public Service," Kathleen Hale and Mitchell Brown, note that as perhaps the quintessential public service, election administration is primarily a function of local governments. Hale and Brown point out that since the 2000 Presidential election, this area of public service has come under intense national scrutiny and become increasingly complex. Elections have also undergone radical transformation at the local level through local networks of election officials, other government officials, and nonprofit organizations that have changed the public administration of elections. According to Hale and Brown, over the past 15 years, the interactions, collaborations, and innovations that have taken place in and between local networks of election administrators have generated a public service environment that possesses increased capacity to meet public needs and demands. These local networks and the information arrangements that define them are central to the development of innovation, and central to the spread of new ideas from one locality to another. Hale and Brown examine these local networks and the information exchanged within them, and demonstrate the ways in which local networks are central to innovation, key to the spread of new ideas from one locality to another, and fundamental to improving this area of public service across the country.

In Chapter 13, "Are Public and Private Sector Change Efforts Different: Some Answers and Lessons Learned," Ronald R. Sims, William J. Mea, and John G. Veres, III offer answers to the questions: Are forms of private and public sector change different? And, what are some of the various challenges, barriers to and drivers of public sector change? Sims, Mea, and Veres concluded the chapter with a discussion of best practices lessons learned from their own experiences for improving public sector change efforts.

Chapter 14, "Leadership: The Common Thread in Successful Government Transformation," Barry Hoy addresses the application of systems theory in understanding the process of transformation and specifically the human component of the transformation. Hoy also explores the manner in which good *leadership* as separate from good *management* is particularly, and perhaps even singularly essential, in bringing about the transformations of which we speak. The chapter proceeds from the premise that a goal of leadership is to set the stage for transformation initiative completion with minimal investment of management effort.

NOTE

1. The IHI Triple Aim is a framework developed by the Institute for Healthcare Improvement that describes an approach to optimizing health system performance. It is IHI's belief that new designs must be developed to simultaneously pursue three dimensions, which they call the "Triple Aim": (a) Improving the patient experience of care (including quality and satisfaction); (b) Improving the health of populations; and (c) Reducing the per capita cost of health care.

REFERENCES

Andrews, M., & Shah, A. (2003). Citizen-centered governance: A new approach to public sector reform. In A. Shah (Ed.), *Bringing civility in governance* (pp. 6.1–6.5). Washington, DC: The World Bank.

Answers.com. (2009). Civil service reform. Retrieved from http://www.answers.com/topic/civil-service-reform

Appleby, P. (1978). Government is different. In J. Shafritz & A. Hyde (Eds.), *Classics of public administration* (pp. 101–107). Oak Park, IL: Moore.

Asheville City News. (2014). Asheville city manager bolsters change efforts for Asheville police department. Retrieved from http://www.ashevillenc.gov/NewsandEvents/CityNews/tabid/662/articleType/ArticleView/articleId/27359/City-Manager-bolsters-change-efforts-for-Asheville-Police-Department.aspx

Averson, P. (1999). Designing metrics for government agency performance. Retrieved from http://www.balancedscorecard.org/BSCResources/PerformanceMeasurement/DesigningMetrics/tabid/140/Default.aspx

Battaglio, R. P., & Condrey, S. E. (2006). Civil service reform: Examining state and local government cases. *Review of Public Personnel Administration, 26*(2), 116–118.

Battalino, J., Beutler, L., & Shani, A. B. (1994). Large-system change initiative: Transformation in progress at the California Department of Corrections. *Public Productivity and Management Review, 20*(1), 24–44.

Becker, J., Algermissen, L., & Niehaves, B. (2004). Organizational engineering in public administrations. In H. M. Haddad (Ed.), *Proceedings of the 2004 ACM Symposium on Applied Computing* (pp. 1385–1389). New York: ACM Press.

Bhatia, N. (2009). Case study: Public-sector reform in the United Kingdom. *McKinsey Quarterly*. Retrieved from http://www.mckinsey.com/insights/public_sector/the_case_for_government_reform_now

Bouvard, F., Dohrmann, T., & Lovegrove, N. (2009). The case for government reform. *McKinsey Quarterly*. Retrieved from http://www.mckinsey.com/insights/public_sector/the_case_for_government_reform_now

Bouvard, F., Labaye, E., & Tadjeddine, K. (2009). Case study: Undertaking reform in France. *McKinsey Quarterly*. Retrieved from http://www.mckinsey.com/insights/public_sector/the_case_for_government_reform_now

Bozeman, B. (1993). A theory of government "red tape". *Journal of Public Administration Research and Theory, 3*(3), 273–303.

Bridges, W., (1991). *Managing transitions: Making the most of change*. Reading, MA: Addison-Wesley.

Bryson, J. (1995). *Strategic planning for public and nonprofit organizations: A guide to strengthening and sustaining organizational achievement*. San Francisco, CA: Jossey-Bass.

California Faculty Association. (2012). Governor Brown signs pension roll-back legislation. Retrieved from http://www.calfac.org/headline-special-edition/gov-brown-signs-pension-roll-back-legislation

Capacity Development Group, BDP, UNDP. (2006). *Institutional reform and change management: Managing change in public sector organizations*. Retrieved from www.capacity.undp.org

Center for Innovation in Public Service. (2007). *Leading change, managing risk: The leadership role in public sector transformations*. Washington, DC: The George Washington University School of Public Policy and Public Administration.

Chandler, A. (1962). *Strategy and structure: Chapters in the history of the American industrial enterprise*. Cambridge, MA: MIT Press.

Chemengich, M. K. (2013). Managing strategic change in the public sector. *Standard Research Journal of Business Management, 1*(1), 1–40.

Child, J. (1972). Organizational structure, environment and performance: The role of strategic choice. *Sociology, 6*(1), 1–22.

Cummings, T. G., & Worley, C. G. (1997). *Organization development and change* (6th ed.). Mason, OH: South-Western College.

Cummings, T. G., & Worley, C. G. (2001). Organization development and change. (7th ed.). Mason, OH: South-Western College.

Cummings, T. G., & Worley, C. G. (2009). Organization development and change. (9th ed.). Mason, OH: South-Western Cengage Learning.

Cummings, T. G., & Worley, C. G. (2015). *Organization development and change*. (10th ed.). Stamford, CT: Cengage Learning.

Davis, J., Cluter, C., Keenan, P., & Roediger, A. (2012). A practical guide to change in the public sector. Retrieved from https://www.bcgperspectives.com/content/articles/public_sector_change_management_practical_guide_to_change_in_public_sector/

de Graaf, G., & van der Wal, Z. (2008). On value differences experienced by sector switchers. *Administration & Society, 40*(1), 79–103.

Esteve, M., & Ysa, T. (2011). Differences between the public and private sectors? Reviewing the myth. Retrieved from http://www.esade.edu/public/modules. php?name=news&idnew=676&idissue=57&newlang=english

*e*Washtenaw. (2014). Board of commissioners strategic planning efforts. Retrieved from http://www.ewashtenaw.org/government/administrator/ budget/2014-2017-budget-process/budget-documents/board-of- commissioners-strategic-planning-efforts

Frederickson, H. G. (1997). *The spirit of public administration*. San Francisco, CA: Jossey-Bass.

Fullan, M. (2003). *The moral imperative of schooled leadership*. Thousand Oaks, CA: Corvin Press.

Golembiewski, R. T. (1969). Organization development in public agencies: Perspectives on theory and practice. *Public Administration Review, 29*(4), 367–377.

Golembiewski, R. T. (1985). *Humanizing public organization*. Mount Airy, MD: Lomond.

Gretschmann, K. (1991). Analysing the public sector: The received view in economics and shortcomings. In F. Kaufmann (Ed.), *The public sector—challenges for coordination and learning* (pp. 481–510). Berlin and New York: de Gruyter.

Halvorsen, T., Hauknes, J., Miles, I., & Roste, R. (2005). On the differences between public and private sector innovation. Retrieved from http://unpan1.un.org/ intradoc/groups/public/documents/apcity/unpan046809.pdf

Hickenlooper, J. (20012, June 6). Gov. Hickenlooper signs legislation to reform pension system. Retrieved from http://votesmart.org/public-statement/703030/ gov-hickenlooper-signs-legislation-to-improve-the-state-personnel-system#. Vhp_bE0QV9M

Howell, R. (2012, September). How will boomers reshape U.S. cities? Retrieved from http://www.governing.com/generations/government-management/gov- how-will-boomers-reshape-cities.html

Institute of Leadership and Management. (2010). Leading change in the public sector. Retrieved from https://www.i-l-m.com/~/media/ILM%20Website/ Documents/Information%20for%20centres/ILM_PS_REP%20pdf.ashx

Jurisch, M.C., Ikas, C., Wolf, P., & Krcmar, H. (2013). Key differences of private and public sector business process change. *e-Service Journal, 9*(1), 3–27.

Klein, A. (2015). No child left behind: An overview. Retrieved from http://www. edweek.org/ew/section/multimedia/no-child-left-behind-overview-definition- summary.html

Kurland, N. B., & Egan, T. D. (1999). Public v. private perceptions of formalization, outcomes, and justice. *Journal of Public Administration Research and Theory. 9*(3), 437–458.

Levy, A., & Lovegrove, N. (2009, June). Reforming the public sector in a crisis: An interview with Sweden's former prime minister. *McKinsey Quarterly*. Retrieved from http://www.mckinsey.com/insights/public_sector/reforming_the_public_ sector_in_a_crisis_an_interview_with_swedens_former_prime_minister

March, J. G., & Olsen, J. P. (1984). The new institutionalism: Organizational factors in political life. *American Political Science Review, 78*(3), 734–749.

March, J. G., & Olsen, J. P. (1989). *Rediscovering institutions: The organizational basis of politics*. New York, NY: Free Press/Macmillan.

Mares, J. (2013). 25 differences between private sector and government managers. Retrieved from http://www.powermag.com/25-differences-between-private-sector-and-government-managers/

Miles, J. (2014). Government vs. private-sector procurement: An unfair comparison. Retrieved from http://www.govtech.com/state/Government-vs-Private-Sector-Procurement-An-Unfair-Comparison.html

Morris, W. (1981). *The American heritage dictionary of the English language*. Boston, MA: Houghton-Mifflin.

Mort, G. S., Weerawardena, J., & Carnegie, K. (2003). Social entrepreneurship: Towards conceptualization. *International Journal of Nonprofit & Voluntary Sector Marketing. 8*(1), 76–88.

Nablandian, J. (1998, July 10). City council-city manager partnerships (presentation to the California City Managers Conference). Monterey, CA.

Nutt, P. C. (2006). Comparing public and private sector decision-making practices. *Journal of Public Administration Research and Theory*. Retrieved from http://www.highbeam.com/doc/1G1-144435969.html

Nutt, P. C., & Backoff, R. W. (1993). Organizational publicness and its implications for strategic management. *Journal of Public Administration Research and Theory, 3*(2)., 209–231.

Olsen, J. P. (1992). Analyzing institutional dynamics. *Staatswissenschaften und Staatpraxis 2*, 247–271.

Perry, J. L., & Rainey, H. G. (1988). The public-private distinction in organization theory: A critique and research strategy. *Academy of Management Review, 13*(2), 182–201.

Pew Research Center. (2013). Trust in government nears record low, but most federal agencies are viewed favorably. Retrieved from http://www.people-press.org/2013/10/18/trust-in-government-nears-record-low-but-most-federal-agencies-are-viewed-favorably/

Popovich, M. G. (1998). *Creating high-performance government organizations*. San Francisco, CA: Jossey-Bass.

Powell, W. W., & DiMaggio, P. J. (Eds) (1991). *The new institutionalism in organizational analysis*. Chicago, IL: The University Press of Chicago.

Public Sector Commission. (2015). Structural change management. Retrieved from https://publicsector.wa.gov.au/public-administration/structural-change-management

Salerno, A., & Brock, L. (2008). *The change cycle: How people can survive and thrive in organizational change*. Oakland, CA: Berrett-Koehler.

Schwenk, C. R. (1990). Conflict in organizational decision making: An exploratory study of its effects in for-profit and not-for-profit organizations. *Management Science, 36*(4), 436–448.

Scott, J. (1992). *Social network analysis*. Newbury Park, CA: Sage.

Scott, P. G., & Falcone, S. (1988). Comparing public and private organizations: An exploratory analysis of three frameworks. *American Review of Public Administration, 28*(2). 126–145.

Sims, R. R. (2009). Civil service reform in action: The case of the Personnel Board of Jefferson County, Alabama. *Review of Public Personnel Administration. 29*(4), 382–401.

Sims, R. R. (2010). *Change (transformation) in government organizations.* Charlotte, NC: Information Age Publishing.

Surbhi, S. (2015. May 20). Difference between public sector and private sector. Retrieved from http://keydifferences.com/difference-between-public-sector-and-private-sector.html

Tabor, L., Shiras, T., & Kaye, N. (2015, July). Dynamic vision is a cornerstone of state payment reform initiatives. Retrieved from http://healthaffairs. org/blog/2015/07/28/dynamic-vision-is-a-cornerstone-of-state-payment-reform-initiatives/

Trust-Government. (2007). In T. G. Cummings & C. G. Worley (Eds.). *Organization development and change.* Mason, OH: South-Western Cengage Learning.

van der Voet, J. (2015, March). Change leadership and public sector organizational change: Examining the interactions of transformational leadership style and red tape. *The American Review of Public Administration.* Retrieved from http:// arp.sagepub.com/content/early/2015/03/18/0275074015574769.abstract

Vavreck, L. (2015, July 3). The long decline of trust in government, and why that can be patriotic. Retrieved from http://www.nytimes.com/2015/07/04/upshot/ the-long-decline-of-trust-in-government-and-why-that-can-be-patriotic. html?_r=0

White House. (2011). Revising government regulations. Retrieved from https:// www.whitehouse.gov/economy/reform/resources

Wodzicki, M. (2007). Public sector reform and democracy assistance: A literature review. Retrieved from http://www.gordonfn.org/resfiles/wodzicki_PSR%20 and%20Democracy%20Assistance.pdf

Workforce Performance Directorate. (2015). Structural change management: A guide to assist agencies to manage change. Retrieved from https://publicsector. wa.gov.au/document/structural-change-management-guide-assist-agencies-manage-change

World Bank. (1999). *Civil service reform: A review of World Bank assistance* (Operations Evaluation Department Report no. 19599). Washington, DC: Author.

World Health Organization. (2015, September). Launch of the world report on ageing and health 2015. Retrieved from http://www.who.int/ageing/en/

Zucker, L. (1983). Organizations as institutions. In S. B. Bacharach (Ed.), *Research in the sociology of organizations* (pp. 1–42). Greenwich, CT: JAI Press.

CHAPTER 2

HUMAN RESOURCE MANAGEMENT AND CIVIL SERVICE REFORM

Change (Transformation) in Government

Ronald R. Sims

INTRODUCTION

There is perhaps no area of public administration that has experienced greater change, professionalization, and controversy over the past four decades than public human resource management (PHRM) (Condrey, 2012; Sims, 2010b). And given the reality that government or public sector organizations continue to experience pressure to reinvent, reform or to radically change or transform (Sims, 2010a) as discussed in the chapters throughout this book it goes without saying that PHRM will have no choice but to continue to reinvent, reform, radically change and transform in kind.

According to Ban and Gossett (2010), efforts to reform the way in which governments handle the personnel management function have a long

Transforming Government Organizations:
Fresh Ideas and Examples From the Field, pp. 31–74
Copyright © 2016 by Information Age Publishing
All rights of reproduction in any form reserved.

history in the United States. Kellough and Selden (2003) suggest that there have been at least 12 major administrative reforms in the 20th century alone. Ban and Gossett also note that the last 35-year period has seen almost continuous calls for reform, many of them leading to significant changes in how the human resource management (HRM) function is organized and managed in the federal government, starting with President Carter's Civil Service Reform Act of 1978 and moving through the Grace Commission's recommendations under President Reagan (Hansen, 1985; Levine, 1985) to the National Performance era of reinventing government led by Vice President Gore (National Performance Review, 1993; Thompson, 2001) and to President George Bush's President's Management Agenda (Office of Management and Budget [OMB], 2002), which James Pfiffner (2007, p. 7) has characterized as containing possibly "the broadest human resource management changes since the Pendleton Act." With the election of President Barack Obama in 2008 there was every indication his administration would have (and has had) an active policy agenda concerning federal HRM reform.

Condrey (2012) recently noted in answering the question "where is the field PHRM headed?" that

> while the path is not directly clear, this writer believes that public human resource management is on the way toward revitalization and increased importance in the management of public organizations. HRM expertise is not only required for those staffing agency human resources offices but is also an essential part of the job of every public manager. As sound human resource management practices are diffused throughout public organizations, the challenges is for central human resources departments to be viewed as credible and viable sources of human resource management expertise. (p. 11)

And there is no doubt that in the coming years the effectiveness of public sector organizations will depend on how well they are able to respond to major demographic, social, political, economic, technological, and managerial trends which affect their work force and citizens. To effectively respond to these and other trends, challenges and pressures public sector organizations will have to find ways to run differently; jobs must be redefined; and learning and on-going reform, change or transformation must become second-nature for PHRM professionals who will play a role in the implementation of PHRM and civil service reform.

Historically, calls for civil service reform (CSR) in general, and PHRM in particular have resulted in increased pressures on PHRM professionals' to implement reform or change in these areas as well. Consider the following: The traditional role of the PHRM professional focused on knowledge of rules, regulations and techniques; emphasized the values of neutrality and efficiency; found its source of power in rewards and punishments associated with manipulation of rules and procedures; and finally, adopted a problem-solving orientation to management. In contrast, PHRM employees and their agencies have increasingly evolved to a more of a consultative role which centers on productivity-related knowledge; its source of power grows from expertise related to this knowledge; it values efficiency and effectiveness; and it is predisposed to find and identify problems as well as solve them. This transition in professional identity from the compliance to consultative role has both enhanced (a) the status of PHRM professionals and their departments who continue to bring valued expert knowledge of HRM to their agencies and (b) increased organizational effectiveness as partners with agency managers who jointly apply this knowledge within and as part of PHRM or civil service reform efforts.

This chapter first takes a historical look at CSR and PHRM in the United States. Next, the chapter focuses on some lessons and limits to reform in CSR and public HRM reform, change management, and a number of principles applicable to reform in public HRM. Finally, the chapter concludes with some lessons learned from the field on reform, change and transformation of civil service and public HRM.

PUBLIC HUMAN RESOURCE MANAGEMENT AND CIVIL SERVICE REFORM OVER THE YEARS

While there are some suggestions that public personnel administration has been practiced for at least 2,500 years, if not longer (Farazmand, 2007), attempts to reform PHRM systems (i.e., CSR interventions) can be traced back to the early 19th century. Such interventions have typically been designed to address institutional weaknesses associated with public administration in general, and civil service HRM and processes in particular.

Public administration is a labor-intensive enterprise. Hence, the processes used to recruit, select, develop, compensate, motivate, evaluate, and discipline public employees are crucial to effective public management and must continue to change and evolve. This is especially the case given that there is every indication that as we move further into the 21st century it will increasingly be characterized by rapid environmental, technological, social, demographic, political and cultural changes that pose challenges to government and PHRM throughout the world. Coping with and managing these challenges require new capacity building and development in human capital as a key asset of today's modern governments and within the PHRM itself. There is no escape from these challenges and PHRM has to play a critical role in proactively reforming or changing themselves if government agencies are to successfully fulfill their missions in the years to come.

CSR is processes designed to improve the capacity of governments to formulate and implement effective, efficient and accountable public policies and programs (Sims, 1998, 2010a). Policies and programs that meet these criteria are those which foster the adequate provision as well as the effective and efficient delivery of basic public services by the relevant level of government, stimulate the appropriate functioning of the private sector, and/or promote a mutually beneficial relationship between government and civil society. HRM, on the other hand, encompasses the traditional personnel functions of recruitment, selection, training, motivation, compensation, evaluation, discipline, and termination of employees. Each of those tasks demands particular skills. Increasingly, HRM is being recognized for its strategic importance to organizations and jurisdictions, and continues to move beyond its traditional position as a monitor of compliance.

Within the public sector, many of the most visible and interesting controversies, such as affirmative action, employee ethics, sexual harassment, drug testing, and labor-management relations, are part of HRM. Human resources also account for the largest percentage of the operating budget for most public agencies, and public administrators must have both an appreciation for the costs of human resources decisions and the ability to project those costs. In addition, constitutional, statutory and regulatory requirements often constrain personnel decisions and actions in the public sector, and public administrators must have a working knowledge of these legal guidelines.

Public administrators must recognize the political aspect of HRM. HRM policies and techniques are developed, implemented and evaluated in a public (read *political*) context. Public sector HRM practices effect the selection and experiences of government employees which, in turn, affects public policy. In order to make and implement effective HRM policies, administrators need an appreciation of the political and historical context in which the policies have developed to date.

In the current environment, a professional public administrator must be prepared to advocate for the strategic importance of human resources, find ways to be flexible and responsive to change, adapt to changing patterns of employment and intersectoral relations, utilize technology to more effectively communicate with prospective and existing employees, and develop more sophisticated and effective methods of measuring and rewarding performance (Ingraham & Rubaii-Barrett, 2007). In addition, they and others have a profound role to play in PHRM and civil service reform efforts in the years to come.

In order for such reform to take place it is important to understand some of the history of HRM and civil service reforms in the United States. With this in mind, the remainder of this section first takes a historical look at public HRM before providing a selective look at CSR efforts over the past few decades.

PUBLIC HUMAN RESOURCES MANAGEMENT AND CIVIL SERVICE REFORMS: A HISTORICAL PERSPECTIVE

PHRM in the United States can be viewed from at least four perspectives (Klingner & Lynn, 2005; Klingner & Nalbandian, 2003; Klingner, Nalbandian, & Llorens, 2010). First, it is the functions (planning, acquisition, development, and discipline) needed to manage human resources in public agencies. Second, it is the processes by which public jobs, as scarce resources, are allocated.

Third, it is the interaction among fundamental social values that often conflict. These values are responsiveness, efficiency, employee rights, and social equity. Responsiveness means a budget process that allocates positions and therefore sets priorities and an appointment process that considers political or personal loyalty along with education and experience as indicators of merit. Efficiency means staffing decisions based on ability and performance rather than political loyalty. Employee rights mean selection and promotion based on merit, as defined by objective measures of ability and performance, and employees who are free to apply their knowledge, skills, abilities, and other characteristics (KSAOCs) without partisan political interference. And social equity means public jobs allocated proportionately, based on gender, race, and other designed criteria.

Fourth, PHRM is the embodiment of human resource systems (i.e., the laws, rules, and procedures) used to express these abstract values—political appointments, civil service, collective bargaining, and affirmative action under the traditional model; and alternative mechanisms and flexible employment relationships under the emergent privatization and partnership paradigms (Klingner, 2016). Klingner (2016) notes that historically U.S. public HRM systems developed in at least five evolutionary stages (see Table 2.1).

Reform at the Federal Level

In the patrician era (1780–1828), the small group of upper-class property owners who had led the fight for independence and established a national government held most public jobs. With the passing of this generation—marked by the symbolically coincidental deaths of John Adams and Thomas Jefferson on July 4, 1826, the 15th anniversary of the Declaration of Independence—the emergence of political parties spawned

Table 2.1. Evolution of Public HRM Systems and Values in the United States

Stage of Evolution	Dominant Values	Dominant Systems	Role of Human Resource Management	Pressures for Change
Past Stages Patrician (1789–1828)	Responsiveness	"Government by elites"	None	Political parties + patronage
Patronage (1829–1882)	Responsiveness	Patronage	Recruitment + political clearance	Modernization + democratization
Professionalism (1883–1932)	Efficiency + individual rights	Civil service	"Watchdog" over agency managers and elected officials to ensure merit system compliance	Responsiveness + effective government
Performance (1993–1964)	Responsiveness + efficiency + individual rights	Patronage + civil service	Collaboration + legislative limits	Individual rights + social equity
People 1965–1979)	Responsiveness + efficiency + individual rights + social equity	Patronage + civil service + collective bargaining + affirmative action	Compliance + policy implementation + consultation	Dynamic equilibrium among four competing values and systems
Current Stages Privatization (1980 to present)	Responsiveness + efficiency + individual rights + accountability + limited government + community responsibility	Patronage + civil service + collective bargaining + affirmative action + alternative mechanisms + flexible employment relationships	Compliance + policy implementation + consultation + contract compliance + strategic thinking about HRM	Dynamic equilibrium among four progovernmental values and systems and three antigovernmental values and systems
Partnerships (2002 to present)	Responsiveness + efficiency + individual rights + accountability + limited government + community responsibility + collaboration	Patronage + civil service + collective bargaining + affirmative action + alternative mechanisms + flexible employment relationships	Compliance + policy implementation + consultation + contract compliance + strategic thinking about HRM + tension management + boundary spanning	Dynamic equilibrium among four progovernmental values and systems and three antigovernmental values and systems

an era of patronage (1829–1883) during which public jobs were awarded according to political loyalty or party affiliation (Lynn & Klingner, 2010). The increased size and complexity of public activities led to an era of professionalism (1993–1932) that emphasized efficiency (modernization) by defining personnel management as a neutral administrative function and individual rights (democratization) by allocating public jobs, at least at the federal level, on merit (Heclo, 1997; Sims, 2007). The unprecedented demands of a global depression and World War II led to the emergence of a hybrid performance model (1933–1964) that combined the political leadership of patronage systems and the merit principles of civil service systems because even pure merit systems must be responsive to political leadership if government is to be effective (Condrey, 2010; Fischer, 1945; Sayre, 1948).

Social upheavals presaged the emergence of the people era (1965–1979), in which collective bargaining emerged to represent collective employee rights (the equitable treatment of members of management through negotiated work rules for wages, benefits, and working conditions) and affirmative action emerged to represent social equity (through voluntary or court-mandated recruitment and selection practices to help ameliorate the underrepresentation of minorities and women in the workforce), for example, through the application of the Civil Rights Act of 1964 to state and local governments by the Equal Employment Opportunity Act of 1972 (Condrey, 2010; Klingner, 2016; Lynn & Klingner, 2010; Sims, 2007).

Following the passage of the Equal Employment Opportunity Act of 1972, there was a great deal of introspection by central HRM agencies, civil service systems, government managers, and citizens about the relevance of traditional hiring practices and their results as seen in the composition of U.S. workforces. Condrey (2010) notes that in some cases this introspection was voluntary; in other cases, it was not. Numerous charges of unfair recruitment, testing, and performance appraisal techniques were brought to light through lawsuits, consent decrees, and the like. Government agencies, now forced to defend their respective HRM systems, were obligated to prove their techniques' validity and viability in cases where adverse impact on protected groups was detected (Sims, 2010a). Traditional practices such as the rule of three (hiring restricted to the top three candidates for a position as measured by a civil service examination) and written tests based on scanty or nonexistent job analyses came crashing down. When HRM managers were required to justify their methods, in many cases these methods were found to be sorely lacking. This increased scrutiny forced HRM agencies to rethink time-honored practices and to become acquainted with more readily defensible, sophisticated psychological methodologies: validated assessment centers often replaced written tests, broad banding of test scores replaced strict rules of one or three, and performance appraisal systems moved from trait-based systems toward more job-related and interactive measures. In this way, implementation of the Equal Employment Opportunity Act of 1972 helped professionalize and energize a once dormant field. Conversely, it also laid the groundwork for a serious questioning of the role that HRM professionals had in managing modern organizations.

While the Equal Employment Opportunity Act of 1972 ultimately revealed tried-but-not true HRM practices the Civil Service Reform Act of 1978 (CSRA) initiated a steady call to reform PHRM and more specifically to decentralize HRM functions and decisions. Enacted during President Jimmy Carter's administration, the CSRA sought to bring businesslike procedures to the federal government, most notably through a merit pay experiment for federal midlevel managers. Promoted as a proven private sector technique, merit pay sought to link managerial performance to compensation, eliminating time-in-grade step increases (which, ironically, were first designed to be associated with individual performance). Condrey (2010) has pointed out that although time has proved the federal government's merit pay experiment a failure, merit pay and, more important, a view of the private sector as a model for public sector HRM diffused and continues to diffuse to many state, city, and county government organizations. Merit pay, like many of the provisions of the CSRA, was born of the idea that government bureaucracies and the public personnel administrators that had great influence in controlling them had become insulated from executive and political input and control.

By 1980, U.S. public HRM could be described as dynamic equilibrium among the four competing values, each championed by a particular system for allocating scarce public jobs (Ban & Riccucci, 1991; Freedman, 1994; Nalbandian, 1991). In the privatization era (starting in 1980), public HRM still works consultatively with agency managers and employees and with compliance agencies. More specifically, with the advent of the Reagan administration and a coinciding era of cutback management, government organizations at all levels began to question bureaucratic structures and processes. Organizations were instructed to do more with less and to become more efficient, effective, and accountable to executive and public oversight and control (Condrey, 2010; Klingner et al., 2010). Soon government organizations were called on to reinvent themselves. In many instances, reinvention focused on HRM practices; this, for example, was the case for the National Performance Review. Headed by Vice President Al Gore, the National Performance Review called for decentralizing many federal human resource management functions and encouraged the empowerment of managers to act with discretion rather than purely through applying rules and regulations (Gore, 1993).

The mid-1990s saw the emergence of radical reform of PHRM systems which continues to shape the field today (Condrey, 2010; Klingner et al., 2010). Condrey (2010) suggests that an outgrowth of the new public management (NPM) movement led to new pressures for reform: for example, the State of Georgia's abolition of property rights for civil service employees hired or promoted after July 1, 1996 and the Sate of Florida's Service First initiative which abolished tenure for upper-level managers, increasing the opportunity for gubernatorial influence and controls. Condrey and Battaglio (2007) and Hays and Sowa (2007) also note that the reforms started in Georgia and Florida spread to many other states in some fashion or another.

With the emergence of the partnership era (since 2002), public HRM is increasingly expected to operate within a framework of structures, processes, and people that are to a large extent beyond immediate control yet are part of the collective enterprise (Klingner & Lynn, 2005). Consider for example the legislation authoring the recently formed Transportation Security Administration (TSA) which privatized and outsourced almost all important HRM functions, including recruitment and selection (Condrey, 2005). Thus, there is every reason to believe that it will become commonplace for public sector organizations to contract for work that in the past was performed by career employees.

Thompson and Seidner (2016) have recently noted that the period 2006–2014 (i.e., the last 2 years of President George W. Bush's and the first 6 years of the Obama administration) could be characterized as one of instability in federal HRM practices and policies. Further, the most significant reforms of the preceding period, the creation of separate personnel systems at the Departments of Homeland Security and Defense, were repealed. Additionally, the substantial immunity that the federal workforce had enjoyed from the effects of the economic recession that began in 2008 ended when employee pay was frozen and pension contributions for new employees increased in 2011.

As noted earlier, PHRM comprises the functions needed to manage human resources in public agencies. Civil service is the predominant public HRM system because it has articulated rules and procedures for performing the whole range of HRM functions. Other systems, though incomplete, are nonetheless legitimate and effective influences over one or more HRM functions. Although HRM functions remain the same across different systems, their organizational location and method of performance differ, depending on the system and the values that underlie it.

Notwithstanding budget concerns, CSR in the United States has produced a uniquely open system, in contrast to the closed career system common to other nations—which one enters only at a relatively early age and remains within for a lifetime, in the manner associated in the United

States mainly with a military career. The Pendleton Act of 1883 established this original approach, providing that the federal service would be open to persons of any age who could pass job-oriented examinations (Van Riper, 2003). Persons may move in and out of public service, from government to private industry and back again, through a process known as lateral entry. It is this openness to anyone who can pass an examination, this constant availability of lateral entry that has set the tone and character of public service in the United States at all levels. One consequence of U.S. civil service policy has been to provide a notable route for upward mobility, especially for women and Blacks. Thus, the U.S. civil service has reflected the open, mobile nature of American society and, in turn, has done much to support it (Answers.com, 2009).

In more recent years, considerable attention has been given to CSR. Given the centrality of HRM to questions of government performance, such attention is both understandable and warranted. Coggburn, Battaglio, Bowman, Condrey, Goodman, and West (2010) also noted that along with reform proposals, a number of important questions have been raised about the potential effects of reforms and their fit with the public sector's traditional HRM practices and values.

Through the administrations of Jimmy Carter, Ronald Reagan, Bill Clinton and George W. Bush—the policy was to reform, shrink, get a better handle on or outsource government activities. All cited statistics and examples (sometimes overblown, sometimes just flat out wrong) to prove their point (Sims, 2010a).

The Carter administration sought "reform" by depicting the government as a place where nobody, no matter how incompetent, ever got fired. As pointed out previously, President Carter initiated the most sweeping reforms of the U.S. federal civil service in 95 years when he signed the Civil Service Reform Act (CSRA) on October 13, 1978. The substantive reforms of the CSRA began with creation of the U.S. Office of Personnel Management (OPM), on January 1, 1979. CSRA's provisions were wide-ranging. They included reorganization of the agencies tasked with civil service management and regulation, establishment of a Senior Executive Service, creation of performance appraisal and merit pay programs, and clarification and simplification of appeal procedures for personnel actions.

The Reagan administration held back on pay raises and perks because it said feds had it pretty good. The Clinton administration said government needed to be reinvented and went to the media with examples of silly, outdated programs and practices. It jump-started outsourcing by eliminating a couple of hundred thousand jobs that were often contracted to the private sector. The G.W. Bush administration continued outsourcing efforts as well as the Clinton administration program of holding down federal pay raises (Sims, 2010a, 2010b).

While legislation has been a major driver of CSR over the years it is only as effective as the people who administer it, and some of President Reagan's appointees had a devastating impact on the civil service, particularly in the Department of Housing and Urban Development, where they were unsympathetic to needy citizens while lining the pockets of corrupt partisans. A similar concern was recently raised by some of the critics of CSR's efforts introduced under former President George W. Bush (Sims, 2010a).

The election of Barack Obama in 2008 ushered in a new commitment to CSR. According to Condrey (2012), the election of President Obama may have signaled a reversal or, at least, a halting of the antibureaucratic themes of the past 4 decades. President Obama, unlike his recent predecessors, ran for office on a campaign that embraced public service as a high calling. He also appointed John Berry as OPM Director. Berry was the highest profile director of that office since its initial director, Alan Campbell. It appeared to be clear early on in his tenure as president that Obama's call to public service harkened back to President Kennedy's administration. As John Berry (2009) stated:

> I believe this is an historic opportunity for comprehensive reform of our civil service system. The stars are aligned in a way that occurs only once in a generation. We have a President who deeply values service and wants to restore the dignity and respect for our civil service to what it was during Kennedy's stirring call. We have a congress that is willing to help and a public that increasingly recognizes that our current approaches to hiring, rewarding, appraising and training our employees are inadequate. (p. 9)

Condrey (2012) recently suggested that there were six areas that the Obama administration had, or likely would address, concerning federal HRM:

- Recruitment
- Pay system reform
- Performance management
- Training and development
- Improved labor management relations
- In-sourcing

All of these areas are important to the ongoing success of public sector organizations. Consider, for example, the Obama administration has recently called for reeling in of the excessive spending on defense contractors (Harrow, 2008). The National Security Personnel System (NSPS), unveiled under George W. Bush as a way to introduce pay-for-performance, has folded into the General Schedule under Obama's watch. Congress passed The Defense Authorization Act of 2010, which effectively ended the NSPS (Thompson, 2009, p. 18).

The Obama administration has also focused attention on hiring reform. More specifically, President Obama issued a memorandum on "Improving the Federal Recruitment and Hiring Process." The primary goal was to improve the notoriously complex hiring process while simultaneously making working for the government "cool again" (Thompson & Seidner, 2016). President Obama's mandate made explicit demands that agencies overhaul the technical and structural aspects of hiring. Specifically, it mandated "plain language" and shorter job announcements, resume-only applications, expanded assessment and applicant referral (known as "category rating"), and significantly reduce time-to-hire periods.

As one would expect, a variety of stakeholders or constituents continues to voice concerns about the need to revamp or reform the federal civil service system. For example, in 2013 the Partnership for Public Service (PPS) (2014) articulated a vision for creating a federal government that acts as a single, integrated enterprise—not a set of disconnected agencies and programs—in tackling the nation's biggest problems and challenges. The PPS noted that "in no area is this need for a unified, whole-of-government approach more critical than in the way the government manages its talent" (p. i). Based on discussions with numerous current and former federal officials, academics and stakeholders about how to make government more effective, one theme that emerged early and often centered on the inadequacy of the civil service system in helping our federal government recruit, hire, develop, retain and reward our nation's top talent.

According to the PPS the current civil service system makes it harder to attract highly qualified and skilled employees in this age of pay freezes, ad hoc hiring freezes and tight budgets. Additionally, they note that only 9% of the federal workforce is made up of people younger than 30—compared to 23% of the total U.S. workforce. And, that by 2017 nearly two-thirds of the Senior Executive Service, our nation's career leadership corps, will be eligible for retirement and about 31% of the government's permanent career employees will be able to head out the door. Further, according to the PPS (2014) "given the state of the economy over the past several years, government has held on to its experienced employees for longer than anticipated, but retirements are back on the rise" (p. i).

The PPS suggested that there is both an opportunity and an imperative to plan for the future federal workforce, but to do it properly will mean revamping the system that supports it. The PPS pointed to the General Schedule, the pay and job classification system under which the majority of the federal workforce still operates (dating back to 1949) as an example of an area ripe for reform. More specifically, the PPS argued that the General

Schedule reflects the needs and characteristics of the last century's workforce—not those required for today's complex, interagency challenges.

Like others, previous administrations and in particular members of the current Republican congress, the PPS believes that (1) the work of government has changed; (2) the way we work and the skills needed have changed; and (3) the world has changed. However, the civil service system has not kept pace. The PPS also pointed out that to cope, some agencies, many of whom experienced a crisis during the most recent economic recession, were able to cut their own deals with Congress that enabled them to operate under separate systems, with higher pay rates and more hiring flexibilities. And, these deals have resulted in a patchwork quilt of "have" and "have not" agencies, where government competes with itself for high-caliber employees instead of approaching talent at a strategic, enterprise level on behalf of all of government.

In his 2015 budget proposal, President Obama reiterated a commitment to taking executive actions that will "attract and retain the best talent in the federal workforce and foster a culture of excellence" (Partnership for Public Partnership, 2014, p. 2). A possible outgrowth of President Obama's 2015 budget is commitment of a series of initiatives aimed at reforming, improving and rewarding the federal government's Senior Executive Service. For example, one of the suggested initiatives was to create the White House Leadership Development Program, aimed at cultivating career executives. The program would allow "top civil servants and SES candidates" to participate in rotating assignments at agencies across government to address government's "highest priority, highest impact changes" (Katz, 2014, p. 1). Additionally, with Republicans controlling both the senate and congress there have been increased calls for civil service reform in federal hiring, firing, pay, benefits, and conflict adjudication (Clark, 2015). Any such changes, however, would need the approval of President Obama, whose term of office extends to January 2017.

The PPS believes that the steps outlined in the Obama administration budget are critical to reforming the federal civil service system. Additionally, the PPS believe we are long overdue for fundamental reforms that go beyond executive action for the civil service system (PPS, 2014). And, as one would expect, no reform effort will be successful, however, without strong leadership to drive its successful implementation (Sims, 2010b).

Reform at the State Level

Selden (2016) and Condrey (2012) have noted reform efforts in HRM and civil service at the state level. For example, civil service reformers have sought to remove civil service protections from a critical mass of state employees (e.g., Crowell & Guy, 2010; Goodman & Mann, 2010; Kellough & Nigro, 2006). These reforms sought to redefine the relationship between public employees and their employers by allowing for at-will termination without the protection of procedural due process (Kellough & Nigro, 2006). In practice, although some states have implemented system-wide civil service reforms, the percentage of employees covered by the civil service system has fluctuated over time as administrations have changed (Goodman & Mann, 2010). Some administrations may grant employees in the nonclassified service civil service protections before leaving office. Other states may exempt particular departments, employee classes, or agencies either permanently or temporarily to create more personnel flexibility to manage their workforces if state employees serve "at-will" and therefore, do hold a property interest in their positions (Selden, 2016).

Historically, in a traditional classified civil service system, the authority to administer HRM activities belonged to a central HRM department. According to Selden (2016), the purported benefits of this approach include equitable treatment of employees, consistency in the delivery of services, efficiency gains through economies of scale, and clearly delineated roles between central HRM departments and state agencies. In the 1990s many scholars and practitioners pushed for state central HRM departments to decentralize their control over some HRM practices and provide more flexibility to public agencies and their managers (see Kellough & Nigro, 2006, for a more detailed discussion of this). Selden (2016) has noted that states have reduced their HRM staff between 2007 and 2012. Additionally, over the past decade or so, state civil service systems have undergone considerable changes. The underlying philosophy that has driven public dialogue emerged as part of the NPM philosophy discussed earlier (Condrey & Battaglio, 2007). Like advocates for reform at the federal level, those at the state level have pushed for HRM systems that reduce civil service rules and emulate private sector HRM practices. Consider the following:

- Georgia and Florida implemented radical system-wide CSRs in the 1990s and 2000s that changed the nature of civil service within those states.
- The state of Washington adopted system-wide changes in 2002 to its personnel system but without abolishing its civil service system.
- Arizona, Indiana and Tennessee adopted sweeping CSR in the past few years, and
- Colorado continues to pursue similar reforms.

States have also implemented structural changes within their HRM systems. According to Selden (2016) between 2007 and 2012, states implemented an array of HRM restructuring initiatives that are consistent with Rainey's (2006) observation that "the continuing complaints about the rigidity of the civil service personnel system" have motivated government to pursue flexibility using many different paths (p. 36). These structural changes have focused on shared services while decreasing efforts to improve specific HRM processes. A shared services model of HRM creates a centralized service function that considers employees and agency-based HRM professionals as internal customers. This approach is designed to enable a state to better leverage existing resources, to reduce duplication of HRM activities across state agencies, and to provide more consistent, higher-quality services to internal customers by concentrating existing resources and streamlining processes (Selden & Wooters, 2011).

Like federal CSRs, changes in state civil service systems have to a great extent been driven by the underlying philosophy that has driven public dialogue which emerged as part of the new public management (NPM) (Condrey & Battaglio, 2007; Selden, 2016). While civil service has been a cornerstone of the American public sector and traditionally a professional civil service was deemed essential for government performance (Kellough & Nigro 2006; Selden, 2006) such importance and linkage has been (and there is every indication that it will continue to be) challenged by the increased incidence of radical CSR at the state and federal levels (Sims, 2010a). And the calls will continue to come in many forms and for many reasons like those highlighted throughout this selective historical review of PHRM and civil service reform in the United States.

Some are skeptical of CSR and will oppose change. Others have encouraged recent presidential administrations "to blow the whole thing up and start over" (Sims, 2009, 2010a). Neither option is realistic or advisable. Instead, it would seem to make the most sense to chip away at the most regressive characteristics of civil service systems—those which impede the effective delivery of public services to national, regional, state and local citizens and those which fail to motivate and inspire employees. With adequate cooperation from employee organizations, there is the increased likelihood that significant reforms to civil service systems can be made.

As we look to the future, HRM reform and CSR should be selective and focused, and designed to address perceived weaknesses associated with civil service. The civil service—understood as nonmilitary public personnel who work for government applying its laws and regulations—has long been a feature of government management; but it is a civil service based on merit and relevant skills, and therefore, one in which qualifications and expertise are critical to gaining and maintaining public employment in government organizations.

The PHRM function reflects a governmental agency's incentive systems for staff and employees and has an important impact on motivation, morale and commitment to performance. When managers in government fail to fill positions with the most qualified individuals, are unable to suit-ably motivate public employees, and do not work toward the most efficient and effective public service, the opportunity and real costs for society are incalculable (Sims, 1998). Hence, the most important goal of CSR is to set up or strengthen merit systems in a systematic fashion in a move to ensure that both long-term and temporary personnel are competitively recruited as required, swiftly selected, and properly rewarded, trained (or retrained), motivated, utilized, promoted, and dismissed, along the lines of missions and objectives of the relevant government organization.

Modern CSR, for example, regards merit as an important principle to maintain, as it is a precondition to granting managers and employees the discretion, empowerment and flexibility typical of result-oriented admin-istration. Thus, civil service entities or functions committed to maintaining merit systems—at the national, regional or local level—or revitalizing and strengthening their principles and practices in settings where relevant rules are already in place but have not been properly implemented must continue to innovate and improve across the board. The flourishing of innovative ideas also requires constant improvement in agency members' knowledge, skills, attitudes, and motivation, which makes training and retraining of managers and employees essential to support changes in personnel and agency needs.

The development of and reform of civil service entities or PHRM func-tions should be coupled with appropriate HRM planning, transparent definitions of performance requirements, accurate comparative perfor-mance evaluations, and performance-based incentives. Since one of the reasons for the strengthening of HRM or merit systems or CSR is to fill positions with qualified candidates, traditional control management becomes redundant and makes the downsizing of such positions—in the medium run—particularly useful to generating savings that may then be reinvested in training and retraining of employees, benchmarking and/or improved communication technology.

Albeit necessary for adequate agency performance, systematic CSR is not in itself a sufficient condition for improved organizational productiv-ity, as skills are utilized (or not utilized) in agency or group contexts: it is very difficult to foster performance-based HRM if the target agency is poorly structured or culturally unfit. This means that HRM or CSR tools, such as training and retraining of personnel, changes in personnel rules or practices, modifications in position classification, restructuring of per-sonnel categories, streamlining of recruitment and selection procedures are essential to institutional performance, but that to be really effective, other agency systems—such as budgetary management, communication systems, and so on, must be working appropriately. Thus, the systematic and simultaneous diagnosis of, and attention to, other core agency' functions is important for maximizing HRM reform or CSR impacts.

Public Human Resource Management Models or Frameworks

Battaglio and Condrey (2006) have noted that the past two decades have seen a renewed interest in reforming the structure and nature of civil service systems (Condrey, 2010). In the United States, these reform efforts were spearheaded by the concepts of "reinventing government" and new public management. Additionally, Naff (2002) noted that during the 1990s, many public sector jurisdictions sought to reform their civil service systems in order to make them more flexible and responsive. The success of those efforts depended to a large extent on political factors such as the extent to which there were active constituencies backing such reforms. The federal government provides an example in that while in 1978, the Carter administration was able to enact reform legislation, efforts by the Clinton administration died for lack of support.

According to Naff (2002) state governments that have sought reform have taken one of two approaches: either modernization or the complete abolishment of the system. In their discussion of reform in four states and two local governments Battaglio and Condrey (2006), on the other hand, offered that state (and local) governments have sought reform using one of four models: traditional, reform, strategic, and privatization/outsourcing. A brief description of each based upon the work of Condrey (2010, 2012) and Battaglio and Condrey (2006) and others (see for example, Black & Upchruch, 1999; Brown, 2004) are discussed in the next few paragraphs. We will briefly revisit reform efforts at the state level later in this chapter.

According to Brown (2004) the public sector developed a distinctive approach to HRM over time and featured many innovations that delivered significant rights and entitlements to employees. The public sector has been perceived as the "model employer" and conditions of service have been at the forefront of employment reform and innovation. The notion of the model employer encapsulated the principles of best practice and was argued to set an example to the private sector in terms of fair treatment of employees and providing good conditions of service including high levels of job security, superior leave entitlements and generous pensions (Black & Upchurch, 1999).

In the traditional model of HRM in the public sector the focus is on a central HRM organization dictating rules and procedures, ostensibly to achieve fairness and equity in public sector organizations. The HRM model is an outgrowth of the traditional model of the public sector organization, a bureaucratic employment policy matched the operation of Weberian practices and principles of rule-governed rational action. The administrative system was subjected to a bureaucratization of procedures to ensure that decisions and actions were consistent, formalized, and systematically addressed activities through a predefined application of rules and processes. Aspects of a rational-legal bureaucracy that reflected concern with employees and their administration included specialization through functional responsibility, formalized rules to prevent arbitrary dismissal, a reliance on organizational position to confer authority, selection by merit and, generally, a career service (Schroeder, 1992).

Condrey (2005) notes that little thought is given to line functions of the organization, whether they be paving roads, providing recreation services to citizens, delivering social services to clients, or fostering diplomatic relations with a foreign country. In this setting, according to Brown (2004) and Alford (1993), the employment system was highly centralized and run by powerful central agencies that were responsible for all the hire decisions, setting establishment numbers and formulating rules for employment, training and career development. Employment in the public sector was based on the notion of a "career service" of security of tenure and lifelong employment and was framed through the operation of an internal labor market (Gardner & Palmer, 1997). Employees were recruited to the public service at the lower ranks of departments and promotion to higher-level positions was restricted to internal public sector applicants, unless the position was highly specialized.

The demands for a new approach to management that allowed greater flexibility in dealing with employee issues were based in the rhetoric of the need for greater government agency responsiveness and efficiency. Condrey (2005, 2010) notes that this model is most closely associated with strong civil service systems such as the U.S. civil service system in existence prior to the Civil Service Reform Act of 1978 or those employed today by local and state governments.

The reform model is almost exactly like the traditional model and seeks to decentralize HRM authority and decision making to line managers. This model values dispersal of real HRM authority to various organizational units, allowing them to make crucial decisions concerning employee recruitment, selection, classification, and remuneration. In many instances, these decisions may be made by line managers having little formal knowledge of or training in modern HRM practices and techniques. Condrey (2005) notes that the result may be responsive to the immediate needs of the organization; however, with no central organizing focus, problems of equity and fairness within and among organizational units may appear. For example, effective and consistent management of equal employment opportunity goals may be hampered, pay disparities may become prevalent, and employee assessment inequities may arise.

The strategic model seeks to blend positive features of the traditional and reform models. Perry (1993) highlights the positive space that such an arrangement makes for human resource professionals. Under the strategic model, HRM is closely aligned with the overall management of a public sector organization. Thus, the HRM professional's focus is on helping management achieve organizational objectives instead of enforcing rules and regulations. In the strategic model, the HRM function is shared between HRM staff and the line departments that use human resource services and the HRM staff serves more as a consultant to management.

The privatization or outsourcing model of public HRM is closely associated with new public management (NPM) and seeks to have specific functions performed by private organizations rather than public sector organizations. This model of public HRM has emerged over the past several decades.

The introduction of NPM with an emphasis on transferring private sector management techniques into the public sector shifted the emphasis in the public sector from administration to management and was part of a broad strategy to achieve efficiency, effectiveness, and quality of service. Changes to the public sector were introduced in response to the perceived need to reduce government expenditure, provide more efficient services and decrease the scope and reach of government provided public goods and services (Brown, 2004; Weller, 1996). Elements of NPM included managing for results, performance measurement, corporate planning, user pays, devolution of authority, decentralization of activities and risk management. Managerialism under a NPM model involved the application of physical, financial and human resources to realize government objectives. It was argued that the NPM model of public management was to be a "flexible, market-based form" (Hughes, 1994). The rhetoric of NPM denoted it as the "arts of private sector management" extended into the public sector (Brown, 2004; Gray & Jenkins, 1995). Thus HRM was included in the public sector reform agenda both in the United States and internationally.

Internationally, the *World Public Sector Report* (WPSR) (UN/DESA, 2005) advocated a HRM framework that was impartial, professional, and responsive, drawing where appropriate on the skills and resources of the private sector. It argued that countries should first establish an effective institutional framework for HRM as an underlying infrastructure to achieve high performance in the public sector. A strategic HRM system should then build on this base using the fundamental values of impartiality, professionalism and responsiveness. The report noted that HRM professionals in the public sector, as well as the private, had long advocated the need for input in the strategic decision processes of their respective organization, but these calls had begun to take on the language of the NPM. In addition to calls for the upgrading of their own influence in these discussion, PHRM managers increasingly pointed to the need for merit-based appointment; competence-based development; competence-based appraisal and performance management; equity vis-á-vis the private sector; the embrace of a total pay approach; and, in the retention field, rightsizing and effective labor management (Goldfinch & Wallis, 2009; Kim & Hong, 2006; UN/DESA, 2005).

In the HRM area per se, one of the most stunning aspects of marketized public administration prior to the Obama administration came in those states—most notably Florida, Georgia, and Texas—where "radical civil service reform" (henceforth, RCSR) commenced (see, e.g., Battaglio & Condrey, 2006; Bowman, West, & Geertz, 2006; Coggburn, 2006; Condrey, 2002; Gossett, 2002; Hays & Sowa, 2006; Kellough & Nigro, 2002; Kuykendall & Facer, 2002; Lasseter, 2002; West, 2002; Wilson, 2006). Couched in the neomanagerialist tenets of the NPM, RCSR grew popular among government reinventors and resonated as a populist theme among the general public (Barzelay, 1992; Condrey & Battaglio, 2007; Durant & Legge, 2006; Pollitt, 1990; Terry, 1993). Indeed, by 2006, Hays and Sowa found that at-will employment influences had diffused to a majority of state governments (56%). Additionally, of the 28 state governments reporting at-will policy expansion, 25 also reported some degree of decentralization of their personnel systems to agencies.

Condrey (2012) has recently added a fifth organizing model, the hybrid model, to these four and has suggested that while there are definite historical time periods that each of these models is most clearly associated with, all of them can be found today in varying degrees local, state, and federal governments in the United States. The hybrid model blends positive features of the strategic and the privatization or outsourcing models. That is, the hybrid model retains the importance of in-house HRM expertise, but appreciates that, with proper organizational oversight, increased flexibility as well as privatization is now an established feature of organizational life. The model recognizes that privatization and outsourcing are not only a permanent part of the public HRM landscape but also create a space for HRM professionals to have an active and increased role and influence in the management of the public sector organization.

In looking to the future, one should expect to see all five of these models to some degree in the practice of public HRM. In reality, public HRM departments or units and staff will need to continue to change or transform and develop a business case for the value they add to their agencies. Condrey (2010) suggests that rather than a strict historical analysis, the five organizing strategies offer an opportunity to understand the delivery of HRM services and how they, in turn, influence the role of the human resource manager.

Ban (2005), in discussing the changing role of the PHRM office or function, has suggested that while reformers' descriptions of the problems with the traditional system have much in common, over the years they have proposed a range of new roles for the PHRM office. For Ban, reform can differ along three dimensions. First, reform proposals may focus on how the PHRM does its work. The first model, which Ban calls the *customer service model*, assumes that the PHRM office will perform most or all of the usual functions but exhorts HRM professionals to do what they do better and faster, recognizing that the public manager is their key customer.

Second, reform may focus on the functions of the PHRM office. Model 2, which Ban calls the *organization development and consulting model*, urges HRM professionals to take on new functions within the organization, serving as internal consultants to managers on a wide range of organizational issues. This approach is sometimes combined with the suggestion that PHRM offices give up some of their traditional functions.

Finally, reform can focus on where the PHRM office sits within the organization—on its power and role in organizational policy. In the third model, the *strategic human resource management model*, the role of the PHRM office is to support the strategic mission of the organization or agency as a whole. To meet that goal, PHRM leaders are urged to act as full members of the management team, linking HRM and HRM policy to agency mission, goals, and policy. Clearly, Ban's view of the evolving role of PHRM is consistent with the PHRM models offered by Condrey earlier.

The models offered by both Condrey and Ban help us understand the importance of recognizing that building and reforming an effective PHRM system cannot be accomplished overnight; it requires internal competence and external support. As such, it is necessarily an incremental process whereby major stakeholders in the organization (political leaders, management, employees, and citizens) gain confidence and respect in the HRM function and its professionals and their ability to facilitate an effective and responsive system of HRM. Those seeking an effective PHRM system should not look to the latest management fad or quick fix but rather should concentrate on the proper resources (both monetary and human) and buy-in of the agency's major stakeholders. Additionally, it is important for those who are committed to PHRM and civil service reform to understand the history of such efforts in the United States and especially the politics that both drive and inhibit HRM and CSR interventions be they incremental or transformational.

The challenge for public sector organizations, PHRM professionals and managers alike is to retain coordinative control over the human resources function when privatization and outsourcing occur. With this model, the role of PHRM is diminished and most requires a change in the role of the PHRM professionals. This model has been criticized for the resultant erosion of employment conditions and opportunities for career development. Large-scale downsizing and contracting out also arguably contributed to poorer quality of service delivery. With the major changes and reforms to the public sector under NPM, Brown (2004) and Black and Upchurch (1999) argued that there was a dilution of some of the practices and conditions that had traditionally set the public sector apart from other organizations in the private and non-profit sectors. Thus, the consequences of adopting NPM practices and principles were argued to have meant a cutting back of employees' benefits and wages, staff reductions and changes in organizational culture and structure (Beattie & Osborne, 2008). As proponents of the evolution of contracting in the United States have argued, the implications of these propensities and trends have been profound for HRM at all levels of government in the United States (Condrey, 2010, 2012; Klijn, 2002).

As evidenced by our discussion thus far, changes or reforms in PHRM indicate that HRM (and CSR) have had a major impact on the operation of the public sector. The contribution of HRM to understanding the constituent elements of public sector organizations is significant. The various historical reforms have been centered on change in public sector organizations and the accompanying HRM and civil service systems. Ongoing and new concerns in relation to new directions and approaches for HRM in the public sector will continue as a result of the ever-increasing levels of technology, changes in demographics or the government workforce and new demands on public managers or leaders to be more efficient, effective and accountable, with more quantitative metrics. Some of the areas of concern and challenge to PHRM professionals will continue to be driven by advances being made possible by highly sophisticated information technology including human resource information systems (HRISs), the importance of understanding the implications of demographic trends such as the aging populations (and government workforces), the need for additional attention to public managers/leadership and leadership development, the greater emphasis on workforce capability or capacity and systems of knowledge management and the never ending calls for greater accountability, minimizing costs and the need for fiscal restraint and efficiency of public sector organizations, while being attentive to and responsive to its citizen constituents.

The reality is that PHRM professionals and their host agencies will continue to need to reform or change and seek radically different models for operating and structuring their work. The different orientation of the public sector from the private sector means that while HRM has commonalities across both sectors in its attention to workforce issues, PHRM will exhibit a range of differences to that of private sector HRM. PHRM professionals will need to continue to reform and transform given the prevailing public sector conditions and context. PHRM will continue to be a key platform for reform and driver of change in public sector organizations. And, in continuing in the role as a driver of change within the public sector HRM professionals will need to continue to search and develop different viable HRM models that take into consideration both the particular character of the public sector while also responding to the shifting conditions wrought by new and ever changing expectations of the multiple decision makers or stakeholders.

SOME LESSONS LEARNED AND LIMITS FROM THE FIELD ON HRM AND CIVIL SERVICE REFORM

While the analysis of any reform, change or transformation is complex and often emergent, the type of actions that those responsible for such initiatives may take can be categorized fairly simply into eight sets: (1) changes in mission/purpose; (2) redefinition of strategy; (3) shifts in objectives or performance targets; (4) alterations in agency culture, values, or beliefs; (5) organizational restructuring; (6) technology reforms; (7) task redesign; and (8) changing people. Changes in mission/purpose and strategy involve a realignment of the agency with its environment.

Alterations in the agency culture, values, or beliefs (including its informal systems and processes) may just be a shift in the internal workings of the agency but could also be in response to environmental demands. Agency restructuring includes the redesign of formal systems and processes and is perhaps the most common perspective on agency reform where new reporting relationships are developed. Technology reforms and task redesign are changes inside the agency affecting how the work is accomplished.

People can be changed by altering key competencies; shifting attitudes, values, and/or perspectives; or through adding and/or removing key people from the agency. These broad categories of action suggest simplicity. Those responsible for CSR and PHRM reform should be cautioned against assuming this as the dynamic nature of the agency, and its components make it far from simple.

Clearly, those responsible for CSR or PHRM reform must know what needs to change. However, how to go about making reform, change or transformation happen requires careful thought and planning.

How to Reform

As suggested above, it has been the author's experience that those responsible for CSR or HRM reform very often know what they need to achieve; they may not always know how to get there. An examination of key stakeholder issues and interests provides cues as to what is needed—but moving an agency to successfully addressing these needs often defeats public sector reform leaders.

Why is it so difficult to accomplish reform? One of the common causes lies in practices that have proven effective in the past, and this is often referred to as the "failure of success" (or in learning how to maintain the status quo). Agencies learn what works and what does not. They develop systems that exploit those learnings. They establish rules, policies, procedures, and decision frameworks that capitalize on the success of "business as usual." Further, they develop patterned responses (habits), assumptions, attributions, and expectations that influence the ways they think about how the world works (Sull, 1999). These beliefs and engrained responses form a strong resistant force, which encourages agencies and people to maintain old patterns regardless of feedback or input suggesting that they are inappropriate. In many respects, this is where the questions of what to reform and how to reform intersect (Sims, 2009, 2010b).

The costs of reform are real, while the benefits of reform are uncertain. By holding off investing in reform, an agency's leaders may be able to fend off pressures to reform in the short run. However, if conditions change and the agency's leaders fail to adjust in a timely fashion, they can quickly find themselves and the agency mired in stagnation and unable to create the necessary energy or motivation to move any reform forward. If reform leaders wait too long, they may find it impossible to do so.

By the time the system reaches point A, the need for reform is obvious, but it may also be too late for the agency to survive without experiencing significant trauma. Positive planned agency or HRM or civil service reform needs to be commenced sooner in the process—before things deteriorate to a crisis or disaster stage. Unfortunately, reform typically comes with costs that appear to lessen the positive outcomes in the short run. As many of those responsible for agency, HRM or civil service reform know, convincing anyone that they should incur short-run costs for longer-run benefits is a difficult selling task—particularly when things are going well or there is a comfort level with the status quo.

How to reform is difficult because identifying and demonstrating the need for agency reform is not obvious. If an agency or HRM or civil service system appears to be working or the key various stakeholders are comfortable with the way things are, why on earth reform for an unproven new one that promises something better? It has been the author's experience that many public sector managers or HRM professionals have had experience adopting new technologies or approaches that fail to deliver on the explicit or implied promises—is it any wonder there is skepticism on future efforts to improve their agencies, HRM or civil service?

A number of issues stand for those interested in advancing reform in HRM entities that provide support or services in the public sector arena. It is important to recognize the complex dynamics of "reforms" of public HRM systems. At the root of efforts to reform public HRM entities or functions is a basic issue of knowledge and knowledge integration. The vast body of knowledge in Public Administration, Political Science, Sociology, Anthropology, Behavioral Sciences, Management and Organization Development & Change disciplines address issues of change and the management of change.

Understanding Organization Reform, Change, and Transformation Management Models

As highlighted throughout this book the world of public sector agencies continues to change fast and, as such, agencies must change quickly too. Agencies that handle change well thrive, whilst those that do not may struggle to survive.

Goldfinch (2009) suggests that reform and change are never inevitable. Guy Peters (1996) claims change in the public sector is the rule rather than the exception but it is not smooth, continuous and incremental. It is disjointed, varies in intensity, and sharp episodes of reform are often followed by periods of relative tranquility. Change might proceed through a series of 'punctuated equilibriums' where long eras of stability alternate with short-lived periods of uncertainty and conflict (Baumgartner & Jones, 1993). There have been a wealth of studies that suggest a considerable degree of stability of policies, public organizations and governance structures. There are numerous terms that describe the durability of institutions arrangements: inheritance, lock-in, stickiness, deadlock, path-dependency, reform impasse and reform paradox (Goldfinch & Wallis, 2009). Policies and structures are often protected by dominant coalitions, embedded in laws and constitutions, and sustained by habit and inertia. Reforms may be 'smuggled in' through a series of cumulative and incremental adjustments, but this can be a time-consuming, reversible and possibly drifting process (Goldfinch, 2009). Yet, reforms and significant change management efforts do occur in public sector organizations as evidenced by the other chapters in this book.

The concept of "change management" is a familiar one in most public sector organizations today. But, how agencies manage change (and how successful they are at it) varies enormously depending on the agency, the change and the people involved. And a key part of this depends on how far people within it understand the change process.

Change management provides a structured approach for making changes in a planned and systematic fashion to effectively implement new methods and processes in an ongoing organization. The goal is to prepare stakeholders for the change or reform, ensure that they are knowledgeable to face change in a dynamic work environment, and ultimately ready to embrace the change.

Reform typically refers to making changes in something (typically a social, political, or economic institution or practice) in order to improve it. That is, to improve management and provide better services by government in more efficient and cost-effective manner. In this view, government reform requires constant vigilance and effort because government by its nature tends to expand in both size and scope.

Reform in reality is simply change but is most often used when one considers change in government—local, state, and federal. Change is a common thread that runs through all organizations regardless of sector, size and age. Understanding organizational change involves examining types of change within government or public sector organizations and the history of recent successes or failures of change initiatives (for example, via a change audit) as described by various contributors in this book. At the macro level common organizational changes enhance strategy, structure, and culture, often involving different leadership or reporting lines, expansion or downsizing, or incorporation of new technologies.

These changes may be further defined when viewed from an evolutionary perspective as transitional, transformational, or developmental. *Transitional* change, the most common and basic, simply enhances the current state via reorganization, changing structure or procedures, utilizing technology, or deciding to expand. These changes may be department or division specific, or organization-wide, and are driven by management. *Transformational* change represents a fundamental, radical shift from the current state, involving personal behaviors and mind-sets. Transitional changes include altering the culture, formulating new, drastically different strategy.

Developmental change stems from an overall philosophy of continuous growth and development that taps the synergy of valued, high performing employees engaged in meaningful work. Developmental organizations continually scan their internal and external environments for opportunities, making regular, incremental changes along the way. Motivating, healthy work environments encourage innovation, personal growth and development, renewal, involvement, partnering, and a sense of ownership and commitment among organizational members. Developmental agencies build internal capability or capacity through people by maximizing their talents, incorporating manageable changes gradually, and avoiding large-scale, radical changes so indicative of poor planning and management.

A change audit assesses an organization's past experiences with and present approach to change along with future capabilities (Gilley, 2005, pp. 98–99). The historical perspective of change examines the organization's culture with respect to change, types of changes that occurred in the past (e.g., small, moderate, large-scale), who was responsible, when change efforts occurred, how changes were implemented, barriers at the time (e.g., culture, poor management or communications, insufficient resources), and success or failure rates (results).

Assessing the current state of readiness for change looks at current behaviors (e.g., resistant, aggressive, inconsistent, etc.), current change efforts, types of change in progress, responsibilities, implementation techniques, willingness of participants, ability of those impacted to change, barriers, and conditions that will be necessary for change to exist. In essence, a thorough internal analysis examines organizational strengths and weaknesses including leadership talent, level of cultural dysfunction, effectiveness of structure, policies and procedures, resource availability, and so forth.

A change audit concludes with an action plan that specifies what must happen for change to successfully occur. How can gaps in ability be lessened, barriers reduced or eliminated, and willingness enhanced? An action plan details how success will be measured (e.g., based on impact on people or processes, profitability, congruence with organizational mission and goals, etc.), who should lead future changes and why, how change should be implemented, resource needs, how to overcome obstacles, and how success should be celebrated.

Change Management and Models

Change management is essential to effectively addressing workforce concerns that arise in any change or reform effort. Change management helps to foster organizational acceptance, enthusiasm, and cooperation, despite the uncertainty that any change or reform holds. Change or reform initiatives fail because the people-related aspects are poorly addressed or altogether neglected. Inadequate communications and a lack of stakeholder comprehension often lead to increased risk, poor performance, and increased time to transition, resulting in wasted time and dollars. One way of increasing the likely success of any change or reform effort is to rely on a change management model that helps to minimize the risks of change. And even better to integrate and use several change management models. There are many different change management models (see, for example,

Beckhard & Harris, 1987; Cummings & Worley, 2009; Kotter, 1996; Lewin, 1951).

Models of change management attempt to help change leaders guide their organizations through change. Early change models followed a relatively simple three-step process that entailed evaluating and preparing a firm for change, engaging in change, and solidifying the change into the fabric of employees' daily lives. Lewin's (1951) model, for example, consists of *unfreezing, movement*, and *refreezing*. Unfreezing involves assessment and readying individuals and organizations for change. Movement occurs when individuals engage in the change process. Refreezing anchors new ways and behaviors into the daily routine and culture of the firm.

More extensive, multistep frameworks have evolved that include leadership, employee involvement, rewards, communication, and more. Models by Kotter (1996) and Ulrich (1998) for example, explore the importance of vision, empowerment, guiding coalitions, commitment, and "selling" the change, among others. These models provide valuable guidelines for planning and implementing change, although they assume that change initiatives will be successful provided all steps are followed in sequence. This assumption of success fails to recognize the powerful human resistance factor, nor do these models suggest appropriate actions necessary to overcome obstacles to change. As a result, a more in-depth, comprehensive, realistic guideline for change implementation is:

1. Understand that change is immensely complex.
2. Understand individual and organizational responses (resistance) to change, and how to deal with these responses.
3. Create a culture that supports change.
4. Establish a vision for ongoing change.
5. Build a guiding coalition for the change.
6. "Sell" the need for continuous change to individuals at all levels of the organization; help people understand that the change is necessary, urgent; teach that change is good, desirable.
7. Remove barriers to action.
8. Involve employees at all levels of the organization in change processes (including initial decision making, planning, implementation, monitoring, and rewarding).
9. Communicate proficiently; solicit input and share information with those impacted by the change; lack of information breeds fear.
10. Prepare for and plan responses to resistance; treat resistance to change as an opportunity; understand that resistance is a symptom of a deeper problem (e.g., poor management or strategy, ineffective communication, etc.).

11. Deal with employees and their reactions individually, not as a group.
12. Execute ongoing changes in small increments.
13. Constantly monitor progress of change initiatives and refine/adjust as needed.
14. Reward individuals and groups for engaging in change.
15. Celebrate short- and long-term wins.
16. Solidify changes in the newly emerged culture (Gilley, 2005, p. 36).

Regardless of the change management models used as a basis for organization change (or in our case CSR or PHRM reform) it is important that those who are responsible for change or reform understand the differing approaches available to them to manage or lead the effort. The ability to discern among competing approaches to change and their likely value may be one of the most important skills those responsible for change or reform in the public sector need to understand and learn how to use (Sims, 2010a).

A variety of theories and models can be found that provide road maps for system-wide reform or change. Yet, very little of what is known is always integrated in the change processes (reforming efforts) of civil service or public HRM systems. The discussion that follows is organized in three parts, namely the context and the need, the strategic element and, the reforming change process and is based on a few principles or theses. The discussion demonstrates both the complexity of managing the reform process and the need to integrate the existing body of knowledge to guide reform and especially transformation in the public sector and civil service in general and public HRM entities in particular.

The Context and the Need for Reform, Change, or Transformation

Principle 1: *The greater the civil service or PHRM entity or function's need for reform, the more people will be willing to participate in the reform process.*

Principle 2: *The greater the civil service or PHRM entity or function's need for reform, the more difficult it is to foster the reform process.*

Civil service or PHRM professionals, being aware that there is a threat to the public civil service or HRM entity or function's survival, are likely to be willing to participate in an effort to improve conditions. Corollary, civil service or public HRM personnel that do not perceive a real threat to the entity's survival will not be motivated to take part in the exploration of reform. For example, some employees at one public HRM entity realized that the need for reform was real and were willing to take part in the reform process and supported the transformation toward a more effective and efficient entity. Yet, as the need to support and help the reform process overcome major and difficult roadblocks increased, some of these same employees began to withdraw their support and involvement and turned to outright resistance to the reform effort.

In other instances, the threat to survival was not perceived as real or urgent by many of the employees until the actual introduction of new leadership in the agency. Employees who fall in this latter group were aware of reforms that were taking place in their respective contextual environments, and accordingly took part willingly in committees that attempted to develop ideas for reform. Yet, transferring ideas into actions turned out to be most difficult. Overcoming the HRM agency's inertia and moving the entity closer toward being an "effective entity" as well as an "efficient entity" in the minds of its customers almost failed due to the lack of shared perception of the urgent need to reform.

The Strategic Dimension

Principle 3: *To the extent that the leaders of the PHRM function or entity are able to develop a clear strategic vision for the reform effort and where the agency (or civil service system) would like to see itself in the foreseeable future, the more likely the effort will succeed.*

Principle 4: *The more involved the leaders of the PHRM function or entity in the formulation of the reform effort the more members of the function or agency are likely to get involved in the process.*

Principle 5: *The more people get involved in the process, the more difficult it will be to develop a shared vision for the reform effort.*

Reform appears to be one of the key elements that are likely to influence the long term survivability of civil service systems or PHRM functions or agencies. The decision to initiate reform whether under normal or abnormal circumstances should be a strategic decision that takes place within a changing environment. The reform of the Personnel Board of Jefferson County, Alabama discussed by Sims (2010b) (and the more recent Jefferson County Commission, Alabama) and other reforms or changes discussed in this book demonstrate that the drivers for reform and change are many. The Personnel Board, for example, in 2002 was experiencing unprecedented pressure to change and a need to rapidly respond to an increasingly dissatisfied customer-base. The threat of state and local actions to dismantle or completely revamp the agency along with the threat of court actions served as continuing pressures for system-wide reform and transformation. The Personnel Board was experiencing mounting pressures to increase efficiency and its overall effectiveness. The increasing demands from employees of the merit system and member jurisdictions in Jefferson County, Alabama for the Personnel Board to provide better quality services with less money called for paradigm changes toward much more of an "entrepreneurial agency." The Personnel Board had no alternative but to reform (Sims, 2009). Similarly, the Jefferson County Commission in 2013 faced the same reality after a more than three decade failure to fulfill its responsibility under a consent decree.

The reform process at the Personnel Board (and the Jefferson County Commission in 2013) started with the development of a vision and the articulation of the need to reform the agency by the federal court and parties to the litigation that the Personnel Board had been involved in for decades. The vision and articulation of the need for and plan to reform then was further developed by the court-appointed receiver.

Furthermore, the imposition of the receivership created a structural mechanism-the receiver—that was charged with the development of reform ideas and implementation strategies. Yet, the reform efforts at the Personnel Board and the Jefferson County Commission points toward the heavy investment and energy required to foster system-wide reform in a public sector organization. Furthermore, the ability to demonstrate the relationship between the level of investment and performance improvement is difficult due to the nature and dynamics of the entity. Given the complex and difficult-to-quantify costs and benefits and the system-wide implications of say, the imposition of a receivership, specific evaluation-criteria and approaches may be inappropriate for appraising the investment. A more suitable approach might be to recognize the strategic character of the investments and apply principles of strategic analysis (Grant, Shani, & Krishnan, 1994).

Reform or change effort investments like those resulting from the imposition of a receivership to bring about much needed changes are strategic to the degree that they are important (i.e., critical to the PHRM agency's overall performance and survival), they involve substantial resource commitments, they are long-run and they are not easily reversible (Sims, 2009). Estimating returns on investments like the costs of imposing a receivership is critical, yet difficult because it involves complex interaction among multiple actors.

The Reform/Change Process

Principle 6: *To the extent that the civil service or PHRM personnel are involved in the reform effort, it is more likely that the effect will lead to significant agency improvements.*

Principle 7: *The greater variety of resources represented in the reform effort, the more difficulty there will be in developing a shared understanding and shared solution to common problems.*

Principle 8: *The more the ideas for reform cross organizational boundaries within the civil service system, HRM function or agency, the more difficult it will be for the reform effort to generate a shared understanding and recommend agreed-upon solutions.*

The environmental context within which federal, state, county and local civil service or PHRM agencies function seems to impose improvements in these entities' performance with fewer resources. Yet, agencies' internal resilience to resist change is a phenomenon that has been observed by many scholars. Most of the scholarly research in the change disciplines point toward agency inertia as one of the key contributors (Sims, 2007). Yet, little of what we know is automatically incorporated into civil service or public HRM reform efforts. Furthermore, while civil service or PHRM reform efforts attempt to overcome an entity's inertia, translating the ideas into action is not an easy task.

The field of "organizational change and development" that is devoted to the study of system-wide change draws heavily upon anthropological, sociological, psychological, biological and political concepts and theories and have examined the roles that the contextual environment, organizational complexity and culture, leadership and stakeholders play in the change (reform) process. For example, the organizational complexity of the reforms introduced at the Personnel Board of Jefferson County (Sims, 2009, 2010b) (and the Jefferson County Commission) and the other reforms and change examples discussed in this book support Meyer's (1979) theory that multiple inputs and competing mission drive bureaucratic response. Instead of viewing reform as a "change in the way we do business," too often it becomes viewed as an added responsibility or input thus requiring structure. The presence of barriers to reform requires little explanation: sociology and psychology point to the stability preferences inherent, respectively, in social organisms and individuals, while population ecology points to inertia as a fundamental characteristic of bureaucratic organizations.

The challenge for many of those responsible for civil service and PHRM reform is achieving internal change in response to a changing external environment on a timely and smoothly managed basis. Reforming a civil service system or PHRM function or agency toward more of a "result driven," "customer driven," "market driven" and "enterprising agency" requires understanding and knowledge of the process of change and its phases, the facilitation of change, the change mechanisms and activities, all of which can be found in the relevant academic disciplines. Yet, there is still a great deal of evidence that suggests that CSR and the PHRM function change very often but still stop short of integrating the existing change management knowledge into their efforts. The literature reports on this unique organizational innovation and points toward the possibilities that this kind of mechanism can facilitate system-wide change process, or foster the reform process—from ideas to action (Sims, 2007, 2009, 2010a).

Reference to resistance is frequently found in the context of change (i.e., reform or transformation). The organizational change and development literature often discusses resistance in the context of resistance to change. In the context of bureaucracy and transformation of bureaucratic entities like civil service systems and PHRM one needs to examine the nature of resistance. Borrowing from physics, we can view resistance as roughly analogous to friction. Friction can hinder all movement, yet on an "ideal" surface objects move with little or no friction. As such, friction seems to qualify how and in what direction an object moves. So, understanding resistance, just like understanding friction, is critical to understanding agency reform. For example, as the reader will see in the context of the various change or reform efforts discussed in this book, a variety of forces serve as potential causes for friction. Examples noted by Sims (2010b) were the high degree of dependency on publicly elected political systems that provided the Personnel Board with its funding; the social-political climate within which the Personnel Board functions; the legal culture driven by the federal court system; the internal structures and management processes that evolved over the life of the agency, and the cultural features that emerged as a result of providing services to the employees and appointing authorities of Jefferson County, AL. Understanding friction dynamics both at the individual, PHRM function, and civil service system levels, might provide an insight to the understanding of a change or reform's progression to date and how to continue and navigate the reform in the future.

As is evident in the discussion of the change or reform efforts discussed by other contributors in this book, the environmental context for public sector organizations is constantly changing. Yet, it is not unusual for there not to be a real sense of urgency that is felt throughout the organization to change "the way we do business" prior to the imposition of change or reform from outside the agency. To often the internal structures and cultures seem to be unresponsive to the demands for change or reform. For example, the resistance against the imposition of the receivership at the Jefferson County Commission from fall 2013 through May 2015 with the author's departure and introduction of a new interim receiver was unparalleled from multiple stakeholders or decision makers.

CONCLUSIONS AND FINAL LESSONS LEARNED

Today's civil service systems and PHRM functions reflect the incentive systems for government staff and employees and are critical determiners of motivation, morale and commitment to performance. When public sector leaders or managers fail to fill positions with the most qualified individuals, are unable to suitably motivate public employees, and do not work toward the most efficient and effective public service, the opportunity and real costs for society and particularly taxpayers are incalculable. Hence, the most important goal of HRM or civil service reform is to set up or strengthen merit systems in a systematic fashion in a move to ensure that both long-term and temporary personnel are competitively recruited as required, swiftly selected, and properly rewarded, trained (or retrained), motivated, utilized, promoted, and dismissed, along the lines of missions and objectives of the relevant public entity.

Today, HRM reform and CSR regards merit as an important principle to maintain, as it is a precondition to granting public sector leaders, managers and employees the discretion, empowerment and flexibility typical of result-oriented leadership. Thus, PHRM reform and CSR aims at establishing merit systems where they do not exist—at the national, regional or local level—or revitalizing and strengthening their principles and practices in settings where relevant rules and regulations or policies and procedures are already in place but have not been properly implemented. The flourishing of innovative ideas also requires the constant change and reform of civil service systems in general and in PHRM in particular with an eye toward improvement of employees' knowledge, skills, attitudes and motivation, which makes training, retraining and development of employees at all levels essential to support changes in personnel and agency needs, and in the successful achievement of a public sector organization's stated mission.

Lessons Learned From the Field

An important lesson from efforts to change or reform civil service and PHRM is that any change or reform cannot be accomplished overnight even when the force of a new federal act and imposition of a receivership (as was the case at the Personnel Board from 2002-2006 and the Jefferson County Commission from October 2013 through May 2015), for example, is behind the reform; it requires making change or reform the norm and increasing its velocity. As such, in order for civil service systems and PHRM to fulfill their roles, they must continually reform (and some would say constantly change and transform) themselves within the boundaries of their local, state and federal mandates to deliver on their mission regardless of the method (i.e., the traditional, the reform, the privatization or outsourcing) as defined by Condrey (2005) to deliver its services.

The efforts to change or reform a civil service system or a PHRM function or entity also illustrates that those responsible for leading such change or reform should not look for a "magic change pill" or look to the latest change management fad or quick fix but rather should concentrate on the three components of holistic organization transformation (Walker, 2002)—people, process, and technology. In particular, change or reform in the public sector has as its most significant linchpin—*people*. Nothing gets done without people. And in the end, it is people that are served by a civil service system or public HRM function or agency. All the theories, modeling techniques, analysis, and technology will mean nothing if adequate attention is not given to the real authors and benefactors of civil service or PHRM reform—people. Mutual trust must be established. Trust must be earned. In order to establish a *trust organization*, those responsible for leading reform must first be trustworthy. CSR or PHRM reform professionals must create an environment that embraces open communication. This openness means that critics and supporters have equal voice in any change or reform initiative.

The efforts to change or reform any civil service system or PHRM also illustrates how important it is to understand what radical reform in a civil service system or PHRM means versus process improvements which only create more efficient execution of existing processes. Such change or reform is an ongoing process that permeates the entire civil service system or PHRM function or agency, and represents a sharp break with the past. This break is a major difference between holistic civil service or PHRM change or reform and a simple or a more narrow reform. While the kind of civil service or PHRM reform that takes place at some entities is an attempt to go down the same path more efficiently, such change or reform involves the development or discovery of entirely new paths. This view supports the idea of civil service or PHRM reform and in most contexts the work of change or reform as it is tied to change, innovation and transformation.

Another important lesson from the field on efforts to change or reform civil service or PHRM functions or entities focuses on what Kotter (1996) refers to as the necessity of creating a crisis (or sense of urgency) without creating panic. The importance of this is presented by Burke, Wilson, and Salas (2005) in their study of *Highly Reliable Organizations (HROs)*. In their research, they call this step "unfreezing" based on Lewin's (1951) change management model and it is characterized as a precipatory *jolt* to the agency. Something must occur to convince the function or agency that *business as usual is not working*. Reforms have a greater chance of succeeding if something is done to create a sense of urgency and to convince the agency that the status quo is no longer acceptable (e.g., the imposition of a federal receiver at the Personnel Board of Jefferson County, Alabama (Sims, 2009, 2010b) and the Jefferson County Commission. At the Personnel Board, efforts to unfreeze the system were much more successful over time than efforts at the Jefferson County Commission. Of course, in the author's view it didn't help that the change champion (the federal judge) seemed to consistently send mixed messages to the receiver and the Jefferson County Commission and others on the expectations or goals for the receivership, the receiver's authority and approach to reforming or transforming the system which had refused for more than three decades to fulfill its commitment in the original consent decree.

As has been reported in many sources the biggest barrier to change or reform is the *organizational culture* (Smith, 2003). Kotter (1996) and others (see for example, DiDonato & Gill, 2015; Kippler, 2013; Schraeder, Tears, & Jordan, 2005; Smith, 2003) discussthe challenges and approaches for changing culture. According to Kotter (1996), culture is *very hard to change*. Organizational culture at public sector organizations and HRM functions or entities have been *reinforced* through incentives, human resource policy, and leadership or management style. However, in reality, the strengths and capabilities that have made a civil service system or PHRM entity successful in the past may become irrelevant or even *inhibitors* to future success. In any case, change or reform requires new organizational models that better serve the public sector customers. Successful civil service or PHRM reform demonstrates the success of new approaches that are superior to old methods or more appropriate given a new agency or government context. The challenge is: culture does not change easily.

Changing a culture must begin with *policies and incentives* that *drive behavior*. Incentives and agency, system or human resources policy must align with new approaches that comprise a change or reform initiative. One of the greatest challenges and tools in implementing reform, whether in a civil service system or PHRM entity or other organization, is changing human resources policy. For example, establishing new job titles for new types of jobs can be very difficult for those leading civil service reform. The best situation is where those responsible for reform encounter employees that are also able to be change or reform leaders who are not content with the status quo. In the end, successful civil service or PHRM change or reform has the greatest likelihood of occurring when employees at all levels of the civil service system or PHRM entity have clear policies and incentives which encourage them to be enablers, not barriers to any change or reform effort.

As evidenced throughout this chapter, calls for reform of PHRM and civil service systems and for a redefinition of the role of PHRM have been a perennial part of the dialogue about public management for decades. From before the Civil Rights Act of 1964 and the Civil Service Reform

Act of 1978 through the National Performance Review in the 1990s to the present Obama administration's management agenda, reformers have argued that PHRM organizations should move away from their traditional role, with its focus on routine processing of personnel transactions and on control and enforcement of rigid civil service laws (Ban, 2005; Condrey, 2010; Thompson & Seidner, 2016; West, 2002). PHRM professionals have been exhorted, rather, to be more like their private sector counterparts which includes new roles more aligned with the mission of their host agencies and more responsive to management's needs. The reality, however, is that PHRM and their public sector organizations are not "just like" their private sector counterparts when one considers the structure of the HRM process in the public sector. In the private sector, each business or organization is free to establish its own HRM system, although it must work within the constraints posed by laws governing such issues as affirmative action, labor relations, and family and medical leave. In the public sector, traditionally, individual agencies have had little freedom to design their own personnel systems; they must operate within civil service laws. Traditional civil service systems were complex and highly formalized and stressed uniformity rather than flexibility. Also, traditionally, a centralized body, such as a civil service commission or, at the federal level, the U.S. Office of Personnel Management, not only set the rules but also actually administered the system, developing and administering civil service examinations for hiring and promotion and establishing pay policy, among other functions. These centralized organizations also had the responsibility of oversight over agency HRM functions and the role of these centralized organizations is continuing to change at the federal, state and local levels as highlighted in the discussion found earlier in this chapter, as a result of reforms designed to radically change PHRM and civil service systems. Those reforms are key to understanding the ever changing role of PHRM.

According to Pollitt and Bouckaert (2011) five of the last six presidents (Carter, Reagan, George H. W. Bush, Bill Clinton, and George W. Bush) felt it politically advantageous to include criticism of the federal bureaucracy as a significant element in their electoral campaigns. However, in practice their actions varied from attempts at sympathetic modernization of the federal departments, agencies and civil service system (Carter and Clinton) to attacks on alleged bureaucratic "waste" and duplication, combined with the introduction of more and more political appointees (Reagan, G. W. Bush). Ever expanding contracting out seems to have been a feature of both political parties. This has grown steadily from the (always existing) contracting out for products (computers, military hardware), through contracting for general services (office cleaning, prison management) to contracting for what many would regard as core government functions (including policymaking and monitoring contracts), and contracting for

HRM functions such as recruitment and workforce planning (Durant, Girth, & Johnston, 2009) which is more reflective of the partnership and outsourcing model offered by Condrey (2010) and described earlier in this chapter.

The future of PHRM will only include more and more calls for reform, change or transformation. The expectations of elected officials, citizens and public managers will continue to increase demand on further reform by PHRM professionals. Any efforts to reform PHRM can be justified by the fact that it is an ongoing effort to improve the effectiveness of human resources at the state, local, and federal levels. The success of any reform or change effort always lies in the eyes of those who are impacted most by it. PHRM professionals and the reform efforts that must deal with it are inherently political, constitutional, legal, social, and organizational. Employees and citizens and, of course presidents and other government officials, will expect PHRM professionals to continue to meet their needs and exceed their expectations. Public HRM professionals will have to continue to find ways to respond to the changing elements of the public sector which in itself is ever changing, reforming and transforming given the increased dissatisfaction with and lower public trust of government, and especially at the federal level. As we look to the future, reform, change or transformation for PHRM professionals, their functions and civil service systems will be the norm—no doubt about it!

REFERENCES

Alford, J. (1993). Thinking about the demise of public service boards in commonwealth and state government. In M. Gardner (Ed.), *Human resource management and industrial relations in the public sector*. Melbourne, Australia: Macmillan.

Answers.com. (2009). Civil service reform. Retrieved from http://www.answers.com/topic/civil-service-reform

Ban, C. (2005). The changing role of the human resource office. In S. E. Condrey (Ed.), *Handbook of human resource management in government* (2nd ed., pp. 12–36). San Francisco, CA: Jossey-Bass.

Ban, C., & Gossett, C.W. (2010).The changing role of the human resource office. In S.E. Condrey (Ed.), *Handbook of human resource management in government* (3rd ed., pp. 5–26). San Francisco, CA: Jossey-Bass.

Ban, C., & Riccucci, N. (1991). *Public personnel management: Concerns, future challenges*. New York, NY: Longman.

Barzelay, M. (1992). *Breaking through bureaucracy*. Berkeley, CA: University of California Press.

Battaglio, R. P., & Condrey, S. E. (2006). Civil service reform: Examining state and local government cases. *Review of Public Personnel Administration, 26*(2), 116–118.

Baumgartner, F., & Jones, B. D. (1993). *Agendas and instability in American politics*. Chicago, IL: University of Chicago Press.

Beattie, R. S., & Osborne, S. P. (2008). *Human resource management in the public sector*. New York, NY: Routledge.

Beckhard, R., & Harris, R. T. (1987). *Organizational transitions: Managing complex change*. Reading, MA: Addison-Wesley.

Berry, J. (2009, September 11). *A merit system for the 21st century? Remarks of OPM Director John Berry*. Syracuse, NY: The Maxwell School of Syracuse University.

Black, J., & Upchurch, M. (1999). Public sector employment. In G. Hollinshead, P. Nicholls, & S. Tailby (Eds.), *Employee relations*. (pp. 505–562). London, England: Financial Times Management.

Bowman, J., West, J., & Geertz, S. (2006). Radical reform in the sunshine state. In J. E. Kellough & L. Nigro (Eds.), *Civil service reform in the states: Personnel policies and politics at the subnational level* (pp. 145–170). Albany, NY: SUNY Press.

Brown, K. (2004). Human resource management in the public sector. *Public Management Review*, 6(3), 303–309.

Burke, C. S., Wilson, K. A., & E. Salas (2005). The use of team-based strategy for organizational transformation: Guidance for moving toward a high reliability organization. *Theoretical Issues in Ergonomics Science*, 6(6), 509–530.

Clark, C.S. (2015, January 21). A ripe time for civil service reform? *Government Executive*. Retrieved from http://www.govexec.com/magazine/magazine-analysis/2015/01/ripe-time-civil-service-reform/103347/

Coggburn, J. D. (2006). At-will employment in government: Insights from the state of Texas. *Review of Personnel Administration*, 20(2), 158–177.

Coggburn, J. D., Battaglio, R. P., Jr., Bowman, J. S., Condrey, S. E., Goodman, D., & West, J. P. (2010). State government human resource professionals' commitment to employment at will. *The American Review of Public Administration*, 40(2), 189–208.

Condrey, S. E. (2002). Reinventing state civil service systems: The Georgia experience. *Review of Public Personnel Administration*, 22(2), 114–124.

Condrey, S. E. (2005). Toward strategic human resource management. In S. E. Condrey (Ed.), *Handbook of human resource management* (2nd ed., pp. 1–14). San Francisco, CA: Jossey-Bass.

Condrey, S. E. (2010). *Handbook of human resource management in government*. San Francisco, CA: Jossey-Bass.

Condrey, S. E. (2012). Public human resource management: How we get where we are today. In N. M. Ricussi (Ed.) *Public personnel management* (5th ed., pp. 1–13). London, England: Routledge.

Condrey, S. E., & Battaglio, R. P., Jr. (2007). A return to spoils? Revisiting radical civil service reform in the United States. *Public Administration Review*, 67(3), 424–436.

Crowell, E. B., & Guy, M. E. (2010). Florida's HR reforms: Service first, service first, service worst, or something in between? *Public Personnel Management*, 39(1), 15–46.

Cummings, T. G., & Worley, C. G. (2009). *Organization development and change* (9th ed.). Mason, OH: South-Western Cengage Learning.

DiDonato, T., & Gill, N. (2015, July 15). Changing an organization's culture, without resistance or blame. *Harvard Business Review*. Retrieved from https://hbr.org/2015/07/changing-an-organizations-culture-without-resistance-or-blame

Durant, R. F., Girth, A. M., & Johnston, J. M. (2009). American exceptionalism, human resource management, and the contract state. *Review of Public Personnel Administration, 20*(3), 207–229.

Durant, R. F., & Legge, J. S., Jr. (2006). Wicked problems, public policy, and administrative theory: Lessons from the GM food regulatory arena. *Administration & Society, 38*(3), 309–334.

Farazmand, A. (2007). *Strategic public personnel administration: Building and managing human capital for the 21st century*. Westport, CT: Praeger.

Fischer, J. (1945, October). Let's go back to the spoils system. *Harper's, 362*–368.

Freedman, A. (1994). Commentary on patronage. *Public Administration Review, 54*(3), 313.

Gardner, M., & Palmer, G. (1997). *Employment relations: Industrial relations and human resource management in Australia* (2nd ed.). Melbourne, Australia: Macmillan.

Gilley, A. (2005). *The manager as change leader*. Hartford, CT: Praeger.

Goldfinch, S. F. (2009). Introduction. In S. F. Goldfinch & J. E .Wallis (Eds.), *International handbook of public management reform* (pp. 15–28). Cheltehnah, England: Edward Elgar.

Goldfinch, S. F, & Wallis, J. E (2009). *International handbook of public management reform*. Cheltehnah, England: Edward Elgar.

Goodman, D., & Mann, S. (2010). Reorganization or political smokescreen: The incremental & temporary use of at-will employment in Mississippi state government. *Public Personnel Management, 39*(3), 183–209.

Gore, A. (1993, September 7). Remarks by the president and vice president in presenting the national performance review. Retrieved from http://govinfo.library.unt.edu/npr/library/status/endnotes/endnotes.htm

Gossett, C.W. (2002). Civil service reform: The case of Georgia. *Review of Public Personnel Administration, 22*(2), 94–113.

Grant, R., Shani, A. B., & Krishnan, R. (1994). TQM's challenge to management theory and practice. *Sloan Management Review, 35*(2), 25–35.

Gray, A., & Jenkins, B. (1995). From public administration to public management: Reassessing a revolution. *Public Administration, 73*(1), 75–99.

Hansen, M. G. (1985). Review: Management improvement initiatives in the Reagan administration: Round two. *Public Administration Review, 45*(3), 441–446.

Harrow, R., Jr. (2008, November 11). Like Clinton, Obama calls for fewer federal contractors to cut spending. *Washington Post*. Retrieved from http://www.washingtonpost.com/wp-dyn/content/article/2008/11/10/AR2008111002427.html

Hays, S. W., & Sowa, J. E. (2006). A broader look at the "accountability" movement: Some grim realities in state civil service systems. *Review of Public Administration, 26*(2), 102–117.

Hays, S. W., & Sowa, J. E. (2007). Changes in state civil service systems: A national survey. In J. S. Bowman & J. P. West (Eds.), *American public service: Radical reform and the merit system* (pp. 3–23). United States: CRC Press.

Heclo, H. (1997). *A government of strangers*. Washington, DC: Brookings Institution.

Hughes, O. (1994). *Public management and administration*. London, England: St Martin's Press.

Ingraham, P. W., & Rubaii-Barrett, N. (2007). Human resource management as a core dimension of public administration. *The Foundations of Public Administration Series*. Retrieved from http://www.aspanet.org/scriptcontent/pdfs/fpa-hrm-syllabus.pdf

Katz, E. (2014, December 9). Obama announces plans to reform and modernize the senior executive service. *Government Executive*. Retrieved from http://www.govexec.com/management/2014/12/obama-announces-plans-reform-and-modernize-senior-executive-service/100818/

Kellough, J. E., & Nigro, L. G. (2002). Pay for performance in Georgia state government: Employee perspectives on GeorgiaGain™ after 5 years. *Review of Public Personnel Administration, 22*(2), 146–166.

Kellough, J. E., & Nigro, L. G. (2006). Dramatic reform in the public service: At-will employment and the creation of a new public workforce. *Journal of Public Administration Research and Theory, 16*(3), 447–466.

Kellough, J. E., & Selden, S. C. (2003). The reinvention of public personnel administration: An analysis of the diffusion of personnel management reforms in the states. *Public Administration Review, 63*(2), 165–176.

Kim, P.S., & Hong, K.P. (2006). Searching for effective HRM reform strategy in the public sector: Critical review of WPSR 2005 and suggestions. *Public Personnel Management, 3*, 199–216.

Kippler, T. (2013, November 26). The 9 clear steps to organizational culture change. Retrieved from http://www.eremedia.com/tlnt/the-9-clear-steps-to-organizational-culture-change/

Klijn, H.E. (2002). Governing networks in hollow state: Contracting out, process management or a combination of the two? *Public Management Review, 4*(2), 149–165.

Klingner, D. E. (2016). Competing perspectives on public personnel administration: Civil service, nonstandard work arrangements, privatization, and partnerships. In R. C. Kearney & J. D. Coggburn (Eds.). *Public human resource management: Problems and prospects* (6th ed., pp. 1–15). Singapore: CQ Press.

Klingner, D. E., & Lynn, D. B. (2005). The politics of the emergent paradigms. In S.E. Condrey (Ed.), *Handbook of human resource management in government* (2nd ed., pp. 37–57). San Francisco, CA: Jossey Bass.

Klingner, D., & Nalbandian, J. (2003). *Public personnel management: Contexts and strategies* (5th ed.). Upper Saddle River, NJ: Prentice-Hall/Simon-Schuster.

Klingner, D. E., Nalbandian, J., & Llorens. J. (2010). *Public personnel management: Context and strategies* (6th ed.). Upper Saddle River, NJ: Prentice-Hall.

Kotter, J. P. (1996). *Leading change*. Boston, MA: Harvard Business School Press.

Kuykendall, C.L., & Facer, R.K., II. (2002). Public employment in Georgia state agencies: The elimination of the merit system. *Review of Public Personnel Administration, 22*(2), 133–145.

Lasseter, R. W. (2002). Georgia's merit system reform, 1996–2001: An operating agency's perspective. *Review of Public Personnel Administration, 22*(2), 125–132.

Levine, C. (1985). *The unfinished agenda of civil service reform: Implications of the grace commission report (Brookings dialogues on public policy)*. Washington, DC: Brookings Institute.

Lewin, K. (1951). *Field theory in social science*. New York, NY: Harper & Row.

Lynn, D., & Klingner, D.E. (2010). The politics of the emergent paradigms. In S. E. Condrey (Ed.), *Handbook of human resource management in government* (pp. 45–71). San Francisco, CA: Jossey-Bass.

Meyer, M. W. (1979). *Change in public bureaucracies*. Cambridge, England: Cambridge University Press.

Naff, K. (2002, August 22). *Prospects for civil service reform in California: A triumph of technique over purpose*. Retrieved from http://bss.sfsu.edu/naff/HRM/calif_%20 paper.pdf

Nalbandian, J. (1991). *Professionalism in local government: Roles, responsibilities, and values of city managers*. San Francisco, CA: Jossey-Bass.

National Performance Review. (1993). *From red tape to results: Creating a government that works better and costs less*. Washington, D.C.: U.S. Government Printing Office.

Office of Management and Budget. (2002).*The president's management agenda, fiscal year 2002*. Washington, DC: Author.

Partnership for Public Service. (2014). *A new civil service framework*. McClean, VA: Booz Allen Hamilton.

Perry, J. L. (1993). Strategic human resource management. *Review of Public Personnel Administration, 13*(4), 59–71.

Peters, G. P. (1996). *The future of governing: Four emerging models*. Lawrence, KS: University Press of Kansas.

Pfiffner, J.P. (2007). The first MBA president: George W. Bush as public administrator. *Public Administration Review, 67*(1), 6–20.

Pollitt, C. (1990) *Managerialism and the public services: The Anglo-American experience*. Oxford, England: Blackwell.

Pollitt, C., & Bouckaert, G. (2011). *Public management reform: A comparative analysis— new public management, governance, and the neo-Weberian state* (3rd ed.). New York, NY: Oxford University Press.

Rainey, H. G. (2006). Reform trends at the federal level with implications for the states: The pursuit of flexibility and the human capital movement. In J. Kellough & L. Nigro (Eds.), *Civil service reform in the states: Personnel policy and politics at the subnational level* (pp. 33–58). Albany, NY: SUNY Press.

Sayre, W. S. (1948). The triumph of techniques over purpose. *Public Administration Review, 8*(2), 134–137.

Schraeder, M., Tears, R. S., & Jordan, M. H. (2005). Organizational culture in public sector organizations: Promoting change through training and leading by example. *Leadership & Organization Development Journal, 26*(5/6), 492–502.

Schroeder, R. (1992). *Max Weber and the sociology of culture*. London, England: Sage.

Selden, S. C. (2006). The impact of discipline on the use and rapidity of dismissal in state governments. *Review of Public Personnel Administration, 26*(4), 335–355.

Selden, S. C. (2016). After the recession: State human resource management. In R. C. Kearney & J. D. Coggburn (Eds.), *Public human resource management: Problems and prospects* (6th ed., pp. 61–78). Singapore: CQ Press.

Selden, S. C., & Wooters, R. (2011). Structures in public human resource management: Shared services in state governments. *Review of Public Personnel
Administration, 31*(4), 349–368.

Sims, R. R. (Ed). (1998). *Accountability and radical change in public organizations.*
Westport, CT: Quorum Books.

Sims, R. R. (2007). *Human resource management: Contemporary issues, challenges, and
opportunities.* Charlotte, NC: Information Age Publishing.

Sims, R. R. (2009). Civil service reform in action: The case of the Personnel Board
of Jefferson County, Alabama. *Review of Public Personnel Administration, 29*(4),
382–401.

Sims, R. R. (2010a). *Change (transformation) in government organizations.* Charlotte,
NC: Information Age Publishing.

Sims, R. R. (2010b). *Reforming (Transforming?) a public human resource management
agency: The case of the Personnel Board of Jefferson County, Alabama.* Charlotte,
NC: Information Age Publishing.

Smith, M. E. (2003). Changing an organization's culture: Correlates of success and
failure. *Leadership & Organization Development Journal, 24*(5/6), 249–261.

Sull, D. N. (1999). Why good companies go bad. *Harvard Business Review, 77*(4),
42–52.

Terry, L. D. (1993). Why should we abandon the misconceived quest to reconcile
public entrepreneurship with democracy: A response to Bellone & Goerl's
"Reconciling public entrepreneurship and democracy." *Public Administration
Review, 53*(4), 393–395.

Thompson, F. (2009). HR strategies for driving change: Finding the right road. *The
Public Manager, 38*(4), 17–18.

Thompson, J. R. (2001). The civil service under Clinton: The institutional consequences of disaggregation. *Review of Public Personnel Administration, 21*(2),
87–113

Thompson, J. R., & Seidner, R. (2016). Human resource management in the federal
government during a time of instability. In R.C. Kearney & J. D. Coggburn
(Eds.). *Public human resource management: Problems and prospects* (6th ed., pp.
49–60). Singapore: CQ Press.

Ulrich, D. (1998). *Champions of change: How CEOs and their companies are mastering
the skills of radical change.* San Francisco, CA: Jossey-Bass.

UN/DESA. (2005). *Unlocking the human potential for public sector performance. World
public sector report 2005.* New Delhi: United Nations.

Van Riper, P. V. (2003). Civil service. *Dictionary of American History.* Retrieved June
21, 2009 from http://www.encyclopedia.com/doc/1G2-3401800847.html

Walker, D. (2002, January 25). *Transformation in government.* Presentation to Association of Government Accountants 13th Annual Leadership Conference,
Washington, DC. Retrieved from http://www.gao.gov/cghome.htm

Weller, P. (1996). The universality of public sector reform. In P. Weller & G. Davis
(Eds.), *New ideas, better government* (pp. 1–10). Sydney, Australia: Allen &
Unwin.

West, J. P. (2002). Georgia on the mind of radical civil service reformers. *Review of Public Personnel Administration*, 22(2), 79–93.

Wilson, G. (2006). The rise of at-will employment and racial inequality in the public sector. *Review of Public Personnel Administration*, 26(2), 178–187.

SECTION I

TRANSFORMATION AT THE FEDERAL LEVEL

CHAPTER 3

CYBERSECURITY MISSION AND MANAGEMENT AT THE DEPARTMENT OF HOMELAND SECURITY

Toward a Model of Integrated Adaptation

Marcia A. Beck and Jonathan P. West

Cyber readiness lags far behind the threat ... American companies' most-sensitive patented technologies and intellectual property, U.S. universities' research and development, and the nation's defense capabilities and critical infrastructure, are all under cyber attack.... One lesson of the 9/11 story is that, as a nation, Americans did not awaken to the gravity of the terrorist threat until it was too late. History may be repeating itself in the cyber realm. (Reflections on the Tenth Anniversary, 2014, p. 7)

In 2014 hackers, using login information stolen from contractors, broke into U.S. Office of Personnel Management (OPM) computer networks and stole personal information of more than 22 million applicants for

Transforming Government Organizations:
Fresh Ideas and Examples From the Field, pp. 77–133

government jobs and their families, friends, and acquaintances (Nakashima, 2015); 5 million of them had their fingerprints stolen (Paletta, 2015). The perpetrator, most likely the Chinese government, was inside the OPM network for 6 months; it took U.S. government authorities 4 months to discover the attack and secure the system. This was the most audacious of hundreds of cyber attacks on government and commercial systems in recent years, including on the Sony corporation, the U.S. State Department, the IRS, the Defense Department, the Joint Chiefs of Staff, and the U.S. Army Corps of Engineers; local governments, private companies, and individuals have all been subject to attacks by state governments, lone wolves, or hacktivist organizations such as Anonymous (Kelly, 2012).

Whether fishing expeditions to see how far and how deep the intruder can penetrate into computer networks, politically motivated actions, or the theft of private data for economic gain, the attacks have so far been limited in scope compared to the potential deleterious effects of malicious assaults on physical and electronic infrastructure, transportation, and communication systems. The massive 2014 OPM breach already signaled the increased capacity of cyber attacks to undermine national security: the hackers may have the means to threaten, bribe, or extort U.S. officials as a way to gain further intelligence. To date, officials have been playing defense, and without much of a game plan—either protecting their position against known threats or strategizing against unknown threats only after the offensive players have scored.

Cybersecurity—"[a] set of activities and other measures intended to protect—from attack, disruption, or other threats—computers, computer networks … and the information they contain and communicate, including software and data, as well as other elements of cyberspace" (Fischer, 2015, p. 1)—has taken on new urgency after the spate of security breaches, cyber attacks on government and private sector computer systems, and preparations for international cyber warfare. (Nolan, 2015; Paletta, Yadron, & Valentino-DeVries, 2015). Cybersecurity responsibilities have been spread across far-flung sectors of government and private industry, in large part because of the difficulty in coordinating intelligence, research, and technical fixes (Trujillo, 2014); turf battles also limit sharing of information, funding, and authority (Priest & Arkin, 2010). Government mandates have increasingly focused on the Department of Homeland Security [DHS] as the operational hub for civilian cybersecurity efforts, directing the Department to protect critical infrastructure sectors against physical and cyber attacks, promote cyber threat information sharing among government, private, and nonprofit sectors, and buttress cyber crime law enforcement. To comply with its cybersecurity mission, DHS has adapted existing programs, created new organizational units, and developed programs, practices, and technologies that engage private business, nonprofit organizations, and the public-at-large. The question this chapter addresses is: *Can the DHS transform its organizational and operational capacity to secure the nation's cyber networks?* (Behn, 2015).

The answer is complicated, as DHS has never been anything other than a department in flux; it began with the transformation of 22 previously independent government agencies into a single organizational structure comprised of different loci and patterns of decision making, organizational cultures, and management practices. The goal since its inception has been to transform multiple government agencies into "a single, cohesive, and effective department that is greater than the sum of its parts" (U.S. Government Accountability Office [GAO], 2015b, p. 209). This goal, according to dozens of reports from the GAO, DHS Office of Inspector General [OIG], congressional committees, and former DHS leaders and managers, has not been attained in over 12 years of operation. DHS missions to protect the homeland have, understandably, superseded DHS organizational management; threats to the nation's security have prompted disparate responses on the part of DHS components and trumped efforts to coordinate management operations (GAO, 2015b). Increasingly, however, weaknesses in DHS organizational management are viewed as detrimental to the Department's effective execution of its missions (S. Rep. 114-1 [Coburn], 2015; Bucci, Rosenzweig, & Inserra, 2015; GAO, 2015b).

This connection between management weaknesses and mission execution affects DHS cybersecurity operations. DHS has five core missions, the fourth of which is to "Safeguard and Secure Cyberspace" (U.S. Department of Homeland Security [DHS], 2014b, p. 7). A separate IT mission, to "Enable the DHS mission through excellence in information technology" (DHS, 2014b, p. 9), supports the core missions by fulfilling five goals: developing an engaged workforce, crafting innovative interoperable technologies, promoting data-driven decisions and high-quality IT services, securing cyberspace, and improving governance, accountability, and performance in the IT environment. The mission of securing cyberspace is thus directly connected to organizational management functions throughout the DHS. In order for the DHS to transform its operational capacity to fulfill the mission of securing cyberspace by adapting to changing threat environments, management operations must first be integrated and coordinated to make "One DHS" greater than the sum of its parts. The DHS must integrate and adapt at the same time in order to support and execute its cybersecurity mission: integrate the disparate processes and cultures in its components, directorates, and offices and adapt its operations to the needs of numerous stakeholders and emerging cyber threats.

"Integrated adaptation"—the model used here as the template for the transformation of the DHS into a cybersecurity powerhouse that combines management with mission—refers to the integration of disparate management practices, cultures, and orientations embedded in its legacy components as a prerequisite for the Department's capacity to fulfill its cybersecurity mission. Only an internally cohesive and integrated DHS can leverage its strong subcultures to effectively adapt to the rapidly changing cyber threat environment. DHS leaders have emphasized both internal integration of mission support functions and organizational adaptation to mission execution needs since the Department's inception, with varying degrees of success. Part I of this chapter examines the difficulties DHS encounters in attempts to integrate and coordinate management practices that impact its cybersecurity mission. Part II then turns to DHS attempts to adapt its organizational, technological, and networking capacity to execute that mission.

DHS ORGANIZATIONAL MANAGEMENT

E pluribus pluram: A Stovepiped Matrix

Problems at DHS since its inception come straight out of a public organizational management textbook: rapid leadership turnover, ineffective political appointees, stovepiping, low worker morale and motivation, a fractured organizational culture, insufficient performance metrics, a focus on performance outputs rather than outcomes, overspending and waste, faulty organizational communication, ineffectual congressional oversight, politicization of decision making. Watchdog and think tank reports have pointed out problems and offered solutions, with only incremental success. DHS officials, over the years, have acknowledged the problems and issued dozens of responses with neatly outlined strategies to move forward. The problem lies in implementation, which lags far behind strategizing and planning. Changes are introduced piecemeal or not at all. Workforce surveys are carried out and never acted on. Plans are made but only partially implemented. DHS leaders, managers, and staff know what needs to be done but not how to do it or who should take responsibility for following through. What follows are the most pressing problems preventing the consolidation of the DHS into a single departmental entity, highlighting potential solutions and progress toward attaining the goal.

Organization. The formation of the Department of Homeland Security in 2002 constituted the most expansive reorganization of government since the creation of the Department of Defense in 1947. The reorganization of 22 distinct U.S. government entities into a single department was a complex process. The functions of various agencies were redistributed into a new organizational framework, with some functions originally housed in one agency dispersed over two or more new DHS components and some functions originally dispersed across multiple agencies consolidated into one new DHS component (Institute of Medicine [IOM], 2013). Seven DHS operational components now constitute the frontline organizations responsible for homeland security: the Coast Guard, the Secret Service, the Transportation Security Administration, the Federal Emergency Management Agency, Citizenship and Immigration Services, Customs and Border Protection, and Immigration and Customs Enforcement. Overseeing the seven components is a variety of directorates and offices—DHS "Headquarters"—charged with coordinating policies and processes to execute department-wide missions (see Figure 3.1).

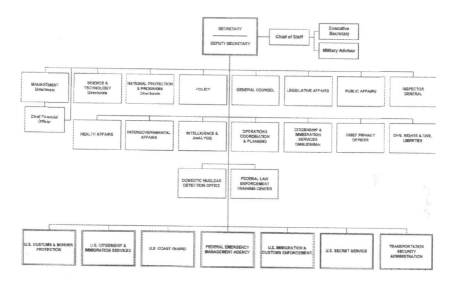

Source: http://www.dhs.gov/sites/default/files/publications/Department%200rg%20Chart.pdf

Figure 3.1. U.S. Department of Homeland Security.

DHS is designed as a matrix organizational structure, or more precisely a "matrix of matrixes," with staff in the components responsible to their component managers and to managers heading up projects that involve cross-component cooperation (IOM, 2014; West, 2012). In addition, the directorates are also organized as matrixes: Science and technology is organized into research project divisions that intersect both with component functions (such as First Responders Group) and functions in other directorates such as the National Protections and Programs Directorate (for example, cybersecurity) (Shea & Morgan, 2009). DHS missions anchored in different departmental components are cross-linked with intelligence collection and analysis units across the Department (GAO, 2014a).

Matrix organizations are crafted to address complex and rapidly-changing environments that demand flexible and coordinated responses to challenges. They are notoriously problematic, especially in public sector organizations with their tensions between political appointees and career civil service staff and bureaucratic requirements that defy organizational flexibility. They can encourage power struggles over turf, the absence of clear lines of responsibility and accountability, inefficient decision making, and a focus on internal operations at the expense of organizational goals and mission (Davis & Lawrence, 1978; Sy & D'Annunzio, 2005). All of these problems have plagued the DHS since its creation, especially those of managing cross-cutting horizontal and vertical integration projects, devising efficient decision-making structures, and assigning responsibility for implementing policies.

Integration in the DHS matrix is undermined by the dogged persistence of stovepiping: each of the seven components brings with it the management, cultural, and decision-making practices of its pre-DHS history; the focus on mission as opposed to unified management operations in its early years meant that few coordinated decision-making structures were put into place. Structural and procedural stovepiping continues to impede management integration, including in the cybersecurity field: a panoply of uncoordinated data centers and IT systems are spread throughout the DHS organization (Gordon, 2015), the seven components have very uneven records in meeting risk mitigation and management requirements of DHS-wide information security systems (Coburn, 2015), and components prove uncooperative at times in providing DHS authorities with necessary data. In 2014, for example, the Secret Service refused to hand over the data produced from the continuous monitoring of its computer networks to DHS authorities, defying Office of Management and Budget [OMB] instructions. This prevented the integration of the Secret Service data with that of the rest of DHS networks and limited the ability of the DHS Chief Information Security Officer to manage the Department's information security plan as required by the Obama Administration's cyber policies (DHS OIG, 2014a). As of late 2015, components independently develop their own cyber training programs in the absence of a DHS-wide training program for cyber staff; this "could hinder DHS from performing its cyber missions in an integrated and effective manner" (DHS OIG, 2015c, p. 6). Stovepiping is caused not only by structural impediments or a culture that privileges the proprietary nature of information collected in different components but often by the sheer volume and complexity of information available for dissemination: intelligence briefers often rely on their own components' information analyses because of the lack of time and resources to collate information from other sources (Priest & Arkin, 2010).

The DHS stovepiped matrix means that the processes to create a nexus of vertical integration of authority between the components and DHS Headquarters and horizontal integration based on functional tasks and projects have not been implemented. The department's seven components, though sharing cross-component missions, too often operate as autonomous units, neglecting to share information and sometimes refusing to cooperate with Headquarters leadership outright; headquarters, for its part, has often failed to effectively ensure compliance with department-wide policies (DHS OIG, 2015b). Before DHS can effectively work toward its mission of securing cyberspace, its leaders have to make the matrix work by integrating cybersecurity mission support functions across the components.

Management. With stovepiping practices hampering matrix organizational integration, DHS management practices have also remained largely uncoordinated. While watchdog reports on DHS management practices conclude that progress has been made, significant management weaknesses continue to hamper the efficiency and effectiveness of DHS operations (GAO, 2015b). A major problem is the lack of coordination across the Department in financial management systems (GAO, 2015a), major acquisitions (GAO, 2015b), information security controls (DHS OIG, 2014a), the assessment of threats to assets and facilities, and oversight of IT licenses and maintenance (DHS OIG, 2015b). The absence of accountability for assessing worker support programs (Coburn, 2015) and insufficient performance metrics (GAO, 2015b; GAO, 2013a; DHS OIG, 2013; Herzog & Counts, 2014) lead to both cost overruns and inefficiencies.

Management problems directly threaten the ability of DHS to fulfill its cybersecurity mission (Assessing DHS' performance, 2015). As of 2015, the GAO noted that the DHS still had not developed a comprehensive strategy to address cyber risks to federal facilities and had failed to include cyber threats to building access control systems in its reports to federal agencies (GAO, 2014b; GAO, 2015a). In addition, DHS had not put in place "outcome-based performance measures related to the cyber protection of key parts of the communications infrastructure sector" (GAO, 2015b, pp. 245–246). A critical 2015 Inspector General's report (DHS OIG, 2015c) detailed management weaknesses that undermine the DHS cybersecurity mission: DHS has not standardized the reporting of cyber threats, coordinated information sharing across the Department, adequately protected the privacy and confidentiality of shared information, or monitored the effectiveness of controls on unauthorized data transfers. More debilitating, as of September 2015, DHS still had no cyber security strategic implementation plan, lacked the capability to provide and share real-time cyber incident information among its components—let alone with federal agencies and the private sector, and failed to ensure that components had installed security fixes to their own information systems (DHS OIG, 2015c, p. 18; see also Coburn, 2015). Some staff members have been operating systems without proper authority, endangering the security of sensitive information (Assessing DHS' Performance, 2015). The DHS Inspector General complains that DHS components fail to abide by Department policies and that DHS Headquarters lacks sufficient oversight and enforcement policies to bring the components into line. When components insist on operating autonomously and refuse to share data or information, "DHS Headquarters does not always enforce its authority and ensure compliance … which limits … coordination of assets and integration of systems and processes" (DHS OIG, 2015a, p. 2). As of late 2015, DHS still lacked a strategy to clarify and coordinate components' cyber responsibilities, to implement cross-component performance measures, and to link cyber staff in the components through department-wide training programs, project collaboration, and operational decision making (DHS OIG, 2015c). Management's inability to overcome stovepiping remains the major impediment to integrating processes and procedures in DHS' complex matrix organization, directly undermining the Department's ability to effectively execute its cybersecurity mission.

DHS management is also constrained by wide-ranging and fractured congressional oversight. By 2014, more than 100 congressional committees, subcommittees, and commissions claimed some form of oversight of DHS, compelling DHS officials to participate in more than four thousand congressional sessions of one form or another (Homeland Security Advisory Council [HSAC], 2015). One analyst argues that this "results in conflicting guidance, micromanagement on low-level issues, [and] a lack of strategic direction and over reporting" (Vicinanzo, 2015, n.p.); former DHS Secretary Tom Ridge calls it "overkill," not "oversight" (Help Wanted at DHS, 2013). The 9/11 Commission Report warned already 1 year after DHS was up and running that the Department was "hamstrung by its many congressional overseers" and recommended reforms to end the "dysfunctional" congressional oversight (National Commission, 2004, p. 395). Ten years later, the 9/11 Commission members complained that the same "Balkanized system of oversight detracts from the Department's mission and has made Americans less safe" (Reflections, 2014, p. 37).

Culture and Workforce Morale. It is thus not surprising that the DHS has consistently failed former Labor Secretary Robert Reich's "pronoun test for success" (Reich, 1993): DHS staff in the various components think of themselves as "we" and staff in other components and at DHS Headquarters as "they" (IOM, 2013, p. 119). The lack of a common "we" throughout DHS perpetuates a fractured culture and prevents the development of a single organizational identity. Staff in DHS components are not only complacent about moving toward a unified culture; they appear to actively resist efforts to do so (Kostro, 2015). The absence of a core departmental culture hinders attempts to compel components to adhere to departmental directives and to leverage component resources to execute DHS missions (DHS, 2014b).

The roots of the failure to create a mission-based department-wide culture can be found in Office of Personnel Management's [OPM] annual Federal Employee Viewpoint surveys [FEVs] through 2015 and interviews with DHS employees (OPM, 2014, 2015; IOM, 2013): a blatant lack of employee engagement, a disconnect between Headquarters staff and front-line employees in the field, employee mistrust of managers and leaders, the dearth of employee recognition and advancement programs, the absence of a performance-based culture, and the lack of department-wide communication about core values, expectations, and behaviors. The absence of sustained leadership commitment to living and communicating a mission-oriented DHS culture that rises above politics, parochial interests, and personal advancement has contributed to the perpetuation of a fragmented organizational culture (IOM, 2013; Tobias, 2011).

Various attempts have been made by DHS leaders and advisors to leverage the strong cultures found in the DHS components (IOM, 2013) and channel them toward a unified mission-oriented DHS culture. The 2007 Homeland Security Culture Task Force, the 2011 DHS Workforce Strategy, the 2012 DHS Employee Engagement Executive Steering Committee, and the 2015 DHS Employee Task Force all recommended the requisite ingredients needed to "blend" component cultures into a unified, integrated Department culture (Tobias, 2011, p. 28): leadership training; employee engagement and recognition; measures to increase trust and strengthen morale; and improved communication and goal alignment between Headquarters and components, as well as between Headquarters staff and field workers. But the reports have come and gone, with no appreciable improvement in employees' assessment of workplace culture.

DHS, as a whole, has had the lowest worker morale throughout the entire federal government for many years running, with some of its components landing at rock bottom on OPM's FEVs. Lack of identification with the organization's missions is not the problem: a majority of the approximately 250,000 DHS employees appear to believe deeply in the DHS core missions to which they devote their energies despite weaknesses in organizational support (HSAC, 2015; IOM, 2013; Coburn, 2015; Vlahos, 2008). Far more responsible for the debilitating and consistent low morale at DHS is bad management: poor leadership, lack of accountability, nontransparent decision-making structures, inadequate training, ineffective performance measures, insufficient employee engagement, limited opportunities for advancement, and a fractured departmental culture that insulates and isolates rather than integrates and motivates. Management, not alienation from mission, is responsible for the abysmal level of work-force morale at DHS (Risher, 2014).

Low DHS scores on the 2009 annual FEVS prompted the Department to create the "DHSTogether Employee and Organizational Resilience" program to support the health and well-being of the workforce (Risher, 2014). In March 2012, DHS' Chief Human Capital Officer testified before Congress that a "concerted effort"—including "improved employee communication, training, emphasis on diversity and inclusion, and employee recognition," as well as improved leadership training—was being made to improve employee morale, although no specific details were provided (Schwemle, 2013, p. 65). The actions didn't match the rhetoric, however, and DHS scores in the 2012 FEVS continued to sink in the areas of leadership and knowledge management, a results-oriented performance culture, talent management, and overall job satisfaction (Schwemle, 2013).

DHS then commissioned a study by the National Academy of Science's Institute of Medicine (IOM) on improving the DHSTogether program. After meetings and interviews with employees, site visits, and a comprehensive analysis of DHS programs, IOM issued a 266-page report concluding that the DHSTogether program was piecemeal and ineffective, with no long-term strategic plan to guide its implementation and no mission focus or alignment with operational needs (IOM, 2013). The IOM committee laid out a specific 5-year program of Department workforce reforms in meticulous detail, recommending that DHS replace DHSTogether with a new, employee-engaged, leadership-supported program. DHS agreed to devise a 5-year strategic plan for workforce readiness and resilience. Two years later, DHSTogether was still in place and no strategic plan was in sight. One DHS employee said that the IOM report was shelved because it cast an unfavorable light on the Department; the DHS Under Secretary for Management responsible for workforce issues claimed never to have seen or heard of the report, which turned out to be just one of many surveys and reports conducted and left on a shelf to gather dust (Markon, 2015).

The failure to devise a workable employee engagement strategy bore the expected fruit in the OPM FEVS through 2015: DHS employee morale remains at abysmally low levels and DHS ranked dead last in the 2014 Partnership for Public Service "Best Places to Work" listings (see Partnership for Public Service, 2015): 19 out of 19 large organizations (HSAC, 2015; Bucci et al., 2015; Markon, 2014a). The 2015 OPM FEVS brought no good news for DHS: engagement index trends based on the quality of leaders, supportive supervisors, and intrinsic work experience were all down from previous years, as were scores measuring effective leadership, feelings of employee empowerment, and overall work satisfaction. The latter score was 13 points lower than the average government-wide score, leaving DHS once again at the bottom of the rankings by a large margin. Even more troubling in light of its cybersecurity mission, DHS' main cybersecurity unit, the National Programs and Protections Directorate [NPPD], ranked 308 out of a total of 315 federal government subcomponents in 2014, with a score measuring employee satisfaction and commitment almost 50 points lower than the top ranking unit. The quality of leadership and lack of performance-based awards and opportunities for advancement drove the low ranking (Partnership for Public Service, 2015). This reflects the conclusion of a 2015 HSAC Task Force report: "lack of confidence in leadership at many levels, perceived shortages of means to carry out job responsibilities, insufficient communications with supervision and higher management, and inadequate career development opportunities are fundamental issues" (p. 3). These factors inevitably affect morale, help explain the high employee turnover throughout the NPPD (DHS OIG, 2013) and make it less likely that young cyber security experts will be tempted to spend their energies in the dysfunctional environment. The GAO (2012c, 2013b) recommended in 2012 that DHS leaders address the causes of low morale at the NPPD; in October 2015, DHS had not fully implemented actions to do so (GAO, 2015c).

Leadership. The biggest leadership problem DHS faces is the preponderance of political appointees who come and go leaving major projects unfinished, lack the managerial and functional experience to effectively operate their organizational units, use their positions for personal, family, or political gain, or undermine morale by skirting Department policies in the service of political favoritism (Coburn, 2015; DHS OIG, 2015a; Rein, 2014). The high number of DHS political appointees is itself a problem: a 2015 HSAC Report assessed DHS' 168 political appointees as "an excessive number, even for a department the size and complexity of DHS," noting that many of them are not qualified for the positions they hold, thus demoralizing staff and dissuading talented civil service applicants from applying for positions (p. 19; see also IOM, 2013, pp. 95–96). The flux in leadership and long term vacancies undermine policy implementation and successful change management, demoralize employees, and discourage potential applicants (Help Wanted at DHS, 2013; Markon, Nakashima, & Crites, 2014; HSAC, 2015).

The high turnover in leadership positions has plagued DHS from the outset: a 2007 Report already noted a "leadership vacuum" (HSAC, 2007, p. 5) and at the end of 2013 more than 40% of DHS' top leadership positions were vacant or filled by what some DHS employees ironically called the "A-team"—"acting" personnel who might work hard at their jobs but whose temporary status undermines the continuity necessary for the implementation of effective long-term policies (Help Wanted at DHS, 2013; HSAC, 2015). During his nomination hearings in the Senate, Jeh Johnson acknowledged the alarming number of leadership vacancies and vowed to fill senior positions during his term (K. Johnson, 2013). The number of vacancies began to decrease after he was confirmed as DHS Secretary in December 2013, although a 2014 *Washington Post* article lamented that a 4-year trend of DHS employees leaving the Department at a rate "nearly twice as fast as in the federal government overall" was only accelerating (Markon et al., 2014, n.p.]. Johnson retorted that the DHS had been significantly reconstructed in the 9 months since he assumed office, including a reduction in the number of vacancies. But his remark that each of the twelve senior DHS officials who had been appointed during that time had "pledged to serve until at least the end of this Administration" (Markon, 2014b, n.p.), meaning a little over 2 years hence, did little to allay concerns about the lack of continuity in DHS leadership.

Leadership and staff problems have dogged attempts to establish a DHS state of the art cybersecurity enterprise structure: turnover in one DHS cybersecurity unit in 2013 prevented the development of a strategic plan to implement network security systems in civilian federal agencies (DHS OIG, 2013). Specifically, "a parade of high level departures ... exacerbated turf battles and other problems that delayed Einstein 3, a program to block malicious software before it enters the dot-gov networks" and "has at times hampered the Department's ability ... to serve as the federal point of contact for critical industries, such as energy and transportation, and for state and local governments" (Markon et al., 2014, n.p.). One respected DHS deputy secretary for cybersecurity—the Department's first "cyber czar" who had been successful in coordinating DHS efforts with various government agencies and industries in the private sector—left in 2013 after only a year and a half on the job (Sternstein, 2013). There were periods when staff throughout DHS cybersecurity offices left the department "in droves" (Miller, 2015c, n.p.). The lure of the private sector—with its higher pay, advancement opportunities, and bureaucracy-free environs —tempted much of the initial executive leadership in the DHS cyber divisions to leave; bureaucratic constraints on hiring, advancement, and pay increases also limit the ability of DHS to hire much-needed staff—especially Millennials—in its cyber divisions.

Strategic Workforce Planning. A significant shortage of skilled cybersecurity experts in the U.S. labor market has the potential to put national security at risk as state and nonstate hackers prove increasingly bold in penetrating private and public computer networks (Guccione, 2015; Libicki, Senty, & Pollak, 2014). Not only must government agencies compete with the private sector for skilled cyber experts, but government agencies compete among themselves to hire the best of the best, especially those upper-tier experts who can identify security vulnerabilities in complex networks and spot "zero day"—heretofore unknown—intrusions. Government entities are at a disadvantage because of complex hiring requirements, employment-delaying security clearances, and limited career development opportunities (Kettl, 2015; Sternstein, 2015a). Even the Department of Defense, which can use the Defense Civilian Personnel System to hire some cybersecurity professionals, has difficulties in hiring mission-critical cyber experts because of the lag time in hiring and extensive background checks (Libicki et al., 2014; GAO, 2011). DHS has an even harder time hiring and retaining cybersecurity professionals, in large part because of the fluctuation of leadership in DHS cyber offices, the insufficiency of training and career development programs, and the overall low morale, which leads to the impression, especially among Millennials, that the Department is not a "cool place" to work. DHS thus depends on contractors for much of its cyber staff; while this provides temporary fixes, it prevents the Department from developing its own pool of cyber experts who identify with DHS' cybersecurity mission and become engaged in organizational operations.

The Bush Administration's Comprehensive National Cybersecurity Initiative of 2008 addressed the shortage of skilled cybersecurity personnel and proposed measures to fill the need through education (Lipicki et al., 2014). DHS Secretary Napolitano followed through in 2009 and 2010, introducing a cross-component Cyber Workforce Initiative and obtaining OPM approval to hire one thousand excepted service ("direct hire") cybersecurity positions in the Department (HSAC, 2012). These were not enough to fill the growing need, in no small measure because some of the hires had no advanced cybersecurity skills and were placed in standard information technology positions (Sternstein, 2014). A Homeland Security Advisory Council, comprised in large part of cyber experts, published the CyberSkills Task Force Report in 2012, advocating enhanced departmental efforts to define mission-critical cybersecurity skills; a comprehensive workforce strategy to recruit, retain, and retrain a cadre of cyber experts; and partnerships with educational institutions, the private sector, and other federal agencies to secure a new generation of cyber experts. The report explicitly listed the national security implications of failing to recruit and retain top-notch cybersecurity personnel and proposed that DHS "build a team of approximately 600 federal employees with mission-critical cyber security skills" (HSAC, 2012, p. 4). The 2012 GAO assessment of the strategy, however, noted the same lack of performance and oversight measures that it cited in other areas (2012b) and in 2013, the DHS Cybersecurity and Communications Office (CS&C) had a vacancy rate of 22% (Rockwell, 2013).

Laborious U.S. government civil service requirements and security clearances are not the only reason that DHS has difficulty recruiting and retaining cybersecurity experts. The Department has not adequately defined the skill requirements attached to mission-critical cyber positions or established cyber employment categories that would facilitate a targeted

direct hire process (NICE, 2013; Rockwell, 2013; Schwemle, 2013). To
engage a highly skilled cybersecurity workforce, DHS has to do a better
job of aligning its workforce strategy with its cybersecurity mission and
IT support structures, reaching out to the private sector to lure recruits,
implementing training programs and career development policies, and
developing long-term plans to educate future cybersecurity experts and
motivate them to serve in government. Aside from policy and outreach, to
mobilize and retain the cyber workforce it needs to fulfill its mission, DHS
must eliminate the perception that it is a dysfunctional workplace (Kostro,
2015; IOM, 2013) and this will happen only when department-wide morale
improves and leadership becomes more stable and effective at engaging
and rewarding employees.

E pluribus unum: Making the Matrix Work

An integrated management system is the key to solving DHS' internal
problems and providing the department the foundation to adapt to an
ever-changing cybersecurity environment. Organization integration
requires coordinated decision-making structures, budget and acquisition
processes, strategic plans, strategies, and cultures to eliminate stovepiping
and to institutionalize cross-departmental cooperation in administration
and operations (GAO, 2004; Dalton & Best, 2007; Noble, 2000; Pardy &
Andrews, 2010). Management integration requires transparent, centralized
decision-making authority and clear responsibility for outcomes, the
lack of which has weakened DHS management since the department's
creation. Unlike a hierarchical "command and control" model, integrated
management is founded on a cooperative governance model based on
cross-Departmental decisionmaking structures.

At DHS, integrated management would entail DHS Headquarters'
senior leaders conferring with component managers to get a full picture
of mission-oriented capabilities throughout the Department. Decision-making structures should bring together component-level managers
with relevant Headquarters, policy, operations, and intelligence leaders.
Authority for decision-making should be clarified, as should responsibility
for decision-making and policy implementation. Given the complexity
of DHS mission-support activities, cooperative decision-making structures must coexist with functional hierarchical decision-making structures
in certain areas, such as incident reporting and acquisition programs
(Wise, 2006; Is DHS Effectively, 2012). Component policies, practices,
and performance metrics need to be more clearly aligned with Headquarters' decisions (GAO, 2012a; IOM, 2014); department-wide performance
measures should be included in component staff evaluations to facilitate

the alignment (IOM, 2014). This is especially important in cybersecurity support to ensure that information technology acquisitions and usage are standardized to facilitate the sharing and safeguarding of information.

In the case of DHS, internal organizational cohesion is a *prerequisite* for the development of an overarching departmental culture that extracts common values, assumptions, and goals from strong component subcultures as a foundation for strengthening mission effectiveness. Attempts to forge a common culture without the organizational interaction to anchor them (Getha-Taylor, 2009), while laudable, are likely to fail in the long term. A fragmented departmental culture that undermines effective internal management will constrain DHS' responses to mission-related external challenges. If the tension embedded in strong component subcultures, on the other hand, can be channeled into mission performance goals in the context of an integrated departmental culture, the divergent ways of assessing critical situations may prove central to adapting to changing mission environments (Schein, 2010).

DHS leaders and advisors have long emphasized management integration and recognized the connection between integrated management and a cohesive departmental culture. The 2007 Culture Task Force recommended the establishment of cross-component leadership teams to "coordinate—and integrate—agency goals and efforts and encourage a universal culture" and proposed more cross-departmental communication to weaken stove-piping and strengthen a mission-oriented culture (HSAC, 2007; Vlahos, 2008, n.p.). When Janet Napolitano took the reins as DHS Secretary in 2009, she coined the term "OneDHS" to refer to integrating management functions and responding to crises (Miller, 2012b); in her Bottom-Up Review (DHS, 2010), she noted that transforming disparate cultures into "OneDHS culture" would require "cohesive horizontal and vertical integration and management of department-wide initiatives" (p. 36).

In January 2011, DHS published its first management integration strategy (DHS, 2012b); subsequent updates emphasized transformative processes that were designed to be "cross-cutting" and "multi-dimensional." A key feature of the strategy was mission-driven management operations emphasizing matrix relationships (DHS, 2012d). In the Department's four-year Strategic Plan published in 2012, Secretary Napolitano focused on management and intelligence integration and emphasized the objective to "enhance and integrate departmental management functions ... both horizontally across missions and functions and vertically within missions and functions" (DHS, 2012d, p. 24). The authority of the Department's Under Secretary for Management, for example, was to be strengthened vis-à-vis the components' management offices (GAO, 2015b) to enhance vertical integration, and employees were to be offered cross-departmental assignment rotations to strengthen horizontal mission relationships (DHS,

2012d). Included in the strategy were plans to eliminate duplication in internet technology services, increase DHS' analytic capability through an "Analytic Agenda" based on cross-component analyses, and strengthen integrated acquisition and investment strategies. Some improvements ensued (GAO, 2015b; Miller, 2012b), but by all accounts the overall goal of transforming a fragmented management system into an integrated whole was largely unsuccessful or, at best, very incomplete (Coburn, 2015; Building One DHS, 2012; GAO, 2015b; Kahan, 2014). When Napolitano left DHS in 2012, many leaders left with her (Beckner, 2013) and yet another leadership vacuum undermined the implementation of management integration reforms.

Unity of Effort. The 2004 9/11 National Commission Report used the term "Unity of Effort" to characterize the goal of creating a unified system of information sharing, agency cooperation, and congressional oversight across the government (pp. 411–423); retired U.S. Coast Guard Admiral Thad Allen referred to it as a model of decision making in an increasingly complex and networked national security environment (Allen, 2012; The Future, 2012). Four months after being appointed DHS Secretary, Jeh Johnson introduced his own "Unity of Effort" initiative in April 2014 to integrate "governance, strategy, processes, analysis, and culture" in DHS management to support mission execution (DHS, 2014b, p. 58). The central concepts in Secretary Johnson's DHS Unity of Effort campaign are integration, coordination, and cohesion—all of which are central to making DHS' organizational matrix work. The goal is to integrate department-wide planning and strategy with component functions to serve DHS missions, moving from a "component-centric" model to a coordinated departmental approach. Johnson's integrated management incorporates component leaders into decision-making processes and adapts decision-making structures to strategic needs. Departmental cohesion would be attained "not by centralizing the decision-making authority and processes within an opaque DHS Headquarters, but rather by transparently incorporating DHS components into unified decision-making processes and the analytic efforts that inform decision-making ... to harness the significant resources of the Department more effectively" (DHS, 2014b, pp. 6–7). One of Johnson's first Unity of Effort initiatives was the implementation of regular Department senior leadership forums to bring together component heads with Headquarters leaders to discuss problems and department-wide policies, strategies, and operations "in an environment of trust" (Johnson, 2014).

An integrated DHS culture, in Johnson's initiative, should follow from integrated management: only if components align their goals with DHS missions, adhere to department standards and procedures, coordinate their resources, and commit to a spirit of collaboration will a department-wide culture ensue (DHS, 2014b). His Unity of Effort campaign foresees a core culture based on high performance standards, innovation, and cross-component mission support and execution. This speaks to earlier recommendations to leverage, not suppress, legacy cultures in DHS' seven operational components by extracting common department-wide values. The DHS Internet Technology Strategic Plan emphasizes the importance of a "mission-focused and results-oriented unified culture" to enhance organizational performance in IT mission support functions through continuous training, "mission-focused discipline, a security mindset, and innovative problem-solving." The effects will be to "strengthen workforce morale and performance through the promotion of a culture of account-ability that recognizes and rewards results" (DHS, 2015c, p. 11).

To integrate mission support functions, Secretary Johnson is reviving the Joint Requirements Council (JRC), which was created in 2004 to ratio-nalize investments and eliminate duplications in acquisitions. It fell into disuse after 2006 (Magnuson, 2011), leaving a fragmented, redundant, and decentralized acquisitions process that led to cost overruns and, in the case of cybersecurity, outdated network security systems (Building One DHS, 2012; Coburn, 2015). Attempts were made to standardize and accel-erate the acquisition of cybersecurity resources in response to emerging threats, but proved unsuccessful (Cummiskey, 2015). Former DHS offi-cials have been advocating for years a coordinated and centralized IT and cybersecurity acquisitions process to support the cybersecurity mission (Is DHS Effectively, 2012; Magnuson, 2011). The revival of the JRC as part of Johnson's Unity of Effort initiative is an attempt to replace compo-nent stovepiping with mission-oriented collaboration. The JRC, located within the office of the DHS Secretary, would strengthen the DHS matrix by bringing together senior leaders from the components to make recom-mendations to Headquarters on aligning acquisitions and investments more closely to DHS missions (Beckner, 2015a; DHS, 2015a). This would improve the foundation for the DHS cybersecurity mission by streamlining a dispersed IT acquisitions system and coordinating cyber training and operations across the whole Department (Beckner, 2015a).

Secretary Johnson's integrated management model, like that of Secre-tary Napolitano's before him, also relies on an "Analytic Agenda" to make management more efficient and effective; whereas Napolitano referred only briefly and very generally to the concept (DHS, 2012d), Johnson refers explicitly to a model already used in the Department of Defense (Stevens & Johnson, 2005). The DOD's Analytic Agenda is an empirically-based model of decision making that adapts to changing environments. A 4-year process, the Analytic Agenda is a "data-driven management of mission" (DHS, 2014b, pp. 11, 16) designed to collate "Big Data" and create different empirical models to "consistently assess strategic/external risk; measure outcomes; forecast such outcomes under different resource allocations, policies, and economic conditions; and use these forecasts to inform strategic planning, programming, acquisition, and operational decisions" (p. 11). The adaptive nature of this strategy is clear: "Maintaining a standing set of empirical models would allow the Department to quickly analyze the causes, likely duration, and the predicted effectiveness of alternative policy options in response to new trends" (p. 12). In combination with the integrated decision-making structures proposed by Secretary Johnson and the emphasis on "risk analytics" highlighted in the DHS 2014 Quadrennial Homeland Security Review (2014a), the Analytic Agenda would allow for cohesion and adaptation in DHS mission support and execution. To further support management integration efforts, DHS introduced the "Management Cube"—a technology tool developed by a private company to facilitate cross-departmental information sharing by "integrating the Department's financial, acquisition, human capital, procurement, asset, and security data into a single location" (DHS, 2015c, p. 15). Overseen by an Executive Steering Committee of members from across the organizational spectrum of DHS, the Management Cube "provides analysts access to an integrated set of enterprise-wide data," improving both the efficiency and effectiveness of organizational decision making (Fulgham, 2014, n.p.).

DHS has been steadily working to improve the pool of cybersecurity applicants for its positions, both in the short and long terms. Its Cyber Management and Support Initiative, a cross-component program created in March 2013 to hire and train cybersecurity experts for mission-critical positions, has helped accelerate both the hiring process (Cummiskey, 2015) and efforts to educate a new generation of cybersecurity experts. One such effort is the National Initiative for Cybersecurity Education [NICE], a public-private partnership that grew out of the 2008 Comprehensive National Cybersecurity Strategy. NICE works closely with DHS to improve the cyber awareness skills of the general population and develop recruiting and retention strategies, as well professional career development standards, for a highly skilled cybersecurity workforce (NICCS, n.d.). DHS also has its own outreach programs to colleges and universities that encourage and support homeland security research and education (DHS, 2013c). Jeh Johnson expanded this outreach in April 2015 when he announced plans to open a DHS recruiting office in Silicon Valley (Hicks, 2015). His goal is to foster more contacts between a government trying to encourage public-private information sharing and a tech industry distrustful of government motives and competencies. To counter the problems inherent in an aging workforce (IOM, 2013; NICE, 2013) DHS will have to learn to appeal to the cadre of Millennials attracted to private sector tech industries both to make the mission of securing the homeland from cyber attacks "cool" and to put the management foundations in place so that "cool" does not turn into "lukewarm" (Katz, 2015).

Homeland security analysts and officials often advocate applying methods used in the 1986 Goldwater-Nichols Act that propelled the DOD into a more unified organization to DHS in order to overcome its fragmented structures, processes, and identities (Gerstein, 2015; Kostro, 2015; Is DHS Effectively, 2012). Secretary Johnson has set strategies in place to move toward this model without the legislative underpinnings. Even those who are very critical of DHS management applaud his efforts. It cannot escape anyone's notice, however, that most of Secretary Johnson's strategies have been attempted in the past—his "Unity of Effort" campaign is just the latest iteration of Secretary Napolitano's "OneDHS" initiative, albeit with more specific underpinnings. The Government Accountability Office applauds Johnson's efforts but is understandably concerned that they result in "demonstrated, sustained progress," with their overall assessment a year after the Unity of Effort initiative was announced being "too early to tell" (GAO, 2015a, p. 13). The failure to institutionalize the policy changes designed to integrate management processes in the past (Beckner, 2015a), a revolving door of leadership and acting leadership appointments, piecemeal performance measures that lacked corrective strategies, a dearth of experts, especially in cyber positions, ineffective use of resources (GAO, 2015b), and low Department morale fueled in part by little employee engagement (HSAC, 2015) have been the main factors preventing DHS from reaping all that its various leaders have sown in attempts to integrate management functions and make the DHS matrix work.

THE DHS CYBERSECURITY MISSION

As massive, debilitating, untraceable hacks on every known computer system proliferate, reinforcing the centrality of cybersecurity to national security, the Obama Administration and Congress have made it a priority to establish rules and produce legislation to protect the nation against cyber attacks. At the same time that it attempts to integrate into a single cohesive department in which a "unity of effort" replaces a disunity of initiatives and orientations, DHS must transform its organizational capacity to effectively execute its cybersecurity mission. To do this, DHS must adapt its resources, intelligence analyses, decision-making processes, organizational structure, technological tools, strategic hiring practices, information sharing strategies, and stakeholder relationships to changing cyber threat environments.

Organizational adaptation is the process of executing missions by developing the capacity to respond to changes in the operational environment. It is based on organizational and technological innovations, collaboration with stakeholders, continual feedback and corrective actions to strategies, and the coordination of networks to attain goals (Wise, 2006). It is especially important in the ever-changing world of homeland security: "The ability to continuously innovate and adapt is fundamental to achieving and sustaining resilient infrastructures, communities and a resilient nation" (Gaynor, 2011, n.p.). This is especially true for DHS' cybersecurity mission, with its kaleidoscope of constantly changing threats and complexity of stakeholder needs and concerns. The second part of this chapter examines how DHS has adapted its organization, policies, and technologies to fulfill its mission of protecting the nation against cyber threats in the context of political and legal support, ambiguities, and impediments.

DHS Cyber Responsibilities

DHS' cybersecurity responsibilities are many and wide-ranging: monitoring the computer networks and safeguarding the information of civilian federal agencies; protecting critical infrastructures from cyber and physical attacks; facilitating the sharing of cyber threat information between the government and the private sector; developing cybersecurity technologies along with the private sector; and sharing cybersecurity intelligence with stakeholders (DHS OIG, 2015b). The first three tasks are carried out under the DHS National Protection and Programs Directorate [NPPD], the fourth under the Science and Technology Directorate, and the fifth under the Office of Intelligence Analysis. The following focuses on the three NPPD tasks (see Figure 3.2).

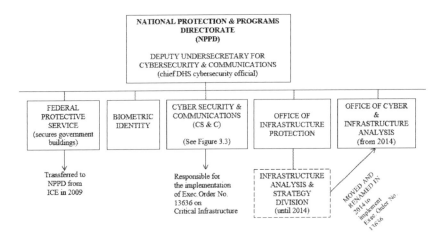

Source: Figure created using information from (dhs.gov; GAO 2014b; Sternstein, 2013).

Figure 3.2.   National Protection & Program Directorate 2007–2015.

Civilian Federal Agencies. In 2010 and 2014 the Office of Management and Budget [OMB] passed the major responsibility for monitoring and securing the computer networks of civilian federal agencies (".gov") to DHS (Coburn, 2015; OMB, 2014; GAO, 2015b). Agencies are responsible for their own network security strategies but are directed to allow DHS to evaluate those strategies, monitor and secure their networks, take measures to eliminate vulnerabilities and thwart attacks, and protect the security of personally identifiable information (PII) on agency networks (DHS, 2012a).

Critical Infrastructure. DHS has been charged since its inception with protecting the nation's physical and cyber critical infrastructures—the 16 sectors vital to U.S. national security and public health: chemical, commercial facilities, communications, critical manufacturing, dams, the defense industrial base, emergency services, energy, financial services, food and agriculture, government facilities, healthcare & public health, information technology, nuclear reactors and material, transportation systems, and waste & wastewater systems (DHS, Critical, n.d.). Responsibility for critical infrastructure cybersecurity is spread among multiple stakeholders: federal, state, local and tribal governments; public and private corporations, and international actors. DHS NPPD is responsible for the cyber and physical protection of U.S. critical infrastructure sectors.

Private and nonprofit sectors. The most problematic part of DHS' cybersecurity mission is facilitating public-private information sharing, the synergy of which is essential to protecting as wide a swath of U.S. communication networks as possible from cyber threats and attacks. Government relies on information from the public and private/nonprofit entities for both access to cyber threats and the technology to counter them; the private sector relies on classified information and the wide-ranging resources of the government to protect critical infrastructures and private networks from cyber attacks. Several obstacles stand in the way of seamless private-public cybersecurity information sharing.

Private companies are concerned about liability for sharing data with the government, or with other companies, that might contain PII (Moteff, 2014). Many fear that complex federal and state laws, regulations, and contracts referring to proprietary information might entail legal risks if shared with the government (Nolan, 2015; Protecting America, 2015) and that data sharing may divulge information that makes them subject to regulatory enforcement by state or federal agencies (Protecting America, 2015). Private companies also worry that sharing information from their networks may put them at a competitive disadvantage with other companies (Norton, 2015) or harm their reputation for being able to protect privacy among their customers (Nolan, 2015; Protecting America, 2015). Technical concerns also impede the motivation to share information: if information about vulnerabilities is shared but not immediately fixed, intruders may have an opening to orchestrate attacks (Protecting America, 2015). The government, for its part, is often reluctant to share sensitive information with private sector entities, whether for security or proprietary reasons; the difficulty of attaining security clearances limits some critical infrastructure entities from having access to DHS cyber threat information (Protecting America, 2015).

Finally, the issue of trust has prevented high levels of public-private cybersecurity information sharing: the Wikileaks episode, Edward Snowden's revelations about National Security Administration (NSA) collection of information, and the general decline of public confidence in the government have lessened the willingness of some private companies and the public at large to condone the widespread sharing of information between the private and public sectors. DHS has attempted to assure stakeholders that their systems go to great lengths to protect PII (DHS, 2012c), but problems remain: it is difficult to completely expunge all PII from critical cybersecurity threat information sharing (Protecting America, 2015) and even more difficult to persuade American citizens that the government should gather and share data that contains their personal information. DHS officials are developing incentives for private companies to share information (DHS, 2013b; DHS, NPPD, 2015; Is DHS Effectively, 2012); the only way to incentivize Americans on the whole is to convince them that national security can be reconciled with privacy and civil rights concerns.

Organizational and Technological Foundations of the DHS Cybersecurity Mission

The National Protections and Programs Directorate [NPPD] was established in 2007 and, with its 3,500 employees, is the main DHS unit responsible for the protection and resiliency of cyber and physical critical infrastructures, federal facilities, and communication networks. Of the NPPD's five offices (until proposed changes in 2015), the Cybersecurity and Communications [CS&C] office, also established in 2007 by merging three existing DHS units, is the most directly responsible for cybersecurity information sharing and threat mitigation across government (see Figure 3.3). DHS announced an NPPD organizational "transformation" in 2015 to improve the Department's cybersecurity mission support and mission execution functions (Examining the Mission, 2015): See Figure 3.4.

Cybersecurity Information Sharing. The National Cybersecurity and Communications Integration Center (NCCIC—pronounced "N-kick"), established in 2009 and one of CS&C's five main units (through 2015), is the physical cyber command center where DHS analysts work with

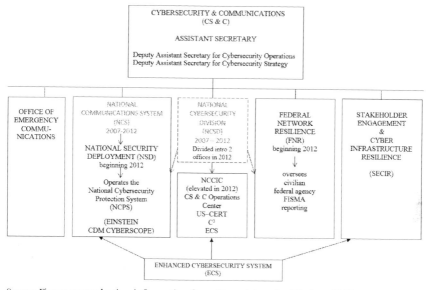

Source: Figure created using information from (Examining the Mission, 2015) and (Miller, 2012a; DHS OIG, 2014b; DHS 2012c).

Figure 3.3.   Cybersecurity and Communications 2007–2015.

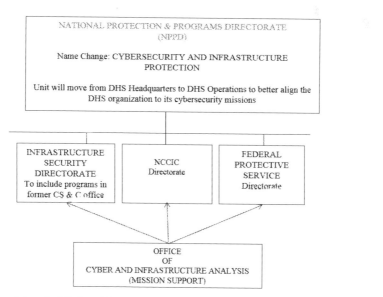

Source: Examining the Mission (2015).

Figure 3.4.   Proposed Changes to NPPD October 2015.

representatives of federal agencies, all levels of government, critical infra-structure sectors, private companies, and international entities to share information relating to cybersecurity and to identify and address potential and actual threats. It is charged with integrating information about cyber vulnerabilities and threats, coordinating responses, and performing onsite incident mitigation (Examining the President's Cybersecurity, 2015). DHS considers NCCIC to be the "national nexus of cyber and communications integration for the Federal Government, intelligence community, and law enforcement" (DHS, n.d., NCCIC, p. 1) and the GAO agrees, propos-ing the Center's expansion as "the central focal point for leveraging and integrating the capabilities of the private sector, civilian government, law enforcement, the military, and the intelligence community" (GAO, 2015b, p. 238).

Some were surprised, then, when in February 2015, the Obama Admi-nistration announced the creation of the Cyber Threat Intelligence Integration Center (CTIIC) in the Office of the Director of National Intelli-gence (ODNI), stressing the new Center's role in coordinating information and strategies from the nation's cybersecurity hubs, including the NCCIC. Members of Congress complained that they received little, or last-minute, advance notice of the White House's proposed new cyber integration center (Volz, 2015); questions arose as to whether the CTIIC would require legis-lative action (Beckner, 2015b). The CTIIC's purpose is to integrate and analyze cyber threat intelligence from across the government to support policymakers, network operators, and law enforcement. Administration officials emphasize that the goal is not to supplant the role of the NCCIC, but rather to support it in its information sharing and cybersecurity stra-tegizing (Bejtlich, 2015). Some observers welcome the CTIIC as a cyber command hub; the DHS Deputy Secretary projected that the new Center will "ensure consistent downgrading of intelligence to the lowest classifi-cation level to make government-held, classified information actionable and more widely available" (DHS, 2015d). Others worry that the CTIIC will create "mission overlap" and only add to confusion about responsi-bility for collating and sharing cyber threat information (Kimery, 2015a; Nakashima, 2015; Volz, 2015). Given the central coordinating and integ-rating role of the NCCIC as viewed by DHS cyber officials (Examining the President's Cybersecurity, 2015) and the GAO, the precise function of the CTIIC remains unclear. Competing legislation in 2015 (see below) mirrors the potential confusion.

Information Sharing Analysis Centers (ISACs; see National Council of ISACs, n.d.) were created by President Clinton's 1998 Presidential Decision Directive-63 as a forum in which critical infrastructure sector owners and operators can share information about any type of threats, incidents, or vulnerabilities (ISAC Council, 2009). Each of the 16 designated critical infrastructure sectors eventually developed its own ISAC (Moteff, 2014). ISACs are nonprofit groups formed directly by companies, contracted out to security firms, or added to existing critical infrastructure industry associations (Moteff, 2014; Sternstein, 2015e). In 2003, Homeland Security Presidential Directive-7 superseded PDD-63 to formally establish an information sharing partnership among "information sharing analysis mechanisms," the DHS, and government agencies involved in critical infrastructure sectors in order to facilitate threat information and coordinate the protection of the nation's cyber and physical infrastructure sectors (Homeland Security Presidential Directive 7, 2003, p. 1743).

ISACS have helped to mitigate cyber threats to critical infrastructure sectors. They were mobilized along with company incident response teams, government employees, and a cyber incident working group to craft a coordinated response to the Conficker worm that used advanced malware strategies to slip through a vulnerability in the Microsoft operating system to hack into computers and steal PII. Scott Charney, a corporate vice president at Microsoft, credits the collaboration with defusing the potentially devastating malware relatively quickly. Microsoft also collaborated with the Financial Services ISAC and law enforcement to destroy botnets such as Zeus and Citadel that had resulted in hundreds of millions of dollars in financial fraud. "The collective efforts of industry and government," he testified, "freed millions of infected computers from the control of cybercriminals" (Protecting America, 2015, pp. 3–4).

Information Sharing Analysis Organizations (ISAOs) are also designed to collect, analyze, and share information about potential or existing threats to the nation's critical infrastructure sectors without being organized along sector lines. Their purpose is to create a mechanism through which industries, businesses, and firms, including those that serve critical infrastructure sector clients, can share cyber threat information and have access to DHS threat mitigation strategies (DHS, Frequently, n.d.). ISAOs were established by the authority of the Homeland Security Act (2002; Fischer & Logan, 2015), but remained dormant until February 2015, when President Obama issued Executive Order 13691 on promoting public-private sector cybersecurity information sharing. The Executive Order directs the DHS Secretary to encourage the formation of ISAOs, coordinate cybersecurity information sharing with the organizations through NCCIC, develop an efficient strategy for granting clearances to private sector ISAO members (so they can participate in NCCIC sessions), and select an ISAO Standards Organization to develop a set of voluntary, consensus industry standards, in place of government regulations, for the groups' functioning (DHS, ISAOs, n.d.; Fischer & Logan, 2015).

The DHS emphasizes that ISAOs should complement ISACs in the realm of cybersecurity information sharing and threat mitigation (DHS,

ISAOs, n.d.). The goal is to combine ISAOs with ISACs to offer a kind of matrixed-based information sharing system that taps into industry-specific needs while at the same time offering a cross-sector view of potential vulnerabilities and threats (DHS, 2015b; Norton, 2015). Others, however, are concerned that ISAOs will only complicate the information sharing process, add information-sharing breadth without offering security depth, privilege large companies that can afford ISAO set-up and administration costs (Libicki, 2015), and leave companies open to lawsuits for the sharing of PII (Edwards, 2015).

DHS has developed other information sharing protocols to encourage public-private collaboration to fend off cyber threats. The Enhanced Cybersecurity System [ECS] is a voluntary cybersecurity information sharing protocol between DHS and private sector entities that began as a pilot program in both the Department of Defense and DHS to protect private companies involved in defense activities (DHS OIG, 2014b; DHS, n.d., Enhanced). DHS took over ECS from the DOD in 2013, allowing security-cleared commercial service internet providers [CSPs] to offer ECS services to their customers, including those in the 16 critical infrastructure sectors (DHS, n.d., Enhanced). ECS shares unclassified, "sensitive," and classified government cybersecurity information with security-cleared private entities (Nolan, 2015) through an internet service provider add-on feature (Coburn, 2015). As of May 2014, 40 critical infrastructure entities were participating, and 22 companies had signed memorandums of agreement to join (Coburn, 2015; DHS OIG, 2014b). As of April 2015, three CSPs had signed up to offer ECS: AT&T, CenturyLink, and Verizon (DHS, n.d., Enhanced; see also DHS OIG, 2015b).

In January 2014 the DHS NPPD introduced the Critical Infrastructure Cyber Community C3 Voluntary Program ("C-Cubed" or C^3) to coordinate efforts among governmental and private entities involved in critical infrastructure functions to improve cybersecurity and resilience against attacks. This program is founded on the three "C"s of convergence (of resources dedicated to the protection of critical infrastructures), connections (of critical infrastructure stakeholders to cybersecurity experts in DHS and throughout the cyber community), and coordination (of cross-sector cybersecurity strategies). One of the program goals is to promote the "Cybersecurity Framework" standards, guidelines, and best practices established by the National Institute of Standards and Technology [NIST] to help critical infrastructure stakeholders manage cybersecurity risks (DHS, 2015e; DHS, U.S. CERT, n.d.; NIST, 2014).

DHS continues to develop cybersecurity information sharing techniques with a wide network of stakeholders in government and the private and nonprofit sectors. To be effective, its efforts must be complemented by laws that protect companies from liabilities and lawsuits over shared personal information, standards for protecting the privacy and rights of people whose PII is shared, and the trust of the American public in government's ability to uphold those standards. These are daunting tasks, especially since, as becomes clear below, even government does not trust government to share and protect information.

National Cybersecurity Protection System. The National Cybersecurity Protection System [NCPS] was established at DHS in 2008 as a "suite of capabilities that monitor and analyze cyber threat data transiting to and from civilian government networks" (DHS, 2012c, p. 4). It includes an array of technical capabilities to analyze data, detect and prevent intrusions, share information, and report threat incidents. The major reporting and analysis tools are CyberScope, CyberStat, and the U.S. Cyber Emergency Readiness Team [U.S.CERT]; two of the most important monitoring, detection and intrusion prevention instruments are the EINSTEIN tool, various iterations of which are a key part of DHS technical innovation in fulfilling its cybersecurity mission, and continuous diagnostics and mitigation [CDM].

U.S. CERT was created within DHS in 2003 to protect U.S computer and communication networks against cyber attacks; it is considered "the front line against cyber threats" (DHS, 2012c, p. 3). U.S. CERT analysts receive cyber vulnerability, threat information, and incident reports and disseminate the means to secure networks. U.S.CERT analyzes EINSTEIN data from civilian federal agencies and works through the NCCIC to pursue a wide range of activities and relationships with public and private stakeholders to analyze threat information, encourage cyber-information sharing, coordinate with national security intelligence, and disseminate cyber threat and defense information to government agencies, critical information sectors, businesses, and the general public (DHS, U.S.CERT, n.d; Moteff, 2014; Nolan, 2015). U.S.CERT was codified in law in 2014.

Cyberscope is an automated network security reporting tool developed by DHS together with the Department of Justice and NIST to aid civilian federal agencies in fulfilling their requirement to allow DHS to monitor their networks for vulnerabilities and malicious activity. OMB mandated that agencies submit metrics concerning their networks' security through the CyberScope application once a month beginning in November 2011 (Miller, 2011); once a year agencies must submit a report about their networks' security, including how they protect PII, through CyberScope (OMB, 2014). The goal of implementing technology to continuously monitor agency networks and send relevant data automatically to CyberScope was attained by the end of 2015. CyberStat sessions are face-to-face reviews conducted by OMB, DHS, and National Security Council personnel with staff from civilian federal agencies using CyberScope reports to hold agencies accountable for their network security posture, identify problems, and recommend solutions and best practices (OMB, 2014). The CyberScope tool and CyberStat sessions support DHS' responsibility to help agencies protect their computer networks (DHS, 2012c).

EINSTEIN, a technical tool first developed in 2003, is used by DHS to augment civilian federal agency efforts to detect and prevent malicious intrusions into their computer networks. EINSTEIN monitors network traffic to and from federal civilian agency networks and feeds information to U.S.CERT for analysis and mitigation strategies. Since its development, two updated iterations of this tool have increased its capacity to detect and prevent malicious cyber threats. EINSTEIN 1 collects computer network flow records from those civilian federal agencies on which it is installed; it can't target malicious activity or provide real-time mitigation solutions. EINSTEIN 2 adds an intrusion detection function to the initial version, allowing it to identify the signatures of known or suspected malicious malware; like EINSTEIN 1, it has no real-time capability to protect against these threats but sends information to U.S.CERT for analysis (DHS, 2012c). The latest (2013) version of the tool, EINSTEIN 3 Accelerated (E^3A), builds on the first two versions by blocking malicious activity in near real time before it can do significant damage, using classified information to do so (Johnson, 2015).

Technical, commercial, and legal impediments hamper DHS' ability to prevent malicious hack attacks in federal agencies. E^3A, like the earlier versions, can block cyber threats only against known and suspected threats; DHS is using this as the foundation to develop technology that can protect against unknown threats (DHS' Efforts, 2015). E^3A is deployed through the private sector internet service providers [ISPs] that serve civilian federal government agencies; not all of them have the technical or security clearance capabilities to fully deploy the tool (Johnson, 2015; Serbu, 2015). Legal concerns have been the key sticking point in preventing DHS from deploying its technology across federal civilian agencies to counter cyber threats and attacks. Federal agency heads have been uncertain as to their statutory authority to provide DHS access to information on their computer systems, especially when it comes to PII (Sternstein, 2015b). When EINSTEIN was first deployed on a voluntary basis, many agencies refused or neglected to grant DHS the authorization to run the tool. Several DHS cybersecurity officials relate the story of the 2014 Heartbleed encryption malware to illustrate how legal concerns hampered DHS efforts: when this encryption malware threatened to compromise stored data and passwords in the nation's computer systems, some agency lawyers hesitated in giving DHS the go-ahead to scan their networks for the bug (Lyngaas, 2014). The DHS deputy undersecretary for cybersecurity noted DHS' frustration at the inability to quickly jump the legal hurdles:

Everybody remembers Heartbleed.... We wanted to look and make sure that no one was running that version of OpenSSL.... It took the better part of just over a week to get the legal side of some of the agencies to be OK with it while the technical side sweated bullets knowing that the whole world knew about this vulnerability now and all the wannabes were trying to exercise it. (as cited in Boyd, 2014, n.p.)

In October 2014, partly in response to the Heartbleed fiasco, OMB empowered DHS to scan civilian agency networks using EINSTEIN and required agencies to provide DHS with their authorization to do so (OMB, 2014). Legislation to anchor these instructions from the Executive Office in law was introduced in 2015.

OPM, at the time of the 2014 hack, was covered by EINSTEIN 2 but not E³A, because the agency had no agreement with its ISP to do so (Serbu, 2015). It is unlikely that E³A would have been able to prevent the hack in any case, because it was not a known threat signature and because the hackers had gained the administrative credentials necessary to access OPM networks (Serbu, 2015; Sternstein, 2015c). DHS detected the specifics of the hack only after the fact, using EINSTEIN 2 technologies once OPM had identified an intrusion, and sent the relevant information to be analyzed in the DHS NCPS. Armed with the authorization to scan all federal civilian agencies, DHS hopes to expand its deployment of EINSTEIN and add technology that is even more effective at intercepting unknown threats in real time. By 2015, only 45% of civilian federal agencies had EINSTEIN running (Johnson, 2015; Serbu, 2015); the goal is to have E³A in place and employed to protect the 52 largest agencies against threats and attacks by 2016, two years ahead of the original schedule (Miller, 2015a).

DHS collaborates with commercial companies to complement EINSTEIN with a continuing diagnostics and mitigation [CDM] tool to secure civilian federal agency networks. EINSTEIN checks traffic between agency networks and the web; CDM directly assesses agency networks for vulnerabilities and threats. The goal is to prevent perpetrators who get through EINSTEIN from setting up shop on agency computer networks, thus providing increased "situational awareness" that aids efforts to mitigate risks (DHS OIG, 2014a). CDM is a package of software that automatically scans networks in a period of 72 hours through a multilayered process that establishes sensors to automatically search for vulnerabilities, sends results to a dashboard that illustrates risks to agency networks, alerts administrators of the risks, sends reports to agencies, and collates results across all agencies on a government-wide dashboard so that vulnerabilities and risks can be compared (DHS, CDM, n.d.). The OMB required civilian federal agencies to work with DHS to implement CDM systems on their networks in 2013 (OMB, 2013). Implementation occurs in three phases; as of July 2015, 97%

of federal civilian agencies had the tools to implement phase one of the CDM program (Johnson, 2015).

The DHS 2014–2018 Strategic Plan goes one step further by establishing the goal of "enabling the NCCIC to receive information at machine speed" so that networks can be "more self-healing, using mathematics and analytics to mimic restorative processes that occur biologically" (DHS, 2014b, p. 30). DHS is moving toward this capability by adopting machine-to-machine "STIX"—structured threat information eXpression—and "TAXII"—trusted automated eXchange of indicator information—to "create automated, machine-readable threat and security information that can be shared across industries and groups in near real-time" (Protecting America, 2015, p. 9). The Obama Administration's 2015 cybersecurity legislative proposal directs DHS to adopt these protocols to share threat indicators with ISAOs, civilian federal agencies, and law enforcement; in 2014 NCCIC developed a program to "test automated delivery of STIX indicators via TAXII" (Examining the President's Cybersecurity, 2015, n.p.).

Executive and Legislative Branch DHS-Related Cyber Initiatives

The transformation of DHS into a central hub of civilian cybersecurity strategy is taking place at the nexus of executive and legislative initiatives and support. The major Executive Office effort to connect national security to cybersecurity began in January 2008 with the Bush administration's Comprehensive National Cybersecurity Initiative [CNCI] (Rollins & Henning, 2009). President Obama built upon and expanded that foundation in his 2009 updated CNCI and vowed to make cybersecurity efforts a keystone of his administration's agenda (White House, 2009a, 2009b), warning that "the cyberthreat [is] one of the most serious economic and national security challenges the nation [faces]" (Nakashima, 2012, n.p.). When Obama announced plans in May 2009 to establish an Executive Office position of Cybersecurity Coordinator, a debate ensued about whether the DHS or the Executive Office should be the center of the nation's cybersecurity efforts (Gorman, 2009; Gross, 2009; Vijayan, 2009b). The decision was made to combine efforts. The position of "Cybersecurity Coordinator and Special Assistant to the President," the White House's own "cyber czar," was formally established in December 2009 to help prepare the President's cybersecurity legislative agenda, set priorities for the DHS cybersecurity mission, and encourage federal agencies to work with DHS to secure the .gov computer networks.

In 2011, President Obama introduced his cybersecurity legislative proposal to encourage information sharing between the private sector and government; this was followed by the administration's 2012 "Information Sharing and Safeguarding Strategy" (DHS, 2013a). This calls for coordinated efforts to balance between sharing and protecting information, interoperability of data sharing and network capabilities, national standards to guide information sharing and protection processes, the development of enhanced technological solutions to cyber problems, and efforts to guarantee privacy, civil rights, and civil liberties (DHS, 2013a). The administration followed through with two executive orders: the February 2013 EO 13636, "Improving Critical Infrastructure Cybersecurity," and the February 2015 EO 13691, "Promoting Private Sector Cybersecurity Information Sharing," both of which raise DHS' profile in sharing and protecting cybersecurity-related information.

Defending against a major cyber attack on the US homeland would require seamless collaboration between the public and private sectors given their shared assets and control over cyber defenses. EO 13636 thus calls for measures to facilitate the government's sharing of unclassified and classified information with critical infrastructure sector entities to protect against cyber threats. This EO directs the DHS secretary, along with the Director of National Intelligence and the U.S. Attorney General, to disseminate security reports to stakeholders and the National Institute of Standards and Technology (NIST) to develop a "Cybersecurity Framework" that aligns processes and procedures to protect against and mitigate the impact of cyber attacks. The DHS Secretary is charged with encouraging the voluntary participation of private entities in the Framework and fast-tracking security clearances for private sector stakeholders. DHS, along with the DOD, is authorized to expand the ECS program to entities in all 16 critical infrastructure sectors. Privacy, civil rights, and civil liberties protections are to be built into all aspects of information sharing procedures (Exec. Order No. 13636, 2013; Moteff, 2014).

Obama's January 2015 cyber legislative update, which he announced on a visit to the NCCIC (Examining the President's Cybersecurity, 2015), emphasizes the role of the NCCIC in public-private cybersecurity information sharing, calls for universal standards to protect PII, promotes law enforcement to combat cyber crime, and proposes the first federal statute to require businesses to notify customers of hacks to their computer networks (White House, 2015). A month later, the White House created the E-Gov Cyber and National Security Unit ["E-Gov Cyber"] in the Office of Management and Budget and proposed the new CTIIC, both designed to work in tandem with the DHS in overseeing civilian federal agencies' cybersecurity responsibilities. E-Gov Cyber is specifically charged with strengthening OMB's oversight of agency compliance with

DHS' cybersecurity monitoring through CyberStat reviews, EINSTEIN applications, and CDM scans (Miller, 2015b).

To jumpstart the Administration's push to promote cybersecurity information sharing between the private sector and government, Obama held a summit in February on "Cybersecurity and Consumer Protection" at Stanford University, where he signed Executive Order 13691, "Promoting Private Sector Cybersecurity Information Sharing." This EO revitalizes the dormant ISAOs referenced in the 2002 Homeland Security Act and encourages private organizations to participate in these cross-sector entities to facilitate coordinated government-private sector cybersecurity information sharing and threat mitigation. The EO formally designates DHS' NCCIC as a "critical infrastructure protection program" and grants it authority to engage in voluntary agreements with ISAOs to share information (Exec. Order No. 13691, 2015). From business leaders' point of view, however, the EO provides no protections against the dissemination of PII and no guarantees against liability for doing so (Kimery, 2015b) and thus does little to substantively promote meaningful cyber information sharing between private companies and the government. Doing so requires legislation grounding protections in the law and, although Congress stepped up to the plate in late 2014 to pass five cybersecurity laws, issues related to information sharing liability protections and government access to personal information have proven the hardest to resolve.

While political and jurisdictional conflicts hampered congressional action on cybersecurity laws in the past (Coburn, 2015), the OPM and Sony hacks in 2014 spurred Congress into action in 2014 and 2015, when a spate of cybersecurity initiatives flooded on to the scene (Fischer, 2014). Although five cyber bills passed in December 2014 are relatively narrow in scope (Fischer, 2015), they set the stage for congressional efforts to establish the organizational, legal, and technical foundations for advancing cybersecurity and provide the DHS with some of the tools necessary to lead the way. Prior to 2014, the law guiding cybersecurity measures throughout the civilian part of the federal government was the *Federal Information Security Management Act of 2002*, Title III of the E-Government Act of 2002, which designated the OMB as the central agent in overseeing federal government agencies' efforts to secure their communication systems against unauthorized access, vulnerabilities, and threats. The only reference to the newly created DHS, which would not be operational until 2003, was listing its Secretary as one of many federal officials who should be consulted in developing standards to secure federal information networks (E-Government, 2002).

The OMB has transferred many of its cybersecurity monitoring functions to the DHS since 2010 and the GAO consequently recommended that Congress codify the responsibilities of both DHS and OMB in order to avoid legal confusion over agencies' responsibilities to share information, especially that containing PII (GAO, 2015b). This process ensued with the the Federal Information Security Modernization Act of 2014 [FISMA 2014], which revised FISMA 2002 by formalizing DHS' role in partnering with OMB to promote cybersecurity in civilian federal government agencies—a role that the Department had increasingly been assuming since 2009. This law authorizes the DHS Secretary, in consultation with the OMB Director, "to administer the implementation of [civilian and non-national security] federal agency security policies and practices for information systems' (FISMA, 2014, n.p.). It gives the DHS Secretary the power to issue "Binding Operational Directives" (BOD) to agencies to follow cybersecurity guidelines and policies issued by OMB in consultation with the National Institute of Standards and Technology. DHS Secretary Johnson issued the first BOD in May 2015. This update of FISMA 2002 requires civilian agency heads to maintain cybersecurity standards, holds their Chief Information Security Officers responsible for compliance to those standards, allows DHS monitoring and OMB reporting of agency electronic networks, and stipulates a workforce with the skills necessary to ensure agency compliance. FISMA 2014 establishes specific requirements for agencies to report data breaches (GAO, 2015b) and mandates that DHS provide a federal cybersecurity incident reporting center, which DHS had already been operating since 2003 with its creation of U.S. CERT. FISMA 2014 upgrades the continuous monitoring of agency networks mandated in FISMA 2002 to continuous diagnostics and mitigation, a more robust method of protecting computer networks from malicious threats (FISMA, 2014; Jackson, 2012; Patel, 2014).

A bipartisan bill introduced in the Senate in 2015, *the Federal Information Security Management Reform Act of 2015* (S.1828), would go even further in empowering DHS to oversee cybersecurity efforts, threat mitigation, and incident response at federal civilian agencies (Boyd, 2015b). The bill would give the DHS Secretary the power to authorize efforts to protect an agency's computer networks from an imminent threat "without prior consultation with the affected agency" if the agency fails to respond to the threat in a timely manner. DHS would also be charged with conducting vulnerability scans of both agency and contractor networks (Sternstein, 2015d). Secretary Johnson urged passage of this bill from the start; as of late 2015 no further action had been taken.

The National Cybersecurity Protection Act of 2014: PL 113-282 (NCPA) anchors DHS' cybersecurity functions more deeply in federal law. The Act codifies the operations of the NCCIC as the "federal civilian interfaces for cybersecurity information sharing" (NCPA, 2014). The goal is to facilitate the cross-sector interaction of representatives of government, the intelligence community, the private sector, ISAOs, and law enforcement agencies in a single physical space to share cyber threat and cyber security information and analysis (GAO, 2015b). The NCPA allots to the Under Secretary of the DHS NPPD wide authority to determine the composition of the NCCIC but requires the inclusion of federal, state, and local government representatives, as well as private sector critical infrastructure owners and operators. The DHS Secretary acquires the authority to grant any government or private entity immediate temporary access to the NCCIC in case of a cybersecurity incident that presents an imminent threat, foregoing the usual security clearances required for access to the government's sensitive and classified information. The threshold for information sharing established in the 2002 Homeland Security Act was the presence of a terrorist threat or any menace to the operation of the nation's physical or cyber critical infrastructure; the NCPA widens the scope of DHS's authority to share any information linked to cybersecurity risks and incidents very broadly defined. The broadened scope of DHS' information sharing function in combination with the ability of DHS officials to determine who gets a seat at the NCCIC table, including private sector representatives not associated with critical infrastructure centers, gives the DHS a significant amount of say in who receives what information related to cybersecurity (Nolan, 2015).

The Cybersecurity Enhancement Act of 2014: PL 113-274, promotes the voluntary sharing of cybersecurity information, analyses, and mitigation strategies between government and the private sector, much of which would be carried out at the NCCIC. The law calls on the director of NIST to work closely with public and private sector entities, including ISACs, to develop strategies and establish best practices to "identify, assess, and manage cyber risks" (Cybersecurity Enhancement, 2014) and to improve and standardize interoperable cloud computing services (GAO, 2015b). To assuage private companies' concerns about information sharing, the law directs NIST to develop methods to protect business confidentiality, individual privacy, and civil liberties in the sharing of information and mandates that governments at all levels not use shared information for regulatory purposes. This fails to alleviate private businesses' concerns about liability for sharing PII (Kimery, 2015b) and the law in general is viewed as relatively narrow in scope, basically codifying NIST's existing role in developing a national Cybersecurity Framework to standardize and share cybersecurity strategies and best practices (Patel, 2014). But the law does provide DHS, along with other federal agencies, some latitude in skirting civil service personnel hiring requirements in the field of cybersecurity, allowing them to hire recipients of government scholarship-to-service awards for "excepted service" positions. Two laws passed in December 2014 deal more directly with helping DHS hire a workforce with the cybersecurity skills necessary to fulfill the Department's mandates:

The Cybersecurity Workforce Assessment Act of 2014: P.L. 113-246 requires the DHS Secretary to assess the readiness and capacity of the existing workforce to meet DHS' cybersecurity mission and to develop strategies to recruit, train, and retain a highly skilled cyber workforce (Cybersecurity Workforce, 2014). Since Washington watchdogs know by now that DHS talks a good game when it comes to plans but falls short on implementing them, the law mandates that the workforce strategy include a 5-year implementation plan, specific indications of how to fill existing gaps in the DHS cyber workforce, and a 10-year projection of both DHS' cyber workforce requirements and obstacles to the hiring and retention of cyber experts. The law requires very specific skill classifications, directing DHS to identify cybersecurity positions and vacancies and specify whether positions are filled by permanent DHS employees, contractors, or staff employed in other federal agencies. To help correct the fragmented and insufficient DHS cyber training efforts noted in Part I of this chapter, DHS must specify the number of cybersecurity staff who received essential training, and reasons if training was not provided. The law also directs DHS to report on the viability of establishing a Cybersecurity Fellowship Program, which would offer tuition payment for undergraduate and graduate students in return for their commitment to work at DHS for a specific period of time. This law mostly codifies practices that were already in place at DHS, adding reporting and assessment measures that compel DHS to be accountable for its workforce policies.

The Homeland Security Cybersecurity Workforce Assessment Act, Section 4 of the *Border Patrol Agent Reform Act of 2014*: PL 113-277 directs the DHS to classify its cybersecurity positions in accordance with OPM standards as aligned with NIST's National Cybersecurity Workforce Framework and to identify "critical need" cybersecurity positions at DHS, where there are extant and potential skill shortages (Moore, 2013). To make it somewhat easier for DHS to hire cybersecurity professionals, this law provides for two strategies long sought by DHS officials to be a competitive cybersecurity employer: it amends the 2002 Homeland Security Act to establish "excepted service" cybersecurity positions, including senior-level and Senior Executive Service [SES] positions, and it allows the DHS Secretary to set pay rates and provide additional compensation and incentives for employees in these excepted positions in line with Department of Defense practices (Border, 2014). One likely motive for these provisions is to facilitate DHS' ability to directly hire cybersecurity experts, rather than indirectly through contractors (Libicki et al., 2014).

Legislation proposed in 2015, but not passed into law as of this writing, would further impact DHS' cybersecurity mission by (1) adding liability protections for businesses that share cybersecurity information with the government (*The Cyber Threat Sharing Act of 2015*, S. 456), (2) authorizing

DHS to employ EINSTEIN to monitor all civilian federal agency compu-
ter networks for existing and potential threats (*The Federal Cybersecurity
Enhancement Act*, S. 18696), (3) augmenting DHS' ability to implement
Binding Operational Directives to secure civilian federal agency networks
(*Cyber Defense of Federal Networks Act*, H.R. 3313), (4) strengthening oversight of civilian federal agencies' ability to secure their computer networks
and protect PII when sharing information (*Federal Computer Security Act*,
S.1990), (5) streamlining the process of hiring a skilled cybersecurity workforce (*2015 Competitive Service Act*, S. 1580), (6) strengthening the role of the
NCCIC (*The National Cybersecurity Protection Advancement Act*, H.R. 1731),
(7) spreading responsibility for cybersecurity information sharing among
several agencies under the auspices of the Director of National Intelligence (DNI) (*The Cybersecurity Information Sharing Act [CISA]* S. 754), and
(8) authorizing the operation of the Executive Office CTIIC, giving the
DNI a major role in developing cybersecurity information sharing procedures (*Protecting Cyber Networks Act of 2015 [PCNA]*: HR-1560. The latter
two proposals may confuse the role of the DHS as the central location of
the government's efforts to share cyber threat information and mitigate
attacks by highlighting the role of the DNI and the new CTIIC. Although
the DHS and privacy advocates have strongly criticized CISA as potentially
undermining the safeguarding of PII (Hagemann, 2015; Waddell, 2015),
CISA has a good chance of becoming law in 2016.

As DHS' cybersecurity responsibilities have expanded via a combination
of executive branch initiatives and congressional action, its leaders have
engaged in several organizational realignments to match matrix to mission.
The following section highlights the Department's attempts, beginning in
2005 and ending with a major transformation in 2015, to integrate mission
support processes and adapt to mission execution requirements.

DHS Organizational Adaptation

DHS Secretary Chertoff engaged in a major organizational restructuring called the "Second Stage Review" (S2R) in 2005. The three changes
most relevant to DHS' cybersecurity mission were the creation of the
Office of Policy, the Operations Department, and the position of Assistant
Secretary for Cyber and Telecommunications. The new offices were established to integrate capabilities and institutionalize collaboration across the
Department (Carafano & Zuckerman, 2012; Relyea & Hogue, 2005) and
the new cyber position was to coordinate the Department's cybersecurity
efforts. IT groups welcomed the position as a "high-level champion" for
cyber at DHS and hoped the position would stem the tide of turnover
in cyber staff (Gross, 2005). While the Policy Office proved important in

coordinating policy development (Carafano & Zuckerman, 2012), operational planning remained anchored in the components (Allen, 2012; The Future, 2012). The cyber position remained without a full-time occupant for a year (Beckner, 2006), however, and did little to stop the high turnover of cybersecurity experts. In 2007 three DHS offices were consolidated into the new Cybersecurity & Communications Office (CS&C), the seat of the renamed Assistant Secretary for Cybersecurity & Communications, under the auspices of the newly established NPPD.

Organizational reforms continued in 2010 with DHS' first Bottom-Up Review [BUR], the main purpose of which was to examine the alignment of the Department's organization with its mission (DHS, 2010). The BUR advised strengthening both the capability and the authority of DHS to protect information networks by adding an operational unit to buttress infrastructure resilience, improving predictive and forensic cybersecurity technology, and increasing public awareness of cyber issues (DHS, 2010). A year later Secretary Napolitano created the position of Deputy Secretary of Cybersecurity housed in the NPPD (the DHS' own "cyber czar")—DHS' top cybersecurity official. The organizational reforms would come to fruition in 2012. In the BUR, Napolitano complained about Congress chipping away at the authority of the Secretary, granted in the 2002 Homeland Security Act, to make organizational changes and she requested restoration of that authority (DHS, 2010), an interesting prelude to Congress' complaint in 2015 that DHS planned changes without informing Congress (see below). The Secretary also requested that Congress streamline its oversight of DHS to allow the Department to focus on its missions; the request went unheeded.

The year 2012 saw another major reform when, in response to Executive Order 13618 on "Assignment of National Security and Emergency Preparedness Communications Functions," the DHS Office of Cybersecurity and Communications (CS&C) was reorganized to better provide support for the Department's mission of protecting the country's cyber and communications infrastructure (DHS OIG, 2013). A DHS official's description of the reorganization's purpose illustrates the dual goal of integrating internal operations, on the one hand, and adapting to external needs, on the other: "[centralize] common support functions of budget, finance, acquisitions, information management, and human capital" and be "more capable of agile operations, of forming stronger partnerships" in securing the country's cyber networks and infrastructure (as cited in Miller, 2012a, n.p.).

The 2012 realignment added two units to the CS&C division to consolidate the collection of cyber threat information and establish a government-industry partnership to share threat and network vulnerability data. The reorganization also highlighted DHS' emphasis on cybersecurity resilience—the capacity to respond to and recover from threats and attacks—as opposed to simple prevention. The Stakeholder Engagement and Cyber Infrastructure Resilience unit [SECIR] is the organizational foundation for DHS outreach to the public and increased efforts to protect critical infrastructure. The NCCIC, formerly part of a broader National Cybersecurity Division, was elevated to comprise its own unit and became the operational arm of CS&S—in effect the DHS' cybersecurity operational center, housing U.S. CERT, as well as other national communications offices. The NCCIC has become an important part of the transformation of the DHS into the central hub of civilian cyber threat reporting and mitigation. It began as DHS' coordinating center for monitoring and analyzing cyber risks among federal agencies (DHS OIG, 2013; OMB, 2010), and by 2015, in addition to 13 federal departments and agencies, representatives of 16 private sector entities have a seat at the NCCIC table, with more than 100 routinely sharing information with the Center (Oversight, 2015).

At the end of 2014, DHS established the Cyber, Infrastructure, and Resilience [CIR] Division within the Office of Policy to strengthen its organizational matrix by improving cross-departmental information sharing and collaboration, eliminating duplication in components' execution of the DHS cybersecurity mission, and developing "cross-departmental cyber strategies to effectively capitalize on the Department's cyber capabilities and workforce" (DHS OIG, 2015c, p. 4). Soon after, in 2015, the status of the Office of Policy was elevated to an executive office in DHS Headquarters and took on planning functions previously performed in the Operations Department. The Joint Requirements Council was resurrected to enhance cross-component investments, training, and operations, leading to "the most significant reorganization of the Department's headquarters since the 2005 2SR" (Beckner, 2015a).

Several blistering reports on uncoordinated, inefficient, and ineffective DHS cybersecurity efforts from Congress and the DHS Inspector General cast a negative light on the Department's ability to execute its responsibilities. The reports noted, among other deficiencies: (1) the lack of an updated and finalized Continuity of Operations Plan at NPPD to establish procedures for keeping security operations in place during emergencies (DHS OIG, 2015b), despite the emphasis on "resilience" in DHS strategic plans; (2) only a small minority of federal agency personnel find CyberStat sessions useful in learning how to improve their networks' cybersecurity (Sternstein, 2015a); (3) the CyberScope tool does not run efficiently, in large part because of the ineffective training of the contractors who administer the system; a lack of training may prevent the tool from working as it should, including the securing of PII (DHS OIG, 2013); (4) management and oversight of EINSTEIN is inefficient (Coburn, 2015; DHS OIG, 2013; Sternstein, 2015c); (5) the NCCIC lacks sufficient staff and training opportunities (DHS OIG,

2015b) and its operators often fail to use best practices and performance measures in simulating cybersecurity problems (Coburn, 2015), all of which undermine the Center's potential to respond to actual vulnerabilities and threats. While the Center has expanded to include more representatives from the private sector, because of laborious security requirements and the inability of nonprofit groups to finance ISACs, still only 4 of the 16 critical infrastructure sectors have permanent representatives on the floor of NCCIC (Sternstein, 2015e).

Cybersecurity information sharing also fails to run at peak levels: U.S.CERT does not perform as well as private companies, such as Google and Microsoft, in providing information to the private sector about cyber threats (Coburn, 2015); private entities are deterred from joining the Enhanced Cybersecurity Sharing [ECS] program because of the long application process, the lack of clear PII controls, the fact that only known threats can be deterred (Coburn, 2015); and the "quality of DHS cyber threat indicators" is still uncertain (DHS OIG 2015b, p. 19). The lack of sufficient outreach from DHS about the program has also limited the number of critical infrastructure sector companies that take part in ECS (DHS OIG, 2015b). The lack of uniform rules and procedures for establishing privacy controls for shared information throughout DHS cyber operations is a big concern of both private companies and privacy advocates (Coburn, 2015; DHS OIG, 2015b). Finally, the networking component of DHS' mission to secure cyberspace—so crucial to the strategy of adaptation to protect the homeland (Wise, 2006)—remains weak: DHS' NPPD is part of the nation's "Information Sharing Environment" with other federal information sharing centers (GAO, 2015b). Like them, it is charged with attaining interoperability of technologies, procedures, standards, and communications to secure cyberspace. NPPD, along with other centers, however, lacks a common incident reporting and management system that prevents the coordination of cybersecurity information sharing practices and response to problems (DHS OIG, 2015b).

After these reports, and as the fallout of the massive OPM hack unfolded throughout 2015, Secretary Johnson announced plans to completely reorganize and rename the NPPD in order to better align it to mission execution and elevate the status of the NCCIC, in part by creating a direct incident reporting line to the DHS Secretary (Boyd, 2015a). This put the Department's tools for cybersecurity information sharing and threat mitigation center stage. The changes create dual leadership of NCCIC: the managerial head responsible for oversight and mission support, a position vacant for an entire year up to the reform, is now the Assistant Secretary of the CS&C office; the position of NCCIC director of daily operations was newly filled in August 2015 (Bartley, 2015; Boyd, 2015a).

Members of the U.S. House of Representatives Homeland Security Committee and its subcommittees, drafting a bill to reorganize the NPPD in September 2015, complained in a letter to the DHS that Department leaders were holding back information on their plans for the NPPD reorganization, viewing Congress as an obstruction rather than a partner in streamlining NPPD to make it more effective (Bennett, 2015). At a hearing a month later, the Chairman of the House Cybersecurity Subcommittee admonished DHS cyber officials for failing to inform Congress of the proposed NPPD reorganization and complained that DHS planned to move forward on organizational realignment without the input of Congress or private sector stakeholders. Committee members, he averred, heard about the proposal only through leaks in the media and ran up against roadblocks when attempting to get information from DHS. The House Homeland Security Committee sent a bipartisan letter to DHS complaining about the process and the House unanimously passed legislation in October 2015 to prohibit DHS from reorganizing NPPD without congressional approval (Examining the Mission, 2015).

At the hearing about the proposed changes in October 2015, DHS' cybersecurity leaders described the reorganization as a "transformation" of culture, governance, and processes to integrate cybersecurity efforts across the DHS. The NPPD would move from Headquarters to Operations to better adapt to an increasingly aggressive threat environment and more effectively streamline cybersecurity mission support activities (Examining the Mission, 2015). The changes would entail more outreach to external stakeholders and more matrixed processes throughout DHS, including increased collaboration with the Science & Technology Directorate and coordination with field staff. Though still in the planning stages as of this writing, the organizational transformation measures will involve a significant shuffle of units that were formerly a part of the NPPD, especially its CS&C office. The new cyber operations center would have three subordinate directorates: Infrastructure Security with a focus on protecting critical infrastructures, an elevated NCCIC to guard against threats in the private, government, and federal.gov arenas, and the Federal Protective Service to protect federal facilities, with all three collaborating to protect against cyber threats and supported by an enhanced Office of Cyber and Infrastructure Analysis. DHS cyber leaders and House Homeland Security Committee members agree that NPPD needs a facelift and a name change, most likely to "Cybersecurity and Infrastructure Protection," to more accurately reflect the unit's mission.

CONCLUSION

The Introduction to this volume refers to the "why, what, and how" of transforming government organizations. The "why" in the case of DHS is that the Department increasingly has become a key player in securing the nation's cyber networks. The "what" is twofold: the internal processes necessary to support DHS' cybersecurity mission, on the one hand, and DHS' responses to the cyber threat environment to execute the mission, on the other. The "how" corresponds to the "what:" integrate organizational and managerial processes to channel component resources into departmental capacity to support the mission and adapt DHS operational capacities to prevent, respond to, and be resilient in the face of cyber attacks.

Part I of this chapter illustrates that efforts have been made to "make the DHS matrix work" by integrating organizational and managerial processes, but a series of problems has impeded progress in the implementation of reforms, most notably a political appointee-heavy leadership structure and the difficulty in hiring and retaining a skilled cybersecurity staff. The interruptions in both policy implementation and the development of a comprehensive cybersecurity strategy caused by these problems undermine execution of the DHS' cybersecurity mission. Causes and consequences of these problems are a demoralized workforce, a fragmented culture, and a dysfunctional congressional oversight system based on political interests and mistrust of DHS leaders to follow through on promises and commitments. DHS leaders know what they have to do to integrate internal operations, engage their workforce, and forge a core Department culture; now they have to show the wherewithal to do it. Secretary Johnson's Unity of Effort campaign is a major step forward toward integrating DHS organizational and managerial support functions for the cybersecurity mission; following through on the reforms when he leaves DHS will be the deciding factor. Toward that end, internal integration management at DHS can be facilitated through two changes recommended by the 2015 HSAC DHS Employee Task Force: decrease the number of political appointees by transferring positions to the career civil service and create an Ombudsman office responsible for the implementation of reforms during changes of leadership.

Part II of this chapter illustrates that DHS has been more successful with adaptation to the cyber threat environment than with internal integration, though much work still needs to be done. The Department is developing state-of-the-art technologies with the private sector and other federal agencies to counter cyber threats and has engaged with stakeholders across all sectors to share cyber threat information and establish procedures to respond to vulnerabilities and attacks. Executive Office mandates and congressional legislation have begun to grant DHS the authority it needs to effectively carry out its cybersecurity mission responsibilities and to hire and retain a skilled cyber workforce. A series of departmental reorganizations has reinforced DHS' cybersecurity mission and granted a more central role to the Department's Center for analyzing cyber threat information, the NCCIC, as well as emphasized the management integration necessary for mission support. Creating a synergy between internal integration and adaptation to the cyber threat environment is key to DHS' transformation as a central hub of cybersecurity.

In addition to the problems caused by incomplete internal integration, DHS' ability to adapt its resources to the changing cyber threat environment is undermined by several external factors. In the absence of overarching cybersecurity framework legislation (Fischer & Logan, 2015) and uncertainty about the balance of power between the executive and legislative branches in mandating cybersecurity actions (Rollins & Henning, 2009), the authority of DHS to monitor civilian federal agency networks and share information with government and the private and nonprofit sectors remains unclear, pieced together as it is in different federal laws and made uncertain by redundancies (Vijayan, 2009a). The position of the Cybersecurity Coordinator in the Executive Office and the newly announced CTIIC in the Office of the Director of National Intelligence render the role of the DHS "cyber czar" and its NCCIC unclear (Nolan, 2015). The reorganization of the NPPD to raise the level of the NCCIC in 2015 appears to be an attempt, in part, to put information sharing and incident response squarely in the hands of the DHS; whether Congress and the President will concur is an open question. As the cybersecurity environment, like the rest of the world, becomes more complex, there needs to be more of a concerted attempt on the part of Congress, the President, and the DHS to marshal their combined forces to respond to cyber threats with the active participation of stakeholders (Allen, 2012; Fuerth & Faber, 2012; Kamarck, 2007). This will be accomplished only if the enervating forces of politicization and bureaucratization can be transformed into the energizing force of cooperation in the pursuit of national security, and this depends largely on the elusive factor of trust.

Perhaps most potentially deleterious to DHS' effective transformation as a key player in securing the homeland against debilitating cyber attacks is the lack of trust endemic to American society in the second decade of the third millennium. Distrust between DHS and Congress bogs the department down in overlapping and redundant hearings; antipathy between the political parties and the executive and legislative branches turns DHS into a political football; doubts on the part of private companies about government's intentions prevent the sharing of cyber threat information that may be necessary to thwart future attacks; the American public's general lack of trust and confidence in the government over the collection and use of personally identifiable information render DHS' cybersecurity mission more difficult. If government and citizens do not find ways to eliminate the mistrust that affects all aspects of this mission, a cyber 9/11 might do it for them.

REFERENCES

Allen, T. (2012). Confronting complexity and creating unity of effort: The leadership challenge for public administrators. *Public Administration Review, 72*, 320–321. doi:10.1111/j.1540-6210.2012.02585.x

Assessing DHS' performance: Watchdog recommendations to improve Homeland Security. Hearings before the Committee on Homeland Security, Subcommittee on Management and Oversight Efficiency, House, 114th Cong. (2015). Retrieved from http://homeland.house.gov/hearing/assessing-dhs-s-performance-watchdog-recommendations-improve-homeland-security

Bartley, R. (2015, August 12). DHS expands role of NCCIC, taps Andy Ozment to head federal cybersecurity hub. *Fierce Government IT*. Retrieved from http://www.fiercegovernmentit.com/story/dhs-expands-role-nccic-taps-andy-ozment-head-federal-cybersecurity-hub/2015-08-12

Beckner, C. (2006, July 13). The Second-Stage Review, one year later. *Homeland Security Watch*. Retrieved from http://www.hlswatch.com/category/dhs-news/page/6/

Beckner, C. (2013, July 12). 15 top slots at DHS now vacant with Napolitano's resignation. *Foreign Policy, The Cable*. Retrieved from http://foreignpolicy.com/2013/07/12/15-top-slots-at-dhs-now-vacant-with-napolitanos-resignation/

Beckner, C. (2015a, February 3). A quiet but notable reorganization at DHS headquarters. *Homeland Security Watch*. Retrieved from http://www.hlswatch.com/2015/02/03/a-quiet-but-notable-reorganization-at-dhs-headquarters/

Beckner, C. (2015b, February 11). A new cyber threat intelligence center: Is legislation needed? *Security Insights*. The GW Center for Cyber and Homeland Security. Retrieved from http://www.securityinsights.org/2015/02/a-new-cyber-threat-intelligence-center-is-legislation-needed/

Behn, R. D. (2015, June 11). Rule #1: Policy design starts with operational capacity. *Government Executive*. Retrieved from http://www.govexec.com/excellence/promising-practices/2015/06/rule-1-policy-design-starts-operational-capacity/115051/

Bejtlich, R. (2015, February 19). What are the prospects for the Cyber Threat Intelligence Integration Center? *Brookings Tech Tank*. Retrieved from http://www.brookings.edu/blogs/techtank/posts/2015/02/19-cyber-security-center-bejlich

Bennett, C. (2015, September 17). Lawmakers accuse DHS of stonewalling on cybersecurity plans. *The Hill*. Retrieved from http://thehill.com/policy/cybersecurity/254096-lawmakers-accuse-dhs-of-stonewalling-on-cyber-plans

Border Patrol Agent Reform Act of 2014, Pub. L. No. 113-277, 128 Stat. 2995 (2014).

Boyd, A. (2014, October 3). New policy requires DHS to scan civilian systems. *Federal Times*. Retrieved from http://archive.federaltimes.com/article/20141003/CYBER/310030017/New-policy-requires-DHS-scan-civilian-systems

Boyd, A. (2015a, August 10). DHS cyber center gets new leadership. *Federal Times*. Retrieved from http://www.federaltimes.com/story/government/cybersecurity/2015/08/10/nccic-leadership/31427695/

Boyd, A. (2015b, July 23). New bill strengthens DHS role in federal cybersecurity. *Federal Times*. Retrieved from http://www.federaltimes.com/story/government/cybersecurity/2015/07/23/fisma-reform-act/30564001/

Bucci, S. P., Rosenzweig, P., & Inserra, D. (2015, January). Reforming DHS: Missed opportunity calls for Congress to intervene. *Heritage Foundation Research Reports*. Retrieved from http://www.heritage.org/research/reports/2015/01/reforming-dhs-missed-opportunity-calls-for-congress-to-intervene

Building "One DHS". (2012). Why can't management information be integrated? Hearings before the Committee on Homeland Security, Subcommittee on Oversight, Investigations, and Management Retrieved from http://www.gpo.gov/fdsys/pkg/CHRG-112hhrg76599/html/CHRG-112hhrg76599.htm

Carafano, J. J., & Zuckerman, J. (2102, February 3). DHS Office of Policy: Misguided reorganization threatens Homeland Security Strategic Planning. *The Heritage Foundation*. Retrieved from http://www.heritage.org/research/reports/2012/02/dhs-office-of-policy-misguided-reorganization-threatens-homeland-security-strategic-planning

Coburn, T. (2015, January). A review of the Department of Homeland Security's missions and performance. This U.S. Senate report is commonly referred to as "the Coburn report." A complete citation is found below under "S. Rep. 114-1 (2015)."

Cummiskey, C. (2015, July 15). How DHS can improve federal cybersecurity now. *Federal Times*. Retrieved from http://www.federaltimes.com/story/government/dhs/blog/2015/07/15/how-dhs-can-improve-federal-cybersecurity/30196705/

Cybersecurity Enhancement Act of 2014, Pub. L. No. 113-274, 128 Stat. 2971 (2014).

Cybersecurity Workforce Assessment Act of 2014, Pub. L. No. 113-246, 128 Stat. 2880 (2014).

Dalton, C., & Best, N. (2007). *Integrated management*. Burlington, MA: CIMA.

Davis, S. M., & Lawrence, P.R. (1978, May). Problems of matrix organizations. *Harvard Business Review*. Retrieved from https://hbr.org/1978/05/problems-of-matrix-organizations

DHS' efforts to secure .Gov. Hearings before the Committee on Homeland Security, Subcommittee on Cybersecurity, Infrastructure Protection and Security Technologies, House, 114th Cong. (2015) (Written testimony of Andy Ozment).

E-Government Act of 2002, Pub. L. No. 107-347, 116 Stat. 2899 (2002).

Edwards, H.S. (2015, February 13). Obama's new plan for online security faces some big questions. *Time*. Retrieved from http://time.com/3708958/obama-cyber-security-hackers/

Examining the Mission, Structure, and Reorganization Effort of the National Protection and Programs Directorate. Hearings before the Committee on Homeland Security Subcommittee on Cybersecurity, Infrastructure Protection and Security Technologies, House, 114th Cong. (2015) (Written testimony of Suzanne E. Spaulding, Ronald J. Clark, and Phyllis A. Schneck) (Opening Statement by John Ratcliffe)

Examining the President's Cybersecurity Information Sharing Proposal. Hearings before the Committee on Homeland Security, House, 114th Cong. (2015). (Written testimony of Suzanne Spaulding and Phyllis Schneck).

Exec. Order No. 13618, 78 Fed, Reg, 649 (January 3, 2013).

Exec. Order No. 13636, 78 Fed. Reg. 33 (February 19, 2013).

Exec. Order No. 13691, 80 Fed. Reg. 34 (February 20, 2015).

Federal Information Security Modernization Act of 2014, Pub. L. No. 113-283, 128 Stat. 3073 (2014).

Federal Information Security Management Reform Act of 2015, S. 1828, 114th Cong. (2015).

Fischer, E. A. (2014, December 12). *Federal laws relating to cybersecurity*. (Congressional Research Service Report No. R42-114). Retrieved from ProQuest Congressional website: http://congressional.proquest.com/congressional/docview/t21.d22.crs-2014-rsi-0586?accountid=14585

Fischer, E. A. (2015, April 29). *Cybersecurity issues and challenges: In brief*. (Congressional Research Service Report No. R43831). Retrieved from ProQuest Congressional website: http://congressional.proquest.com/congressional/docview/t21.d22.crs-2015-rsi-0245?accountid=14585

Fischer, E. A., & Logan, S.M. (2015, June 15). *Cybersecurity and information sharing: Comparison of legislative proposals in the 114th Congress*. (Congressional Research Service Report No. R44069) Retrieved from ProQuest Congressional website: http://congressional.proquest.com/congressional/docview/t21.d22.crs-2015-rsi-0322?accountid=14585

Fuerth, L. S., & Faber, E.M.H. (2012, October). *Anticipatory governance. Practical upgrades*. The Project on Forward Engagement, The George Washington University. Retrieved from https://www.gwu.edu/~igis/assets/docs/working_papers/Anticipatory_Governance_Practical_Upgrades.pdf

Fulgham, C. (2014, May 29). DHS innovating with business data integration. Chief Financial Officers Council. Retrieved from https://cfo.gov/dhs-innovating-with-business-data-integration/

Gaynor, J. (2011, September 1)." Resolving a clash of cultures—a mission versus organizational focus. *Security Debrief*. Retrieved from http://securitydebrief.com/2011/09/01/resolving-a-clash-of-cultures-a-mission-versus-organizational-focus/#axzz3kiJJbkDK

Gerstein, D. M. (2015,January 27). Go back to basics to reform Homeland Security. *Politico Magazine*. Retrieved from http://www.politico.com/magazine/story/2015/01/homeland-security-reform-114657?o=1

Getha-Taylor, H. (2009). Managing the "new normalcy" with values-based leadership. *Public Administration Review, 69*, 200-206. doi: 10.1111/j.1540-6210.2008.01965.x

Gordon, H. (2015, March 30). Congressman wants to curb copycat IT systems at DHS. *NextGov*. Retrieved from http://www.nextgov.com/cio-briefing/2015/03/heres-how-reduce-it-duplication-dhs/108718/

Gorman, S. (2009, August 4). Security cyber czar steps down. *The Wall Street Journal*. Retrieved from http://www.wsj.com/articles/SB124932480886002237

Gross, G. (2005, July 13). DHS reorganization creates a new cybersecurity position. *Network World*. Retrieved from http://www.networkworld.com/article/2313048/lan-wan/dhs-reorganization-creates-new-cybersecurity-position.html

Gross, G. (2009). Experts disagree on cybersecurity role for DHS. *Network World*. Retrieved from http://www.networkworld.com/article/2255249/data-center/experts-disagree-on-cybersecurity-role-for-dhs.html

Guccione, D. (2015, August 24). With a major cybersecurity job shortage, we must act like we are at war. *NextGov*. Retrieved from http://www.nextgov.com/technology-news/tech-insider/2015/08/major-cybersecurity-job-shortage-we-must-act-we-are-war/119370/

Hagemann, R. (2015, August 4). CISA steps into the limelight with a manager's amendment and agency discontent. Niskanen Center. Retrieved from https://niskanencenter.org/blog/cisa-steps-into-the-limelight-with-a-managers-amendment-and-agency-discontent/

Help Wanted at DHS: Implications of Leadership Vacancies on the Mission and Morale. Hearings before the Committee on Homeland Security, House, 113th Cong. (2013) (Testimony of Max Stier).

Herzog, R. J., & Counts, K. S. (2014). Administrative ironies and DHS performance reporting. *International Journal of Organization Theory and Behavior, 17*(1), 1-30. Retrieved from http://search.proquest.com/docview/1520757268?accountid=14585

Hicks, J. (2015, April 22). Homeland Security is laying roots in Silicon Valley and you might not like its reasons. *The Washington Post*. Retrieved from https://www.washingtonpost.com/news/federal-eye/wp/2015/04/22/homeland-security-is-laying-roots-in-silicon-valley-and-you-might-not-like-its-reasons/

Homeland Security Act of 2002. Pub. L. No. 107-296, 116 Stat. 2135 (2002).

Homeland Security Advisory Council. (2007). Homeland Security Culture Task Force (Report). Retrieved from http://www.dhs.gov/xlibrary/assets/hsac_ctfreport_200701.pdf

Homeland Security Advisory Council. (2012, Fall). CyberSkills Task Force (Report). Retrieved from http://www.dhs.gov/sites/default/files/publications/HSAC%20CyberSkills%20Report%20-%20Final.pdf

Homeland Security Advisory Council. (2015, May 21). DHS Employee Task Force (Report). Retrieved from https://www.dhs.gov/sites/default/files/publications/DHS-HSAC-Employee-Task-Force-Report-May-2015.pdf

Homeland Security Presidential Directive/HSPD - 7. (2003, December 17). *Critical infrastructure identification, prioritization, protection*. Public Papers of the Presidents of the United States: George W. Bush (2003, Book II). 1739-1745. Retrieved from http://www.gpo.gov/fdsys/pkg/PPP-2003-book2/pdf/PPP-2003-book2-doc-pg1739.pdf

Information Sharing and Analysis Centers Council (ISAC) Council. (2009, January). The role of Information Sharing and Analysis Centers (ISACs) in private/public sector critical infrastructure protection. ISACCouncil.Org (January). Retrieved from http://www.isaccouncil.org/images/ISAC_Role_in_CIP.pdf

Institute of Medicine. (2013). A ready and resilient workforce for the Department of Homeland Security: Protecting America's front line. Washington, DC: The National Academies Press. Retrieved from http://www.nap.edu/catalog/18407/a-ready-and-resilient-workforce-for-the-department-of-homeland-security

Institute of Medicine. (2014, July 3). Advancing workforce health at the Department of Homeland Security. Protecting those who protect us. Washington, DC. The

National Academies Press. Retrieved from http://www.nap.edu/catalog/18574/ advancing-workforce-health-at-the-department-of-homeland-security-protecting

Is DHS Effectively Implementing a Strategy to Counter Emerging Threats? Hearings before the Committee on Homeland Security, Subcommittee on Management, Investigations, and Oversight, House, 112th Cong. (2012). (Testimony of Paul A. Schneider).

Jackson, W. (2012, September 21). CyberScope falls flat on improving IT security, feds say. *GCN: Public Sector Media Group*. Retrieved from http://gcn.com/ articles/2012/09/21/cyberscope-continuous-monitoring-it-security-datapoint. aspx

Johnson, J. (2014, April). Strengthening departmental unity of effort. (Memorandum for DHS Leadership). Retrieved from http://www.hlswatch.com/ wp-content/uploads/2014/04/DHSUnityOfEffort.pdf

Johnson, J. (2015, July 8). Securing the .gov. Remarks by Secretary of Homeland Security Jeh C. Johnson at the Center for Strategic & International Studies. Retrieved from http://www.dhs.gov/news/2015/07/08/remarks-secretary-homeland-security-jeh-charles-johnson-securing-gov

Johnson, K. (2013, November 13). Homeland Security nominee heading toward confirmation. *USA Today*. Retrieved from http://www.usatoday.com/ story/news/politics/2013/11/13/homeland-security-jeh-johnson-secretary-confirmation/3515487/

Kahan, J. (2014). One DHS revisited: Can the next Homeland Security secretary unite the department? *Journal of Homeland Security and Emergency Management, 11*(1), 1-24. doi:10.1515/jhsem-2013-0088

Kamarck, E. (2007). *The end of government as we know it*. Boulder, CO: Routledge.

Katz, E. (2015, September 3). How government techies can usher in the next generation of federal workers. *Government Executive*. Retrieved from http:// www.govexec.com/management/2015/09/how-government-techies-can-usher-next-generation-federal-workers/120248/?oref=relatedstories

Kelly, B. B. (2012). Investing in a centralized cybersecurity infrastructure: Why "hacktivism" can and should influence cybersecurity reform. *Boston University Law Review, 92*(5), 1663-1711. Retrieved from http://search.proquest.com/ docview/1328333278?accountid=14585

Kettl, D. F. (2015, July 20). Why plugging the cyber breach is the 2nd biggest problem at OPM. *Government Executive*. Retrieved from http://www.govexec. com/excellence/promising-practices/2015/07/why-plugging-cyber-breach-2nd-biggest-problem-opm/117844/

Kimery, A. L. (2015a, February 10). Administration announces cyber equivalent of National Counterterrorism Center. *Homeland Security Today*. Retrieved from http://www.hstoday.us/briefings/daily-news-analysis/single-article/ administration-announces-cyber-equivalent-of-national-counterterrorism-center/fe05e50722adeecf42c7f514ff98ba87.html

Kimery, A. L. (2015b, February 13). Obama's cyber info-sharing Executive Order applauded, but legal protections still required. *Homeland Security Today*. Retrieved from http://www.hstoday.us/focused-topics/cybersecurity/

single-article-page/obamas-cyber-info-sharing-executive-order-applauded-but-legal-protections-still-required.html

Kostro, S. S. (2015, April). The Department of Homeland Security Unity of Effort initiative. *Center for Strategic and International Studies*. Retrieved from http://csis.org/files/publication/150407_Kostro_DHSUnityofEffort.pdf

Libicki, M. C. (2015, March 4). Sharing information about threats is not a cybersecurity panacea. RAND, Office of External Affairs. Retrieved from http://www.rand.org/content/dam/rand/pubs/testimonies/CT400/CT425/RAND_CT425.pdf

Libicki, M. C., Senty, D., & Pollak, J. (2014). Hackers wanted: An examination of the cybersecurity labor market. RAND. Retrieved from http://www.rand.org/content/dam/rand/pubs/research_reports/RR400/RR430/RAND_RR430.pdf

Lyngaas, S. (2014, October 31). Cybersecurity: Can DHS get it together? *FCW: Federal Computer Week*. Retrieved from https://fcw.com/articles/2014/10/31/cybersecurity-can-dhs-get-it-together.aspx

Magnuson, S. (2011, December). DHS considers reviving dormant Joint Requirements Council. *National Defense Magazine*. Retrieved from http://www.nationaldefensemagazine.org/archive/2011/December/Pages/DHSConsidersRevivingDormantJointRequirementsCouncil.aspx

Markon, J. (2014a, October 10). DHS morale sinks further despite new leadership at the top, survey shows. *The Washington Post*. Retrieved from https://www.washingtonpost.com/news/federal-eye/wp/2014/10/10/dhs-morale-problems-grow-worse-during-secretary-johnsons-brief-tenure/

Markon, J. (2014b, September 22). Homeland Security secretary objects to article about employee exodus. *The Washington Post*. Retrieved from https://www.washingtonpost.com/news/federal-eye/wp/2014/09/22/homeland-security-head-objects-to-report-about-exodus-of-employees/

Markon, J. (2015, February 20). DHS tackles endless morale problems with seemingly endless studies. *The Washington Post*. Retrieved from http://www.washingtonpost.com/politics/homeland-security-has-done-little-for-low-morale-but-study-it--repeatedly/2015/02/20/f626eba8-b15c-11e4-886b-c22184f27c35_story.html

Markon, J., Nakashima, E., & Crites, A. (2014, September 21). Top-level turnover makes it harder for DHS to stay on top of evolving threats. *The Washington Post*. Retrieved from https://www.washingtonpost.com/politics/top-level-turnover-makes-it-harder-for-dhs-to-stay-on-top-of-evolving-threats/2014/09/21/ca7919a6-39d7-11e4-9c9f-ebb47272e40e_story.html

Miller, J. (2011, September 15). Agencies must use CyberScope tool for FISMA reports. *Federal News Radio*. Retrieved from http://federalnewsradio.com/all-news/2011/09/agencies-must-use-cyberscope-tool-for-fisma-reports/

Miller, J. (2012a, October 19). DHS realigns cyber office into five divisions. *Federal News Radio*. Retrieved from http://federalnewsradio.com/in-depth/2012/10/dhs-realigns-cyber-office-into-five-divisions/

Miller, J. (2012b, September 4). Management successes pave the way for "One DHS". *Federal News Radio*. Retreieved from http://federalnewsradio.com/in-depth/2012/09/management-successes-paving-the-way-for-one-dhs/

Miller, J. (2015a, June 8). Cyber attack against OPM was 1 of 9 DHS recently discovered targeting "bulk PII." *Federal News Radio*. Retrieved from http://

federalnewsradio.com/technology/2015/06/cyber-attack-against-opm-was-1-of-9-dhs-recently-discovered-targeting-bulk-pii/

Miller, J. (2015b, February 12). OMB reaffirms cyber oversight role. *Federal News Radio*. Retrieved from http://federalnewsradio.com/technology/2015/02/omb-reaffirms-cyber-oversight-role/

Miller, J. (2015c, January 29). Stempfley leaving DHS for private sector position. *Federal News Radio*. Retrieved from http://federalnewsradio.com/technology/2015/01/stempfley-leaving-dhs-for-private-sector-position/

Moore, J. (2013, July 12). OPM hopes cyber job database will help agencies fill workforce gaps. *Federal News Radio*. Retrieved from http://federalnewsradio.com/technology/2013/07/opm-hopes-cyber-job-database-will-help-agencies-fill-workforce-gaps/

Moteff, J. D. (2014, February 21). *Critical infrastructures: Background, policy, and implementation*. (Congressional Research Service Report No. 7-5700, RL 30153). Retrieved from ProQuest Congressional website: http://congressional.proquest.com/congressional/docview/t21.d22.crs-2014-rsi-0102?accountid=14585

Nakashima, E. (2012, May 16). White House's cybersecurity official retiring. *The Washington Post*. Retrieved from https://www.washingtonpost.com/world/national-security/white-houses-cybersecurity-official-retiring/2012/05/16/gIQAX6fmUU_story.html

Nakashima, E. (2015, February 10). New agency to sniff out threats in cyberspace. *The Washington Post*. Retrieved from https://www.washingtonpost.com/world/national-security/white-house-to-create-national-center-to-counter-cyberspace-intrusions/2015/02/09/a312201e-afd0-11e4-827f-93f454140e2b_story.html

National Commission on Terrorist Attacks Upon the United States. (2004). The 9/11 Commission Report. Retrieved from http://www.9-11commission.gov/report/911Report.pdf

National Cybersecurity Protection Act of 2014, Pub. L. No. 113-282, 128 Stat. 3066 (2014).

National Council of ISACS. (n.d.). Information Sharing and Analysis Centers (ISACs). Retrieved from http://www.isaccouncil.org/aboutus.html

National Initiative for Cybersecurity Careers and Study (NICCS). (n.d). About the National Initiative for Cybersecurity Education (NICE). Retrieved from https://niccs.us-cert.gov/footer/about-national-initiative-cybersecurity-education

National Initiative for Cybersecurity Education (NICE). (2013, March 14). 2012 Information Technology Workforce Assessment for Cybersecurity (ITWAC) (Summary Report). Retrieved from https://cio.gov/wp-content/uploads/downloads/2013/04/ITWAC-Summary-Report_04-01-2013.pdf

National Institute of Standards and Technology (NIST). (2014, February 12). Framework for improving critical infrastructure cybersecurity. Retrieved from http://www.nist.gov/cyberframework/upload/cybersecurity-framework-021214.pdf

Noble, M. T. (2000). *Organizational mastery with integrated management systems*. New York, NY: John Wiley & Sons.

Nolan, A. (2015, March 16). *Cybersecurity and information sharing: Legal challenges and solutions.* (Congressional Research Service Report No. 7-5700, R43941). Retrieved from ProQuest Congressional website: http:// congressional.proquest.com/congressional/docview/t21.d22.crs-2015-aml-0108?accountid=14585

Norton, S. (2015, February 17). Information sharing orgs weigh in on Obama's executive order. *The Wall Street Journal.* Retrieved from http://blogs.wsj.com/cio/2015/02/17/information-sharing-orgs-weigh-in-on-obamas-executive-order/

Oversight of the U.S. Department of Homeland Security. Hearings before the Committee on the Judiciary, House, 114th Cong. n.p. (2015) (Written testimony of Jeh Johnson).

Paletta, D. (2015, September 24). Federal cyber breach was worse than first believed. *The Wall Street Journal,* p. A6.

Paletta, D., Yadron, D., & Valentino-DeVries, J. (2015, October 12). Cyberwar ignites new arms race. *The Wall Street Journal,* A1, A12.

Pardy, W., & Andrews, T. (2010). *Integrated management systems.* Lanham, MD: Government Institutes.

Partnership for Public Service. (2015). National Programs and Protections Directorate (DHS). (Agency Report). Retrieved from http://bestplacestowork.org/BPTW/rankings/detail/HS20

Patel, S. (2014, December 18). Congressional passage of cybersecurity bill is a triumph for automation, groups say. *Power: Business and Technology for the Global Generation Industry.* Retrieved from http://www.powermag.com/congressional-passage-of-cybersecurity-bill-is-a-triumph-for-automation-groups-say/

Priest, D., & Arkin, W.M. (2010, July 19). Top secret America: A hidden world, growing beyond control. *The Washington Post.* Retrieved from http://projects.washingtonpost.com/top-secret-america/articles/a-hidden-world-growing-beyond-control/

Protecting America from Cyber Attacks. Hearings before the Committee on Homeland Security and Governmental Affairs, Senate, 114th Cong. (2015) (Testimony of Scott Charney).

Reflections on the Tenth Anniversary of the 9/11 Commission Report (2014). Report by the members of the 2004 9/11 Commission. Bipartisan Policy Center, Annenberg Public Policy Center. Retrieved from http://bipartisanpolicy.org/wp-content/uploads/sites/default/files/%20BPC%209-11%20Commission.pdf

Reich, R. B. (1993, July 28). The pronoun test for success. *The Washington Post.* Retrieved from http://www.washingtonpost.com/archive/opinions/1993/07/28/the-pronoun-test-for-success/e45f3343-8b9b-444c-b7c2-2afa235c53e3/

Rein, L. (2014, April 9). DHS officials broke hiring rules, watchdog alleges. *The Washington Post.* Retrieved from http://www.washingtonpost.com/blogs/federal-eye/wp/2014/04/09/exclusive-dhs-officials-broke-hiring-rules-watchdog-alleges/

Relyea, H.C., & Hogue, H.B. (2005, August 19). *Department of Homeland of Security reorganization: The 2SR initiative.* (Congressional Research Service Report No. RL 33042). Retrieved from Proquest Congressional website: http://

congressional.proquest.com/congressional/docview/t21.d22.crs-2006-gvf-0042?accountid=14585

Risher, H. (2014, September 30). Front-line morale problems are threatening homeland security. *Government Executive*. Retrieved from http://www.govexec.com/management/2014/09/front-line-morale-problems-are-threatening-homeland-security/95441/

Rockwell, M. (2013, September 20). Does DHS need an acquisitions oversight board? *FCW: Federal Computer World*. Retrieved from https://fcw.com/articles/2013/09/20/dhs-procurement-oversight.aspx

Rollins, J., & Henning, A.C. (2009, March 10). *Comprehensive National Cybersecurity Initiative (CNCI). Legal authorities and policy considerations*. (Congressional Research Service Report No. R 40427). Retrieved from Proquest Congressional website: http://congressional.proquest.com/congressional/docview/t21.d22.crs-2009-fdt-0222?accountid=14585

S. Rep. 114-1 (Coburn) (2015). Retrieved from http://congressional.proquest.com/congressional/docview/t21.d22.cmp-2015-hsg-0001?accountid=14585

Schein, E. H. (2010). *Organizational culture and leadership* (4th ed.). San Francisco, CA: Jossey-Bass.

Schwemle, B. L. (2013, February 27). Department of Homeland Security personnel issues. In *Issues in Homeland Security Policy for the 113th Congress*, William L. Painter, Coordinator. (Congressional Research Service Report No. R42985), pp. 63–66. Retrieved from ProQuest Congressional website: http://congressional.proquest.com/congressional/docview/t21.d22.crs-2013-dsp-0168?accountid=14585

Serbu, J. (2015, July 25). DHS rushes to complete cyber defense programs for agencies. *Federal News Radio*. Retrieved from http://federalnewsradio.com/cybersecurity/2015/06/dhs-rushes-complete-cyber-defense-programs-agencies/

Shea, D. A., & Morgan, D. (2009, June 22). *DHS Directorate of Science & Technology: Key issues for Congress*. (Congressional Research Service Report No. RL34356). Retrieved from ProQuest Congressional website: http://congressional.proquest.com/congressional/docview/t21.d22.crs-2009-rsi-0533?accountid=14585

Sternstein, A. (2013, March 17). DHS cyber czar Mark Weatherford to step down. *NextGov*. Retrieved from http://www.nextgov.com/cybersecurity/2013/03/dhs-cyber-czar-mark-weatherford-step-down/61922/

Sternstein, A. (2014, May 21). Bill would let DHS pay cyber workers as much as the Pentagon pays. *NextGov*. Retrieved from http://www.nextgov.com/cybersecurity/2014/05/bill-would-let-dhs-pay-cyber-workers-much-pentagon-pays/84958/

Sternstein, A. (2015a, May 14). Cyber pay equals out at $112,000 in government and industry, survey says. *NextGov*. Retrieved from http://www.nextgov.com/cybersecurity/2015/05/cyber-pay-equaling-out-112000-government-and-industry-survey-says/112756/

Sternstein, A. (2015b, July 31). DHS secretary OKs bill to monitor federal networks. *NextGov*. Retrieved from http://www.nextgov.com/cybersecurity/2015/07/administration-leader-oks-senate-panels-bill-monitor-federal-networks/118760/

Sternstein, A. (2015c, July 23). Senate committee poised to upgrade agency anti-hacking laws, again. *NextGov*. Retrieved from http://www.nextgov.com/cybersecurity/2015/07/senate-committee-poised-upgrade-agency-anti-hacking-laws-again/118512/

Sternstein, A. (2015d, July 22). Senators want to give DHS new Cybercom-like powers to thwart civilian agency hacks. *NextGov*. Retrieved from http://www.nextgov.com/cybersecurity/2015/07/senators-want-give-dhs-new-cybercom-powers-thwart-civilian-agency-hacks/118368/

Sternstein, A. (2015e, August 24). The nation's 24-hour Cyber Watch Center still has some empty seats. *NextGov*. Retrieved from http://www.nextgov.com/cybersecurity/2015/08/nations-24-hour-hack-watch-center-missing-three-quarters-industry/119392/

Stevens, J. G., & Johnson, R. E. (2005, June 22). Joint Data Support to the Analytic Agenda. Military Operations Research Society Symposium. Retrieved from http://www.dtic.mil/dtic/tr/fulltext/u2/a448559.pdf

Sy, T., & D'Annunzio, L. S. (2005). Challenges and strategies of matrix organizations. *Human Resource Planning, 28*(1), 39–48. doi:GALE%7CA131500184&v=2

The Future of Homeland Security: The Evolution of the Homeland Security Department's Roles and Mission. Hearings before the Committee on Homeland Security and Government Affairs, Senate, 112th Cong. (2012). (Testimony of Thad Allen).

Tobias, R. (2011). Leading differently: Can reorganizations change things? *Public Manager, 40*(2), 28–29. Retrieved from http://search.proquest.com/docview/889955019?accountid=14585

Trujillo, C. (2014, September 30). The limits of cyberspace deterrence. *Joint Force Quarterly 75* (4th Quarter), 43–52. Retrieved from http://ndupress.ndu.edu/Portals/68/Documents/jfq/jfq-75/jfq-75_43-52_Trujillo.pdf

U.S. Department of Homeland Security. (2010, July). Bottom-up review. (Report). Retrieved from http://www.dhs.gov/sites/default/files/publications/bur_bottom_up_review.pdf

U.S. Department of Homeland Security. (2012a, February 15). FY 2012 reporting instructions for the Federal Information Security Management Act and agency privacy management. (Federal information security Memorandum). Retrieved from http://www.dhs.gov/xlibrary/assets/nppd/fism12-02-signed.pdf

U.S. Department of Homeland Security. (2012b, June). Integrated strategy for high risk management. Implementation *and* transformation. Retrieved from https://www.dhs.gov/sites/default/files/publications/priv-gao-report-june-2012-final-redacted-caps.pdf

U.S Department of Homeland Security. (2012c, July 30). Privacy impact statement for the National Cybersecurity Protection System (NCPS). (DHS/NPPD/PAI-026). Retrieved from http://www.dhs.gov/sites/default/files/publications/privacy-pia-nppd-ncps.pdf

U.S. Department of Homeland Security. (2012d, February). Strategic plan: Fiscal years 2012-2016. Retrieved from http://www.dhs.gov/xlibrary/assets/dhs-strategic-plan-fy-2012-2016.pdf

U.S. Department of Homeland Security. (2013a, January). DHS information sharing and safeguarding strategy. Retrieved from http://www.dhs.gov/sites/default/files/publications/12-4466-dhs-information-sharing-and-safeguarding-strategy-01-30-13--fina%20%20%20.pdf

U.S. Department of Homeland Security. (2013b, June 12). Executive Order 13636. Improving critical infrastructure cybersecurity. (Incentives Study Analytic Report). Retrieved from http://www.dhs.gov/sites/default/files/publications/dhs-eo13636-analytic-report-cybersecurity-incentives-study.pdf

U.S. Department of Homeland Security. (2013c, November 5). Readout of DHS' and White House officials' participation in cybersecurity workforce roundtable. Retrieved from http://www.dhs.gov/news/2013/11/05/readout-dhs-and-white-house-officials%E2%80%99-participation-cybersecurity-workforce

U.S. Department of Homeland Security. (2014a, June 18). The 2014 quadrennial Homeland Security Review. Retrieved from http://www.dhs.gov/sites/default/files/publications/qhsr/2014-QHSR.pdf

U.S. Department of Homeland Security. (2014b). Fiscal years 2014-2018 strategic plan, 1-61. Retrieved from http://www.dhs.gov/sites/default/files/publications/FY14-18%20Strategic%20Plan.PDF

U.S. Department of Homeland Security. (2015a, June 4). DHS makes significant strides in management initiatives. Retrieved from http://www.dhs.gov/news/2015/06/04/dhs-makes-significant-strides-management-initiatives

U.S. Department of Homeland Security. (2015b, March 8). Information Sharing and Analysis Organizations (ISAOs) public meeting. (Transcript). Retrieved from http://www.dhs.gov/sites/default/files/publications/March%2018%20Information%20Sharing%20and%20Analysis%20Organizations%20Public%20Meeting.pdf

U.S. Department of Homeland Security. (2015c). Information technology strategic plan FY 2015-2018. Retrieved from http://www.dhs.gov/sites/default/files/publications/dhs-itstratplan-508_0.pdf

U.S. Department of Homeland Security. (2015d, February 25). Statement by Deputy Secretary Alejandro Mayorkas on the Cyber Threat Intelligence Integration Center. Retrieved from http://www.dhs.gov/news/2015/02/25/statement-deputy-secretary-alejandro-mayorkas-cyber-threat-intelligence-integration

U.S. Department of Homeland Security. (2015e, February 17). Summary of performance and financial information Fiscal Year 2014. Retrieved from http://www.dhs.gov/sites/default/files/publications/DHS%20FY%202014%20SPFI_0_0_0.pdf

U.S. Department of Homeland Security. (n.d.). Continuous diagnostics and mitigation (CDM). Retrieved from http://www.dhs.gov/cdm

U.S. Department of Homeland Security. (n.d.). Critical infrastructure sectors. Retrieved from http://www.dhs.gov/critical-infrastructure-sectors

U.S. Department of Homeland Security. (n.d.). Enhanced cybersecurity services. Retrieved from http://www.dhs.gov/enhanced-cybersecurity-services

U.S. Department of Homeland Security. (n.d.). Frequently asked questions about Information Sharing and Analysis Organizations. Retrieved from http://www.dhs.gov/isao-faq

U.S. Department of Homeland Security. (n.d.). Information Sharing and Analysis Organizations. Retrieved from http://www.dhs.gov/isao

U.S. Department of Homeland Security (n.d.). National Cybersecurity and Communications Integration Center (NCIIC). Retrieved from http://www.dhs.gov/national-cybersecurity-communications-integration-center

U.S. Department of Homeland Security. (n.d.). US-CERT (Info Sheet). Retrieved from https://www.us-cert.gov/sites/default/files/publications/infosheet_US-CERT_v2.pdf

U.S. Department of Homeland Security, National Protection and Programs Directorate. (2015, June). Enhancing resilience through cyber incident data sharing and analysis (White Paper). Retrieved from https://www.dhs.gov/sites/default/files/publications/Data%20Categories%20White%20Paper%20-%20508%20compliant.pdf

U.S. Department of Homeland Security, Office of Inspector General. (2013, June). DHS can take actions to address its additional cybersecurity responsibilities. (Report No. OIG-13-95). Retrieved from https://www.oig.dhs.gov/assets/Mgmt/2013/OIG_13-95_Jun13.pdf

U.S. Department of Homeland Security, Office of Inspector General. (2014a, December 12). Evaluation of DHS' information security program for Fiscal Year 2014. (Report No. OIG-15-16). Retrieved from https://www.oig.dhs.gov/assets/Mgmt/2015/OIG_15-16_Dec14.pdf

U.S. Department of Homeland Security, Office of Inspector General. (2014b, July). Implementation status of the Enhanced Cybersecurity Services program. (Report No. OIG-14-119). Retrieved from https://www.oig.dhs.gov/assets/Mgmt/2014/OIG_14-119_Jul14.pdf

U.S. Department of Homeland Security, Office of Inspector General. (2015a, March 24). Investigation into employee complaints about management of U.S. Citizenship and Immigration Services' EB-5 program. Retrieved from https://www.oig.dhs.gov/assets/Mga/OIG_mga-032415.pdf

U.S. Department of Homeland Security, Office of Inspector General. (2015b, February 23). Major management and performance challenges facing the Department of Homeland Security (Revised). (Report No. OIG-15-09). Retrieved from https://www.oig.dhs.gov/assets/Mgmt/2015/OIG_15-09_Feb15.pdf

U.S. Department of Homeland Security, Office of the Inspector General. (2015c, September 4). DHS can strengthen its cyber mission coordination efforts. (Report No. OIG-15-140). Retrieved from https://www.oig.dhs.gov/assets/Mgmt/2015/OIG-15-140-Sep15.pdf

U.S. Department of Homeland Security, U.S CERT. (n.d.). Critical Infrastructure Cyber Community Voluntary Program. Retrieved from https://www.us-cert.gov/ccubedvp

U.S. Government Accountability Office. (2004, August). Department of Homeland Security. Formidable information and technology management challenge requires institutional approach. (Report No. GAO-04-702). Retrieved from http://www.gao.gov/assets/250/243876.pdf

U.S. Government Accountability Office. (2011, November). Cybersecurity human capital initiatives need better planning and coordination. (Report No. GAO-12-8). Retrieved from http://www.gao.gov/assets/590/586494.pdf

U.S. Government Accountability Office. (2012a, February 3). DHS: Additional actions needed to strengthen strategic planning and management functions. (Report No. GAO-12-382-T). Retrieved from http://www.gao.gov/assets/590/588195.pdf

U.S. Government Accountability Office. (2012b, December). DHS strategic workforce planning. Oversight of departmentwide efforts should be strengthened. (Report No. GAO-13-65). Retrieved from http://www.gao.gov/assets/660/650479.pdf

U.S. Government Accountability Office. (2012c, September). Information sharing. DHS has demonstrated leadership and progress, but additional actions could help sustain and strengthen efforts. (Report No. GAO-12-809). Retrieved from http://www.gao.gov/assets/650/648475.pdf

U.S. Government Accountability Office. (2013a, April). Communications networks, outcome-based measures would assist DHS in assessing effectiveness of cybersecurity efforts. (Report No. GAO-13-275). Retrieved from http://www.gao.gov/assets/660/653515.pdf

U.S. Government Accountability Office. (2013b, December 12). DHS' efforts to improve employee morale and fill senior leadership vacancies. (Report No. GAO-14-228T). Retrieved from http://www.gao.gov/assets/660/659642.pdf

U.S. Government Accountability Office. (2014a, June). DHS intelligence analysis. Additional actions needed to address analytic priorities and workforce. (Report No. GAO-14-397). Retrieved from http://gao.gov/assets/670/663794.pdf

U.S. Government Accountability Office. (2014b, December). Federal facility cybersecurity. DHS and GSA should address cyber risk to building and access control systems (Report No. GAO-15-6). Retrieved from http://www.gao.gov/assets/670/667512.pdf

U.S. Government Accountability Office. (2015a, February 26). DHS: Progress made, but more work remains in strengthening management functions. (Report No. GAO-15-388T). Retrieved from http://gao.gov/assets/670/668716.pdf

U.S. Government Accountability Office. (2015b, February). High-risk series, an update. Report to congressional committees (Report No. GAO-15-290). Retrieved from http://www.gao.gov/assets/670/668415.pdf

U.S. Government Accountability Office. (2015c, October). National Protection and Programs Directorate. Factors to consider when reorganizing (Report No.GAO-16-140T). Retrieved from http://www.gao.gov/assets/680/672944.pdf

U.S. Office of Management and Budget. (2010, July 6). Clarifying cybersecurity responsibilities and activities of the Executive Office of the President and the Department of Homeland Security (DHS) (Memorandum No. M-10-28). Retrieved from https://www.whitehouse.gov/sites/default/files/omb/assets/memoranda_2010/m10-28.pdf

U.S. Office of Management and Budget. (2013, November 18). Enhancing the security of federal information and information systems. (Memorandum No.

M-14-03). Retrieved from https://www.whitehouse.gov/sites/default/files/omb/memoranda/2014/m-14-03.pdf

U.S. Office of Management and Budget. (2014, October 3). Fiscal Year 2014-2015 Guidance on improving federal information security and privacy management practices (Memorandum No. M-15-01). Retrieved from https://www.whitehouse.gov/sites/default/files/omb/memoranda/2015/m-15-01.pdf

U.S. Office of Personnel Management. (2014). 2014 Federal employee viewpoint survey results. Employees influencing change. Retrieved from http://www.fedview.opm.gov/2014FILES/2014_Governmentwide_Management_Report.pdf

U.S. Office of Personnel Management. (2015). 2015 Federal Employee Viewpoint Survey Results. Employees influencing change. Retrieved from http://www.fedview.opm.gov/2015FILES/2015_FEVS_Gwide_Final_Report.PDF

Vicinanzo, A. (2015, March 2). Watchdog calls for DHS reform to improve homeland security. *Homeland Security Today*. Retrieved from http://www.hstoday.us/single-article/watchdog-calls-for-dhs-reform-to-improve-homeland-security/2a88f664ecb42b9e6175907ff8b595b5.html

Vijayan, J. (2009a, March 9). Federal cybersecurity director quits, complains of NSA role. *Computerworld*. Retrieved from http://www.networkworld.com/article/2264463/data-breach/federal-cybersecurity-director-quits--complains-of-nsa-role.html

Vijayan, J. (2009b, April 28). Senator questions White House role over cybersecurity. *Computerworld*. Retrieved from http://www.networkworld.com/article/2255336/data-center/senator-questions-white-house-control-over-cybersecurity.html

Volz, D. (2015, February 11). Lawmakers not briefed about Obama's new $35 million cyber agency. *National Journal*. Retrieved from http://www.nextgov.com/cybersecurity/2015/02/lawmakers-not-briefed-about-obamas-new-35-million-cyber-agency/105102/

Vlahos, K. (2008, June 23). DHS: A clash of cultures. *Homeland Security Today*. Retrieved from http://www.hstoday.us/channels/dhs/single-article-page/a-clash-of-cultures/c96258fc3b805fbd4eb94266b6f57bfb.html

Waddell, K. (2015, August 3). The Homeland Security Department issues a big warning about the Senate's cyber bill. *National Journal*. Retrieved from http://www.nationaljournal.com/s/70687/homeland-security-department-issues-big-warning-about-senates-cyber-bill

West, D. M. (2012, June 26). A vision for Homeland Security in the Year 2025. *Governance Studies at Brookings*. Retrieved from http://www.brookings.edu/~/media/Research/Files/Papers/2012/6/26-security-homeland-west/26_homeland_security_west.pdf

The White House. (2009a, May). The Comprehensive National Cybersecurity Initiative. Retrieved from https://www.whitehouse.gov/issues/foreign-policy/cybersecurity/national-initiative

The White House. (2009b, May 29). Cyberspace Policy Review. Assuring a trusted and resilient information and communications infrastructure. Retrieved from https://www.whitehouse.gov/assets/documents/Cyberspace_Policy_Review_final.pdf

The White House. (2015, January 13). Securing cyberspace—President Obama announces new legislative cybersecurity proposal and other cybersecurity efforts. Retrieved from https://www.whitehouse.gov/the-press-office/2015/01/13/ securing-cyberspace-president-obama-announces-new-cybersecurity-legislat

Wise, C. R. (2006). Organizing for homeland security after Katrina: Is adaptive management what's missing? *Public Administration Review, 66*(3), 302–318. Retrieved from http://search.proquest.com/ docview/197175662?accountid=14585

CHAPTER 4

PUBLIC SECTOR RETIREMENT SYSTEMS

Change or Consider Bankruptcy?

William J. Woska

INTRODUCTION

Although employer-provided retirement systems are relatively recent in the private sector, dating from the late 19th century, public sector plans go back much further in history. From the Roman Empire to the rise of the early-modern nation state, rulers, and legislatures have provided pensions for the workers who administered public programs. Military pensions, in particular, have a long history, and they have often been used as a key element in attracting, retaining, and motivating military personnel. In the United States, pensions for disabled and retired military personnel predate the signing of the United States Constitution (Craig, 2003).

In the United States, public sector pensions are provided by federal, state, and local government including cities, counties, and special districts established by state legislatures. The retirement programs are generally funded by contributions made by both the employee and the employer.

Transforming Government Organizations:
Fresh Ideas and Examples From the Field, pp. 135–151
Copyright © 2016 by Information Age Publishing

Most full-time public sector employees are covered by a retirement program. Nearly all states have some kind of protection for public sector pensions, either in state constitutions or through a court's interpretation of the constitution. Most protect pensions under contract theory which prohibits states from passing a law that impairs a contract. Unlike the private sector, once a public sector employee is hired, most courts have found that the terms of the retirement benefit cannot be changed. (See the United States Constitution, Article 1, Section 10, Clause 1 for an example of language prohibiting a change of contract provisions at the federal level. Most state constitutions have a similar prohibition.)

Detroit, Michigan, and Vallejo, and Stockton, California, appear to be examples of a growing list of public agencies that file for bankruptcy. When an employee earns pension benefits, the agency creates a long-term liability. A majority of public jurisdictions have defined benefit retirement programs that are underfunded. Municipalities have found it difficult to offer new retirement plans due to the fact that retirement benefits are a mandatory source of collective bargaining and that a large number of public employees are unionized. Labor unions have been ideologically inclined toward defined benefit pension systems. For example, organized labor in Detroit fought to keep a defined benefit retirement program for new employees even as benefits were being reduced for current retirees. With the above in mind, this chapter provides the background with respect to public employee retirement systems and the significance and impact of retirement programs that are not fully funded.

TYPES OF PUBLIC SECTOR RETIREMENT PROGRAMS

Public sector retirement programs are generally referred to as either defined benefit (DB) or defined contribution (DC) pension plans. Since the 2008 financial crisis, several public agencies have introduced cash balance plans.

Defined Benefit Retirement Plan

A DB plan promises a specified monthly benefit at retirement. DB pension plans are employer-sponsored retirement plans in which workers are promised a fixed pension after retirement in the form of an annuity. The benefit is typically linked to the participant's final wage and the number of years of service, with the exact formula varying by employer. DB pension plans are offered by some private employers, as well as by the federal, state, local government, and other public agencies. In the private sector, the use of DB plans has been declining since the early 1980s. In March, 2013, about 16% of private sector workers participated in a DB plan (U.S. Department of Labor, 2013). In contrast, in the public sector, most workers participate in DB pension plans.

A DB pension plan provides an older employee with a greater benefit for each year of employment as opposed to retiring at a younger age. For example, a pension plan referred to as 2% at age 60 would provide the individual retiring at age 60 with 2% of his/her highest monthly compensation over a period of time for each year of employment. If the individual retired earlier than age 60, the percentage for each year of service would be less. Conversely, if retirement occurs after age 60, the benefit for each year of service may be more.

Figure 4.1 provides an example of a 2% at age 60 retirement benefit.

Referring to Figure 4.1, an employee who retired at age 57 would be eligible for a pension benefit equal to his/her highest monthly compensation over a period of time (e.g., generally one to three years depending on pension plan) for each year of employment. For example, an employee with 25 years of service retiring at age 57 would receive a benefit of 41.25% (25 x 1.65 %) of his/her highest monthly compensation.

Defined Contribution Retirement Plan

A defined contribution (DC) pension plan is specified as a:

> plan which provides for an individual account for each participant for benefits based solely on the amount contributed to the participant's account, and any income, expenses, gains and losses, and any forfeitures of accounts of other participants which may be allocated to such participant's account. (26 U.S.C. §414(i))

It does not promise a specific benefit at retirement. In these plans, the employee or the employer (or both) contribute to the employee's individual account. Benefits are determined on the amounts credited to the account plus any earnings on the funds placed in the account. The value of the account will fluctuate due to the changes in the value of investments. The amount of the distribution of the funds in the account will be determined by the individual. Examples of DC plans include Individual Retirement Accounts (IRAs) and 401(k) plans in the private sector, and 457 plans in the public sector.

While there are similarities between the features of 401(k) and 457 plans, there are also differences in the ways the plans are being used. Most public sector employees will have a significant portion of their retirement income

PERCENTAGE OF FINAL COMPENSATION

Age	50	51	52	53	54	55	56	57	58	59	60	61	62	63+
Benefit Factor	1.092	1.156	1.224	1.296	1.376	1.460	1.552	1.650	1.758	1.874	2.000	2.134	2.272	2.418
Years of Service						Percentage of Final Compensation								
5	5.46	5.78	6.12	6.48	6.88	7.30	7.76	8.25	8.79	9.37	10.00	10.67	11.36	12.09
6	6.55	6.94	7.34	7.78	8.26	8.76	9.31	9.90	10.55	11.24	12.00	12.80	13.63	14.51
7	7.64	8.09	8.57	9.07	9.63	10.22	10.86	11.55	12.31	13.12	14.00	14.94	15.90	16.93
8	8.74	9.25	9.79	10.37	11.01	11.68	12.42	13.20	14.06	14.99	16.00	17.07	18.18	19.34
9	9.83	10.40	11.02	11.66	12.38	13.14	13.97	14.85	15.82	16.87	18.00	19.21	20.45	21.76
10	10.92	11.56	12.24	12.96	13.76	14.60	15.52	16.50	17.58	18.74	20.00	21.34	22.72	24.18
11	12.01	12.72	13.46	14.26	15.14	16.06	17.07	18.15	19.34	20.61	22.00	23.47	24.99	26.60
12	13.10	13.87	14.69	15.55	16.51	17.52	18.62	19.80	21.10	22.49	24.00	25.61	27.26	29.02
13	14.20	15.03	15.91	16.85	17.89	18.98	20.18	21.45	22.85	24.36	26.00	27.74	29.54	31.43
14	15.29	16.18	17.14	18.14	19.26	20.44	21.73	23.10	24.61	26.24	28.00	29.88	31.81	33.85
15	16.38	17.34	18.36	19.44	20.64	21.90	23.28	24.75	26.37	28.11	30.00	32.01	34.08	36.27
16	17.47	18.50	19.58	20.74	22.02	23.36	24.83	26.40	28.13	29.98	32.00	34.14	36.35	38.59
17	18.56	19.65	20.81	22.03	23.39	24.82	26.38	28.05	29.89	31.85	34.00	36.28	38.62	41.11
18	19.66	20.81	22.03	23.33	24.77	26.28	27.94	29.70	31.64	33.73	36.00	38.41	40.90	43.52
19	20.75	21.96	23.26	24.62	26.14	27.74	29.49	31.35	33.40	35.61	38.00	40.55	43.17	45.94
20	21.84	23.12	24.48	25.92	27.52	29.20	31.04	33.00	35.16	37.48	40.00	42.68	45.44	48.36
21	22.93	24.28	25.70	27.22	28.90	30.66	32.59	34.65	36.92	39.35	42.00	44.81	47.71	50.78
22	24.02	25.43	26.93	28.51	30.27	32.12	34.14	36.30	38.68	41.23	44.00	46.95	49.98	53.20
23	25.12	26.59	28.15	29.81	31.65	33.58	35.70	37.95	40.43	43.10	46.00	49.08	52.26	55.61
24	26.21	27.74	29.38	31.10	33.02	35.04	37.25	39.60	42.19	44.98	48.00	51.22	54.53	58.03
25	27.30	28.90	30.60	32.40	34.40	36.50	38.80	41.25	43.95	46.85	50.00	53.35	56.80	60.45
26	28.39	30.06	31.82	33.70	35.78	37.96	40.35	42.90	45.71	48.72	52.00	55.48	59.07	62.87
27	29.48	31.21	33.05	34.99	37.15	39.42	41.90	44.55	47.47	50.60	54.00	57.62	61.34	65.29
28	30.58	32.37	34.27	36.29	38.53	40.88	43.46	46.20	49.22	52.47	56.00	59.75	63.62	67.70
29	31.67	33.52	35.50	37.58	39.90	42.34	45.01	47.85	50.98	54.35	58.00	61.89	65.89	70.12
30	32.76	34.68	36.72	38.88	41.28	43.80	46.56	49.50	52.74	56.22	60.00	64.02	68.16	72.54
31	33.85	35.84	37.94	40.18	42.66	45.26	48.11	51.15	54.50	58.09	62.00	66.15	70.43	74.96
32	34.94	36.99	39.17	41.47	44.03	46.72	49.66	52.80	56.26	59.97	64.00	68.29	72.70	77.38
33	36.04	38.15	40.39	42.77	45.41	48.18	51.22	54.45	58.01	61.84	66.00	70.42	74.98	79.79
34	-	39.30	41.62	44.06	46.78	49.64	52.77	56.10	59.77	63.72	68.00	72.56	77.25	82.21
35	-	-	42.84	45.36	48.16	51.10	54.32	57.75	61.53	65.59	70.00	74.69	79.52	84.63
36	-	-	-	46.66	49.54	52.56	55.87	59.40	63.29	67.46	72.00	76.82	81.79	87.05
37	-	-	-	-	50.91	54.02	57.42	61.05	65.05	69.34	74.00	78.96	84.06	89.47
38	-	-	-	-	-	55.48	58.98	62.70	66.80	71.21	76.00	81.09	86.34	91.88
39	-	-	-	-	-	-	60.53	64.35	68.56	73.09	78.00	83.23	88.61	94.30
40	-	-	-	-	-	-	-	66.00	70.32	74.96	80.00	85.36	90.88	96.72

Figure 4.1. Two percent at age 60 defined benefit schedule.

provided through their defined benefit plan and can therefore use their 457 plan assets to supplement this income. In contrast, for most employees in the private sector, the 401(k) plan will serve as their primary retirement benefit. This distinction is important with respect to how employees are structuring their retirement benefits.

Cash Balance Plans

Cash balance plans are DB plans where each member has a notional account to which the employer and the employee each make contributions, and the employer credits a return annually. These plans differ in two important ways from traditional DB plans. First, they enhance the likelihood of making required contributions, thereby, preventing the future buildup of large unfunded liabilities. Second, they allocate benefits more evenly between short and long-term employees than the traditional back-loaded DB plans (Munnell Aubrey, & Cafarelli, 2014).

PENSION PLAN FUNDING

Retirement plans are generally funded through contributions made by both the employer and the employee. Funding a pension plan involves determining appropriate contribution amounts at specific points in time and determining how to invest the assets of the plan until benefits are paid. In the private sector, minimum contribution requirements are set by federal law (Employee Retirement Income Security Act of 1974 (ERISA)). In the public sector, each local governing body (e.g., city, county, school district, special district) sets its own contribution levels within whatever requirements, if any, the state may have established for local jurisdictions. Decisions about what to contribute and when are usually made by a retirement board or plan sponsor within the boundaries of any established contribution requirements similar to ERISA in the private sector (American Academy of Actuaries, 2014).

When an employee earns pension benefits, the government creates a long-term liability. If the employer puts aside enough money to cover that liability, pension benefits will be sufficiently funded. But if the employer underestimates the costs, then there is a problem. If there is an impact on the economy, such as the recession beginning in 2008, pension plan funding may be affected depending on investments made on behalf of the retirement fund.

In principle, pension plans need to employ actuarial consultants to project the cost of the benefits pledged. These projections rely on many assumptions, but the most important are those regarding rates of return on fund assets, contribution rates, pay raises, longevity and cost-of-living adjustments (COLAs). When the first two factors (rates of return on fund assets and contribution rates) turn out to be lower and the rest higher than originally assumed, the actuary has underestimated the costs and underfunding is the result (Atanasov, 2014).

PUBLIC SECTOR PENSION LIABILITY

On a continuing basis, newspapers, journals, and financial reports address unfunded public sector pension liability. Sometimes there is a significant difference as to information reported reflecting different calculations, reporting dates, and other assumptions. However, irrespective of the differences, all reports agree that most public sector pension plans are underfunded.

Unfunded pension liabilities have increased significantly during the first part of this century. The average public pension plan was fully funded in 2001, but the ratio of funding to pension liabilities has subsequently steadily declined. This chronic underfunding of public pensions was largely a consequence of investment portfolio returns that were well below the rates of return assumed in the plans' actuarial calculations (Triest & Zhao, 2013).

The Federal Reserve Board (FRB) provides periodic reports of actuarial liabilities and funding status of DB plans. On October 31, 2014, the FRB reported the funding status of state and local DB pension funds beginning in 1974 and ending with the second quarter of 2014, a period of 40 years. Figure 4.2 identifies the status of DB pension funding during this period.

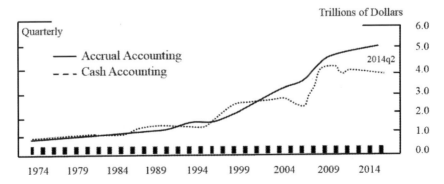

Figure 4.2.   Liabilities of state and local defined benefit pension funds under accrual and cash accounting.

DB pension plans were generally 100% funded between 1974 and the late 1990s. In fact, during a 5-year period beginning around 1997 public sector DB pension plans were more than 100% funded. However, a perilous drop in funding occurred with the 2008 recession and there has been little if any recovery. It is estimated that DB pension plans are underfunded by $1.3 trillion dollars in the second quarter of 2014 (Stefanescu & Vidangos, 2014). Some estimates are considerably higher.

PENSION PLAN UNDERFUNDING:
A FACTOR IN MUNICIPAL BANKRUPTCY FILINGS

There are approximately 89,000 municipal governments in the United States (U.S. Census Bureau, 2012. Municipalities are defined to include cities, towns, counties, school and taxing districts, and utilities. Among all U.S. municipalities there were 239 bankruptcy filings between 1980 and 2010. Most of these cases included smaller entities such as utilities and special districts According to the most recent information based on federal court records, as of July, 2012, 27 cities and municipal agencies have filed for Chapter 9 bankruptcy protection since 2010, among which six were cities or localities (Maciag, 2012; The National Association of State Budget Officers, 2012). On July 18, 2013, Detroit, Michigan, filed for bankruptcy, the largest municipal bankruptcy filing in U.S. history, by debt, estimated at $18 to 20 billion dollars (Davey & Walsh, 2013).

Pension plan underfunding has been a significant factor relating to bankruptcy filings by municipalities. On May 6, 2008, the city council for the City of Vallejo, California, a city with a population of almost 120,000, voted to file for Chapter 9 bankruptcy. "Unsecured claims" included $84 million dollars for pensions (Mendel, 2009), On August 1, 2011, Central Falls, a small city in Rhode Island with unfunded pension and health insurance programs totaling more than $80 million dollars filed for bankruptcy (Bidgood, 2012). Less than a year later, Stockton, California, a city with a population approaching 300,000 filed for bankruptcy. Stockton has an unfunded pension obligation of more than $900 million dollars (Cone, 2013). On July 10, 2012 two weeks later, the City of San Bernardino, California, with an unfunded pension plan of $50 million dollars, filed for bankruptcy (Esquivel & Mozingo, 2015). On July 18, 2013, Detroit, Michigan, a city with a population exceeding 700,000, filed for Chapter 9 bankruptcy. Detroit had an unfunded pension obligation of more than 9 billion dollars (Brownfeld, 2014).

Detroit may be the first of the major cities to file for bankruptcy. A George Mason University study identified other large cities facing similar problems with pension costs including Chicago, Baltimore, and Pittsburg

(McClain, 2013). The City of Chicago's four pension funds were only 36% funded as of December 31, 2012, and had an unfunded liability of $19.5 billion dollars. The city estimates that without pension reform, its required contribution to the funds will more than double in the next 2 years, from $479.5 million in 2013 to $1.087 billion in 2015. "The pension crisis is no longer around the corner. It has arrived at our schools," says Chicago Mayor Rahm Emanuel, referring to pension underfunding (Klepper, 2013).

PUBLIC SECTOR RETIREMENT SYSTEMS MUST CHANGE WITH THE TIMES

Pensions and health care are the major contributors to postemployment retirement costs. Although retirement benefits are generally a small percentage of a municipality's total budget, pensions constitute the largest portion of long-term debt. The pension costs are increasing exponentially. For example, the state of Illinois pension debt increased 79% between 2009 and 2014, from $62 to $111 billion dollars (VanMetre, 2014). In California, a decade of financial data posted in 2015 by Betty T. Yee, the state's Controller, shows that the state's 130 public pension systems are carrying approximately $200 billion in unfunded liability in 2013, compared with $6.3 billion of unfunded liability in 2003 (Yee, 2015).

Public agencies throughout the United States are beginning to realize that because of the continuing increase in the unfunded liability of pension plans, change must occur. With increasing pension costs combined with the need to balance a budget, the cost of retiree benefits is crowding out other local government services, including public safety. "Crowd out" has become a feature of defined benefit pension systems. Reductions in staffing, at all levels including police, fire, and other public safety positions, are occurring because of the need to balance budgets in light of increasing pension costs.

Across the country, state government and other public agencies are introducing pension reforms in an attempt to address unfunded liability issues. These reforms include a combination of increased pension contributions by employees, reductions in pension contributions by employers, reductions in benefits, increases in age and service requirements for normal retirement, cost-of-living adjustment reductions, increased vesting requirements, and adjustments in the calculation of final salary for retirement purpose (Snell, 2012).

Prior to the 2008 financial crisis, the states of Alaska and Michigan introduced retirement plans that required all new hires to participate solely in a DC plan. Since the financial crisis several additional states including Georgia, Oregon, Rhode Island, Washington, Tennessee, and Virginia have adopted hybrid plans that require participation in both DB and DC plans.

Utah, Florida, and Ohio offer employees the option of participating in either a DB or DC plan. Kansas and Louisiana have adopted cash balance plans (Sanford & Franzel, 2012).

The state of Nebraska has had a cash balance plan for state and county workers for several years. Texas also has a cash balance plan for the Texas Municipal Retirement System and the Texas County and District Retirement System. The states of Kansas and Kentucky have recently introduced cash balance plans (Munnell et al., 2014).

California's Pension Reform Act of 2013

Since the market collapse of 2008–2009 and resulting pension fund investment losses, all but a handful of states have adopted significant changes to their public employee retirement plans aimed at reducing unfunded liabilities and bringing contribution rates down to manageable levels (Snell, 2012). California Governor Jerry Brown viewed pension reform not only as a fiscal necessity, but also as a political imperative to win voter support for his November 2012 ballot initiative to close the state's long-standing budget deficit with temporary sales and income tax increases. In September 2012, the California State Legislature passed, and Brown signed into law, AB340, the Public Employee Pension Reform Act of 2013 (PEPRA). The State of California's Public Employees' Retirement System (CalPERS) is the nation's largest public pension fund with a market value of over $281 billion dollars in 2013. CalPERS had an unfunded liability, calculated by dividing the plan's assets by its obligations, of more than $57 billion dollars (Yee, 2015). Following the 2008 recession, the market value of CalPERS decreased from $253 to $183 billion dollars, a loss of more than 38% (CalPERS, 2015).

PEPRA applies to nearly all public employers in California except the University of California, charter cities and charter counties, unless these entities participate in their own retirement systems governed by state statute, like San Francisco and San Jose.

PEPRA, like many other states changing their pension systems, applies primarily to new members hired on or after January 1, 2013. The following are examples of some of the significant changes resulting from PEPRA:

- Reduces pension benefit formulas and increases retirement ages.
- Final average salary calculation based on regular recurring pay (eliminates any increase added on to increase a retirement benefit).
- Final average salary calculated over three years (some employees hired prior to January 1, 2013 had a final average salary calculation based on the highest single year of service).

- Increases contribution rates for all employees, including those hired prior to January 1, 2013.
- Establishes limitations on maximum compensation for pension purposes (CalPERS, 2012).

The overall savings over the next 30 years for all employers impacted by PEPRA are expected to be between $42 and $55 billion dollars (Worgan, Lamoureux, & Milligan, 2012).

A Movement Away From Defined Benefit Plans?

Public and private sector retirement plans have evolved along divergent paths. DB plans have historically been the dominant retirement incentive in both the private and public sectors. In 1975, 73% of private sector workers, and 98% of public sector workers were covered by DB plans (Munnell, Haverstrick, & Soto, 2007). In 2005, only 36% of currently employed private sector workers participated in DB plans, while public sector participation increased (Employee Benefit Research Institute, 2007).

Figures 4.3 and 4.4 provide a comparison of the contrasting movements between the private and public sectors with respect to pension plan design. Figure 4.3 provides a 30 year history of the change in the private sector from primarily a DB programs to a DC pension system (Anumeha, Ballard, Moore, & Rendon, 2013).

As illustrated in Figures 4.3 and 4.4, unlike the private sector, public sector participation in DB plans has remained stable. However, as reflected in Figure 4.3, public sector employers have been increasingly redesigning pension plans to include DC plans, hybrid plans, and other alternative plans including cash balance, 401(k), and 457 deferred compensation plans.

As policymakers evaluate retirement plans offered to public sector employees, it is important to understand the fundamental issues that have resulted in the different retirement plan trends observed in the public and private sectors. These issues include broad structural differences in revenue generation between private and public entities, differences in the costs of regulatory compliance, and compensation parity (Anumeha et al., 2013).

Policymakers must also understand a key difference between DB and DC pension plans. The critical difference between the two pension plans is not necessarily in whether employers or employees contribute to the fund or how assets are invested, but in who bears the investment risks in the timing of benefit promises and payouts—the employee or the taxpayer?

Generally speaking, in a DB system, benefit promises are made well before they must be paid out, and the employer bears the risks of the

Pension Sector Plan Design Trend

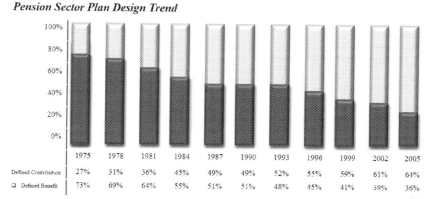

	1975	1978	1981	1984	1987	1990	1993	1996	1999	2002	2005
Defined Contribution	27%	31%	36%	45%	49%	49%	52%	55%	59%	61%	64%
Defined Benefit	73%	69%	64%	55%	51%	51%	48%	45%	41%	39%	36%

Figure 4.3. Private sector change from a defined benefit to a defined contribution pension system between 1975 and 2005.

Pension Sector Plan Design Trend

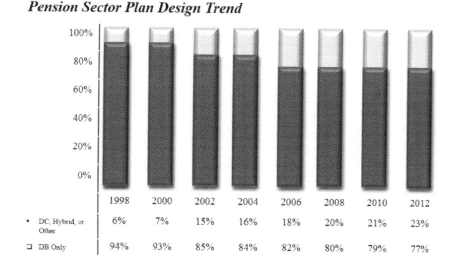

	1998	2000	2002	2004	2006	2008	2010	2012
DC, Hybrid, or Other	6%	7%	15%	16%	18%	20%	21%	23%
DB Only	94%	93%	85%	84%	82%	80%	79%	77%

Figure 4.4. Private sector change from a defined benefit to a defined contribution pension system between 1998 and 2012.

investment returns (as pension benefits are guaranteed regardless of the fund's returns). In contrast, in a DC system, the employee and/or the employer is obligated to deposit money into employee accounts each pay period and employees bear the risks of the investment returns. This crucial distinction between the two pension plans explains why DC pension plans provide considerably less risk for a public sector employer (Christensen, Bui, & Gilroy, 2014).

THE END ROAD FOR
DEFINED BENEFIT PLANS—BANKRUPTCY?

It is significantly more difficult for the public sector to move away from DB pension plans than the private sector. The contract clause of the United States Constitution mentioned above has been interpreted to provide protection against any type of unilateral change affecting the vested rights of current employees. Also, almost 36% of public employees are represented by unions or other organizations for collective bargaining purposes as compared to less than 7% in the private sector (U.S. Department of Labor, 2015). Given the value of today's pension plans, there is little incentive for current employees to make significant concessions to their plans, except to prevent cuts, such as salaries or employment, where the government has more leeway. Moreover, unions are loathe to create pension plans for new employees that are different from current plans because it creates an "us" versus "them" scenario within their bargaining units (Kramer & Holm, 2013). Nevertheless, since the 2008 recession, with bankruptcy filings and the spiraling effects of unfunded liability caused by DB plans, public agencies are considering other alternatives.

During the last 30 years, there has been a significant shift in the private sector away from DB pension plans. In the public sector there has not been much change with more than 90% of employers with either DB plans or a combination of DB and hybrid pension plans (Anumeha et al., 2013.) Following bankruptcy filings in a number of public agencies, and reports from actuaries reflecting a continuing increase in unfunded liability of their pension plans, a number of other public jurisdictions are now considering changes to their DB pension plans similar to California's PEPRA legislation and/or hybrid plans shifting liability issues from the public agency (Snell, 2012).

There are public agencies throughout the country considering different options to address shrinking revenues and increasing pension liability. These options include the possibility of a bankruptcy filing. Issues regarding the bankruptcy process are being addressed by legal counsel including the impact upon different creditors.(11 U.S.C. § 109(c). However, bankruptcy is not an option for all public agencies (Jacob, 2012).

There are six basic types of bankruptcy cases provided under the Bankruptcy Code. (11 U.S.C. § 501 *et seq*). Bankruptcy filings by municipalities are filed under Chapter 9 entitled "Adjustment of Debts of a Municipality." (11 U.S.C. § 901 *et seq*,) The public agency continues operations and concurrently pays creditors through a court-approved plan of reorganization.

The 10th Amendment to the U.S. Constitution grants each state full autonomy over its local governments. It is for this reason that municipalities must receive legal authority from the state to be eligible to file for bankruptcy under Chapter 9. In 2011, there were 26 states with laws that authorized municipalities to file for bankruptcy. Among these, 14 states required that the municipality obtain permission from a state authority before filing, while the other 12 imposed no filing restrictions. Meanwhile, 23 states have yet to pass laws on municipal bankruptcies, effectively disallowing municipalities in these states from filing for bankruptcy. Only one state, Georgia, expressly prohibits municipalities from filing (Delisle, 2010).

The several steps that must be satisfied to file for municipal bankruptcy are as follows:

1. The municipality must have specific authority to file for Chapter 9 bankruptcy under state law.
2. The municipality must be insolvent.
3. The municipality must prove its desire to adopt a plan to adjust its debt.
4. The municipality must satisfy at least one of four specified conditions to demonstrate that it has obtained or tried to obtain an agreement with creditors, that it is not feasible to negotiate with its creditors holding at least the majority of the claims in each class that the entity intends to impair under its debt adjustment plan, or that it has reason to believe its creditors might attempt to obtain preferential payment or transfer of the entity's assets.
5. The municipality must be able to show that it filed for bankruptcy in good-faith (Dabney, Darby, Egan, Levinson, South, & Tidmore, 2012).

Between 1980 and 2010 there were 239 bankruptcy filings by municipalities (public agencies) in the United States (DeAngelis, & Tian, 2013). Municipalities are defined to include cities, towns, counties, school and taxing districts, and utilities. Figure 4.5 identifies bankruptcies filed each year during this period.

Between 2010 and August, 2012, there were an additional 27 public agency filings for bankruptcy. During the next 2 years, Detroit, Michigan, and nine other public agencies filed for Chapter 9 protection. Increasing unfunded liability caused be DB pension plans will be a continuing issue for other public agencies when faced with staff reductions, reducing and/or eliminating services, and other funding limitations, as these government entities consider change and/or modifications to DB pension plans and/or a Chapter 9 bankruptcy filing in the future (DeAngelis, & Tian, 2013).

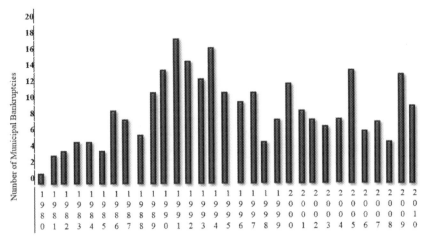

Figure 4.5.   Municipal bankrupticies 1980 to 2010.

CONCLUSION

With public sector pension costs straining the budget of state and local governments, fundamental reform of the way in which public employees receive retirement benefits is necessary. Even considering significant modifications to DB pension plans, such as California's PEPRA legislation, recessions, actuarial assumptions on investments, and other economic factors will continue to expose DB pension plans to increasing liability. Public sector officials understand the significance of the relationship between a DB pension plan and the term "unfunded liability." However, unlike the private sector where the movement from DB plans to DC plans (401(k)) has been significant due largely to the decline of companies with DB plans and the establishment of new companies with 401(k) plans, the public sector continues in perpetuity so conversions are more difficult (Munnell et al., 2007). Also, public sector employees are older, more risk adverse, and more unionized than the private sector causing further difficulty for elected pubic officials to consider change until all other options are exhausted.

A number of states, like California, have enacted pension reforms that rely on the creation of a new pension tier for new employees. However, the reforms will not have a noticeable impact on net pension liabilities for many years. Nevertheless, these reforms should reduce the rate at which new liabilities accrue and may reduce employer costs in the near term. The timing of reform impacts will depend on employer demographics and turnover, among other factors (Moody's Investor Service, 2013).

It is imperative that elected officials understand that, irrespective of pension reform measures occurring throughout the country, the continuing increase in the unfunded liability of DB pension plans eventually consumes a larger portion of an annual budget. Balanced budgets, or those with little increase, are important to elected officials, and with a greater portion of a budget allocated to pensions, reductions elsewhere have an impact on services. At a certain point in time the "reduction" of services may change to the "elimination" of services.

Since elected officials hold office for a limited time, and the unfunded liability of a DB pension system grows over a much longer period of time, it is not unusual that the issue of pension reform to other than a DB pension plan is passed on to a successor. This and other political pressures are reasons that there has been an insignificant reduction in DB pension plans in the public sector. Perhaps the only solution to resolving the need for movement from the DB plan occurs when it is necessary to follow Detroit, Michigan; Central Falls, Rhode Island; Stockton, Vallejo, and San Bernardino, California; and other public agencies, into a filing for bankruptcy.

REFERENCES

American Academy of Actuaries, Issue Brief. (February, 2014). Objectives and principles for funding public sector pension plans. Retrieved from www.actuary.org/.../academy-unveils

Anumeha, B. N., Moore, D., & Rendon, A. (2013). Retirement benefits in the public and private sectors: A comparison of trends, regulatory environments, and related issues. Pension Review Board, Research Paper No. 13-002. Retrieved from http://www.texastransparency.org/pension-benefits-in-the-private-and-public-sectors

Atanasov, I. (2014). Why public pension plans are left unfunded. *Public Sector, Inc.* Retrieved from www.publicsectorinc.org/2014/10/why-public-pension-plans-are-left-unfunded

Bidgood, J. (2012). Plan to end bankruptcy in Rhode Island city gains approval. *The New York Times.* Retrieved from http://nyti.ms/NPvVAs

Brownfeld, A. (2014). The unfunded public pensions and corruption that broke Detroit's back. *Communities Digital News.* Retrieved from www.commdiginews/politics.com

CalPERS. (2012). Summary of public employees' pension reform act of 2013 and related changes to the Public Employees' Retirement Law. Retrieved from https://www.calpers.ca.gov/page/employers/policies-and-procedures/pension-reform-

CalPERS, (2015). Facts at a glance. Retrieved from www.calpers.ca.gov

Christensen, L., Bui, T., & Gilroy, L. (2014). Addressing common objections to shifting from defined benefit pensions to defined contribution retirement plans. Reason Foundation. Retrieved from http://reason.org/news/show/pension-reform-defined-contribution.

Cone, T. (2013). Stockton pensions present problem in bankruptcy. Associated Press. Retrieved from http://huffingtonpost.com.san-francisco

Craig, L. (2003). Public sector pensions in the United States. *EH Net*. Retrieved from https://eh.net/encyclopedia/public-sector-pensions-in-the-united-states

Dabney, H., Jr., Danby, P., Egan, D., Levinson, M., South G., III, & Tidmore, E., (2012). *Municipalities in peril: The ABI guide to chapter 9* (2nd ed.) Alexandria, VA. American Bankruptcy Institute.

Davey, M., & Walsh, M., (2013). Billions in debt, Detroit tumbles into insolvency. Retrieved from www.nytimes.com/.../detroit-files-for-bankruptcy.html?_r=0

DeAngelis, M., & Tian, X. (2013). United States: Chapter 9 Municipal Bankruptcy–Utilization, Avoidance, and Impact. American Bankruptcy Institute. Retrieved from http://www.abiworld.org/municipal_bankruptcy_utilization_avoidance_and_impact.pdf

Delisle, E. (2010). Fiscal stress faced by local government. Congressional Budget Office, Economic and Budget Issue Brief. Retrieved from https://www.cbo.gov/sites/files/2-09-municipalities.brief.pdf.mployee

Employee Benefit Research Institute (EBRI). (2007). Retirement trends in the United States over the past quarter-century. Retrieved from www.ebri.org/research/?fa=retirement-

Employee Retirement Income Security Act of 1974 (ERISA), Pub. L. 93-406; 29 U.S.C. Chapter 18 (1974).

Esquivel, P., & Mozingo, J. (2015). San Bernardino's bankruptcy plan favors CalPERS. *Los Angeles Times*. Retrieved from http://www.latimes.com/local/california/la-me-san-bernardino-bankruptcy-20150519-story-html

Jacob, M., (2012). Is bankruptcy the only option? California Public Agency Labor & Employment Blog. Retrieved from http://www.calpublicagencylaboremploymentblog.com/bankruptcy/is-bankruptcy-the-only-option/

Klepper, D. (2013). Not just Detroit's problem: American cities and counties' unfunded liability totals $574 billion. Retrieved from http://www.huffingtonpost.com/detroit

Kramer, D., & Holm, B. (2013). Nebraska's public pension system, repeating our successes will lead us to solvency. Platte Institute for Economic Research. Retrieved from www.platteinstitute.org/.../20130621_Kramer__Pension_Paper.pdf

Maciag, M., (2012). Governing the states and localities. Mapping municipal bankruptcies. Retrieved from www.governing.com-municipal-cities-counties-bankruptcies.

McClain, B., (2013). New study analyzes fiscal health of six major U.S. urban centers. George Mason University. Retrieved from https://newsdesk.gmu.edu/2013/09/new-study-analyzes-fiscal-health-six-major-u-s-urban-centers

Mendel, E., (2009). Bankrupt Vallejo eyes CalPERS. Retrieved from http://calpensions.com

Moody's Investor Service. (June 27, 2013). Adjusted pension liability medians for US states. Retrieved from https://www.moodys.com/adjusted_pension_liability_medians_for_us_states.pdf

Munnell, A., Aubry, J., & Cafarelli, M. (2014). Defined contribution plans in the public sector: An update. Center for Retirement Research at Boston College. Retrieved from www.crr.bc.edu/defined-contribution-plans-in-the-public-sector-an-update

Munnell, A., Haverstick, K., & Soto, M. (2007). Why have defined benefit plans survived in the public sector? Center for Retirement Research at Boston College. Retrieved from crr.bc.edu/content/uploads/2007/12/slp_2.pdf

National Association of State Budget Officers. (2012). Municipal bankruptcy & the role of the states. Retrieved from www.nasbo.org/sites/default/filespdf/Municipal%20%26%20the%

Sanford, P., & Franzel, J., (2012). The evolving role of defined contribution plans in the public sector. National Association of Government Defined Contribution Administrators. Retrieved from www.nagdca.org/the-evolving-role-of-defined-contribution-plans-in-the-public-sector

Snell, R. (2012). State pension reform, 2009–2011. National Conference of State Legislatures (2012). Retrieved from http://www.ncsl.org/research/fiscal-policy/state-pension-reform-2009-2011.aspx

Stefanescu, I., & Vidangos, I. (2014). Introducing actuarial liabilities and funding status of defined-benefit pensions in the U.S. financial accounts. Board of Governors of the Federal Reserve System, FED Notes (October 31, 2014). Retrieved from www.federalreservegov/introducing-actuarial-liabilities-and-funding-status-of-defined-benefit-pensions.

Triest, R., & Zhao, B., (2013). The Role of Economic, Fiscal, and Financial Shocks in the Evolution of Public Sector Pension Funding. Federal Reserve Bank of Boston, Working Paper No. 13-26. Retrieved from http://www.bostonfed.org/economic/wp/wp2013/wp1326.htm

U.S. Census Bureau. (2012). Census Bureau reports there are 89,004 local governments in the United States. Retrieved from https://www.census.gov/govs/cog2012/.

U.S. Department of Labor, Bureau of Labor Statistics. (2013, September). Retirement benefits: Access, participation, and take-up rates, private industry workers. National Compensation Survey, Table 2 (March, 2013). Retrieved from www/bls.gov/ncs/ebs/benefits/2013/ebb/0052.pdf

U.S. Department of Labor, Bureau of Labor Statistics, Union Members Survey (2015, January). Retrieved from http://www.bls.gov/news.release/union2.nr0.htm

VanMetre, B. (2014). Illinois pension debt balloons to $111 billion. *Illinois Policy*. Retrieved from http://illinoispolicy.org/illinois-pension-debt-still-ballooning/

Worgan, K., Lamoureux, D., & Milligan, A., (2012). Actuarial cost analysis California Public Employees' Reform Act of 2013. *CalPERS*. Retrieved from www.calpers.ca.gov/eip-docs/about/pubs/cost-analysis.pdf

Yee, B., (2015). Government financial reports. California State Controller's Office. Retrieved from https://bythenumbers.sco.ca.gov

CHAPTER 5

FEDERAL CHANGE

Difficult But Doable for the Effective Leader

William J. Mea[1]

INTRODUCTION

Americans have the expectation that their government will respond to its citizens' core needs, and when this requires change, that progress will be straightforward. However, in reality, achieving successful transformation and change in government can be exceptionally challenging. Sometimes political or economic conditions have changed; sometimes methods for achieving progress are outdated or obsolete; and sometimes the public's expectations have changed.

The federal government can be trusted to reliably do much good for its citizens. Year in and year out, the government provides essential services without a hitch. Examples include retirees receive their Social Security checks on time, medical support is provided for the poor, and our Nation's security apparatus provides globally-deployed defense forces across all time zones. Despite these benefits, some citizens have grown to expect

Transforming Government Organizations:
Fresh Ideas and Examples From the Field, pp. 153–197
Copyright © 2016 by Information Age Publishing
All rights of reproduction in any form reserved.

instantaneous results from a system that was not designed for speed. This could be anticipated if one's expectations are influenced by the experience of using modern apps on an iPhone or Android to instantly contact a ride, buy a new suit, or find a restaurant. To people unfamiliar with the inner workings of government, political change seems to be stymied by complexity and confounded by process. But our government was designed to be careful and deliberative, with the legislative process being sometimes contentious. Within this context, government leaders need to discern how to manage achieving the art of what is possible.

Chapter Purpose and Focus

This chapter examines why achieving major change and transformation in the public sector is perceived as so difficult. While the public expects the federal government to be able to resolve issues quickly, there are many barriers. The chapter examines how barriers to making rapid change are woven into the fabric of the governing process. It also examines factors that have emerged over time, such as the role of associations as discussed later that make it surprising the government accomplishes as much as it does. In contrast, there are multiple positive case examples of change that show how agencies can achieve positive transformation. These examples will be examined in greater depth later in the chapter. The last section is a discussion of principles and lessons learned that have proved effective for achieving transformation. The chapter also offers ideas as to what can be done to make efforts in the federal sector more effective. By the end of the chapter, the reader will have gained perspective on how to achieve organizational change amidst the context of many challenges.

Approach and Chapter Organization

This chapter explores challenges to transformation, and reviews relevant literature and examples. The author will revisit questions posed in a prior article he wrote with others (Mea, Sims, & Veres, 2000) on public-sector transformation, but with the new intent of creating greater understanding and offering workable solutions. The main questions posed are: "Why is change so difficult in U.S. Federal organizations?", "What are the foundational and constitutional factors that make government so difficult to transform?", and finally, "What are the factors and principles to consider when attempting to implement transformation or change projects?"

The first section sets the stage for an in-depth examination of why achieving change and transformation within government is so arduous.

The foundations of federal government are by their nature a compromise, and the purposes served by our government cannot be as focused nor efficient as those of private-sector companies, because the government serves multiple purposes and stakeholders. Private entities have the bottom line goal of profit, while government is tasked with providing far more diffuse and shifting goals without a singularly clear bottom line. This section will review the constitutional basis and related historical developments that make transformation challenging, thus providing useful background for change practitioners.

The second section discusses other factors that have emerged in government over the course of time that make transformation difficult. Issues such as associations, the Congressional iron triangle, and rent-seeking are some of the topics discussed.

The third section will share some positive examples of government transformation and change projects at both defense and nondefense agencies. The author will explore the nature of successful case examples and what made them successful.

The final section explores some of the key principles that public-sector leaders can apply to make government transformation and change possible. By public-sector leaders we mean staff in federal, state, county, or local municipalities who are in a position to have a positive influence. They could be elected officials, appointees, or career civil servants. A few important themes are elaborated in some detail, and this includes a consideration of the role of information technology as a critical enabler. Another key theme is the importance of correctly measuring change while offering insights into the common errors in misreading change results (Buckley, Mea, Weise, & Carraher, 1998). This final section will also offer a list of lessons learned that can serve as a reference to which change agents can refer in their own efforts to build successful change in their organizations. Some of these lessons could potentially apply to the private sector, but the focus is on helping public sector leaders do better the important work that they already do.

Reexamining the Author's Prior Assessment on Public Sector Transformation

Over a decade ago the author published an article that compared organizational transformation efforts in the public and private sectors (Mea, Sims, & Veres, 2000). This article defined the essential elements for change and provided vignettes from failing and successful projects in both sectors. At the time of publication the author was a "Big Five" management consultant who worked primarily with successful Fortune 1000 companies, but who occasionally was assigned to federal projects. Management consultants of that period typically valued rapid decision making, decisive action, analytical precision, and simplicity—values that drive business profitability and that reflected the most profitable markets. The author noted that government contains significant restrictions on action and noted that a different set of values and skills may be needed to make change achievable within the public sector. Other assumptions, competencies, and wisdom, need to be brought to the table when helping government organizations transform themselves.

Shortly after the 2000 article was published both in English and in French, a French political science professor criticized several of the article's premises. He noted that the authors failed to fully appreciate the benefits of bureaucracy. At the time, the senior author quickly dismissed this observation, but in retrospect appreciates this criticism. One might reasonably argue that it is easy for someone outside of government to criticize it, but once inside a federal organization, one must take ownership for making it better. The author, now an experienced federal program examiner, would agree with the critic's objection that government structures require a greater appreciation of complexity if change is to become possible. Public-sector transformation efforts require a particularly nuanced understanding of the institutional assumptions and challenging circumstances in which progress must take place. These challenges are embedded in the foundation of the way government must conduct its business, and in many respects have evolved over time to provide a system of checks and balances for the system. The challenges are also embedded within the culture that has evolved to cope with emerging issues of governance. This requires a more finely nuanced understanding of change levers, one that looks beneath the surface.

Government and Private Sectors, a Contrast in Style

As a young consultant, the author noted a striking contrast between private-sector firms' leaders and federal managers. With regard to style and decision-making, private sector executives communicated quickly; they were decisive when making decisions, and they focused on the bottom line. Success for private-sector leaders is the result of an entrepreneurial spirit, a diligent climb up the rough and tumble corporate ladder, determination, and sometimes a dose of good luck. Great leaders have a unique combination of cheer and direct no-nonsense focus. They are upbeat, creative, and will fire a consulting firm in a heartbeat if tangible profits are not achieved as a direct outcome of the service.

The federal managers with whom the author met in his early consulting days were also hard working, bright, and dedicated to their agency's missions. But the challenges they faced—decision making, strategy, operations, budgets, Congressional oversight, new legislation and regulations—were often more complex than those faced in the private sector where corporate profitability provides a clear focus. This, in part, explains why it is so difficult for federal leaders to make progress and for change to happen in federal organizations.

To understand the difficulty federal leaders' face when instituting change in their organizations, it is necessary to explain what factors established at America's founding place limits on the way the federal government works. These factors will offer an explanation as to why it is difficult implement change in the federal government organizations. Stated in the terms of questions that might be used by behavioral scientists that study organizational dynamics, what forces limit efficient process and speed of action in government organizations, and what are the forces for and the forces against government change and transformation? The answer in part is due to the way our founders established the form of governing in the U.S. Constitution. Our government was designed from the outset to be deliberative, an attribute that contributes to making government change difficult to achieve.

What Is Meant By Change and Transformation?

When discussing transformation and change in the context of this chapter the author is taking a broad rather than narrow view of these concepts. Transformation is defined in Merriam-Webster.com, 2015) as "a complete or major change in someone's or something's appearance, form, etc." To transform is to "to change something (completely) and usually in a good way" or to "change in character or condition" and synonyms are to alter, convert or revamp. Change is defined (Merriam-Webster.com, n.d.) as "to become different in some particular way" make "radically different" or "to shift" or "undergo a modification." Synonyms included to modify, adjust, or transition.

One might best conceptualize transformation and change as existing on a continuum and as operating at several levels. Transformation implies a radical change. One might visualize these as axes, with transformation and change on a horizontal (x) axis while the size of the institution impacted could be depicted on a vertical (y) axis. For instance, a particular change could impact a region of the globe, a nation, an agency, a particular citizen stakeholder group, or a work group at the lowest level. The case examples that are used later in this chapter cover a broad representation of these, but would generally tend to illustrate major changes that impact a few stakeholder groups.

THE ROLE OF THE NATION STATE AND INHERENT CONSTITUTIONAL CHALLENGES TO RAPID CHANGE

In order to create effective government transformation, one must first understand the proper role of government in the nation state. The founding fathers' view of the state is a social contract between citizens and the government, which provides national security and the essential goods and services that the private sector cannot provide for itself. The Constitution is unique to America's founding. In order to understand what the framers of the Constitution had in mind, one must first understand the proper role of the nation state.

The Nation State

Thomas Hobbes, as cited by Fukuyama (2011), provides a useful, if dark, vision of the state as a social contract that our founders would appreciate:

The basic social "deal" underlying the state (is): in return for giving up the right to do whatever one pleases, the state (or Leviathan) through its monopoly on force guarantees each citizen basic security. The state can provide other kinds of public goods as well, like property rights, roads, currency, uniform weights and measures, and external defense, which citizens cannot obtain on their own. In return, citizens give the state the right to tax, conscript, and otherwise demand things of them (p. 82)

From an anthropological perspective, the nation state, as compared to earlier social units (the family and tribe) is, "by contrast ... coercive, domineering, and hierarchical, which is why Friederich Nietzsche called the state the "coldest of all cold monsters" (Fukuyama, 2011, p. 82). At America's founding, rights were not conferred by a king or parliament but by the Constitution and these are rights "immune to revocation" (Podhoretz, 2012, p. 2).

From a financial standpoint, an effective nation state provides just governance under the rule of law, which provides conditions under which creativity can be fostered. Under these circumstances the collective revenues can be used to improve human capital, build infrastructure, and provide for defense. Some economists, such as Andrew Leith (personal communication, September 12, 2015), would contend that balanced revenues and rule of law foster an environment that leads to technological advancement and an expanding economy.

Mistrust of Corrupting Influences

Our founders purposefully designed conflict into the federal government, through the Constitution, so as to provide checks and balances among the branches of government. In order to ensure that God-given rights were immune to revocation, the founders designed a government that avoided concentrated power because they realized that concentration of power led to corruption. In 1784, in support of a republican form of government, Thomas Jefferson (as cited by Peden, 2000) wrote:

> In every government on earth is some trace of human weakness, some germ of corruption and degeneracy, which cunning will discover, and wickedness insensibly open, cultivate and improve. Every government degenerates when trusted to the rulers of the people alone. The people themselves therefore are its only safe depositories. And to render even them safe, their minds must be improved to a certain degree. (p. 156)

George Washington's words reflected this understanding when writing to John Jay about the flaws of human nature and their impact on the Articles of Confederation. In August of 1798 he wrote:

> We have errors to correct; we have probably had too good an opinion of human nature in forming our confederation. Experience has taught us, that men will not adopt and carry into execution measures the best calculated for their own good, without the intervention of a coercive power. I do not conceive we can exist long as a nation without having lodged somewhere a power, which will pervade the whole Union in as energetic a manner, as the authority of the State Governments extends over the several States. (p. 136)

The three branches of the federal government have functions, defined in the Constitution, that are to some extent overlapping. The result is that each branch constantly vies for dominance and has its own interest and agenda. This creates messiness in the process even during the best of times. The legislature creates laws, but relies on the executive branch to implement them and to faithfully carry them out. For example, the President is Commander-in-Chief, but only the House of Representatives can raise revenues in the form of taxes. James Madison (1788) argued persuasively in Federalist Number 47 that a separation of powers was essential to good governance.

> The accumulation of all powers, legislative, executive, and judiciary in the same hands, whether of one, a few or many, and whether hereditary, self-appointed, or elective, may justly be pronounced the very definition of tyranny. (p. 15)

There is much grousing about the current era's lack of cooperation among the three branches of government. But when a legislative process runs swiftly, as is the case in times of emergency, it can sometimes lead to a lack of full deliberation resulting in poorly vetted statutes with far-reaching, sometimes unintended, consequences. Some have argued that the laws rushed through Congress following 9/11 have led to some of the very issues in privacy that Congress is now trying to remedy.

This lack of concentration of powers can lead to a lack of accountability for failures. President Theodore Roosevelt made an interesting point on how a separation of powers leads to problematic government, in his 1908 State of the Union address when he stated,

> The danger to American democracy lies not in the least in the concentration of administrative power in responsible and accountable hands. It lies in having the power insufficiently concentrated, so that no one can be held responsible to the people for its use. Concentrated power is palpable, visible, responsible, easily reached, quickly held to account. (p. 306)

Roosevelt was arguing, of course, for power in the executive branch that he controlled. At the same time, there is wisdom in this statement because diffused responsibility for successes or failures makes it more difficult for the public to understand who is responsible.

Resourcing the Nation's Needs

Providing and investing resources is done differently in the private and public sectors. In the private sector resourcing is more straightforward. In the federal government, the responsibility for obtaining and deploying capital is shared between the executive and legislative branches. The President can propose a budget, but only Congress can appropriate money, and all appropriations bills must originate in the House of Representatives. Article 1, Section 9 of the Constitution states,

> No Money shall be drawn from the Treasury, but in Consequence of Appropriations made by Law; and a regular Statement and Account of the Receipts and Expenditures of all public Money shall be published from time to time. (Cornell, n.d., p. 536)

The President's capacity for leadership in relationship to Congress depends on his or her reputation, skills in communicating with the public, and ability to successfully build coalitions (Rosati & Scott, 2011, pp. 72–73). Though he or she can veto legislation, it is in his or her best interest to influence laws in advance, as they are being prepared.

There are a number of unique features in the legislative process, ones that are seemingly laborious but absolutely essential to proper representation of "the governed." The key processes involve legislative deliberation on policy as well as oversight of how appropriations are made and laws implemented.

Legislative Deliberation and Parochial Interests

Former Congressman Lee Hamilton, director of the nonpartisan Center for Congress at Indiana University, notes that the public is often frustrated with traditions of the deliberative process—committee work, floor action, amendments, endless debates, voting on changes, and conference committees—that may result in a bill taking years to be approved (Hamilton, 2003).

> The process of deliberation guarantees that their voices are heard and freedom protected. Committees are where members of Congress with different backgrounds, political philosophies and regional outlooks build consensus—in essence, where they make sure that legislation meets the needs of a broad array of Americans.... Committees are also where members and staff use expertise they've developed in particular policy arenas to ask hard questions, consider the merits of proposals and smooth out problems....To a large extent, every stage is designed to allow Congress to explore all aspects of a problem, accommodate different interests, reduce points of friction, and build a consensus in support of a bill. This is how Congress knocks out bad ideas and proposals, and adjusts good ideas to make them better laws. (paras. 3–4)

Hamilton notes, further, that "short-cutting—increasingly the norm on important initiatives in recent years—hurts the quality of legislation, and makes the Congress a less representative body" (paras. 3–4). Alexis de Tocqueville, as cited by Hamilton observed that,

> The electors see their representative not only as a legislator for the state but also as the natural protector of local interests in the legislature; indeed, they almost seem to think that he (or she) has a power of attorney to represent each constituent, and they trust him (or her) to be as eager in their private interests as in those of the country. (de Tocqueville, n.d., para. 1)

The relationship between a Senator or Congressman is similar to the relationship between leaders and the led in earliest forms of governing. According to Francis Fukuyama (2011),

> Tribalism exists (... in) the underlying social relationship between the politi-
> cian and his or her supporters is the same as in a kinship group: it is based
> on a reciprocal exchange of favors between leaders and followers, where
> leadership is won rather than inherited, based on the leader's ability to ad-
> vance the interests of the group. (p. 79)

In other words, the relationship of a citizen to his or her representative is
anthropologically rooted, and like the relationship of a parent to a child.
There is a deeply rooted expectation that the representative advocates for
them rather than the larger nation as a whole. Unlike a family relationship, however, Members of Congress understand that they can be quickly
replaced if they do not serve parochial interests.

The Benefit of Argumentation

One of the unsettling features of the legislative process is the bickering
that accompanies legislative argumentation, but there is a great benefit
in this seemingly futile process. Currently the situation is better than was
the case in some earlier Congresses, such as when in 1856 Congressman
Preston Brooks caned Senator Charles Sumner into unconsciousness.

> The fact is, it is very difficult to get agreement among a broad cross-section
> of Americans on major political issues. Most years there is little agreement
> on what the main issues are, let alone what specific steps should be taken to
> address them. ... Most bills passed by Congress actually receive fairly broad,
> bipartisan support. Yet dispute and delay often occur because it's a tough
> and tedious job making policy for a country of this vast size and remarkable
> diversity.... It's the job of the House and Senate to give the various sides
> a chance to be heard and to search for a broadly acceptable consensus....
> There is bound to be bickering when you bring together 435 Representatives
> and 100 Senators, all duly elected to Congress—all of whom feel strongly
> about issues and want to push their views and represent the best interests of
> their constituents. (Hamilton, 2003, pp. 1–2)

Providing a forum for strongly held opinions in an environment of intense
debate ensures that differences are surfaced and that all sides have a chance
to present the interests of their stakeholders. To some, watching Congress
on C-SPAN looks like a baroque form of road rage. They might wish that
an all-wise leader or small group would make a decision and move on to the
next agenda item. However, that is precisely how decisions are made in an
autocracy. Dispute is not dysfunction and the spirited conflict of democracy
ensures that difficult issues are fully aired.

Benefits of Congressional Oversight

Another feature of our legislative process designed by our founding fathers is Congressional oversight that, although burdensome, is a process that provides for important checks and balances. This oversight is a frequent source of conflict between the executive and legislative branches that leads to what may appear on the surface to be inefficiencies. In the private sector there would be no perfectly corresponding function, although chief financial officers, corporate boards, and auditors might have somewhat corresponding roles. While the President has significant discretion in carrying out federal policies through the bureaucracy of his or her cabinet agencies, Congress retains oversight. Congress can hold hearings, fail to approve nominations, prescribe reports, and direct constraints on the use of funds. Former Congressman Lee Hamilton remarks,

> There is a world of meaning to be read into Senator Warner's passing reference to Congress as "a co-equal branch of government." ... The White House, Pentagon and executive agencies are not the only shapers of official U.S. policies and activities. Congress—the people's branch of government —has not just the right, but the duty, to be at the table as well. It especially has both the right and the duty to be the body asking those hard questions.... Good congressional oversight is fundamental to our democracy. At its best, it helps Congress - and, through it, the American people—evaluate how well our government and its representatives, whether they're soldiers or bureaucrats, are performing. It can ferret out malfeasance, compel executive-branch policy-makers to explain their policies and substantiate the reasoning that underlies them, and ensure that our federal government is truly acting in the best interests of the nation. Done well, oversight protects the country from bureaucratic arrogance, prevents misconduct, and gives voters the information they need to judge the activities of an administration. (Hamilton, 2004)

Congressional oversight of the executive branch is a necessary, but sometimes a burdensome process.

OTHER STRUCTURAL FACTORS THAT MAKE GOVERNMENT TRANSFORMATION DIFFICULT

Political forces have shaped the government process in ways that the founders might not have expected. Normative political theory tries to explain how the policy process should behave in ideal terms, helping explain what ought to be. Although theoretically true, in reality there are many outside factors and influences on public policy that do not hold to the ideal. Positive political theory explains what happens in the real world and it helps make predictions about what might happen in reality. It explains the motivations and interests of the actors in a real world.

The Role of Associations

The first such factor in real world politics is the influence and participation of associations in the public policy process. Associations form out of the need to give a louder voice to specific interest groups. Examples include grassroots groups, coalitions, business and trade associations, and lobbyists. In the ideal society, one assumes that people form groups to represent their respective interest without negatively affecting the interests of others. In reality, interests often conflict. Alexis de Tocqueville praised Americans' fluid association forming when he observed that,

> Americans of all ages, all stations of life, and all types of disposition are forever forming associations.... In democratic countries knowledge of how to combine is the mother of all other forms of knowledge; on its progress depends that of all the others. (de Tocqueville, 1835, p. 350)

One might assume that public officials benevolently carry out the will of the people (Shugart, n.d.), but the conflicting voice of people banding together in competing associations make it challenging. The founders wanted people to have a voice, and associations provide this, but this has been achieved in a conflict-ridden way that the founders might not have fully anticipated.

Public Choice. Public choice is a term for applying economic method and theory to political behavior. But, according to author William Shugart, the reality of this is more complicated (Shugart, n.d.). People in groups act as individuals, and public officials act out of their own parochial economic interest. Individuals are driven by utility maximization and come together in groups to serve their self-interests. They are driven by their pocketbooks, and if they can, will get the broad public to pay for a public good that disproportionately benefits them, working with their legislative representative to advocate for that public good. Because interests tend to be geographically based, legislators team with others to achieve their narrow objectives. These narrow objectives fall under three broad categories: rent-seeking, logrolling, and iron triangles.

Rent-Seeking. Rent-seeking is a term coined by the economist David Ricardo (as cited by Shugart) defined as, "the payment to a factor in excess of what is required to keep that factor in its present use" (Shugart, n.d., p. 2). "Privilege seeking" might be a more apt term to describe expenditures to seek legislative privileges, but the aggregate cost of seeking these gains is inefficient. It not only results in a transfer of resources, but also adds to loss in the economy.

Logrolling. Logrolling is an example of cooperative rent-seeking in which legislators exchange favors with their colleagues by voting for a narrower interest in exchange for later favoring a bill that favors their constituents. Somewhat surprising and counterintuitive to logic, smaller and more homogenous groups can work more effectively in concert than can larger and more diffuse interest groups. The joint benefit at the intersection of corn farmers and the ethanol manufacturers comes quickly to mind. Somewhat surprisingly, Angora goat farmers carved out a subsidy for mohair in World War II and have continued to receive special subsidies even though military uniforms are no longer made from mohair. They continue to be a small and dedicated constituency with an outsized impact (Ip, 2013). If these were the only examples, it would not be a problem. In aggregate, the impact of many small groups' subsidies is large. The net result is to raise the cost of all products and services for the populace at large. It creates a burdensome distortion of the market and a drag on efficient government. There are numerous forces arrayed against making positive changes within government, and these forces make any transformative effort difficult to achieve.

Iron Triangles. Paul Johnson of Auburn University described the relationships in government as being "iron triangles" (Johnson, n.d.). The three sides of the iron triangle are Congress, interest groups, and the bureaucracy. An iron triangle forms when a group lobbies specific legislative committees with jurisdiction over a special issue or function. Executive branch bureaucrats with specific expertise do whatever they can to support such programs. The lobbies may have significant resources that they use to fund research and mobilize public opinion and opinion makers. Lobbyists can serve a useful function in providing legislators with expertise and depth on an issue, but sometimes the iron triangle works at odds with the executive branch interests. The Defense Base Closure and Realignment Commission (BRAC) was one effort to avert these problems. According to Shugart, bureaucracies naturally conform to the desires of the committees who oversee their area of public policy because they control the budget and can prescribe additional reports and constraints (Shugart, n.d.). Rather than being forces for transformation, the committees and the bureaucracies have a shared interest in continuation of the *status quo* – elected officials to return to office, and agency personnel to influence their programs and future agenda.

Regulations. Regulations are a necessary part of the public policy process. Regulations are developed in a process by which an administration creates more detailed instructions to implement laws that Congress passes.

There is always a period for public comment before regulations go into effect, giving the public and interest groups an opportunity to submit input with regard to a proposed regulation. In a retrospective view on problems with regulation, Dr. Bruce Yandle (1999) described how interests groups promoting laudable public policy sometimes team with narrow interests to starve out competition in the marketplace. In Yandle's example, he noted how religious groups teamed with bootleggers to limit alcohol sales on Sundays. In Yandle's theory of bootleggers and Baptists, bootleggers worked behind the scenes to limit alcohol, not for the purpose of limiting consumption, but to limit competition and to get religious groups to strictly enforce regulations. The same principles can be applied in other areas of regulation, such as ethanol content in gasoline, prescription drugs, environmental protection, and technological performance standards. In each of the areas noted, values-focused groups can team with industries that have an interest in locking out competition and bureaucrats who have an interest in developing ever-stricter regulations that ensure their control.

Other Influences & Constraints

In addition to the more overarching general influences of associations noted in the prior section, one can identify a host of specific influences on policy and programs that are often outside the influence of an administration. The impact of these sources is often unclear to most citizens, but they are strong influencers nevertheless.

Think Tanks. Even with an avalanche of available information, there are limits to the depth of analysis that elected officials and bureaucrats can achieve. Think tanks fill that gap by providing analysis and advice from private entities in specialized areas of expertise. They have gained "prominence (for research and analysis) due to the institutions' demonstrated efficiency, independence, relevance, and access to key government officials" (McGann, 2010, p. 41). In the process though, agencies sometimes privatize expertise, purchasing services from contractors, and thus they surrender command of this expertise.

Business Groups, Monied Elites, and Foundations. There is some evidence in empirical studies that organized business groups and monied elites have a separate but outsized impact on policymaking. By comparison to mass citizen groups and coalitions as well as average citizens, they employ different avenues of influencing policy. Their ability to work through opinion-shaping institutions, such as foundations, think tanks, the press, lobbies, and political campaigns contributes to their potential to dominate the agenda accepted for legislative consideration (Gilens & Page, 2014, p. 566). It does not remove the capacity of ordinary citizens to make an impact. However, average citizens' may only benefit when they share the same position as "the economically-elite citizens who wield the actual influence" (Gilens & Page, 2014, p. 576).

In summary, there have been many developments over the course of the nation's experience that complicate the environment in which leaders must institute change. Federalist paper Number 51 anticipated this difficulty:

> In framing a government which is to be administered by men over men, the great difficulty lies in this: you must first enable the government to control the governed; and in the next place oblige it to control itself. (Madison, 1787, para. 4, p. 322)

Regardless of the complexities, this chapter will show in the next section that effective leaders make change possible. The public expects more and deserves more from its government.

CASE EXAMPLES OF EFFECTIVE PUBLIC-SECTOR TRANSFORMATION

Having reviewed factors that make it difficult for new and transformative government initiatives, this chapter now turns its attention to a few positive examples of public-sector transformation and change projects. The author has relied on his experience, interviews with public-sector consulting executives, and historical cases as his sources. Some of these examples demonstrate major transformations in government; others represent smaller examples of change management victories. All demonstrate that, despite the many obstacles to effective government, changes that serve the public are possible with the right combination of leadership and willingness to serve the public. Just a few illustrative cases are provided, though many more exist than might be presumed from news headlines. Within this section, each case example will describe the challenge, what happened, the elements that made it successful, and what was unique about the case.

The case examples used in this section cover a broad representation of transformation and change, but they generally tend to illustrate major changes that impact a few stakeholder groups or specific projects in the government. Some, on the other hand, are broad sweeping. The section begins with a legislative case example that resulted in broad transformational changes for the Department of Defense (DOD). It is important to point out that these examples could all be considered change successes, but at different levels of change. Moreover, there are many successes in federal government operations and results that do not get wide attention in the media.

Defense-Related Case Examples

Goldwater-Nichols. Failings in military logistics in the 20th century exposed weaknesses in the way the Services' coordinated with each other. The Goldwater-Nichols DOD Reorganization Act of 1986 (P.L. 99-433), commonly referred to as simply "Goldwater-Nichols," led to one of the most positive and monumental government transformations. As historical context leading up to the act, America experienced many difficulties throughout its history due to Defense organizational coordinating challenges. The Spanish-American War highlighted logistics coordination difficulties between the Army and the Navy, two Services with different cultures and ways of operating. During World War II, significant difficulties were encountered in coordinating seaborne, land, and air activities across the military services. Logistics were poor and the nation struggled to synchronize purchasing, transportation, and maintenance.

President Roosevelt created the Joint Chiefs of Staff in 1942 to help overcome the difficulties evident in logistics, procurement, construction, and transportation (Locher, 2001). However, the system still required consensus operational decisions from services that worked independently of each other (Locher, 2002) (Lederman, 1999). The Navy embraced independent action and decentralized command decisions, a system consistent with millennia of small-deployed units operating at sea far from the nation (Locher, 2001). The Army embraced centralized action and decision-making, a system consistent with doctrine for land-based operations of ground forces that often required a mobilization and training buildup prior to deployment. Later events exposed more extensive flaws in coordination. Interservice rivalry in Vietnam and later in the Iranian hostage rescue demonstrated the need for sweeping changes to make the DOD's structure more responsive. A number of Congressional voices from both parties and Reagan-era influential think tanks (such as the Center for Strategic and International Studies and Heritage Foundation) called for major re-organization (Lederman, 1999, p. 69). Many senior military personnel objected to a call for major reorganization, but the forceful voice of support from Admiral William Crowe (Chairman of the Joint Chiefs of Staff from 1985 to 1989) helped override the forces against jointness and clear chain-of-command (Locher, 2002, p. 209).

The passage of Goldwater-Nichols in 1986 instituted dramatic changes in the way that the services interact. The operational chain of command was unified, streamlining the chain of command from the President to Secretary of Defense to combatant commanders. It clarified that combatant commanders were responsible for operations in their geographic regions as well as the supporting role of each service. Each service was to organize, train, and equip its members and provide forces to regional commanders who conducted operational planning. From an organizing standpoint, the Act forced military services to participate in joint commands and education. From a cost perspective, the Act forced the services to integrate development of technology and purchasing.

By the time of Operation Desert Storm, the Act's benefits were well demonstrated in the overwhelming success and coordination in that short war. According to William Campbell (personal communication, June, 12, 2015. 2015) one of the chief benefits was that combatant commanders now had true operational control of area forces. They were given the supporting resources they needed to carry out their operations. James Locher (2002), who served on the Senate Armed Services Committee and played a key role in drafting the Act, pointed out that, "The overarching objective ... as it was ultimately formulated was to balance joint and service interests" (Locher, 2001, p. 105). It strengthened civilian authority while improving military advice to the President, improved joint officer training and assignments, and increased the attention needed to formulate strategy and planning contingencies. The most important outcome was to create clear roles—unified command and responsibility for successfully carrying out military missions. According to Locher (2001), Les Aspin (former Congressman and later Secretary of Defense under President Clinton) called Goldwater-Nichols "one of the landmark laws of American history ... probably the greatest sea change on the history of the American military since the Continental Congress created the Continental Army in 1775" (Aspin, 1986, as cited in Locher, 2001, p. 108). The Act has not been without its critics since joint staffs have become bloated and the procurement process often has had difficulty fielding low-cost and highly technical weapons as fast as they are needed (Anderson, 2012). One of the challenges that resulted from the Act has been the tendency for more requests for forces than the Services can reliably supply (Campbell, personal communications, June, 12, 2015). However, the Act has influenced many of the achievements made possible and helped generate the world's most powerful and integrated military force.

The challenge of DOD reorganization and the transformation made possible by Goldwater-Nichols demonstrate that resistance to change may be the greatest obstacle, even in the face of deadly coordination failures. Working across party lines was possible in this situation; but internal support for the change was made possible in no small part by the efforts of a few military leaders who were willing to help shift the Service culture from interservice rivalry to serving a higher purpose.

DOD Auditability. Beginning in the early 2000s, successive Secretaries of Defense and DOD Comptrollers have been working, with some positive successes, to transform the way business is conducted by ensuring that the financial statements are auditable. It is difficult to contemplate how any

U.S. company could survive without a clean audit. Shareholders need to know that a going concern has represented its financial statements in an accurate manner, and that the statements tell the public about the quality of management and operations. It would be even more difficult to imagine a private firm saying that it could not undergo an audit, but unfortunately that is the case for the Department of Defense. The Department not only does not have a clean financial audit opinion; it does not at present have the full capacity to conduct an audit.

While DOD's leadership, management, and staff are reliably carrying out their missions in an effective manner, the absence of an audit opinion undermines the confidence the public deserves to have in DOD's financial representation. After all, the Department is responsible for the expenditure of half of the discretionary budget. Given that Defense conducts operations across the world, in all time zones and on every continent, it is not surprising that accounting for all expenditures would be a challenge, but the public deserves to have confidence in the way that the Department spends its money, ensuring that it is efficient and effective in carrying out its mission.

Given that DOD auditability is perhaps the most gargantuan financial accounting challenge in history, there is hope from the author's perspective. Successive Secretaries of Defense have affirmed that the Department will be in a position to conduct a full audit of all its financial statements, which is now expected by September, 2017 (DOD Comptroller, 2015). A significant milestone was reached by the Department when in December 2014; it engaged with three accounting firms to conduct audits, thus signaling a shift from auditability alone to going under an audit for Schedules of Budgetary Resources (SBR) (DOD Financial Improvement & Audit Readiness (FIAR) Plan, n.d., p. 9). In addition, DOD leadership has been working to ensure that there is a link between more accurate financial data and performance outcomes such as readiness.

Throughout the history of the Department, its focus has been on executing effective operations and getting resources to troops. Accounting for and tracking each dollar's accounting transactions has been a concern but less of a focus. Shifting the concerns to a greater focus on financial accountability involves a cultural shift, a change management challenge that commanders are now fully absorbing. The responsibility resides not just with the Department's 53,000 financial management personnel, but also with others who support the troops to strengthen their "internal control, processes, and financial systems" (McCord, n.d.). Given that the military services will each subject their schedules of budgetary resources (a type of financial statement) to an audit, signals that "an important culture change is underway, requiring both military and civilian personnel across

the Department to learn and understand the business of being audited"
(DOD Financial Improvement & Audit Readiness Plan, n.d., p. 9).

DOD's plan for achieving auditability, in existence since the early 2000s, is a monumental challenge calling for transformational behaviors at every level of the organization. One of the most important lessons of the experience thus far has been to strike the balance between a sense of urgency to gain momentum, while at the same time discovering what needs to be done. A common metaphor used is driving a high-speed racecar while trying to repair the tires. It has been difficult to strike the balance of the need to create urgency and cultural ownership while at the same time discovering issues and focusing energy on the appropriate priorities. Despite the many challenges, it appears that momentum has been building through the four Secretaries of Defense (Sec Def) who have committed to achieving an audit for the Department. It would be unimaginable for a corporation even one thousandth the size DOD to survive without auditable financial statements. Making steady progress toward achieving an audit should help the public have more confidence that tax revenues are being spent effectively. Just as is the case with major changes for private sector organizations, the visible involvement of top leadership is an essential ingredient for success.

Civilian Expeditionary Workforce. Early on during operations in Operation Iraqi Freedom and Operation Enduring Freedom, the military began to rely more on civilians in theaters of war to support direct operations. As the need grew in the mid-2000s, the DOD began to experience significant challenges providing resources and developed its Civilian Expeditionary Workforce (CEW), a trained and ready cadre of civilians to fill roles in the theater of conflict. The program was initially challenged, but after reengineering was employed, there was a successful change.

When people are involved in building a new process under highly pressured circumstances, especially in the public sector, it is sometimes hard to see the big picture. It can become disheartening to the staff participants. While a critical mission at the outset may inspire them, they may lose momentum when they run into challenging obstacles. Such was the case for the CEW program office. It was hard to create an organization while the CEW was simultaneously expected to execute a mission. The project management office struggled to provide qualified and capable personnel at a time of high operational tempo, working with four military services at the same time, all of whom had their own cultures, different ways of conducting business, and different methods that worked for them. According to Lyn McGee (personal communications, May 6, 2015), the Army in particular had already developed a great deal of expertise, but relying on a new centralized function was a difficult adjustment.

Sometimes the solution to resolving a vexing problem in government is a matter of taking a step back to see the big picture, in order to understand how culture plays a key role in influencing the breakdowns or inefficiencies. The DOD CEW in 2009 needed to quickly recruit and get boots on the ground for work in Iraq and Afghanistan, but they experienced unexpected and vexing delays that undermined critical theater support to troops. Each request for a civilian position was handled sequentially even if ones that entered the system later were of a higher priority or had more complex requirements. The central program office struggled to fulfill a variety of needs using processes adopted from the different services, but sometimes the steps were neither efficient nor effective. This serial approach led to delays in resourcing high-priority needs as the office was "trying to be fair" to all requests.

A key challenge of this project was the definition of key performance indicators and the way they were measured. One key metric—time to fill open positions—created two challenges. The first was that the program office was getting "beaten up" for long "average" hiring intervals for open positions. This was caused by averaging across all open positions—a brain surgeon position taking 180 days to fill was averaged with a supply clerk that took 20 days to fill. The second challenge, and far more damaging to the program, was the impact on resources of trying to solve the wrong problem. An across the board focus on applying more pressure to the screening and placement processes was not going to make a significant difference. Performing a volatility analysis that combined time to hire with position criticality allowed the program office to focus resources on the key, hard-to-fill positions.

DOD engaged an organizational consulting firm to apply system tools to improve the throughput, but a closer inspection revealed that a "compliance-focused culture" had made the process more complex than was really needed. The program office was attempting to fulfill the needs of each service with the processes defined by each service, and in a serial fashion.

The consulting partner helped to define predeployment policies and to redesign operational tools used to support predeployment activities (e.g., posting, selection, medical screening, training, and family support). The team took an agnostic approach as to what worked best and mapped the entire predeployment process from beginning to end. These process maps were used to identify and reduce redundancies and eliminate steps that were not truly essential. A project team paired with a CEW Integrated Process Team (IPT) to identify problematic steps in the process. It then developed actions to resolve the problems.

Solutions included the development of "functional" predeployment sub-teams where an individual CEW processor was responsible for one subset of the process (such as passport processing or medical requirements tracking). As a result of this effort, DOD increased the throughput for recruitment, selection, predeployment, and eventual deployment of CEW personnel—a 76% increase in 6 months.

The lessons to be learned in this case are multiple. First, despite a "burning platform" need to perform, where highly dedicated people are applying their best efforts, it is often difficult to see the forest through the trees. Second, a culture of compliance with well-established and customized processes is apt to get in the way of revealing the underlying problem, no matter how great the effort to overcome the obstacles. Third, sometimes an outside perspective is needed to strip away processes that are unnecessary and to work with an agency to develop processes that meets the true needs.

Fallujah Water District. In 2008, the Government of Iraq was challenged to convince al Anbar residents that it was capable of taking care of the needs of all Iraqis. A skillful Texas civilian showed how cultural understanding made the difference in an important water project.

There are many examples of transformational success in al Anbar Province that demonstrate the value of shared cultural understanding when embarking on a major change. U.S. State Department representatives in cooperation with the U.S. Marine Corps and its embedded Navy medical assets employed sometimes-unorthodox tactics in a winning alliance with local authorities.

In 2008, Fallujah's water distribution system was degraded and failing. The local populace needed reliable and safe water distribution, an essential service for creating confidence in the central government. This particular issue took place while the author was serving as an officer in charge of a small Marine medical unit in Iraq and who was peripherally involved in discussions with the local health ministry. The Fallujah Water Minister, a jovial and engaging engineer, having a sense of U.S. military customs and market-based approaches, brought a PowerPoint proposal to a key decision meeting to request American funding. The proposal provided what appeared to be a reasonable cost, deliverables, and milestones that would set up plants at districts throughout the city. It seemed from the author's perspective to make sense that decentralized processing would be more cost effective, engage neighborhoods in ownership, and provide redundancy in cases of individual plant failures. The U.S. State Department lead for the project (a member of the Provincial Reconstruction Team on loan from the City of Austin, Texas), however, said in a very low-key manner that there were a few things that would need to change. As a former consultant, the author advised the lead to waste no more time and to instruct the Iraqi's to develop a proposal that met the technical requirements by next week. The State Department representative said, "That would make sense in the U.S. private sector; watch what I do and back me up" (author's personal experience).

The lead surprisingly kept asking questions—for 3 hours. During a break in discussions, the State Department representative explained some complexities of Iraqi governance to the author. Failures of Iraqi central governance and providing basic infrastructure had fanned the flames of animosity (some tribally-based) between local districts. The State Department representative was keenly in tune with the nuances of Iraqi culture and saw the bigger picture. He understood that the objective of the project was not to deliver water in an efficient and low-cost fashion but to hold the central government responsible to the public at large. If water was treated and delivered from one central location, the government would be forced into a position in which it could not fail. Different constituencies would never have faith in the central government if the government had a way to squeeze out of its basic obligations. The populace would hold the central ministry responsible and there would be no avoiding the needs of people, even those in districts with tribes out of favor.

The solution Fallujans and the Iraqi government needed was to build and maintain a reliable central distribution from one plant. For the next three hours (including numerous sociable cigar breaks) the State Department representative asked questions of the water Minister in a friendly way that permitted the Iraqi official to propose a revised solution—one that would commit the central authority to consistent delivery to all neighborhoods and would communicate that the central government was reliable and serving all citizens. It would create the perception that the central government was interested in their welfare. This case lesson demonstrated a principle, regardless of the country, that when working with public-sector personnel it is critical to understand the assumptions of the culture. Cutting to the chase may be effective in most business circumstances where the endpoint is known. However, a wise leader in government must also have a sense of the endgame, and he or she must work within the framework of that particular agency's culture, providing as much time as is needed to work out a plan with which all will agree.

Veterans Benefits Administration. Under the leadership of Assistant Secretary Hickey since 2011, the Veterans Benefits Administration (VBA) has been embarked on a successful large-scale agency change effort to improve the way VA processes veteran disability benefits. Despite the good work that is being done every day to serve the public and meet an agency's mission there has been no shortage of dispiriting stories, especially to this author, who worked treating patients at a Veterans Affairs medical center for 3 years. Good news does not make for flashy front-page news. There is hope, however, as demonstrated by the tremendous progress that the Department of Veterans Affairs (VA) has made in processing veterans' disability compensation claims.

The VA had been trying for over a decade to reform its outdated paper-based disability claims processing process, one that required some veterans to wait lengthy periods to receive compensation. Veterans are entitled, by law, to make a claim for disability compensation in cases where they were injured in service or developed a lingering illness whose underlying conditions presumptively occurred while in military service. Not surprisingly, due to recent wars, new presumptive conditions (such as Agent Orange), and VA outreach to veterans, claims had increased, as did an accompanying backlog. The problem was placed on the General Accountability Office's High Risk List as one of the federal government's major management problems (Stofko, personal communication, May 8, 2015; VBA, n.d.).

Allison Hickey, a retired Air Force Brigadier General, has led the Veterans Benefits Administration (VBA) in an effort to transform the organization in a way that demonstrates a real commitment to veterans, along with the capacity to resolve a vexing problem within a federal bureaucracy. New to President Obama's Administration in June 2011, she committed to deploying the right resources, engaging with stakeholders, and employing modern technology to reduce the late backlog (over 125 days) and increase the accuracy of evaluations by 2015.

The VA had been processing claims at 56 regional offices throughout the U.S. and Manila (in the Philippines) using paper claim forms that were often misplaced or misdirected when a veteran moved to a new location and files were mailed between offices. Rather than relying on a few specialists to solve the problem, the VA engaged a wide group of stakeholders to solicit ideas to resolve the issues—including employees, veteran service organizations, and Congressional staff. As a result of this discovery process, the VA implemented digital claims processing and encouraged digital claim filing and the inclusion of all private records at the time of filing to allow quick and easy access, regardless of processing location. In terms of process, the VBA developed standardized procedures for examining the files for claim determination and instituted rules-based calculations. The process is being standardized across all locations, accompanied by standardization and improvement in employee training. However, the process can still be customized for the most complex or simplest claims, for veterans having more acute financial or medical problems or those which can easily processed through a more streamlined work flow.

As a result, the backlog was decreased from 611,073 in FY 2014, to fewer than 125,000 in 2015, and is expected to be effectively eliminated by the end of this year. Most significantly, General Hickey demonstrated that it was possible in a legacy organization, to rally people around a worthy mission to serve veterans (Stofko, personal communication, May 8, 2015).

There are a number of lessons to be learned from this case example. First, even in the face of what appears to be an intractable process problem that appears to be getting more problematic, it is possible to reverse the tide. Second, process redesign and technology applied effectively in a coordinated effort can strip the barnacled ship of decades of encrusted inefficiency and bureaucratic process. Third, an energetic leader who stays calmly positive about the future, in spite of the many difficulties, has a way of inspiring a dispirited workforce.

Nondefense Examples

The following section covers nondefense case study examples. Although there are fewer examples, but this reflects practical limitations of space without diminishing the lessons to be drawn.

Occupational Safety and Health Administration Compliance. Challenges to worker safety led to creative thinking in the Clinton administration, and an Occupational Safety and Health Administration (OSHA) program for workplace safety training led to a change in the way the agency works with employers and reduced injuries and illnesses. Amidst the rush to serve the public interest the work of an agency can sometimes overtake the underlying purpose for which it was established in the first place. Created in 1970 by President Nixon, the OSHA is mandated to help establish standards and protect the nation's one hundred plus million workers. Over its first two decades, the agency began to develop a reputation for a culture that rewarded its workers for racking up enforcement actions over its core mission, ensuring safe working conditions. Clinton Administration Assistant Secretary, Joseph Dear, reported to Congress that employers were complaining bitterly that OSHA was less concerned about worker safety than it was about "inflexible punishment" (Syverson, 2003). Dear initiated the idea of working with company safety committees, trade associations, and expert safety consultants to shift the culture from a focus on punishment to one focused on safety enhancement.

The concept of working with stakeholders was expanded in the next administration under Assistant Secretary John Henshaw, and later under Assistant Secretary Ed Foulke, both with whom the author worked while he served at the Department of Labor in the early 2000s. Henshaw enhanced the decades old OSHA Voluntary Protection Program (VPP), an effort to recognize best-in-class companies for their workforce safety culture and records. By 2003 the program implementation was resulting in a 52% lower rate of lost workday incidents from the 2001 baseline as a result of extending and expanding the Clinton-era partnership model. This model, which had begun with Vice President's Gore's "reinventing government" plan gave OSHA officials a new opportunity to communicate with employers, the public, and interest groups.

The VPP program was incorporated as a core feature within OSHA's 2003 Five-Year Strategic Plan amidst the Department of Labor's initiative to streamline OSHA's structure. This burning platform to save costs and streamline effort providentially became the mechanism for making a transformation possible. OSHA continued to execute strict enforcement mechanisms, but within the new approach employers were given a week to resolve a complaint and an illegal condition was eliminated. In addition to inspections, OSHA staff focused more on compliance assistance that trained employers to focus on doing the right thing from the beginning. In addition to enforcement inspections, a new focus was to reach more employers and industry groups through outreach and training. While the enforcement mechanisms remained and were by no means diminished, the nonenforcement programs reached a larger stakeholder network. Compliance assistance ramped up during this period as did OSHA's use of data for enforcement.

A core feature of the strategic plan was to focus on performance metrics. Both Henshaw and Foulke were strong proponents of employing a balanced set of metrics to focus the organization and employees on measuring and tracking progress toward goals. Henshaw, as quoted in Syverson (2003, para. 19) stated,

> We have to stay focused and on target. We have to be results oriented, not activities oriented. We have to measure how effective we are on an ongoing basis, so we can fine tune our process to get the maximum impact for the resources we have, then evaluate how we've done.

Government organizations are often criticized for focusing on process instead of results. Given that agencies receive criticism in the press from Congress in its oversight role and General Accountability Office reports, it is not surprising that agency leaders would feel stretched. Having a core set of integrated metrics helps the agency focus on the most meaningful things instead of losing focus. In this case, improving the bottom line of worker safety served as a unifying goal.

This case demonstrates a number of attributes in a change program which federal leaders can employ to overcome the forces against change, helping to transform the organization in a way that better serves the public and engages employees. In this OSHA example, the agency leadership carried over a promising program from the previous administration. Where politics might make it easier to scrap the program and focus on something entirely indifferent, it was instead enhanced. A second feature of this agency program was that its leaders shifted the focus from punishment to education and training in order to meet the core mission. A final feature, and a lesson for other leaders attempting to change the organization, is that they used a strategic plan with a set of integrated metrics on which they focused to increase worker safety.

President's Emergency Plan for AIDS Relief. The President's Emergency Plan for AIDS Relief (PEPFAR) program, a large-scale health intervention, has helped the U.S. make transformative positive impacts since its beginning in 2003. Our nation often rises to a level of extraordinary leadership in the face of international crises to devastated regions, sometimes taking an approach that employs a fresh start and creates a federal program that is effective for international aid. Such was the case with the Marshall Plan in Europe following World War II, and more recently with the President's Emergency Plan for AIDS Relief. PEPFAR was codified in the "United States Leadership Against HIV/AIDS, Tuberculosis, and Malaria Act of 2003" (P.L. 108-25).

In the early part of this century, acquired immune deficiency syndrome (AIDS) was a devastating illness, killing multitudes in sub-Saharan Africa and undermining their economies. Congress initially passed a 5-year, $15 billion authorization, to fight this destabilizing pandemic. The PEPFAR program was started in May 2003 to control AIDS in Africa and the Caribbean. Beginning with an organization unencumbered with typical bureaucratic processes, PEPFAR set up treatment sites, testing and counseling centers, low-cost purchasing of antiretroviral drugs, supply chains for treatment, and educational outreach to prevent the transmission of human immunodeficiency virus (HIV). The U.S. Global AIDS Coordinator and Special Representative for Global Health Diplomacy is a Presidentially-appointed and Senate-confirmed position to coordinate and oversee America's global response. The PEPFAR Coordinator was given strong foreign assistance authorities in the implementing legislation. The legislation gave the Coordinator full authority over strategic planning, program planning, and budgets of agencies responsible for international HIV and AIDS relief (PEPFAR, n.d.). This brought an unprecedented measure of enforceable coherence to the global HIV and AIDS response (Ash, 2015).

As has been the case in other successful programs, there was a clear focus on integrated metrics and achieving demonstrable outcomes. According to Nazanin Ash (2015) at the Center for Global Development, the President's Emergency Plan for AIDS Relief program had specific, measurable, time-bound goals built into the program from the outset in the authorizing legislation. This gave leadership the parameters within which to make the difficult choices. If a specific program proved direct quantifiable treatment results, care, or prevention outcomes, it was supported. If not, it was eliminated. Consistent with a theme of focusing on metrics, PEPFAR launched what is still one of the deepest and broadest international aid data collection efforts, assessing the performance of every partner/grant recipient/country program and aggressively managing for results. Since the program leadership had concrete information available with which to explain why deviations from the original PEPFAR strategy would compromise the goals agreed to in the original legislation, the Coordinator was able to work constructively with Congress to maintain the focus (Ash, 2015).

As a result of this program, millions of people have been treated, orphans have received care, and infants have been saved from infection (CRS, n.d.). Most importantly, people with AIDS can live productive lives and a generation in sub-Saharan Africa has been saved from death. After a decade since its initiation, Amanda Glassman and Jenny Ottendorf (2013, para. 5) remarked:

> PEPFAR has helped changed the equation on what was once—not too long ago—seen as an insurmountable plague. This is evident from looking at the change in treatment coverage over the last decade alone ... since PEPFAR was created in 2003. (p. 1)

In keeping with the Obama Administration's goals of sustainable development and building country capacity, PEPFAR has evolved to the next phase, helping countries build ownership of their long-term response. Congress has reauthorized the program (CRS, n.d.) in the "PEPFAR Stewardship and Oversight Act of 2013" (P.L. 113-56), which extended many of the existing authorities and strengthened program oversight through updated reporting requirements (Kaiser Foundation, 2014).

What are the key lessons of PEPFAR from a transformation change management standpoint? The original legislation must be simple, providing clear goals and overarching authority for a program coordinator. In the case of PEPFAR, a key principle for guiding its success was using scientifically validated investments to scale up prevention and treatment, and also setting benchmarks to ensure that the goals were being met. Focusing on demonstrable outcomes and employing validated metrics is essential. In order to be considered a useful investment, an international program should be sustainable, in the sense that nations benefiting from the program themselves begin to absorb direction and support. The best programs are widely supportable and they endure across administrations; by this standard PEPFAR has met the goal. It has "managed to maintain bi-partisan support that bridged two U.S. administrations, six U.S. congressional sessions, and one global economic crisis" (Glassman & Ottendorff, 2013, p. 1).

Food Safety and Inspection Service. The Food Safety and Inspection Service (FSIS) leadership in 2001 initiated an organizational change effort continuing through 2004 that ultimately achieved new efficiencies and improvements to enable frontline employees to better accomplish their jobs. Sometimes a subcabinet agency fulfills its mission primarily through enforcement mechanisms, but like police work, carrying out work through punitive measures is neither cost effective nor gets at the heart of the issue. Like many other federal agencies working with more constrained budgets, the U.S. Department of Agriculture (USDA) centralized many of its functions in an effort to reduce overhead costs and achieve uniformity of results in the mid-1990s.

While the reorganization was successful in flattening the organization and streamlining operations, FSIS had issues including high travel costs and complaints about plant inspections that were not addressed. The time for travel reduced the time inspectors could be at food processing plants. They typically flew out to plants for inspection, an expensive approach that emphasized looking for infractions.

The compliance-oriented culture of the agency at the time focused on measuring the extent to which plants met FSIS regulations and identified infractions. A similar orientation existed at OSHA, where the more infractions identified, the more it would be clear that inspectors were diligent in performing their duties. Once the inspection was reported at the central office, the inspector would later return to the plant to check on remediation and find additional violations. It created a "gotcha" culture of acrimony between plants and inspectors, driving many plants to spend time hiding issues rather than seeking a means of ensuring safety by bringing problems to the attention of FSIS inspectors.

The agency sought consulting assistance for this initiative, beginning with a focus on developing performance metrics. In the course of developing the metrics, it became clear that centralizing this function had exposed a deeper problem, one in which the agency was in part undermining its mission to improve food safety. Because the culture focused on infractions it created exactly what it did not want, a lack of transparency and an increased potential for undetected violations instead of improvements in food safety.

Not surprisingly, by deconstructing the organization and relocating inspectors from a central location to a district office close to or at the plants, the agency was able to save costs. More importantly, work on the process itself yielded many positive outcomes. The agency was able to recognize that, like OSHA, it could focus federal employees' efforts on making them partners with the plant. With leadership's support and new initiatives in education and compliance assistance, the orientation of inspectors shifted to a cooperative partnership with plant operatives, focused on prevention and safety instead of targeting violations. This resulted in fewer infractions because of improved conditions. These leadership actions resulted in a significant reduction in costs as well as a reduction in the violation of safety standards. From a culture perspective, it resulted in a reorientation to the real mission, safer food for the public. The lesson to be learned in this federal context is that initially unsettling attempts to save costs can have very positive impacts. Once one looks beneath the surface, in this case cost issues, it can reveal a host of hidden cultural and process issues that can be transformative (McGee & Sechriest, personal communication, January 25, 2015).

Recovery Act Transparency

At the time when the American Recovery and Reinvestment Act (ARRA) (Public Law 111-9) was passed in early 2009, America was in the midst of the Great Recession. The Obama Administration, beginning with the Office of Management and Budget (OMB), developed an overarching "ethics infrastructure" that simplified the process for capturing cost and performance data. This made it possible to ensure integrity throughout the period of the effort.

Also known as the "Stimulus" or "Recovery Act," the legislation in ARRA aimed to save or create jobs through funding a wide variety of programs such as infrastructure and education. The ethics infrastructure was composed of representatives drawn from OMB, the President's Economic Advisory Recovery Board, a Recovery Accountability and Transparency Board (RATB), state representatives, and major grantees to bring transparency to $840 billion in spending. President Obama named Interior's Inspector General Earl Devaney to establish RATB, whose mission was to provide transparency of ARRA-related funds and to detect and prevent fraud, waste, and mismanagement of those funds. The overall ethics infrastructure carried out successful administration of the Act and avoided the kind of scandal associated with fraud and waste that sometimes accompanies rapid expenditure. Moreover, the ethics infrastructure ensured a new, much higher level of transparency than had been the case in the past.

The program established a web-based portal where agencies and recipients reported in centrally on their ARRA expenditures. The detailed and standardized information format enabled the sort of transparency that had been envisioned in the 2006 Federal Funding Accountability and Transparency Act (Public Law 109-282), an act aimed at holding government accountable for spending decisions and reducing waste (Pasquantino, personal communication and interview on administration of the American Recovery and Reinvestment Act, July 7, 2015). Wood and Siempelkamp (2010) report that,

> To implement its mission of transparency and accountability, the (organization) created two game-changing systems—Recovery.gov and FederalReporting.gov—that have reformed the standards and transformed government and transparency as well as risk assessment and accountability for federal spending.... From October 1 through October 10, 2009, for the

first time in the history of government, recipients of federal awards publicly reported on the money they received. (p. 3)

Successful implementation resulted in several transformative federal and state achievements. First, it developed and deployed a technology-based reporting portal that showed transparency could be achieved. Second, the success of the endeavor inspired many states to implement their own new portals for transparency reporting (Pasquantino, personal communication and interview on administration of the American Recovery and Reinvestment Act, July 7, 2015). Third, the ethical infrastructure and transparency board paved the way for the Digital Accountability and Transparency Act of 2014 (Public Law 113-101). If anything, this case demonstrates that a determined team can deploy policy and technical solutions that bring new transparency to government spending, and by doing so, increase trust in the government. Even the vocal critics of ARRA in the Congress applauded the new level of transparency.

This section has reviewed a number of case examples demonstrating, despite the forces against change noted in prior sections, that it is possible for effective leaders to implement transformation within the federal context. The next section will discuss some of the lessons learned, some of which were mentioned within these case examples.

PRINCIPLES FOR TRANSFORMATION AND MANAGING PUBLIC-SECTOR CHANGE

Thus far this chapter has reviewed in depth the forces that make it difficult to make change and transformation possible. On the other hand, it has also provided some case examples of the many instances where major change was achieved despite the challenges. This final section explores principles that public-sector leaders can apply in their day-to-day work to make government transformation and change possible. The recommendations could be applied by elected officials or appointees at the start of their tenure, but it is aimed primarily at career senior-level and program managers who have responsibility for making their organization work. Many of the challenges begin with the nature of the legislative process, and "threading the needle" to make change happen in agencies requires inspiring leaders. The section begins by describing "kludgeocracy," an overarching term that summarizes the challenges of getting the outcomes the public seeks through policy and programs. It then shifts to ways to help make transformation and change possible, even in the face of difficulties. This portion is divided into three sections related to who are effective leaders, what effective leaders do, and how effective leaders shape the organization. The categories are not mutually exclusive and the concepts overlap to some degree.

Kludgeocracy

Steven Teles, a political scientist at Johns Hopkins University who is interested in the interaction of policy and organizational change, provides a handy overarching concept to many of the difficulties encountered in federal policy and programs described throughout this chapter (Teles, n.d.). He uses the term "kludgeocracy" to describe the current state of government policy and programs, when the fundamental policy mechanism is substantially more complicated than the problem it is trying to solve (Klein, 2013). Kludge, a term drawn from coding, is "an inelegant patch put in place to solve an unexpected problem and designed to be backward-compatible with the rest of an existing system" (Teles, 2013, p. 98). Teles (2013) argues that the complexity of government rather than its size is the greatest challenge, with government practices hiding "from view the tendency of public policy to redistribute resources upward to the wealthy and organized at the expense of the poorer and less organized" (p. 97).

The costs built into programs due to kludgeocracy are often "hidden, indirect, and ... corrupt the distribution of its costs" (Teles, 2013, p. 98) so that many of the outcomes are disconnected with the original intent. A fitting example was confusion during Hurricane Katrina about which agency (federal or local) should be responsible for New Orleans' levees. Policy complexity and extracting rents make it difficult to understand who benefits and who pays. Complexity obscures what is intended (Klein, 2013). This leads to loss of public trust and a corrosive political process that seeks to find backdoor avenues to advance hidden interests.

The next subsections reflect lessons learned to make effective transformation and change possible in the federal context, that is, ways in which to build successes that overcome kludgeocracy.

What Makes a Great Leader?

Regardless of the challenges—Constitutional, evolutionary, or kludgeocracy—there are means by which effective leaders can help achieve transformation and change. The following subsections outline principles that leaders can employ in government to make change possible. This subsection focuses on the nature of leaders themselves, their attributes and how they communicate.

Optimism. Effective leaders in government service need to be optimistic. That is not to say they are unrealistic and unaware of risks. There is a Marine saying that, "Hope is not a COA (course of action)" (America's Sergeant Major, 2009, p. 1). On the other hand, if a leader's frame of mind is cynical from the outset, then small barriers add up quickly and can lead to defeat. For example, Ed Gamache, the director of a Veterans Affairs Medical Center faced steep challenges when initiating one of the VA's first reengineering efforts, changing the way in which the hospital operated. The medical chief of staff, a powerful and forceful figure, was initially opposed to this initiative. Ed optimistically pressed for system changes, focusing on improving care for veterans, even though many forces were organized against making the transformation. Ed held the key staff responsible for selecting and tracking quality care metrics, relentlessly but positively pointing out the advances that were being made. In the end, Ed prevailed and the initiative proved successful. The chief of staff left the VA system to head up an even larger reengineering at one of the nation's largest medical centers. As was noted in the OSHA and PEPFAR examples, a positive face at the outset, as well as maintaining a positive outlook is an important characteristic of leaders responsible for instituting transformation. Maintaining optimism in the face of critics and the inevitable setbacks is a choice.

Mission Focus. Private sector leaders have an advantage in their ability to make speedy decisions when compared to government organizations. In the private sector, there is a clear bottom line—to make profit. In the public sector leaders must serve broader objectives and stakeholders. In the private sector an organization is profitable or not, and the profit forecast against competitors provides a clear point of comparison to check if a company is moving in the right direction. The investing public rewards the more profitable companies. The absence of a similar bottom line in the public sector can make it more challenging for its leaders to maintain focus. Achieving the mission serves as an effective proxy for profit, and prudent federal leaders focus the organization's workers on a clearly communicated mission. In many federal agency situations, the mission can be so broad and the constituency it serves so diffuse, that it creates confusion in the workforce about priorities. An effective leader creates clarity about their understanding of the mission in ways that people can easily understand and on which they can focus their energies. Furthermore, as will be discussed later in this chapter, achievements against the mission objectives are translated into metrics against which progress is assessed. Several examples in previous sections showed ways in which leaders clarified the mission. For example, in the midst of reorganizations, leadership at OSHA and at FSIS clarified what the mission meant to the workforce—in these cases a focus on improved worker and food safety as the highest mission priority.

Creating Necessity. In the private sector, it typically is necessary to use what John Kotter, a noted expert on change management, calls a "burning platform" to create a sense of urgency for change and transformation. (Kotter, 1995; Kotter & Cohen, 2002) In the private sector, especially in companies whose business models rely on shifting technologies, creating a sense of urgency for change may mean the difference between great success and bankruptcy. In the public sector agencies may shift but they are rarely if ever eliminated.

Nevertheless, it is possible for skilled federal leaders to create a sense of urgency. This involves a more subtle and consistent form of communication than for the private sector. Public sector jobs are rarely eliminated, so it is important to capture people's imagination about what is possible, linking the mission with people's actions each day. For instance, while the VBA backlog created frustration on the part of both veterans and the VA workforce, General Hickey worked with multiple stakeholders to communicate that it was possible to tackle this challenging issue and to better serve veterans. Likewise, successive Secretaries of Defense have communicated with operations personnel about the importance of achieving auditability to reassure the public that its funds are being spent as intended.

Leadership Activities

Strategy, Goals, and Metrics. Having a well-integrated strategy and supporting metrics can play an important role in the success of a private enterprise. Building a strategy forces leadership to look at the organization from a different standpoint and come to a shared understanding, while metrics serve as guideposts against which to measure progress against one's plan. These activities are essential in the realm of national defense.

Some essential core references for these exercises include Porter (1980) for strategy and Kaplan and Norton (1993, 1996a, 1996b) for metrics. Mea, Robinson, and Handlon (2002) provide a useful summary for these. The lesser-known but highly useful Ascher and Overholt (1983) approach to strategy provides a more robust extension of Porter's work.

This chapter cannot explain the strategic process within the space provided, but it can be summarized as follows. Strategy begins with an assessment of the environment, including a clarification of the core mission (or core business) with an unvarnished assessment of the environment and or organizational capabilities. The next step involves forecasting trends to assess where the environment will be at some point in the future 10 or more years out. The following step involves clarifying potential environments— from those that are favorable to the ones where exogenous contingencies may even threaten the existence of the organization. Having detailed out environments with the associated risks and opportunities, the next steps involve creating goals and supportive integrated and balanced metrics. The metrics serve as signposts to clarify progress toward the goals.

Setting realistic goals is an essential element in strategic planning. Private sector organizations generally have much clearer, easier to measure goals with well-defined timeframes. In practice, goal setting in government-related entities often tends to be less quantitative, more social or political environment oriented and heavily qualitative in nature. This makes it harder to establish highly measureable goals with clear timelines for expected outcomes.

A key role for leaders in the strategic planning process is to set demanding, yet realistic goals (Handlon, personal communication, May 6, 2015). Creating overly lofty visions can result in goals that are too diffuse and accompanying metrics that are both hard to measure and impractical. Shooting for the stars is laudable, but goals need to be practical and achievable. A strategy, its goals, and its associated metrics need to be clear, attainable, measurable (i.e., have simple metrics), and integrated (i.e., support each other). Once defined, the goal attainment needs to be measured at the right intervals in order to drive accountability in operations. Execution of long-term strategic plans and goals in private sector organizations are routinely driven by day-to-day operational execution details synchronized across the organization (Eicher, 2006). In the private sector, multiple small groups of people are aligned against a clear mission, detailed execution activities are defined, and results are measured in reported outcomes to the top leaders and the board.

The first PEPFAR coordinator, a former pharmaceutical executive, exhibited strong command of these concepts. He worked with his leadership to develop a strategy they owned and that was clearly tied to goal attainment. Programs and projects that did not demonstrate a clear and direct link to well-defined outcomes were dropped. When members of Congress attempted to support alternative district-sponsored programs with indirect links or of lesser quality, he convincingly engaged with them to clarify the issues. Because the strategy employed clearly defined outcome metrics, he was able to demonstrate with precision when programs favored by members would result in subpar performance. The relationship he developed with legislators was always upbeat and convincing. Rather than argue, he convincingly used data to make the argument, letting Congress decide. OSHA's strategy also demonstrated similar characteristics in that it employed well-balanced and integrated metrics focused strictly on safety outcomes.

Diagnosis. Effective leaders are always taking the temperature of their organization, and they do so in many ways. This challenge is greatest if one is new to a federal organization. For those who have come from a high-paced bottom-line private sector position, there is a temptation to launch into a specific direction without appropriately understanding the nature of the organization—its strengths and weaknesses, the styles of interaction, and where the sources of influence are. While a new leader may have specific agenda items he or she wants to accomplish, the wise leader initially communicates that he or she will take a reasonable period of time (a "listening tour" of perhaps 45 to 60 days) in which to learn and form an assessment, to keep from drawing hasty conclusions. This approach provides the staff with the assurance that the new leader will listen to what they have to say, giving them an opportunity to speak with enthusiasm about the work they have accomplished in the past and to express their hopes and desires for the future.

In the private sector, hires at an executive (C-level) or director level would be expected to have a specific agenda of accomplishments for the near term and longer term, and staff might feel rudderless if the new incumbent did not communicate that clearly from the outset. In the public sector, at a subcabinet level position, the intent would be communicated with the cabinet secretary, but in order to earn the trust of agency staff it is critical to be in a "listening mode" at the beginning in order to earn trust. The failure to act this way can be, "like laying your own landmines" in the public sector, because in government change comes slowly.

In a business context, measuring change begins with clearly defining today's current state. This means defining the current situation, and how things work together to achieve the outcomes today. Defining the current state includes detailed documentation of the current processes, people, technology, financials, quantitative and qualitative measures, outcomes, policies, communications, and products and services to be delivered to customers. This can be part of the activity for the initial "listening period" in a public services organization as well. After one has completed the initial listening tour and formulated a strategy, it is appropriate to formulate a "future state" of desired end-results. Both in the private and public sector this describes future desired outcomes, new and refined processes, technology enablement, economic outcomes, quantitative and qualitative measures, and a host of new or refined support systems needed for new desired outcomes.

One of the best guides to the process of diagnosing public sector agency situations is available in the Peter Daly and Michael Watkins (2006) book, *The First 90 Days in Government*. The authors categorize situations into four groups. Turnarounds, the first grouping, involve situations in which an organization has disturbing performance deficiencies that need to be resolved. The second grouping, realignment, involves less difficult situations in which the organization is meeting its mission in part, but structural or resource allocation issues suboptimize efficiency or consistent results.

Sustainment situations, the next grouping, is one in which the organization is performing near peak, and is an enviable position in which to be. However, even high-performing public sector organizations experience some drift and it is difficult to lead even high-performing organizations when they must adapt to additional constraints, regulations, tightening budgets, or new resource challenges. The fourth grouping, start-up situations, are rare in government and they offer the unique situation in designing the organization and its business processes. PEPFAR was a unique start-up case in which the coordinator could assert control over AIDS resources regardless of the agency.

Technology Implementation & Process Redesign. In both the private sector and in the public sector, major technology implementations are means by which to achieve significant transformations. Both sectors struggle to be effective, and the cost of failure is high but the rewards for a successful technology implementation can be huge. Information technology implementation projects within the government represent a somewhat unique situation, one that can speed change while transforming the way business is conducted. One of the unique features of transformations in government in the past few decades has been the degree to which many of these transformations depended on an accompanying systems implementation. Systems implementations are all about adding new technology into existing business processes in order to achieve dramatically improved mission accomplishment. That is, they automate and smooth out the processes to free up people for more productive uses of their energy. Systems implementations should be viewed within the strategy as an "enabling" initiative for a larger purpose. Technology in this case is a means, or a pathway, to refine business operating processes while employing new technologies to achieve goals like "cheaper, faster, better, more effective" services for government customers.

Systems implementations not only change the technologies employed; they change how people do things, and how the new processes will work. Thus, the four critical factors, all equally weighted, that make the difference in any successful systems implementation are: people, processes, technology, and outcomes, with goals and results that must be defined more clearly.

People need to be trained on the new operating processes and technology uses. More importantly, direct personal input from people (customers, employees, vendors and third-party contractors) are all highly valuable in the design and implementation of new systems. Technology that is easy to use, is intuitive for people to understand, has navigation mechanics that are easy to employ, and has the look and feel of tools created, are all people-related factors that make a big difference in systems implementations. Also important is giving those who will use the new technology "input" into the process early on.

As processes get changed and refined the workers help design improvements to the workflow process. Early involvement of people whose jobs are impacted is necessary in order to get them invested in a positive outcome. When a process is designed without the involvement of stakeholders (such as employees, customers, employees, or vendors) it often leads to failure of an attempted technology transformation effort. The IRS Modernization and the Health and Human Services (HHS) Financial Systems implementation offer contrasting approaches and results. The early IRS systems modernization failed due to its scope and failure to fully engage stakeholders; the HHS implementation took a successful stepwise approach over a more easily digested period while engaging stakeholders.

How Leaders Shape the Organization

Engaging Stakeholders. If any transformation or change effort is to be successful it must engage with the key stakeholders. Stakeholders are those individuals and groups with an interest in or who will be affected by the change. Even if one is undertaking a straightforward technology initiative in the private sector, such as an enterprise resource plan (ERP), it is necessary to engage with and gain the support of stakeholders within the organization (e.g., executives, operations managers, and impacted workforces, etc.) as well as allied stakeholders (board of directors, financial analysts, suppliers, and sales channels).

In the context of federal sector agencies, engaging external and internal stakeholders is of even greater importance (Ostroff, 2006). In the process of designing any transformative program, reaching out to and engaging with Congress is of highest importance. A slow and deliberative process may appear ponderous, but failure to get all viewpoints represented or to get the support of legislators can lead to a backlash and undermine a program's implementation. As noted in the PEPFAR example, the coordinator worked closely with Congress to make the case for permitting only the best programs to be funded. In preparing Goldwater-Nichols, key Congressional staff members worked closely with military leaders to seek wider support for the resulting reorganization.

Engaging with internal stakeholders should also be a high priority when seeking a major program change. Government staff members often stay in their organizations for a long time, sometimes for an entire career (Ostroff, 2006). Long-term federal employees develop an intuitive sense of how to get things done in their culture—what will work and what will not—and gaining their trust and their input can be an essential factor in creating success. This was the approach used at OSHA, bringing in employees for the design of its reengineering to make sure that their knowledge was tapped. This helped make the changes successful and helped to detect any potential landmines in advance of implementation. Bringing in the team may seem to slow down forward progress, but unless a leader builds trust and emotional commitment, programs tend to fail.

One of the more creative stakeholder interventions the author has observed was when a vice president (VP) at a ship manufacturer formed a group of the most vocal critics of a reengineering effort, calling them the "Grumpy's Gripers Team"—named after the most vocal critic. The VP first charged the group with the mission of interviewing and analyzing the organization to fully discover problems with the proposed effort. After the team reported back, the VP charged the team with selecting three issues they cared about and coming up with a plan to resolve those issues. As a result of the experience, the team members became known as the most vocal in detecting culture issues and the most creative in overcoming barriers. The author observed a similar approach in government when a chief financial officer put the most vocal critic of a new accounting project in charge of its success, promising a step raise if the person was successful. It worked.

Understanding One's Team. Some experienced federal managers would assert that the most important relationship they have is upward. Some very successful managers simulate a refined obsequiousness in an effort to draw in their leader in order to shape what they believe are the best outcomes. This author would contend, on the other hand, that the most important relationship that a public-sector leader has is with those who report to him or her. The soul of leadership is having a clear vision for the results to be achieved, and the heart of leadership is to understand the people one leads in a way that can help them achieve the goals of the organization. Since goals cannot be accomplished without people resources, effective leaders give their team credit for their accomplishments. Nothing is more deflating, and negative, than a boss taking credit for what someone else did, without giving proper recognition to the persons who accomplished the important end-results.

Assuming that the primary relationship for achieving success is with one's direct reports, understanding the personality of each and what motivates them is essential. The psychology literature shows that there are essentially eight different normal personality styles, and that interacting with them calls for different interpersonal approaches that respond to their unique need (Millon & Everly, 1985). Table 5.1 summarizes these personality subtypes (Mea, 2015). Elaborating on the managerial tactics for interacting with each type is beyond the scope of this chapter, but it is not surprising that each has unique needs. Furthermore, the complexity of balancing the relationship of each to the other types calls for great insight and sensitivity.

Table 5.1.   A Summary of Personality Subtypes

Type	Description of Characteristics
Forceful	Forceful assertiveness in the pursuit of goals.
Sociable	Dramatic and animated with a tendency to be charming but sometimes shallow.
Sensitive	Unpredictable and erratic with pessimism and sense of being unappreciated.
Inhibited	Organized and interpersonally courteous and reliable, but with emotions held in check.
Confident	Poised and confident with flexible thinking, but sometimes lacking thoughtfulness.
Cooperative	Docile, thoughtful and compliant with others; open to others but sense of personal weakness.
Respectful	Shy and interpersonally cautious, often with a sense of being alone.
Introversive	Passive and unobtrusive with a hidden emotional expression.

Both in the private and public sectors, one of the key roles of great leaders is that of mentoring. Much has been made in literature of the past decade regarding the idea that great leaders were themselves mentored. Leaders who help others around them succeed and improve every day are more respected and admired by the teams they lead. It may not be realistically possible to mentor multiple people, but leaders obtain greater loyalty when development and coaching is a priority. Some management experts assert that the social obligations of a leader go beyond merely achieving excellent group outcomes. For leaders, there is a moral obligation to make each person perform better as an individual and within the collective group. This prepares them for a next higher level of responsibility. The practice is woven within the fabric of the U.S. military, where training and education is part of the core mission. Preparation for joint coordination and operations is codified in Goldwater-Nichols and in military doctrine. Some corporations are nearly as committed to development as the U.S. military, and as the State Department found under General Colin Powell, it is a powerful model for other agencies to consider.

Working Within the Culture. Mature leaders understand how to work within the parameters of the organization in which they have to work. Every business or public sector organization has a unique culture that has evolved to cope with the challenges it meets. Private sector entities are more dynamic as they need to adapt to the marketplace as a condition for survival. High tech and small firms are noteworthy for cultures that value innovation and speed of execution. Government cultures typically, on the other hand, have multiple constituencies to serve and the need to provide stable, predictable service.

The federal culture required to support steady but not earth-shattering results operates with a different set of behavioral norms, tacit assumptions, and values than those of the private sector (Schein, 1992). New leaders in government who have previously worked in private sector organizations need to be cautious about rushing into specific agendas without having first taken a pulse of the culture to ensure they understand the rules of the game in which they operate. Sometimes the most important norms for ways in which to conduct operations are hidden below the surface (Egan, 1994).

As noted in the subsection on diagnosis, the prudent manager spends sufficient time to discover and understand the culture. Before one can orchestrate the type of operational implementation that is required for transformation and change, a leader needs to understand the rules of the game if one is to accomplish big goals. Clearly, the State Department leader understood culture in the previously cited Fallujah example. In an interesting example that the author observed, a somewhat mistrustful federal CFO would come late at night to check the kinds of work on people's desk, in order to get a sense of the hidden results. To him, the culture and the rules of the game were as important as the officially reported results. The same CFO informed his managers that he would also be meeting monthly offsite and outside of standard hours with lower level employees to get their view of what was going on behind the scenes. While the approach was initially disconcerting to the managers, it ultimately forced managers themselves to pay attention to the culture and to surface contentious issues with the staff. Ultimately, it led to a more open atmosphere and to managers who were more confident.

Measuring Change. One of the chief problems of evaluating whether change has occurred on government projects involves a vexing measurement problem. This is known as the criterion problem in evaluation research. People involved in transformation or change projects frequently conduct pre- and postintervention assessments, but they fail to rule out alternative hypotheses to what they assume is change. Real change due to an intervention is referred to as *alpha* change. Scale recalibration, called *beta* change, occurs when people change their understanding of what is being measured over the course of time (Buckley et al., 1998).

Examples might include working group effectiveness or leadership skills. Since these concepts are often abstruse at the beginning of training, it is possible to change one's understanding in a way that changes the measurement itself. Another form of change is called *gamma* change, which refers to the error of concept redefinition. This occurs when people involved in the change program are exposed to the measurements and they change the way they measure the change in their heads over the course of time. This would be akin to using a ruler that stretches and alternatively shrinks over the course of time (Buckley et al., 1998). Just the act of being measured on something creates its own expectations, and it is important for leaders who are invested in a transformation project to make sure that they are candid with themselves about the successes and failures in a transformation program.

From the perspective of experienced management consultants who have worked on both private and public sector projects, two things matter when evaluating the effectiveness of organizational transformations or major change projects—understanding and confidence. Related to understanding, the critical question to ask is if the key stakeholders truly comprehend what is going to be changed and what needs to change. This is fairly straightforward. A related question is whether stakeholders involved in the transformation have confidence that the appropriate change will be implemented successfully while it is underway. If the answer is no, then this should trigger refining the approach. A related question is do the stakeholders have a measure of confidence that the change is necessary. It is important to establish key timeframes for measuring the change; these are typically at the baseline, at key milestone intervals, and at the end in order to assess the progress.

SUMMARY AND CONCLUSION

This chapter examined why achieving major change and transformation in the public sector is difficult, provided examples of success, and discussed principles for making change possible. The nation's founders set up a form of government that makes the process slow and cumbersome. Many of the difficulties have their source in the Constitution; others have their source in unexpected structural factors unique to our nation's development. The conflicting relationship among the branches of government is not a design flaw, and the acrimony we see now is not much worse than at other times in the nation's history.

Even within the context of the many current barriers to transformation and change, much good comes about in government. The chapter highlighted a number of federal case transformation and change examples from Defense and nonsecurity agency successes. Goldwater-Nichols is a prime example of national security legislation that has led to a dramatic transformation in the way Defense organizes and operates. PEPFAR is a prime example of how leadership can make an immense impact on the welfare of an entire at-risk population.

Despite the complexity and hidden difficulties in our "kludgeocracy," much can be achieved. By adopting the best principles and practices to be learned from great leaders, today's public sector leaders can themselves do great work and make great contributions to the nation.

NOTE

1. The views expressed in this chapter are those of the author and they do not reflect the official policy or position of the United States Office of Management & Budget, National Defense University, the Department of Defense, or the United States Government.

ACKNOWLEDGMENTS

The author would like to express his sincere appreciation to the many people who played a role in preparing this manuscript. Dr. Mary C. Redshaw (Eisenhower School) reviewed the first draft and provided invaluable criticism. James Handlon (Bottom Line Partners, LLC) provided significant additional insights into business process engineering and systems issues. The author's patient editor, Susan Mea, made significant improvements to the final product. The following professors, consultants, and analysts provided helpful insights on transformation and change: Nazanin Ash (Center for Global Development), William Campbell (Wittenberg Weiner Consulting, LLC), Mark Cancian (Center for Strategic & International Studies), James Capretta (Ethics & Public Policy Center), Roland Demarcellus (U.S. Department of State), James Eicher (IBM), Martin Goldberg (Distant Drummer, LLC), Jeff Goldstein (Office of Management & Budget), Dr. Andrew Leith (Australian Army, Eisenhower School), Barry King (Office of Management & Budget), Lyn McGee (Center for Organizational Excellence), Tracy Mehan (former Administrator for Water, U.S. Environmental Protection Agency), John Pasquantino (Office of Management & Budget), William Rossello (R Partners, LLC), Walter Sechriest (Center for Organizational Excellence), Dr. Ronald Sims (College of William & Mary), COL Samuel Smith (U.S. Army, Eisenhower School), and Gary Stofko (Office of Management & Budget).

REFERENCES

America's Sergeant Major. (2009, September 23). Taking the lead. Retrieved from http://www.americassgtmaj.com/heard-in-the-clear-17/
Anderson, G. (2012, December 27). Face It, Goldwater-Nichols Hasn't Worked. *Foreign Policy*. Face It Goldwater-Nichols Hasn't Worked Comments. Retrieved

May 10, 2015, from http://foreignpolicy.com/2012/12/27/face-it-goldwater-nichols-hasnt-worked/

Ascher, W., & Overholt, W. (1983). *Strategic planning and forecasting: Political risk and economic opportunity*. New York, NY: Wiley & Sons.

Ash, N. (2015). Center for Global Development, Correspondence and phone conference on PEPFAR June 17, 2015.

Aspin, L. (1986). House Armed Services Committee, "House-Senate Conference Wraps Up Defense Reorganization Bill," news release, September 11, 1986.

Buckley, M., Mea, W., Weise, D., & Carraher, S. (1998). Evaluating change in public organizations: An alpha, beta, gamma change perspective. In R. R. Sims (Ed.), *Accountability and radical change in public organizations* (pp. 229–241). Westport, CT: Quorum Books.

Cornell Research Service Annotated Constitution. (n.d.). Retrieved June 27, 2015, from https://www.law.cornell.edu/anncon/html/art1frag92_user.html

CRS. (n.d.). Commonly asked questions: President's Emergency Plan for AIDS Relief (PEPFAR). Retrieved May 12, 2015, from http://www.crs.org/public-policy/pdf/PEPFAR-faq.pdf

Daly, P., & Watkins, M. (2006). *The first 90 days in government: Critical success strategies for new public managers at all levels*. Boston, MA: Harvard Business School Press.

de Tocqueville, A. (1835). Alexis de Tocqueville Quote Quotation, Democracy in America. Retrieved May 7, 2015, from http://quotes.libertytree.ca/quote/alexis_de_tocqueville_quote_20d2

de Tocqueville, A. (n.d.) AZquotes. Retrieved May 7, 2015, from www.AZquotes.com/quote/906906

DOD Comptroller. (2015, May). DOD FIAR Plan Status Report May 2015. Retrieved May 27, 2015, from http://comptroller.defense.gov/Portals/45/documents/fiar/FIAR_Plan_May_2015.pdf

DOD FIAR Plan. (n.d.). FIAR Plan. Retrieved May 27, 2015, from http://comptroller.defense.gov/fiar/fiar_plan.aspx

Egan, G. (1994). *Working the shadow side: A guide to positive behind-the-scenes management*. San Francisco, CA: Jossey-Bass.

Eicher, J. (2006, November/December). Making strategy happen. *Performance Improvement, 45*(10), 31–37.

Fukuyama, F. (2011). *The origins of political order: From pre-human times to the French Revolution*. New York, NY: Farrar, Straus and Giroux.

Gilens, M., & Page, B. (2014). Testing theories of American politics: Elites, interest groups, and average citizens. *Perspectives on Politics, 12*(3), 564–581.

Glassman, A., & Ottendorff, J. (2013, May 13). PEPFAR at 10. Global Health Policy Blog Rethinking US Development Policy PEPFAR, HIV/AIDS, Aid Effectiveness, Value for Money Retrieved June 20, 2015, from http://www.cgdev.org/blog/pepfar-10

Hamilton, L. (2003, August 16). Congressional bickering. Retrieved May 7, 2015, from http://centeroncongress.org/congressional-bickering

Hamilton, L. (2004, June 16). Oversight at last. Retrieved May 15, 2015, from http://centeroncongress.org/oversight-last

Ip, G. (2013). *The little book of economics: How the economy works in the real world.* Hoboken, NJ: John Wiley & Sons.

Johnson, P. (n.d.). A glossary of political economy terms. *Economics.* Retrieved May 6, 2015, from http://www.auburn.edu/~johnspm/gloss/economics

Kaiser Foundation. (2014, June 4). The U.S. President's emergency plan for AIDS relief (PEPFAR). Retrieved June 5, 2015, from http://kff.org/global-health-policy/fact-sheet/the-u-s-presidents-emergency-plan-for/

Kaplan, R., & Norton, D. (1993, March). Putting the balanced scorecard to work. *Harvard Business Review,* 36–38.

Kaplan, R., & Norton, D. (1996a). *The balanced scorecard: Translating strategy into action.* Boston, MA: Harvard Business School Press.

Kaplan, R., & Norton, D. (1996b, January-February). Using the balanced scorecard as a strategic management system. *Harvard Business Review,* 75–85.

Klein, E. (2013, January 26). Is America a "kludgeocracy"? Retrieved June 3, 2015, from http://www.washingtonpost.com/blogs/wonkblog/wp/2013/01/26/is-america-a-kludgeocracy/

Kotter, J. (1995). Leading change: Why transformation efforts fail. *Harvard Business Review.* *73*(2), 59–67

Kotter, J., & Cohen, D. (2002). *The heart of change: Real-life stories of how people change their organizations.* Boston, MA: Harvard Business School Press.

Lederman, G. (1999). *The Goldwater-Nichols Department of Defense Reorganization Act of 1986.* Westport, CT: Greenwood Press.

Locher, J., (2001). Has it worked? The Goldwater-Nichols Reorganization Act. *Naval War College Review,* *54*(4), 95–115.

Locher, J., (2002). *Victory on the Potomac: The Goldwater-Nichols Act unifies the Pentagon.* College Station, TX: Texas A & M University Press.

Madison, J. (1787). The Federalist #51. The Federalist #51. Retrieved May 6, 2015, from http://www.constitution.org/fed/federa51.htm

Madison, J. (1788, January 30). The particular structure of the new government and the distribution of power among its different parts. *Constitution Society.* Retrieved May 7, 2015, from http://www.constitution.org/fed/federa47.htm

McCord, M. (n.d.). FIAR Plan Status Report. Retrieved May 1, 2015, from http://comptroller.defense.gov/Portals/45/documents/fiar/FIAR_Plan_May_2015

McGann, J. (2010, Summer/Fall). The fifth estate: Think tanks and American foreign policy. *Politics & Diplomacy,* 35–42.

Mea, W. (2015, May 22). Sharp elbows: Managing the American princeling on your team (Unpublished manuscript). Eisenhower College for National Resource Strategy at National Defense University. Washington, DC.

Mea, W. J., Robinson, T. L., & Handlon, J. W. (2002). *The balanced scorecard: New strategy applications in B2B commerce.* In R. R. Sims (Ed.), *Changing the way we manage change* (pp. 201–216). Westport, CT: Quorum books.

Mea, W., Sims, R., & Veres, J. (2000). Efforts in organization transformation: Getting your money's worth [Les efforts consentis pour transformer les organisations: Optimiser les dépenses effectuées]. *International Review of Administrative Sciences,* *66,* 479–493.

Merriam-Webster.com. (2015). Transformation. Retrieved from http://www.merriam-webster.com/dictionary/transformation

Merriam-Webster.com. (n.d.). Change. Retrieved from http://www.merriam-webster.com/dictionary/change

Millon, T., & Everly, G. (1985). *Personality and its disorders: A biosocial learning approach*. New York, NY: Wiley.

Ostroff, F. (2006, May). Change management in government. *Harvard Business Review, 84*(5), 141–147, 158.

Peden, W. (2000). *The founders' constitution*. Chapel Hill, NC: University of North Carolina Press for the Institute of Early American History & Culture.

PEPFAR. (n.d.). President's plan for emergency AIDS relief: About OGAC. Retrieved April 9, 2015, from http://www.pepfar.gov/about/ogac/index.htm

Podhoretz, N. (2012). Is America exceptional? *Imprimis, 41*(10), 2.

Porter, M. (1980). *Competitive strategy: Techniques for analyzing industries and competitors*. New York, NY: Free Press.

Roosevelt, T. (1908, January 20). Theodore Roosevelt State of the Union. Retrieved May 23, 2015, from http://www.let.rug.nl/usa/presidents/theodore-roosevelt/state-of-the-union-1908.php

Rosati, J., & Scott, J. (2011) *The politics of United States foreign policy* (5th ed.). Andover, MD: Cengage Learning.

Schein, E. (1992). *Organizational culture and leadership* (2nd ed.). San Francisco, CA: Jossey-Bass.

Shugart, W. (n.d.). Public Choice. Retrieved May 7, 2015, from http://www.econlib.org/library/Enc/PublicChoice.html

Syverson, N. (2003, August 14). OSHA: Views from the inside. Industrial Maintenance & Plant Operation. Retrieved June 25, 2015, from http://www.impomag.com/articles/2003/08/osha-views-inside

Teles, S. (2013). Kludgeocracy in America. *National Affairs*, 97–114. Retrieved May 1, 2015, from http://www.nationalaffairs.com/publications/detail/kludgeocracy-in-america

Teles, S. M. (n.d.). *SSN*. Retrieved June 24, 2015, from http://www.scholarsstrategynetwork.org/scholar-profile/437

VBA claims transformation. (n.d.). Retrieved April 22, 2015, from http://www.benefits.va.gov/transformation/about_transformation.asp

Yandle, B. (1999). Bootleggers and Baptists in retrospect. Retrieved May 7, 2015, from http://object.cato.org/sites/cato.org/files/serials/files/regulation/1999/10/bootleggers.pdf

Washington, G. (1798). The Founders Documents. *The Founder's Documents*. Retrieved May 4, 2015, from http://press-pubs.uchicago.edu/founders/documents/v1ch5s11.html

Wood, M., & Siempelkamp, A. (2010). Transparency in government. *Journal of Public Inquiry, Fall-Winter 2010–2011* Edition, 1–6.

CHAPTER 6

TRANSITION TO A NEW STATE

Consolidating Organizational Resources at Nasa Langley Research Center

Sheri Bias, Donna L. Phillips, and Kathleen N. Cabler

INTRODUCTION

Why do some people fear change and others welcome it? Often times we are not in control of the change and therefore find it hard to adjust, as was the case with the NASA Analyst Consolidation. Managing change means managing people's fear. Change is natural and good, but people's reaction to change is unpredictable. It can be managed if done right.

Organizational change impacts organizational success. The ability to initiate and facilitate change is crucial to the sustainability of organizations, leaders and followers alike. Furthermore, the essence of change is choosing what not to do. This means leaders must know how well it is being implemented, whether it is generating performance success or failure, and if the change needs to be altered. Leaders must be disciplined enough to sort through various competing ideas and alternatives, to stay on course, especially during change. Moreover, leaders are responsible for assuring

Transforming Government Organizations:
Fresh Ideas and Examples From the Field, pp. 199–211
Copyright © 2016 by Information Age Publishing

that change strategy links values with vision and that the change can be successfully implemented; "it falls to the leader to forge a community of employees dedicated to implementing the (change) strategy" (Allio, 2003, p. 8).

In this chapter, we will discuss NASA LaRC Office of Chief Financial Office's adaption to change and ability overcome obstacles faced during the transition to a more efficient and effective organization. The fundamental assumptions underlying *any* change in a human system are analyzed. Two models of change management, William Bridges's (1991) *Transitions* and Salerno and Brock (2008) *The Change Cycle*, are used as lenses for analyzing the initiative. Was this the correct timing? We will explore the timing of introduction of these models. Additionally, we will explore the effectiveness of these models during the change process as compared to other change models. Could other models have been more effective? What process should be used to choose the model that "fits" your organizations' needs? This chapter defines and discusses the principles of change and effective change management to bring the desired vision of the organization to fruition.

CHANGE MANAGEMENT AND LEADERSHIP

One of the most difficult parts of leadership is encouraging and managing organizational change. The management levers that Western-trained business people still customarily reach for when they encounter problems are those wherein change waits. Leaders chance exposure to *incremental change* which bends and adjusts existing ways to improve performance in addition to *transformational change* which results in a major and comprehensive redirection of the organization. As such, leaders must be able to understand each phase of planned change and be prepared to deal with them simultaneously. They should also be willing to engage in the process of *improvisational change* where adjustments are continually made as things are being implemented.

The word change is used so much that the tendency may be to make culture changes seem easy, almost a matter of routine; but that is not always the case. It seems that only a small percent of change efforts actually succeed. There are many reasons for this, some which will be explored in the next section. Indeed, the entire practice of organizational development is based on change management (Schein, 1996) in which practitioners must:

- Gather the information that supports the case for a change effort, and discuss it with those who will be affected by it. Leaders can clarify their vision, anticipate and resolve potential problems, and sometimes even realize that the change is misguided, or that there are far better alternative solutions.

- Use measurement tools: tracking the effectiveness of the change effort both tells people that it is important and provides a way to judge how well it is being implemented, or how well it was designed.

- Avoid eliciting resistance by involving workers from the beginning, clearly explaining the reasons for the change, having clear strategy, direction, and vision, and respecting the viewpoints of other people.

Strong change leaders must be alert to cultures, situations, and people needing change, open to good ideas and opportunities, and ready and able to support the implementation of new ideas in actual practice. While in theory every manager should act as a change leader, the reality is that people show tendencies toward staying with the status quo. A change leader, however, can learn a lot by listening to resistance and then using it as a resource for improving the change and the change process. Change is a continuing theme in our society, and organizations are no exception. A good change strategy cannot guarantee improved performance; however, the wrong change strategy is a guarantee of nonperformance. It pays to get it right. A big factor in getting it right is communication.

Collaborative efforts of communication must align with organizational change. Change challenges our existing paradigms. In order to change we must reorder our thought processes and see the same things in new ways. Leadership plays a key role in building legitimacy and commitment to the change process. To effectively communicate, we must realize that we are all different in the way we perceive the world and leverage this understanding to communicate more effectively with others.

There are insurmountable examples of communication mishaps surrounding change leaving employees to ask questions such as: What does this mean? Are other employees aware of this? What about the leaders? When will it happen? Will I lose my job? Why wasn't I informed? When those impacted by change feel something is done "to" them instead of "for" them they may not fully buy into the vision, subsequently yielding negative results. It is increasingly difficult for change efforts to be realized if they become derailed by seemingly "in the dark" employees concerned about matters deemed critical to their wellbeing. Organizations can implement change more effectively with timely collaborative communication mechanisms and change dialogue inclusive of leaders, followers and customers alike. Regardless of an organization's motive for change, it must be properly communicated.

APPLYING THE LENS OF CHANGE MODELS

Employees must move through the stages or phases of change to fully internalize a change. For those who naturally gravitate to it or who stand to gain from the change, this process is less difficult. However, even these employees will go through the challenge of the change process. Several models exist addressing the nature of change, each with unique language and stages. Two of these models are discussed here: *The Change Cycle* by Salerno and Brock (2008; see also Fernsler, 2011) and William Bridges's (1991) *Transitions* model, both of which were used as a means of introducing employees to the underpinnings of the change process.

Bridges's Model

Bridges (1991) purports that the success or failure experienced with change rides on guiding people through transition. He says "Transition is the psychology process people go through to come to terms with the new situation. Change is a process that leads to an outcome" (p. 4). The change process is where most organizations focus when undergoing change. However, transition is the experience of emotions people move through that aids the organization to successfully achieve the outcome and make the change stick if they are guided appropriately. Bridges's transition model has three phases: (1) Ending/Letting Go, (2) Neutral Zone, and (3) New Beginning. The leaders of change must be prepared to deal with all three transition phases. How transition management is handled often determines the success of the change effort. The first phase of transition, *the Ending*, is the period when individuals must let go of something from the past, so they can embrace what is new (Bridges, 1991). For many individuals, letting go is similar to the grieving process. Creating a space where people are permitted to voice their pain of leaving what they have known behind can aid in their passage through the Ending phase.

Consider this example: In the early 1990s one of the National Aeronautics and Space Administration's locations, Langley Research Center, experienced a major reorganization. In this reorganization some leaders and individuals of status were placed in new positions. Some of them were placed in positions of lesser status. To ease the pain of this experience the Center leaders held a special event to allow employees to express their loss of the old organization. Each person was asked to write on slips of paper what they had to let go of due to the change. Then one-by-one they read their statements aloud to the group and placed the slip of paper into a sealed box with a slit on the top. This event was symbolic of burying the past. It helped individuals to move towards acceptance of the organization's change. By holding this event the leaders were showing sympathy towards their employees and helping with the transition.

The second phase of transition *the Neutral Zone*, "is the time when the old way is gone and the new way doesn't feel comfortable yet" (Bridges, 1991, p. 5). It is like trading a pair of old, comfortable shoes for a new pair that have not been broken in. The old pair of shoes are worn and out of style. So, you buy a new stylish pair of shoes. The new shoes look good, but may feel a little tight and uncomfortable.

In the Neutral Zone, people experience ambiguity and confusion. Because of this, organizations typically suffer a loss of productivity as individuals psychologically work their way through this phase. It is also a time when those least eager to accept the change may try to sabotage the efforts being made to integrate the new way of operating. Communication with employees is just as important in this phase as it is in the Ending phase. While not as much change activity transpires in the Neutral Zone, keeping the lines of communication operational can aid in minimizing rumors and negativity towards the change.

The Neutral Zone also provides an opportunity for organizations to be innovative. As organizations move from the old to the new there are opportunities for thinking outside the box. The organization is more open to trying newer and more efficient processes. Leaders should leverage this transition phase to benefit the overall organization. A key to navigating through the Neutral Zone is to remember it is a journey that cannot be rushed. As such, "the neutral zone is a time when a necessary reorientation and redefinition is taking place and people (including managers) need to understand that" (Bridges, 1991, p. 37).

The third phase of Bridges's (1991) transition model is *New Beginnings*. When change occurs across an organization there is usually a proclamation sent to those impacted stating the specific date and time it is to start as if magically at that specific time, everyone will accept and start operating in the new way. It is like turning off a lamp and the old way disappears, then turning the lamp on and the change has been implemented. Bridges points out that starts and beginnings are two different things. "Starts take place as a result of a decision.... Beginnings ... are the final phase of the transition and ... not measured in the dates written on an implementation schedule" (p. 52).

In this phase Bridges (1991, p. 52) encourages use of the four "P's" (purpose, picture, plan, and part) to assist the organization in achieving the New Beginning. These four "P's" help people's understanding of the change, what the change will look like, where each person fits, and what their role is. In many change efforts managers want to rush to the outcome and often forget that they themselves may have moved through the transition phases before the change was announced. Leaders and managers must remember that all involved in the change are in different places along the transition continuum. There is a lag time between executives and the rank and file in reaching the New Beginning.

Bridges's (1991) *Transitions* model maintains the higher a leader is in the organization the more quickly he or she tends to move through the change. Because they can usually see the destination before others even know the race has begun, senior managers can forget that others will take longer to make the transition: letting go of old ways, moving through the neutral zone, and, finally, making a new beginning. Carefully managing and navigating individuals through the Ending and Neutral Zone phases better ensures the accomplishment of the New Beginning.

Salerno and Brock's Model

The Salerno and Brock (2008) change model, "The Change Cycle," is similar to Bridges's (1991) Transition model in that it addresses the emotions, frustration, and discomfort employees experience in their journey of organizational change. The Salerno and Brock model has six stages.

- Stage 1: Loss
- Stage 2: Doubt
- Stage 3: Discomfort
- Stage 4: Discovery
- Stage 5: Understanding
- Stage 6: Integration

In his review of Salerno and Brock's book, also titled *The Change Cycle*, Fernsler (2011) briefly describes each stage. The *Loss* stage is where people are fearful, cautious and resistant. *Doubt* is when people feel resentful, skeptical and can become defiant. During the *Discomfort* stage, people feel anxious, confused and exhibit unproductive behavior. In the *Discovery* stage people become energized and resourceful. The *Understanding* stage is where people feel confident and their behavior is productive. Finally, in the *Integration* stage people have integrated change into their lives. Salerno and Brock point out individuals pass through each of these stages cyclically. Some move quickly, others take longer and some even get stuck in a specific stage and are unable to find their way out. However, having an understanding of why they are experiencing the emotions and feelings they have in the midst of change can bring comfort to individuals.

In a comparison of change models, the first two stages of Salerno and Brock's model, Loss and Doubt, align with Bridges Ending/Letting Go stage. Salerno and Brock's next two stages, Discomfort and Discovery, are similar to the Neutral Zone phase in Bridges's model. Salerno and Brock's fifth and sixth stages, Understanding and Integration fit with Bridges's New Beginnings phase. The similarities between these two models reveal the significance of the psychological process experienced during change. Emotions, behaviors, productivity, and finally acceptance of organizational change are necessary steps in the journey of change for individuals. It is important for leaders to understand the impact change has on individuals. Through understanding and planning the transition process, leaders can better ensure successful change.

Though different, each model provides the change agent with helpful information to assist employees to move though the stages of change. A change initiative is not really successful until members of the organization have internalized the change and it has become the prevailing culture. In the upcoming section, we reflect upon the challenge of change at NASA Langley Research Center during a major consolidation effort.

NASA LANGLEY RESEARCH CENTER (LaRC)— CHANGE IN THE MAKING

NASA LaRC recently underwent an organization-wide restructuring effort within its financial office. Its initial charter was to develop a comprehensive implementation plan that enabled successful consolidation of financial professionals and optimize financial operations. During this period, the Agency desired to change vertical integration of each Center sustaining all capabilities and move towards a more horizontal integration with inter-dependence across the Agency. Socializing the initiative included talking with diverse professionals across the Center/Agency in addition to other Centers to understand options and models. Other Centers offered lessons learned on transition within a matrix operation.

Operating in a Matrix Structure was one of the stated outcomes of the financial consolidation. The importance of having a management team that really understands how to manage a matrix organization cannot be underestimated. NASA LaRC currently has many matrixed functions at the Center; for example, the Director of the Science Directorate applied his experiences in matrixing engineering competencies to financial pro-fessional's competencies to help leaders further gain knowledge of matrix organizations. The advantages and benefits of the matrixed approach included flexibility for deployment of the workforce, competency steward-ship, and sharing and application of best practices. These benefits are in alignment with the objectives of the Financial Consolidation. With every change, however are risks and fears that must be overcome. Fears of the impacted community are as follows:

1. The operation may not get the "right" people with the "right" skills
2. There is a loss of expertise and continuity when people are moved from one project to another. Retraining new people takes considerable time and resources.
3. The people that they get will not be responsive to their needs. Instead they will be imposing processes and practices that may not be applicable to their particular project.
4. Matrixed people may not have the same level of commitment to a project.

The leaders were further advised that there is more than a perceived loss of control. There is some real transfer of control that they needed to be aware of and plan to manage. It is important to acknowledge this when communicating so they could be clear about how this will be addressed when they implemented the change. The leaders could make this work, but there needed to be a lot of dialog to do it in a way that improved their chance of success.

A three-part transition strategy was adopted—*Transition, Stabilization, Transformation*. Each phase was strategically timed for acceptance of the transition to the new state and to solidify the new processes and expected behaviors. The *Transition* phase was the consolidation of operations of the financial office. During this phase a management plan was documented, a new organizational structure was established, key leadership positions were filled and new communication mechanisms were enabled to keep employees informed of changes. The *Stabilization* phase involved building the team. In this phase leaders ensured communications among the team continued; worked to enable a more collaborative environment among employees; enacted new efficient operations, improved services and leveraged/shared resources. In the *Transformation* phase processes were reinvented. The budget process was restructured, numerous activities were automated, duplicated touch-points were eliminated and operations were streamlined.

From the onset over 200 professionals within the NASA LaRC community were included in collaborative dialogue. The community included a wide-range of diverse professionals such as Organization Unit Managers (OUMs), project managers, business managers, directors, engineers, and analysts as well as consultation with subject matter experts. Not only was insight and understanding into the current state of Center operations gained, but lessons learned on current matrix operations was a beneficial outcome as well. Subsequently, open forums for discussions were held throughout the Center to provide additional opportunity for input into how the operation could be more effective and efficient. Data gathering efforts ensued with other Centers, as well as NASA Headquarters to determine the status of their operations and potential lessons learned from transition to the new organization state.

Given this knowledge and preparation for the implementation of change, it became clearer that in addition to the anticipated benefits of the change, there were also many potential obstacles that needed to be considered. The obstacles identified were:

- Lowest budget in history
- Ongoing workforce challenges
- Growing number of analysts
- Sub-optimized services
- Inconsistent development
- Lack of future pipeline
- Lack of consistent training
- Significant cultural barriers

At first glance, one could say this may not have been the optimal time for such a significant change. However, the realization that LaRC had an amazing opportunity to change and build a stronger community, breakdown walls and enable a more efficient and effective operation was a significant impetus for moving forward. It was determined early on that leadership plays a key role in building legitimacy and commitment to the change process.

Depending on the existing culture the news of change may elicit a variety of responses ranging from fear of the unknown to willing endorsement. "One of the reasons people find change so hard is they have never been taught to understand the emotional and cognitive challenges that change creates" (Salerno & Brock, 2008, p. 9). Although the new organization would provide exceptional customer service, enable flexibility to shift capabilities to meet evolving demands, and ensure employee growth, development and support this did not seem sufficient to calm emotions of the impacted community.

Change takes time and is emotionally intense and stressful for most employees. Most finance employees were directly impacted by the change initiative through encountering changes in roles and responsibilities, new lines of reporting, and modifications in financial operations. The change often results in a need to adjust to new work tasks in addition to new work relationships. To be effective people must be able to understand, change and adapt appropriately to the new work environment.

A critical part of change management efforts is taking the time to reflect on the changes to ascertain any lessons learned by the organization's leadership and employees. Some of the lessons learned from this change endeavor were:

- Change is hard! The existing culture developed over a long period of time and has deep roots in historical norms, beliefs, and perceptions; the culture tends to hold what is current as normal and acceptable
- Personal engagement is critical. It was important to personally engage with individuals and talk about the reason for change, describe a future state, and listen to fears and concerns. Personal engagement required a tremendous investment in time, energy and patience leading change is lonely. The impetus to change falls on the shoulders of the leader/change agent; the leader must be empathetic but also strong to sustain focus; it becomes tempting and easy to retreat and return to the current norm. Most people recognize the overall need to change; many people point out how other organizations should change; few acknowledge that their area should change.
- Change involves emotion. Emotion and culture are major resistance points to enabling change despite what the data, analysis, and information may indicate.
- In hindsight the expertise of organization development professionals being brought into the change effort sooner than later would have benefited the impacted community.

Jacobs, Witteloostuijn, and Christe-Zeyse (2013) maintain "Organizational change is a risky endeavor. Most change initiatives fall short on their goals and produce high opportunity and process costs, which at times outweigh the content benefits of organizational change" (p. 772). These authors present a unified theory of organizational change informed by three main observations of the nature of organizational change. First, organizational change is a risky strategy, as it is often related to the violation of an organization's core cultural values and, potentially, the organization's identity (Hannan, Polos, & Carroll, 2007). Second, the analysis of organizational change needs an approach that can account for the specifics of the organization in question. Third, what works in one organization, culture, or country, may produce failure in another organization, culture, or country. In this culturally diverse world, scholars of organizational change cannot continue to assume that the change patterns in their unique space reflect those experienced on a global stage.

ORGANIZATIONAL CHANGE AND COMMUNICATION

Success of change efforts depends on how effectively the strategy and details of the change are communicated to those who are the targets of change. Lewis and Seibold (1998) investigated how communication affects the successful implementation process, and determined that communication is central to predicting outcomes of planned change. They found that employees within the organization expressed a preference for traditional change communication models; however much of the organizational change communication occurs as an ad hoc response or through informal channels of communication.

Changes to an organization's identity are often experienced as threats to individual identities (Jacobs, Christe-Zeyse, & Polos, 2008). Thus, Van Knippenberg. Van Knippenberg, and Bobbio (2008) note, "a key challenge for change process leaders is to act, not only as change agents, but also as agents of continuity" (p. 175). Success in implementing change requires the ability to communicate, make sound decisions, and get things done with and through people, in other words, building relationships. Culture can have a powerful impact on management and organization behavior. Unfortunately "people are unaware of their culture until it is challenged, until they experience a new culture, or until it is made overt and explicit" (Cameron & Quinn, 2011, p. 19). Thus, "culture change at its root, is intimately tied to individual change; unless managers are willing to commit to personal change, the organization's culture will remain recalcitrant" (p. 7).

Many employees are only vaguely aware that changes are taking place and the ambiguity surrounding these changes opens the door for rumors, anxiety and resistance (Jick, 1993). Significant organizational changes often begin slowly, are incrementally implemented and are subject to change as information is gathered concerning the effectiveness of the process as was the case in the NASA LaRC Financial Analysts scenario. Such change processes may be noninclusive at the start in that only a small fraction of the workforce is involved. Even so, a communication strategy is paramount.

Klein (1996) suggests "there are several empirically founded communications principles that taken together can constitute a communications strategy" (p. 36). These are as follows:

- Message redundancy is related to message retention.
- The use of several media is more effective than the use of just one.
- Face-to face communication is a preferred medium.
- The line hierarchy is the most effective organizationally sanctioned communication channel.

- Direct supervision is the expected and most effective source of organizationally sanctioned information.
- Opinion leaders are effective changers of attitudes and opinions.
- Personally relevant information is better retained than abstract, unfamiliar or general information

To effectively communicate, we must realize that we are all different in the way we perceive the world and leverage this understanding to communicate more effectively with others. In order for leaders to succeed they must motivate and engage others. Internal comunication happens constantly within organizations and is important since clear, consistent and continuous communications builds employee engagement. Leaders must be empathetic, sensitive to feelings of employees and able to establish ways to motivate and foster daily engagement. Communication is always critical but never more so than when you are trying to get others to see and do things differently and if leaders want to change the thinking and actions of others, they must be transparent about their own.

Organizational changes can be derailed because not enough strategic thought is given to communicating the rationale, the progress and the impact of the change. Organizational identity threats elicited by organizational change lie at the core of concerns regarding the legitimacy of change, also driving employee resistance, lack of involvement and weaker commitment to change processes (Van Knippenberg et al., 2008). Leadership plays a key role in building legitimacy and commitment to the change process (Shamir, House & Arthur, 1993). Change can be difficult and communicating it the right way can be equally as challenging.

CONCLUSION

Change can be daunting to employees within an organization when it is not done correctly. Through the discussions in this chapter utilizing the Bridges's (1991) and Salerno and Brock's (2008) models, planned change can be implemented successfully as shown in this example from NASA LaRC. That is not to say that with more planning, more resources, or more time, that it could not have been even better or gone smoother. Change is an evolution and through methodical processes can position the organization for continued success.

REFERENCES

Allio, R. J., (2003). Strategic thinking: The ten big ideas. *Strategy & Leadership,* *34*(4), 4–13.

Bridges, W., (1991). *Managing transitions: Making the most of change.* Reading, MA: Addison-Wesley.

Cameron, K., & Quinn, R. (2011). *Diagnosing and changing organizational culture: Based on the competing values framework*. San Francisco, CA, Jossey-Bass.

Fernsler, T. (2011). Change happens, *Nonprofit World, 29*(2) 26. www.snpo.org

Hannan, M., Polos, L.., & Carroll, G. (2007). *Logics of organization theory: Audiences, codes and ecologies*. Princeton, NJ: Princeton University Press..

Jacobs, G., Christe-Zeyse, J., Keegan, A., & Polos, L. (2008)., Reactions to organizational identity threats in times of change: Illustrations from the German police. *Corporate Reputation Review, 11*, 245–261.

Jacobs, G., van Witteloostuijn, A., & Christe-Zeyse, J. (2013). A theoretical framework of organizational change. *Journal of Organizational Change Management, 26*(5), 772–792.

Jick, T. D. (1993), *Managing change: Cases and concepts*. Boston, MA: Irwin McGraw-Hill.

Klein, S. M. (1996). A management communication strategy for change. *Journal of Organizational Change Management 9*(2), 32–46.

Lewis, L. K., & Seibold, D. R. (1998). Reconceptualizing organizational change implementation as a communication problem: A review of literature and research agenda. In M. E. Rolloff (Ed.), *Communication Yearbook 21* (pp. 93–151). Thousand Oaks, CA: Sage.

Salerno, A., & Brock, L. (2008). *The change cycle: How people can survive and thrive in organizational change*. Oakland, CA: Berrett-Koehler.

Schein, E. H. (1997). *Organizational culture and leadership* (2nd ed.). San Francisco, CA: Jossey-Bass.

Shamir, B., House, R. J., & Arthur, M. B. 1993. The motivational effects of charismatic leadership: A self-concept based theory. *Organization Science, 4*(4), 577–594.

Van Knippenberg, D., Van Knippenberg, B., & Bobbio, A. (2008). Leaders as agents of continuity: Self continuity and resistance to collective change. In F. Sani (Ed.), *Self-continuity: Individual and collective perspectives* (pp. 175–186). New York, NY: Psychology Press.

CHAPTER 7

DRONES IN DOMESTIC LAW ENFORCEMENT

Ethical Issues, Implementation Practices, and Case Studies

Jonathan P. West and James S. Bowman

A drone is a remotely controlled or completely automated aircraft. Initially designed to gather military intelligence, the diffusion of these airborne devices into civilian life is largely due to low-cost microelectronics, lightweight construction materials, as well as advances in computing, global positioning, imaging, signal processing, and communication technologies. Business analysts anticipate a robust market for these machines: by 2020 it is estimated that at least 30,000 unmanned aerial vehicles (UAVs) will be in the nation's skies, serving a wide range of public, private, and commercial functions (Committee on the Judiciary U.S. Senate, 2013; also see Ferris, 2015).[1]

The 2012 Federal Aviation Administration (FAA) Modernization and Reform Act, in fact, required the integration of drones into the national airspace by late 2015. The FAA, as anticipated, missed the deadline due to funding uncertainties (from sequestration, government shutdowns, short-

Transforming Government Organizations:
Fresh Ideas and Examples From the Field, pp. 213–237
Copyright © 2016 by Information Age Publishing

term reauthorization extensions), staff shortages and issue complexity, and is not expected to implement the law until mid-2016 or later. Until then, corporate usage is prohibited without approval[2]; military and civilian agency drones require FAA certification. The Reform Act nonetheless suggests a promising future for aerial robotic craft, one enthusiastically supported by bipartisan drone caucuses in both houses of Congress. Indeed, recent draft regulations "are expected to lead to a revolution in commercial aviation" (Whitlock, 2015). Although the proposed regulations focus on business uses, officials expect that there will be major increase in drone use by government agencies, most notably public safety departments.

The rapid development of this technology suggests the need to shift from what these airborne devices can do to what they should do—namely, decisions about their deployment will be affected by not only technical capacity but also human agency. UAV usage, like any other human activity, is socially constructed as technology can be an enabler of ends, constructive and destructive (Schmidt & Cohen, 2014). Technology is applied in a social context which is never neutral. The issue is not whether UAV engineering will expand, but rather how it will evolve and what changes may be desirable.

As examined below, drone proliferation multiplies both probable benefits and risks. The purpose of this chapter is to explore the ethical implications and implementation issues inherent in surveillance—the primary use of uninhabited aircraft. The background section briefly reviews the ubiquity and types of these domestic droids. The core of the inquiry analyzes the ethical challenges and implementation practices, as well as case studies in drone use. The conclusion discusses guidelines for the present and future use of this technology.

BACKGROUND

Unmanned aerial vehicles are not new (e.g., Villasenor, 2013, pp. 462–464), but since the terrorist attacks of 9-11-01 their worldwide use in military and civil applications has dramatically increased.[3] These machines are the signature weapon of modern warfare, as nearly 90 states and nonstate actors use them for reconnaissance, intelligence collection, and targeting (Saylor, 2015). With the drawdown of wars in Afghanistan and Iraq, the business strategy of UAV manufacturers is to expand their market to civilian uses. Poised to realize this considerable commercial potential are the increasingly influential drone lobby in Washington, D.C., and the large, growing, global trade group the Association for Unmanned Vehicle Systems International (AUVSI). The industry predicts $82 billion in economic benefits, and expects to create 70,000 jobs in the first three years of drone diffusion into the nation's skies and over 100,000 jobs by 2025 (Kesselman, 2015). Customers currently include police departments, universities, Google, state transportation departments, and dozens of federal agencies. Many other organizations including National Geographic, Amazon, insurance companies, real estate firms, detective agencies, the mass media, filmmakers and agribusiness are interested in using this robotic technology.

The growing presence of these devices is driven by their capacity to do "dull, dirty, dangerous" tasks: all-weather, all-terrain search and rescue missions; law enforcement reconnaissance and pursuit; emergency management surveys of fires, volcanic activity, earthquake zones, and nuclear reactor malfunctions; infrastructure inspections of pipelines, towers, and borders; crowd control; oil and gas exploration and mapping; private investigation; and point-to-point deliveries of goods. Before the decade is out, the use of versatile, uninhabited aircraft may become commonplace.

Engineering advances have combined to produce a remarkable differentiation of drone technologies: there are some 1,500 types of unmanned aircraft in production, in a variety of sizes and shapes from extremely small nano machines to those as large as a charter jet with the ability to be nearly anywhere and see anything for any purpose. They vary in weight, range, flight duration, and control systems (Goldberg, Corcoran, & Picard, 2013; Wallace-Wells, 2014). Some are cheap and easy-to-fly so that they can be carried in a backpack, assembled and launched in minutes. Others, as small as insects, can fly undetected into buildings to track, photograph and attack targets with weaponry, both lethal and nonlethal (rubber bullets, gases, tasers, piercing sounds, strobe lights).

Airborne robot technology, then, is characterized by complex, multimodal systems that provide an unblinking eye-in-the-sky coverage carrying high-resolution video cameras, infrared sensors, license plate readers, facial recognition programs, listening devices, weapons, gyroscopes, accelerometers, wireless transmitters, thermal imagining, GPS navigation, and other hi tech capabilities (Finn & Wright, 2012). As the numerous kinds and capabilities suggest, drone missions vary substantially. However just as the Central Intelligence Agency uses these aircraft in foreign countries, many domestic purposes will be for surveillance-like functions such as crime fighting, disaster relief, immigration control, and environmental monitoring.

Following the long-standing link between military technology and subsequent adoption by law enforcement, local and state police departments are expected to be among the largest users of unmanned aerial vehicles (McDougal, 2013). Frequently underwritten by Department of Homeland Security grants, these agencies have employed droids for over 10 years (Salter, 2014, p. 169). In fact, "it's not uncommon," according to the American Civil Liberties Union, "for the police to use a new technology in secret for as long as they can, and then allow the courts to sort out legality once the issue finally comes to them" (Crump, 2013).

In the meantime, it is prudent to consider whether drones are as efficacious as their manufacturers suggest. Domestically, the U.S. Department of Homeland Security Inspector General (2014) found that UAV deployment along the Mexican border is ineffective and five times more expensive than expected. As well, U.S. Department of Justice auditors have questioned Federal Bureau of Investigation, Drug Enforcement Administration, and U.S. Marshal Service drone oversight capabilities (Musgrave, 2015). Abroad, despite dramatic drone strikes, their extensive use in the Middle East has had an uncertain impact on terrorist activities.

In seeking a balance of conflicting claims, the ramifications of drone surveillance is needed because of it protean nature. On the one hand, Talia (2014, p. 737) observes that UAV "capability is exponentially greater than other investigatory tools." On the other hand, Salter (2014, p. 169) argues that, "the role of play, thrill and excitement in militarism ... helps explain police interest ... despite the lack of evidence that such tactics are efficacious in addressing crime and social disorder." What is evident is that uninhabited aerial vehicle technology has evolved faster than the law in part because covert intelligence and military programs have operated with limited oversight and debate.[4] Similarly, previously unreported use of U.S. Customs and Border Patrol drones by the Federal Bureau of Investigation and the Central Intelligence Agency took place without public acknowledgment (Bennett, 2011).

Automated flight technology, in short, holds possibilities that were science fiction a generation ago; in an age of aerial drones and big data, what was once invisible and meaningless is now made visible and meaningful. Observations are more constant, and more and more information goes into a permanent record. Data in many forms, from widely spaced geographical areas, organizations, and time periods can be readily merged and analyzed. As surveillance has become capital—rather than labor-intensive, aerial monitoring of American life will be increasingly easy to do. The line between public and private spheres will be further blurred, and may profoundly change the character of civic culture.

Drone surveillance can be regarded either as a justifiable, impartial practice serving the interests of all or an oppressive technique catering to the interests of some at the expense of others. With the "gold rush" mentality surrounding commercialization of drones—thousands of jobs and billions in revenue are potentially in play—it is critical that stakeholders confront difficult questions, avoid hurried judgments, and employ reliable policymaking processes. Given the adolescence of the drone era, the lack of agreed-upon metrics makes it difficult—and crucial—to scrutinize the advantages and drawbacks of UAV operations. The next section weighs the ethical benefits and problems inherent in the use of these vehicles through the use of a hypothetical, but realistic, case.

ETHICAL ISSUES CASE STUDY

The use of high-tech drones for law enforcement, even to promote public safety, security and productivity, can be controversial and raise important ethical issues. The hypothetical case below illustrates how decisions to use UAVs are complicated and can have significant positive and negative implications.

> *Alonzo Griffith is sheriff of a metropolitan county government. He is intrigued with the idea of using drones for domestic law enforcement. He was aware of the availability of smaller and less expensive versions of the aircraft used in Afghanistan, Iraq, and Iran.*
>
> *His interest was piqued when he learned that UVAs could see through walls, use software for facial recognition, and intercept calls and e-mails, all with little regulation. He thought of several possible uses: helping to locate missing children, identifying marijuana fields, detecting wildfires, reporting highway accidents and hazardous material spills, and tracking dangerous suspects. However, he also knew that surveillance raises controversial privacy issues. He learned some citizen groups strongly opposed their domestic use.*
>
> *Recently Griffith had instructed his staff to buy two unmanned remote control aircraft. Now, he is having second thoughts about the order.*

His decision to order UAVs are examined here, first by using the traditional philosophical approach to decision making, and then by applying behavioral ethics to the case.

Traditional Decision-Making Approach

While a variety of decision-making frameworks could be used to dissect the scenario, one is especially helpful because its scope minimizes the chances of an incomplete and flawed assessment.[5] This approach, the ethics "triad," brings together the competing philosophical schools of thought based on:

- expected *results* of an action (consequentialism or teleology),
- application of pertinent *rules* (duty ethics or deontology), and
- personal character (*virtue* ethics).

When focusing on results, the key question is, "Which decision produces the greatest good for the greatest number?" In contemplating rules, the issue is "Would I want everyone else to make the same decision that I did?" From a virtue ethics perspective, the policymaker asks, "Does this decision improve my character and that of the community?" Relying on consideration of results, rules, and virtues, the triad guides exploration of these distinct perspectives to offer a balanced, defensible assessment (Svara, 2015).

From a *results* perspective, Griffith is confident that his pending purchase could serve the "greater good" and that use of the robotic aircraft would enhance law enforcement capabilities. He believes that using these machines would be an efficient, effective, and safe way to respond to critical situations. He read that in 2012 the FAA had issued more than 300 licenses, and 17 law enforcement units had filed petitions to get permits. The Sheriff expects these numbers will increase rapidly in coming years. He is concerned that his department may become obsolete if he fails to adopt emerging technologies, such as droids. He sees their advantages compared to helicopters because they cost less (approximately $36,000 to $250,000 for a drone versus $3 million for a helicopter and crew). Griffith knows that his counterparts in Mesa County, Colorado and Grand Forks, North Dakota are pioneers at the forefront of this technology. Procuring drones would advance government's core purpose: cost-effective service. The policy, in brief, can be justified as the greatest good for the greatest number.

Yet citizens might perceive the vehicles as a threat to civil liberties and rights. Attorneys and media commentary will likely criticize this initiative as another step toward a surveillance society, raising concerns about "Big Brother" monitoring in an Orwellian police state. Law enforcement offices in Miami-Dade, Los Angeles, Houston, Metro Nashville, and Seattle have purchased or are considering drones, sparking controversy and the scrutiny of policymakers (Seattle officials subsequently cancelled their order after vociferous objections). Smaller cities like Montgomery, TX, North Little Rock, AR,, and Gadsden, AL, have had similar experience with public backlash; Charlottesville, VA and Berkeley, CA ordered a 2-year and 1-year moratorium on citywide use of UAVs, respectively (J. Ferguson, 2015; Watson, 2013).

Griffith knows that an aroused citizenry could threaten his job security and career. Demonstrations by protest groups are already planned throughout the United States; the Sheriff would prefer not to witness such disruptive events in his community. Furthermore, evidence that unmanned machines require ground pilot and maintenance support (with high operational expenses), and have relatively high accident rates, makes him question the cost-effectiveness of drones. Despite his initial enthusiasm, then, he is increasingly concerned about the consequences of using drones.

Concerning the second triad component, *rules*, it may be that it is the department's prerogative to make policy, but ethical rules trump organizational rules. Griffith is mindful that drone technology is currently ahead of the law, as legislation on domestic drones, including FAA guidelines, are in their infancy. While he has heard claims that monitoring may disproportionately fall on marginalized populations (Wall & Monahan, 2011), he is convinced that surveillance can be deployed and used fairly: what is good for one is good for all. Griffin believes it is appropriate to have public input on the purpose and use of drones, and that implementation should include policies on oversight, privacy, and transparency.

Although the county does not have an ethics code, the sheriff—as a member of the National Association of Counties (NACo)—has an obligation to follow its code. He examined NACo's most relevant ethical principles (i.e., to husband public funds, provide the best quality service at minimal cost, and perform duties diligently), and is satisfied that they can be addressed. He also read the International Association of Chiefs of Police Aviation Committee (IACP) recommendations that UAVs operate in a nonnuisance causing, FAA regulation-compliant manner. Griffith recognizes that it is his duty to work responsibly to protect and serve the community, improve citizen safety and advance the public interest. Use of airborne robotic technology for tracking lost children is one example. While it could be viewed positively or negatively (assuring the safety of the child, but intruding on privacy), deployment—following best practices to insure quality service—would include using governmental resources for legitimate purposes and ensuring adequate safeguards against unwarranted surveillance.

He understands that drones if misused could threaten Fourth Amendment rights (to be secure against unreasonable search and seizure) and these aircraft can pose First Amendment risks (chilling the right to express a wide range of viewpoints and freedom to engage in political activities). He is concerned that intrusive monitoring violates certain principles that he tries to uphold, such as the "golden rule" ("do unto others as you would have them do unto you" and "do no harm"). He knows that capturing images of private property without consent diminishes the control people have to live life as they wish. Absent restrictions on data storage and dissemination, Griffith recognizes that a "reasonable expectations of privacy" could be compromised.

He remembers, for instance, the controversy surrounding Whole Body Imaging technology as a screening tool at airports (Vicinanzo, 2014). Problems like this could surface over UAVs, especially if monitoring is conducted clandestinely. In addition, there have also been reports that drones operating in the airspace of commercial or private planes cause safety concerns. Community critics may feel that the results (privacy invasion, safety threats) do not justify the goals (cost-effectiveness, increased security). On balance, though, the Sheriff believes his decision is ethically well-grounded, but acknowledges potential constitutional and safety concerns.

Virtue ethics provides a third lens to assess Griffith's situation. It maintains that people are not moral because of results or rules, but because of what they demand of themselves in character. Virtuous conduct derives from a life-long practice of self-discipline requiring a commitment to ethical values. What is right is that which fosters individual excellence and contributes to collective well-being. Aristotle's encouragement of prudence—to build character requires avoiding both excesses and deficiencies—suggests that the Sheriff could proceed by seeking a middle course that respects privacy and freedom while advancing safety and security. Citizen confidence and public trust are crucial and both are on the decline. Using drones without preparing and involving residents would be imprudent, as would starting a surveillance program without a policy. If he proceeds, it would be only after exercising due diligence, including dialoguing with citizens about the advantages and disadvantages of drones and designing a reasoned approach to surveillance.

Griffith wants to be forthright with the public. He aims to show that drone use is desirable, that the data will not be misused, and that deployment will make him and those in his jurisdiction better citizens. The Sheriff knows that others will disagree that individual and community well-being is advanced by aerial observation; their apprehensions will be weighed, not dismissed. Griffin agrees with critics that heightened levels of control could lead to diminished levels of trust. He does not want law-abiding people to feel they must adjust their behavior because they are being watched. Ultimately, he hopes to successfully balance his law enforcement obligations against citizens' legitimate anxieties about abuse of police power and erosion of individual rights. From a virtue perspective, then, the Sheriff is reasonably confident that his professional values and conduct can serve to reassure the community.

While analysis using the triad may fall short of conclusive solutions, it offers insights about the underlying logic by which decisions are justified. The triad, comprehensive yet succinct, can help provide a defensible judgment derived from evaluation of consequences, rules, and virtues. It offers a conscious attempt to reconcile conflicting values, accomplishing a key function of policy-making: generating alternative viewpoints, systematically evaluating them, and crafting a considered assessment. It cannot, of course, produce a definitive judgment. It should be acknowledged that undue emphasis on one perspective, at the expense of the other approaches, risks distortions—expediency (results-based ethics), rigid rule compliance (rule-based ethics), and self-justification (virtue-based ethics). In view of the limitations of each approach, it is evident that the use of this integrative tool can be worthwhile.

Yet overreliance on rational decision-making models like the triad is the absence of a relationship between moral theorizing and ethical action. As Gazzaniga (2008, p. 148) observes, "It has been hard to find any correlation between moral reasoning and proactive moral behavior. In fact, in most studies, none has been found." The fundamental assumptions underlying the traditional philosophical approach—that people are universally logical, possess complete information, have the willpower to act on it, and to pursue their self-interest—often are absent in real life. For this reason, Bazerman and Tenbrunsel (2011) believe that it is important to identify the unconscious psychological forces that routinely influence decision making.

Behavioral Ethics Approach

Behavioral ethics suggests that factors other than moral reasoning—unconscious biases, moral emotions, and personal intuitions—are likely to affect behavior (Shao, Aquino, & Freeman, 2008). This approach draws on the work of psychologists and focuses on the actual conduct of the individual. While the rational model places considerable cognitive demands on people, it tends to devalue unconscious, emotional, psychological factors that can result in unethical decisions. Behavioral ethics research introduces considerations like:

- ethical fading (unintentional blindness where decision-makers fail to consider relevant information or detect an ethical problem)
- issue framing (the way in which an issue is presented or perceived can affect the outcome)
- action bias (the felt pressure to do something)
- overoptimism (overestimating one's ability to make good decisions)
- confirmation bias (gathering information to confirm preexisting beliefs)
- System 1/System 2 thinking (System 1 is a rapid, intuitive, visceral way to process information and guide action; System 2 is slow-paced, "cool," and deliberative.)

Sheriff Griffith's interest in drones, for example, could be based on the law-enforcement benefits he perceives (efficiency, effectiveness, cost savings), which may reflect the way he understands (frames) and assesses the issue. His fascination with the new technology may be related to his familiarity with its introduction in other jurisdictions and the pressure to not be left behind (action bias), which in turn could desensitize him to the potential privacy threats (ethical fading). The pressure to act could have led to the Sheriff's initial System 1 (gut reaction) to purchase droids; however, his hesitancy to proceed with the order suggests he is rethinking the implications of his decision (System 2). As with any new initiative, there is uncertainty that impairs rational decision making; it is impossible to anticipate all problems; nonetheless, in the present context, Griffith may be overly optimistic about drone benefits. As more information becomes available, he needs to be sensitive to the possibility of confirmation bias—unconsciously seeking data that reinforces existing preferences.

Including insights from behavioral ethics, alongside those derived from the ethics triad, helps to increase awareness of, and account for, the blind spots found in human behavior in each component of the ethics triad. If Sheriff Griffith, at the outset, had applied the prescriptions from the traditional philosophical decision-making analysis, and the descriptions of conduct in the behavioral model, he would have gained a more complete understanding of the dynamics influencing his actions. Responsible decision makers, by definition, are obligated to develop virtues, respect rules, examine results, and heed behavioral biases to craft a considered judgement.

DISCUSSION

Neither drone monitoring nor its absence is problem-free. Reviewing the traditional and behavioral approaches, what then can be concluded? Looking at each part of the triad in sequence, what is the greatest good for the greatest number? As indicated, it may be realized when efficiency, security, and privacy are enhanced to serve both institutions and individuals. This implies that UVA use, initiated for legitimate reasons, produces the promised results, and is not arbitrary or offensive. While courts tend to defer to management, neither the organization nor the individual has absolute rights. The authority to manage can be a seductive rationale for finding the greatest good, exceeding what is reasonable and necessary at the expense of important rights; if so, drone use can be counterproductive.

The second component of the triad, rule-based ethics, focuses on what is good for one, is good for all. Properly designed, surveillance promises fair and objective administration of the social contract, thus mitigating objections to being policed. Opponents, however, believe that surveillance often overreaches; consent is seldom given, violating both the Golden Rule and the categorical imperative and creating unnecessary harm. Because few officials would agree to be monitored, the burden of proof—to establish a well-crafted system—falls on those who would watch others.

Finally, virtue ethics seeks individual excellence and collective well-being. There may be no ready answers based on results or rules, so a person must act in a manner to enhance integrity in decision-making. Activists argue that monitoring can reinforce the autonomy of individuals by emphasizing integrity and the imperative to better one's self. Alternatively, the technology can erode these same characteristics according to critics. In the end, virtue ethics demands a thoughtful decision—neither excessive nor deficient—based on the situation and experience. As such, the choice to use aerial surveillance must enrich the quality of the individual and the community. Yet virtue theory's strength—subjective judgments derived from personal character—is also its limitation: if supporters and opponents of policing behavior believe they are laudable, they are likely to regard what they do as praiseworthy.

The limitations of the ethics triad (results: prediction mistakes; rules: rigidity; virtue: self-righteousness) highlight the significant biases and errors revealed by behavioral ethics. In an example of ethical fading, Mazzetti (2013, p. 319) describes how killing by drone is done without discernment or remorse:

> [T]asked with finding Osama bin Laden, covert strikes came to be morally vacuous matters of routine. As bureaucratic habit overwhelmed ethical sensitivity, lethal force came to be abused ..., even American spies were not certain whom they were killing. Reliant on notoriously inexact intelligence, these ... strikes often resulted in high proportions of non-combatant causalities. [quoting Blee] "In the early days, for our consciences we wanted to know who we were killing before anyone pulled the trigger, now we're lighting those people up all over the place." Immersed in the bureaucracy, people exercised the State's power without qualm, and without a mind to democratic ideals.

It is not difficult to identify civilian parallels, including police monitoring of protest marches and the use of nonlethal weaponry.

By anticipating such forces and deliberately considering their influence, officials may ensure that they do not override personal integrity, the categorical imperative, and the greatest good. The prescriptions of the philosophical decision-making model and the descriptions of conduct in the behavioral model can be seen as mutually beneficial approaches. In essence, both ask decision-makers to think about thinking. Policies that incorporate a synthesis of these two models should enhance the quality of decision-making.

IMPLEMENTATION PRACTICES

To complement the use of the ethics triad and behavioral ethics, those responsible for implementing drone surveillance need to think carefully about selected implementation issues: (1) management concerns, (2) legal compliance, (3) stakeholder analysis, as well as (4) deployment and data policies. To provide practical guidance, Table 7.1 summarizes relevant practices.

Table 7.1.   Selected Domestic Drone Implementation Practices

Management	*Policies*
• Provide training for UAV operators	• Establish policies and procedures on:
• Institute a policy review committee	– deployment decisions
• Track operating costs and benefits	– collection, retention and dissemination of information
• Monitor safety records	– ensuring UAVs are secure against misuse
• Audit flight documentation at regular intervals	– destruction of data collected by drones
• Document drone use and record retention	• Draft city ordinance or police policy on use of pilotless vehicles
• Document flight times, locations, missions and operators	• Develop privacy guidelines
• Ensure data are downloaded securely	• Distinguish between privacy in a public vs. private space
• Know the capabilities of UAVs	• Ban UAV weaponization
• Ensure there are oversight procedures for UAV use	• Decide the types of investigations drones can engage in
• Prevent unauthorized access to the information database	• Decide types of responses UAVs can make
• Assess risks and potential liabilities from drone use.	• Ensure that policies are clear, written and open to the public
	• Clarify information retention and storage practice
Legal Compliance	*Stakeholders*
• Assure adherence to regulations concerning use of UAVs	• Identify key stakeholders
• Know and adhere to:	• Establish a multistakeholder engagement process
– the legal limits on surveillance	• Initiate a public information campaign

(Table continues on next page)

Table 7.1.   (Continued)

Legal Compliance	Stakeholders
– the regulations on obtaining, retaining or using surveillance data	• Engage the community in planning efforts
– 1st and 4th Amendment protections	• Enable review and comment by the public on UAV plans
– court precedents	• Notify the community when drones are used
– statutory requirements on use	
– city restrictions on use	
– restrictions on collecting and sharing information about individuals	
– the conditions under which a warrant is required	

First, program management requires consideration of necessary actions both before and after deployment. In advance of proceeding, it is imperative to assess the risks and liabilities in drone use; knowing the capabilities and limitations of UAVs is crucial. In preparation to launch the program, it is important to: provide operator training, establish oversight procedures, and create a policy review committee to monitor implementation. A process for deciding who is authorized to have access to the information database created by drones must be developed and steps taken to prevent unauthorized access. Action is required to ensure data are downloaded securely. When operating pilotless vehicles, additional decisions arise. It is necessary to provide documentation of UAV use (e.g., flight times, locations, missions, and operators) and record retention arrangements must be made. Such flight information must be audited at regular intervals. Safety records also should be kept, along with operating costs and benefits.

Second, as noted, Constitutional, statutory, and common law requirements must be strictly followed. Assuring adherence to legal mandates includes knowledge of First and Fourth Amendment provisions, statutory requirements on the use of drones, and regulations on obtaining, retaining and using surveillance data. Being conversant with restrictions on collecting and sharing information about individuals is necessary. Law enforcement officials, of course, also must be familiar with the conditions under which a warrant is needed.

Third, an internal and external stakeholder engagement process should be established, as stakeholder support is essential to policy success. These actors can affect law enforcement operations, but their interests often differ: some who may focus on the promise of improved safety and security and others on the erosion or protection of freedoms and privacy. Officials must consider how and when to take stakeholder views into account, and to be willing to adjust policies and practices accordingly. Some jurisdictions succeed at this task, while others fail (see case studies below). If stakeholders are supportive rather than antagonistic, it can considerably influence the ability of law enforcement to advance its UAV initiatives. However, it is not always easy to respond to competing and sometimes contradictory claims, and to create strategies that address the interests of multiple constituencies.

Police officials, then, often operate in a complex political environment that requires them to understand and predict stakeholder activity and gauge the legitimacy, urgency and power of various constituency groups when making high-stakes decisions. The challenge is managing claimant relationships in a way that achieves the mutual objectives of the community and law enforcement. A first step is a public information campaign to alert citizens about what is being contemplated regarding the use of UAVs. This includes mailings to explain what government is doing, why and how it meets local needs. Also public hearings, open meetings, citizen panels, and neighborhood surveys can be used to provide input. It is crucial to engage residents in planning efforts, and arrangements to enable comment on UAV plans. Ultimately, if approved, the public should be notified when drones are used and for what purpose.

Finally, and in addition to managerial, legal and stakeholder issues, law enforcement should establish procedures for: deployment decisions; collection, retention and dissemination of information; safeguards against misuse of UAVs, and destruction of collected data. This may require drafting a city ordinance or police policy on drones, establishing guidelines on issues like privacy, and distinguishing between privacy in a public verses private space. Policies should be clear, written, and open to the community. They need to be specific regarding the types of responses drones can make, the kinds of activities UAVs can undertake and the nature of information retained. In most jurisdictions, there is likely to be a policy banning weaponizing robotic craft.

The general strategies reviewed here illustrate the issues facing law enforcement as they contemplate embarking on drone surveillance. Beyond these broad considerations, contextual factors need to be taken into account in before making decisions. The three cases outlined below include one unsuccessful and two successful examples of law enforcement policy decisions and actions. The cases provide a "reality test" documenting experience with some of the strategies already discussed, and highlight lessons that can be learned from jurisdictions that have experienced diffing results with UAVs.

CASE STUDIES

Seattle, Washington

In 2010, the Seattle police department purchased two 3.5-pound Draganflyer X6 UAVs for $80,000 with funds from a Homeland Security grant, but without city council approval or disclosure to the citizenry (Greene, 2013; Orbanek, 2015). The intended goal was to replace costly manned helicopters by deploying droids to save lives and increase public safety. Specifically it was thought that UAVs would address situations involving hostages, search-and-rescue for missing persons, hazardous material, bomb threats, natural disasters, pursuit of fleeing suspects, collecting traffic data, and fire detection (Claridge, 2013; McGlynn, 2013). However, residents were kept in the dark for 2 years about these plans (Orbanek, 2015). In late 2012, the police department convened a community meeting intending to improve transparency and communicate clearly with citizens so officials could listen to concerns about drone use and shape policy to reflect local preferences (McGlynn, 2013).

They were met with a vociferous outcry from many of the 100 people attending, with shouts of "no drones" and loud cries of "shame" and "murderer" interrupting and drowning out officials. The opposition focused on: "militarization" of police; fears about the overly broad application of drones, invasion of privacy, and the need for limits on police search power; unclear guidelines on who can collect information, how it would be used, and for how long it would be kept; beliefs that mandates should be based on city ordinance not police policy; and the need to require a warrant prior to use of drones (except in emergencies) (Claridge, 2012, 2013; Kaminsky, 2012).

A city council committee held a meeting 4 months later to solicit public input on a proposed ordinance. It would have barred police from using UAVs for surveillance or flying over open-air assemblies. The police department's guidelines indicated that they would not use drones to conduct random surveillance activities and that they would be vigilant in protecting individual privacy (Claridge, 2012, 2013). Notwithstanding these measures, citizens objected to use of pilotless craft under any circumstances. The following day, Seattle Mayor Mike McGinn cancelled the program before it became operational. He did so to enable the police to "focus its resources on public safety and the community building work that is the department's priority" (Claridge, 2012; McGlynn, 2013). The vehicles were returned to the manufacturer.

Mesa County, Colorado

The program in the Mesa County Sheriff's Office became operational in 2010. Between then and 2015, UAVs performed 82 flight missions for a total of more than 300 flight hours. Six trained operators were used on missions ranging from search-and-rescue operations to documentation of crime scenes (Orbanek, 2015). A selling point was cost savings; compared to airplanes, unmanned craft were much cheaper to operate ($25 per hour verses $500 to $1,200 per hour) (Balcerzack & Heigel, 2013; G. M. Ferguson, 2015). The county purchased two small drones. The biggest obstacle encountered was the arduous year-long application and approval process of the Federal Aviation Agency (FAA) in order to obtain a Certificate of Authorization (COA) (Orbanek, 2015).

Once authorization was obtained, drone flights were initially restricted to a one-square-mile area at the County landfill. For two years, testing to perfect the use of the technology was done with a Dragonflyer X6 inside the boundaries of a landfill area. Subsequently, the Sheriff's Office applied for a modified COA to broaden flight area to the entire county, during daytime hours. It was the first jurisdiction to receive approval for such an enlarged area (3,300 square miles) (Unmanned Aerial System Team, 2015). This two-step COA authorization process, starting with a small geographic area and gradually moving to a larger one, is a common strategy used by the FAA.

Unlike the Seattle police, Mesa County officials made every effort from the beginning to proceed with transparency by educating the public using a website, media spots, and a safety fair at a mall (Increasing Human Potential Staff, 2013). They drafted a UAV deployment policy and subjected it to rigorous review and critique by their policy review committee. They worked closely with the University of Colorado Research and Engineering Center for Unmanned Vehicles to provide training in drone use and to increase citizen awareness. To address media and privacy-group concerns, they did not minimize the importance of individual rights under the Fourth Amendment, but stressed their primary responsibility to provide the safest, most efficient aerospace system possible. Sheriff's Office personnel have been working alongside the FAA and Department of Justice to ensure compliance with regulations regarding UAVs by law enforcement units (G. M. Ferguson, 2015).

The primary drone functions in the county have been: (a) accident- and crime-scene reconstruction (the latter using three-dimensional images of crime locations), (b) search-and-rescue operations (generally unsuccessful), and (c) use of cameras to identify "hot spots" in major fires. The Sheriff's office has never employed drones for surveillance (e.g., in the words of one Sheriff's office official "flying around watching people until they do something bad") (Greene, 2013). The most dramatic example of drone use to catch criminals occurred when an armed fugitive with a lengthy record escaped from a halfway house and remained at large. The Sheriff's office operated its unmanned aerial vehicle to search for the felon and spotted him near an acquaintance's house. The location was relayed to the Sheriff's SWAT team; the team sniper shot the escapee. This case shows how use of a UAV can help to keep a safe distance between the police and a fugitive (Orbanek, 2015).

Grand Forks, North Dakota

The Grand Forks County Sheriff's Department is another pioneer in the deployment of UAVs. It followed the same FAA two-step process as Mesa County to receive a COA, but they took it even further by getting permission to fly in 16 counties. Further, they were the first jurisdiction to receive federal approval to operate at night (Pilkington, 2014). Detailed policies have been developed that comply with legal limitations on the use of unmanned aerial vehicles. Grand Forks has a fleet of four small machines. Law enforcement has flown 11 missions, including 5 documenting crime or traffic accidents, 2 focused on a natural disaster (a flooding river), 2 involved in searching for missing people, and 2 entailing searching for criminals (a prison escapee and a rapist) (Pilkington, 2014).

The University of North Dakota helped provide legitimacy and rigorous vetting of remotely piloted aircraft. Oversight of the Sheriff Department's and University's UAV program is provided by the North Dakota Unmanned Aerial Systems Research Compliance Committee, established 2 years ago to establish ethical and privacy boundaries on research and operations. It is composed of professors, law enforcement and community members to ensure, among other things, that activities do not run afoul of Fourth Amendment protections against search and seizure (Orbanek, 2015; Pilkington, 2014).

The Committee conducted surveys of people living in the north-east part of the state that found a relaxed, generally positive attitude about drone applications. Specifically, there was support (90%) for using UAVs in hostage-taking situations, and strong endorsement for using law enforcement drones to hunt for those illegally crossing the border or to track crime suspects. However, support was withdrawn when it came to enforcing traffic violations and only a small majority (58%) approved deployment to identify illegal hunting or fishing activity. There is no claim that these results would be replicated in a national survey; however, they do suggest that in specific parts of the U.S. attitudes are favorable toward drone use by law enforcement. Some civil libertarians may be concerned by certain aspects of the program, even in a conservative locale like Grand Forks. For example, when police were asked how long they stored images (and other drone-gathered data), the obscure reply of the deputy sheriff was "We keep it as long as an investigation is ongoing" (Pilkington, 2014).

Similar to Mesa County, Grand Forks drone action has had dangerous incidents, including two involving criminal pursuit and investigation. The first case involved fleeing suspects who were hiding in a cornfield. A police SWAT team faced difficulty finding them, but was aided by intelligence gathered by a UAV leading to capture of the individuals. The second case involved the rape of two University of North Dakota students. The sheriff's department suspected the perpetrator was a neighbor and flew a pilotless craft outside the suspect's apartment. Pictures from the drone's camera established that the man had a clear line of sight to the women's apartment from his window. The photographs were shown in court and the suspect was convicted (Pilkington, 2014; Orbanek, 2015).

SUMMARY

To summarize, these three cases shed light on the use of the general implementation strategies discussed previously. Mesa County and Grand Forks each took a prudent, cautious approach to drone adoption. In part, this caution was dictated by the FAA's step-by-step COA requirements, which enabled the jurisdictions to comprehend management and legal issues, win the support of their community, and conduct the necessary training and testing to be in compliance with legal mandates. The two law enforcement agencies were careful to develop written policies, to establish effective linkages with universities, and to clearly communicate their intentions to the communities they serve. It helped that the local atmosphere in these two jurisdictions was more welcoming to the use of UAVs in law enforcement than was the case in Seattle. There, well-intentioned police officials were too quick to follow the federal money without having elected officials and residents on board to help decide on the appropriate use of the technology. Police in Seattle were initially secretive in failing to disclose their drone plans. They were also insufficiently attuned to public sentiment to accurately anticipate the reaction their initiative would receive.

CONCLUSIONS

Ethical issues and implementation analysis, as supported by cases, suggests that the domestic use of drones can benefit both institutions and individuals. Because the discussion implies limitations on UAV surveillance, what are some guidelines to ensure effective use? It is challenging to make recommendations without knowing what types of vehicles will fly and the kinds of restrictions that will survive legal review. Conflict occurs when monitoring goes beyond what is sensible, demands precise information about behavior, and when it compromises values. Notably, however, the lack of a policy and the absence of management audits are problematic. Relying solely on the goodwill of officials is not sufficient. The development of a risk-based, neutral regulatory regime is essential.

Generally, drone policy should avoid adding to unequal institutional-individual power relations. An imbalance exists because citizens have few rights as "US law currently provides feeble protections" and offers "a meager right to privacy" (Abril , Levin, & Bel Riego, 2012, pp. 95, 121). The decision to implement surveillance, for example, sometimes does not consider the voice of those surveilled (Vorvoreanu & Botan, 2000). Airborne drone monitoring, it follows, should be evaluated for mutual organization-individual advantage.

Democratic government is about protecting the public good as well as safeguarding individual freedom. The unique utility of UAVs can accomplish much in the public interest, while simultaneously creating moral hazards. The technology can empower people by enlarging their capacities, but without meaningful accountability it can menace democratic ideals. Accordingly, among the proposals are:

- policy transparency and accountability legislation,
- warrants before conducting surveillance,
- restrictions on the kinds of technologies mounted to aerial vehicle platforms,
- an independent body to assess the effect of aerial robots on privacy,
- a public interest advocate (Farber, 2013; McNeal, 2014),
- ethical impact statements on proposed policies (Finn & Wright, 2012),
- limitations on what data is collected by whom and why, how data is collected and processed, and how long it is stored and whether information is available to third parties (Desai & von der Embse, 2008; also see Farber, 2015);
- further development of an "ethical governor" enabling drones to do the right thing (Arkin, 2009; also see Lin, Abney, & Bekey, 2012); and
- a digital bill of rights (Hundt, 2014).

In the short term, the Federal Aviation Administration should consider permitting developers greater latitude in experimenting with UAVs' potential which could assist the agency in finalizing regulations and developing new ones. "Government and industry," according to the drone trade association, "must develop a comprehensive research plan to gather data on expanded use cases and establish recommendations and deadlines to achieve important milestones. This includes an emphasis on developing a UAS traffic management system and coordinating UAS integration efforts" (AUVSU, 2015, p.3).

Clarke (2014, p. 268) argues that joint establishment of codes and standards by industry and government has failed, as criteria for an effective regulatory regime—clarity of purpose, transparency, stakeholder participation, parsimony and enforceability—are not accounted for. He concludes that the industry does "not intend to develop operational standards as a form of industry self-regulation but rather is waiting for governments to initiate such processes" (p. 279).[6] What is needed is robust regulation and oversight to allay concerns that surveillance is based on expediency instead of accountability and legitimacy. Steps in that direction are the 2015 presidential directives mandating that the U.S. Department of Commerce work with the UAV industry to develop a voluntary code of conduct and ordering federal domestic agencies to disclose where they fly drones and what they do with the monitoring data. Similarly, at the local government level effective regulatory regimes are needed. As both the hypothetical case and the real-world cases suggest, codes, policies, and guidelines are necessary to aid local law enforcement officials as they grapple with the ethical, legal and public safety issues raised by domestic drones.

Monitoring is becoming ubiquitous, and the trend is for "more surveillance, more loss of privacy ..., more control ..., and necessarily less concern with ethical treatment" (Rosenberg, 2005, p. 150). Ball (2010, p. 91) argues that there also will be increased use of personal data, biometrics, and covert monitoring. As high-tech invasions of privacy generate litigation, courts and legislatures will be challenged to create sustainable policies. The ethics triad-behavioral ethics discussion here examined important principles and arguments surrounding policy development for robotic aerial surveillance. That analysis—coupled with attention to management concerns, legal compliance, stakeholder analysis and deployment and data policies—may be helpful when decision-makers apply them to specific circumstances to make informed judgments about the use of domestic drones.

NOTES

1. Selected portions of this chapter are adapted from West and Bowman (2014, 2015) and Bowman and West (2015).
2. The Federal Aviation Administration controls the nation's airspace—500 feet over ground level (except in urban areas where it is 1,000 feet over the highest obstacle). Unregulated model aircraft are generally allowed below

400 feet if they remain within the hobbyist's line of sight. Although the agency has studied drones since the 1990s, only case-by-case approval of drone use is permitted (Culver, 2014); before these vehicles can be deployed, they must be FAA sanctioned as airworthy. However, unlike conventional aircraft, uninhabited planes do not have registration numbers and remote pilots are often not licensed. In 2013, the FAA reported that it had issued nearly 1,500 permits since 2007, far more than were previously known (Bennett & Rubin, 2013).

Yet with UAVs available over the Internet, the *Washington Post* reports that "while drone uses are [otherwise] technically prohibited, there is a widespread feeling that in the absence of regulations, anything goes (Whitlock, 2015). Schlag (2013, p. 17) states that "current regulations for drone operations are minimal and largely perfunctory." Draft regulations for commercial drone operations, when finalized in 2 or 3 years, will lift many of the current obstacles for operational approval and clarify issues such as line-of-sight requirements, pilot training and certification, as well as drone speed, flight boundaries, and night use. For now, more than 1,000 commercial exemptions, covering 20 industries, have been granted by the FAA (Kesselman, 2015).

For regular updates on UAV developments, consult the Electronic Frontier Foundation archives (https://www.eff.org), the Center for the Study of the Drone Weekly Roundup (http://dronecenter.bard.edu/weekly-roundup-12615), and the sUAS News site (http://www.suasnews.com).

3. Indeed, the 2004 Central Intelligence Agency investigation into its abuse of detainees was an important reason to start killing terrorist suspects with drones instead of capturing them (Gilsinan, 2014).

4. When controversy has occurred, it has been around the use of armed airborne vehicles and their legal authority and combatant status (Boussios, 2014).

5. The Ockham's Razor rule instructs one to use the simplest possible explanation of a problem, and only make it more complex when absolutely necessary. Adding qualifications and explanations may make a position less elegant, less convincing—and less correct.

6. Thus, the AUVSI (2012) Voluntary Code of Conduct is a brief, aspirational, public relations effort written to assist in the passage of the 2012 Reform Act (Singer & Lin, 2012). Likewise, the International Association of Chiefs of Police Aviation Committee (2012) published recommended guidelines for drone operation, all of which are "preliminary, unenforceable, infinitely malleable, and appear not to have benefited from any consultation with stakeholders" (Clarke, 2014, p. 279).

REFERENCES

Abril, P., Levin, A., & Bel Riego, A. (2012). Blurred boundaries: Social media privacy and the twenty-first century employee. *American Business Law Journal*, *49*(1), 63–124.

Arkin, R. (2009). *Governing lethal behavior in autonomous robots*. Boca Raton, FL: Chapman and Hall/CRC.

AUVSU. (2015). Snapshot of the first 500 commercial UAS exemptions. Retrieved from http://higherlogicdownload.s3.amazonaws.com/AUVSI/f28f661a-e248-4687-b21d- 34342433abdb/UploadedFiles/Section333Report.pdfl

Bazerman , M. H., &Tenbrunsel, A. E. (2011). Ethical breakdowns. *Harvard Business Review*. Retrieved from https://hbr.org/2011/04/ethical-breakdowns

Balcerzack, A., & Heigel, T. (2013). Police forces struggle to incorporate drones. *Northwestern University, Medill National Security Zone (special student reports)*. Retrieved from http://droneproject.nationalsecurityzone.org/headline-police-forces-struggle-to- incorporate-drones-ashley-balcerzak-and-taylor-hiegel/

Ball, K. (2010). Workplace surveillance: An overview. *Labor History, 51*(1), 87–106.

Bennett, B. (2011, December 10). Police employ predator drone spy planes on home front. *Los Angeles Times*. Retrieved from http://articles.latimes.com/2011/dec/10/nation/la-na- drone-arrest-20111211

Bennett, B., & Rubin, J. (2013, February 15). Drones are taking to the skies in the U.S. *LA Times*. Retrieved from articles.latimes.com/2013/feb/15/nation/la-at-domestic-drones-20130216

Boussios, E. (2014). The proliferation of drones: A new and deadly arms race. *Journal of Applied Security* Research, *9*(4), 387–302.

Bowman, J., & West, J. (2015). *Public service ethics: Individual and institutional responsibilities*. Washington, DC: CQ Press.

Claridge, C. (2012). Protesters steal the show at Seattle police gathering to explain intended use of drones. *The Seattle Times; Local New*s. Retrieved from http://www.seattletimes.com/ seattle-news/protesters-steal-the-show-at-seattle-police-gathering-to-explain-intended- use-of-drones/

Claridge, C. (2013). Seattle grounds police drone program. *The Seattle Times; Local News*. Retrieved from http://www.seattletimes.com/seattle-news/seattle-grounds-police-drone- program/

Clarke, R. (2014). The regulation of civilian drones' impacts on public safety. *Computer Law and Security Review, 30*(3), 263–285.

Committee on the Judiciary U.S. Senate. (2013). The future of drones in America: Law enforcement and privacy considerations. *U.S. Government Printing Office, Washington*. Retrieved from http://www.gpo.gov/fdsys/pkg/CHRG-113shrg81775/pdf/CHRG-113shrg81775.pdf

Crump, C. (2103). Capability is driving policy, not just at NSA also in police departments. *American Civil Liberties Union*. Retrieved from https://www.aclu.org/blog/technology-and-liberty-national-security/capability-driving-policy-not-just-nsa-also-police

Culver, K. (2014). From battlefield to newsroom: Ethical implications of drone technology in journalism. *Journal of Mass Media Ethics: Exploring Questions of Media Morality, 29*(1), 52–64.

Desai, M., & von der Embse, T. J. (2008). Managing electronic information: An ethics perspective. *Information Management and Computer Security, 16*(1), 20–27.

Farber, H. B. (2013). Eyes in the sky: Constitutional and regulatory approaches to domestic drone deployment. *Syracuse Law Review, 64*(1),1–48.

Farber, H. B. (2015). Eyes in the sky & privacy concerns on the ground. *TheSciTech Lawyer, 11*(4), 6–9.

Ferguson, G. M. (2015). Eye in the sky: Using unmanned aerial vehicles (UAV) for law enforcement. *Law Officer Magazine: Tactics, Technology, Training, 11*(2). Retrieved from http://www.lawofficer.com/articles/print/volume-11/issue-2/features/eye-sky.html

Ferguson, J. (2015). Drone on drones: A California city issues moratorium on law enforcement use of drones. *BBKnowledge.* Retrieved from http://www.bbknowledge.com/public-safety/drone-on-drones-berkeley-issues-moratorium-on-law-enforcement-use-of-drones/

Ferris, R. (2015, August 6). Do we need to put drones on a tighter leash? *CNBC.* Retrieved from http://www.cnbc.com/2015/08/06/do-we-need-to-put-drones-on-a-tighter-leash.htm

Finn, R. L., &Wright, D. (2012). Unmanned aircraft systems: Surveillance, ethics and privacy in civil applications. *Computer Law and Security Review, 28*(2), 184–194.

Gazzaniga M. (2008). *Human: The science behind what makes us unique.* New York, NY: HarperPerennial.

Gilsinan, K. (2014, December 9). America trades torture for drones. *The Atlantic.* Retrieved from www.theatlantic.com/international/archive/2014/12/the-us-stopped-torturing-terror-suspects-droning-them/383590

Goldberg, D., Corcoran M., & Picard, R. (2013). Remotely piloted aircraft systems and journalism: Opportunities and challenges of drones in news gathering. *Reuters Institute for the Study of Journalism, University of Oxford.* Retrieved from http://reutersinstitute. politics.ox.ac.uk/sites/default/files/Remotely%20Piloted%20Aircraft%20and%20Journali sm.pdf

Greene, S. (2013). Colorado's Mesa county a national leader in domestic drone use. *The Colorado Independent.* Retrieved from http://www.coloradoindependent.com/ 127870/colorados-mesa-county-a-national- leader- in-domestic-drone-use

Hundt, R. (2014, May 19). Saving privacy. *Boston Review.* Retrieved from http://bostonreview.net/forum/reed-hundt-saving-privacy

Increasing Human Potential Staff. (2013). Unmanned "unplugged": Interviews with the people leading the way in unmanned system innovation: Ben Miller, Mesa County Sheriff's Office. *Increasing Human Potential.* Retrieved from http://increasinghumanpotential.org/news/unmanned-unplugged/ben_miller/

International Association of Chiefs of Police Aviation Committee. (2012, August). Recommended guidelines for the use of unmanned aircraft. Retrieved from http://www.theiacp.org/portals/0/pdfs/IACP_UAGuidelines.pdf

Kesselman, S. (2015). Snapshot of the first 500 commercial UAS exemptions. *AUVSI.* Retrieved from http://auvsilink.org/advocacy/Section333.html

Kaminsky, J. (2012). Seattle police plan for helicopter drones hits severe turbulence. *Reuters.* Retrieved from http://www.reuters.com/article/2012/11/27/us-usa-drones-seattle-idUSBRE8AQ10R20121127

Lin, P. Abney, K., & Bekey, G. (Eds.). (2012). *Robot ethics: The ethical and social implications of robotics.* Cambridge, MA: The MIT Press.

Mazzetti, M. (2013). *The way of the knife: The C.I.A., a secret army, and a war at the ends of the earth.* New York, NY: Penguin Press.

McDougal, C. (2013). From the battlefield to domestic airspace: An analysis of the evolving roles and expectations of drone technology. *Public IN Review, 1*(2), 92–102.

McGlynn, D. (2013, October 18). Domestic drones. *CQ Researcher Press, 23*, 885–908. Retrieved from http://library.cqpress.com/cqresearcher/document. php?id=cqresrre 2013101800&type=query&num=domestic+drones&

McNeal, G. (2014, November). Drones and aerial surveillance: Considerations for legislators (Paper for the Brookings Institution, Center for Technological Innovation). Washington, DC. Retrieved from http://www.brookings.edu/research/reports2/2014/11/drones-and-aerial-surveillance

Musgrave, S. (2015, July 15). Homeland security secretary admits border drone goals were "unattainable". *Muckrock*. Retrieved from https://www.muckrock.com/news/archives/ 2015/jul/15/homeland-security-admits-border-drone-goals-were-u/

Orbanek, S. (2015). To protect and serve: Law enforcement agencies make the case for using UAVs to fight crime, while privacy and police overreach concerns abound. *Drone 360, 1*(1), 64–73.

Pilkington, E. (2014, October 1). We see ourselves as the vanguard: The police force using drones to fight crime. *The Guardian News*. Retrieved from http://www.theguardian.com/ world/2014/oct/01/drones-police-force-crime-uavs-north-dakota

Rosenberg, R. S. (2005). The technological assault on ethics in the modern workplace. In J. W. Budd & J. G. Scoville (Ed.), *The ethics of human resources and industrial relations* (pp. 141–172). Champaign, IL: Labor and Employment Relations Association.

Salter, M. (2014). Toys for the boys? Drones, pleasure and popular culture in the militarization of policing. *Critical Criminology, 22*(2), 163–177.

Saylor, K. (2015). *A world of proliferated drones*. Washington, DC: Center for New America Security. Retrieved from http://www.cnas.org/research/world-of-proliferated-drones

Schlag, C. (2013). The new privacy battle: How the expanding use of drones continues to erode our concept of privacy and privacy rights. *Journal of Technology Law & Policy 12*, 123. Retrieved from http://tlp.law.pitt.edu/ojs/index.php/tlp/article/viewFile/123/126

Schmidt, E., & Cohen, J. (2014). *The new digital age: Reshaping the future of people, nations, business and our lives*. New York, NY: Alfred A. Knopf.

Shao, R., Aquino, K., & Freeman, D. (2008). Beyond moral reasoning: A review of moral identity research and its implications for business ethics. *Business Ethics Quarterly, 18*(4), 513–540.

Singer, P., & Lin, J. (2012, July 19). Baby steps: The drone industry's code of conduct skips over key questions. *The Atlantic*. Retrieved from www.theatlantic.com/politics/archive/ 2012/07/baby-steps-industrys-code-of-conduct-skips-over-key-questions/260010

Svara, J. H. (2015). *The ethics primer for public administrators in government and non-profit organizations* (2nd ed.). Burlington, MA: Jones & Barlett Learning.

Talia, A. B. (2014). Drones and *Jones:* The Fourth Amendment and police discretion in the digital age. *California Law Review, 102*(3), 729–780.

Unmanned Aerial System Team (2015). *Mesa County Sheriff's Office: Law Operations Division*. Retrieved from http://sheriff.mesacounty.us/uav/

U.S. Department of Homeland Security Inspector General. (2014). U.S. customs and border protection's unmanned aircraft system program does not achieve intended results or recognize all costs of operations. Retrieved from https://www.oig.dhs.gov/assets/Mgmt/2015/OIG_15-17_Dec14.pdf

Vicinanzo, A. (2014, August 24). Study finds glaring vulnerabilities in TSA's controversial full-body scanners. *Homeland Security Today. U.S.* Retrieved from http://www.hstoday.us/briefings/daily-news-analysis/single-article/study-finds-glaring-vulnerabilities-in-tsas-controversial-full-body-scanners/e8b8834596de4702208a70badeb86d0c.html

Villasenor, J. (2013). Observations from above: Unmanned aircraft systems and privacy. *Harvard Journal of Law and Public Policy 36*(2), 457–517.

Vorvoreanu, M., & Botan, C. H. (2000, June). Examining electronic surveillance in the workplace: A review of theoretical perspectives and research findings. Paper presented at the Conference of the International Communication Association, Acapulco, Mexico. Retrieved from https://www.cerias.purdue.edu/assets/pdf/bibtex_archive/2000-14.pdf

Wall, T., & Monahan, T. (2011). Surveillance and violence from afar: The politics of drones and liminal security scrapes. *Theoretical Criminology, 15*(3), 239–254.

Wallace-Wells, B. (2014, October 5). Drones and everything thereafter. *New York Magazine*. Retrieved from nymag.com//daily/intelligencer/2014/10/drones-the-next-smartphone.html#

Watson, S. (2013, February 5). Charlottesville, VA becomes first city to ban government spy drones. *NBC News: WVIR 29*. Retrieved from http://www.nbc29.com/story/20963560/ charlottesville-city-council-passes-anti-drone-resolution

West, J. P., & Bowman, J. S. (2014, March). *Domestic use of drones: Ethical issues in surveillance*. Unpublished paper presented at the American Society for Public Administration annual meeting in Washington, DC.

West, J. P., & Bowman, J. S. (2015). Electronic surveillance at work: An ethical analysis. *Administration and Society*. doi:10.1177/0095399714556502

Whitlock, C. (2015, February 15). FAA rules might allow thousands of business drones. *Washington Post*. Retrieved from http://www.washingtonpost.com/worldnational-security/faa-releases-proposed-rules-for-domestic-drone-use/2015/02/15/6787bdce-b51b-11e4-a200-c008a01a6692_story.html?wprss=rss_national-security

SECTION II

TRANSFORMATION AT THE LOCAL/STATE LEVEL

CHAPTER 8

DEVELOPING AN ONLINE JOB ANALYSIS QUESTIONAIRE

The Ever Changing Process

Stacey Lange and Martinique Alber

INTRODUCTION

In the field of personnel selection, it can be argued that a job analysis is one of the most critical processes for any agency. It is the foundation which ensures that an agency's selection and evaluation methods are valid and legally defensible. Since the job analysis process can be time consuming and cumbersome for many agencies to complete, new innovations in this area should focus on streamlining the process. One such innovation is to create an efficient and user friendly Online Job Analysis Questionnaire (OJAQ). This chapter will provide guidance for developing an OJAQ as well as discuss the advantages and challenges an agency may encounter along the way.

Transforming Government Organizations:
Fresh Ideas and Examples From the Field, pp. 241–263
Copyright © 2016 by Information Age Publishing
All rights of reproduction in any form reserved.

History of Job Analysis

Job analysis dates back 100 years to the early 1900s when Frederick Winslow Taylor, a mechanical engineer, started conducting efficiency studies by applying engineering principles to work performed by employees on factory floors (Taylor, 1911). These efficiency studies, or worker analysis studies, were the early start to the job analysis process and an entire field of study called *industrial engineering*. In the early 1920s, Morris Viteles used a job analysis method to develop and validate a selection measure for employees of a trolley company (Viteles, 1923). He later published his method so that it could be adapted for use in other areas of employment decisions (Viteles, 1923). Since then, numerous methods have been created and utilized all under the name of job analysis.

In order to fully comprehend the significance of job analysis, it is important to identify whether a process can be defined as a job analysis. The term job analysis refers to the study of a job by breaking it down into various job components such as work behaviors/duties, tasks, or other units or characteristics. Job analysis is defined as a systematic procedure used to identify and determine critical duties required of a job and the characteristics essential to the successful performance of the job duties (Levine, 1983). Levine (1983) explained that one of the most important aspects of defining job analysis is that the procedure used is systematic. In other words, it involves a thorough, methodological plan that is consistently performed. In addition, this systematic process typically results in at least 20 to 30 tasks. The steps utilized in a job analysis may vary depending on the target job, but as long as the job study is systematic, results in 20 to 30 tasks, and is documented, it meets the defined criteria of a job analysis.

Two Approaches to Job Analysis

There is no single unanimously accepted process to complete a job analysis. In fact, the plethora of published job analysis processes available for purchase (e.g., Functional Job Analysis (FJA)) supports the idea that no single procedure works for all jobs or all purposes. However, most job analysis processes can typically be categorized as one of two approaches; a task-oriented approach or a worker-oriented approach.

A task-oriented approach is when the job analysis process focuses on determining the specific activities performed as part of a job. These activities are typically defined by work behaviors, duties, and tasks which provide a detailed picture of what the incumbents do as part of their daily work activities. Many times, the job analysis determines some higher level of work behavior or job duties that define the job and then develop specific tasks which are clearly related to each of the work behaviors or job duties. Subject Matter Experts, commonly referred to as SMEs, then provide ratings or data regarding the work behaviors and tasks to distinctly define the functions of the job. These ratings may be collected in the form of importance, difficulty, frequency and other criteria as needed. A classic example of a task-oriented approach to the job analysis process is the Functional Job Analysis (FJA) which was developed by Fine and Cronshaw in 1944 (Schmitt & Fine, 1983). The FJA requires SMEs to provide ratings related to the target job's work elements. These ratings focus in terms of how the work elements are related to data, people or things.

The worker-oriented approach is a job analysis approach that focuses more on the human attributes job incumbents require in order to perform the job at a successful level. These human attributes are typically categorized into four areas: knowledge (information needed to perform a job), skills (the proficiencies needed to perform the work behaviors and tasks), abilities (stable attributes) and other characteristics (personality factors). The knowledge, skills, abilities and other characteristics (KSAOs) required of a successful job incumbent are inferred through the job analysis data collection process. Data is typically collected regarding the important job duties, as well as which KSAOs are related to important job duties. Some worker-oriented job analysis approaches determine which KSAOs are important, needed on the first day of the job, and have distinguishing value as part of the data collection process. One well-known worker-oriented job analysis process is the Fleishman's Job Analysis System (F-JAS) named after its developer, Edwin Fleishman (1992). He factor-analyzed large data sets of KSAOs across a variety of jobs to determine if there were any common factors across all jobs. Using this method, Fleishman developed 73 specific scales to measure the three common areas or factors which resulted from his study. He called these factors *cognitive, psychomotor,* and *physical.*

Understanding these differences in job analysis approaches is important because of the role the job analysis plays in establishing validity for employment processes used by agencies.

Importance of Job Analysis for Validation of Personnel Decisions

Job analysis is the basis for providing evidence of validity for many personnel decisions made by agencies. If the validity of a selection decision is challenged in court, it is highly likely that the job analysis process and data collected will also be scrutinized. When the procedures used in the job analysis process are not systematic or representative of the job incumbents or the job studied, then the evidence of validity will be weak for any subsequent selection decisions and thus may be challenged.

Some common factors that may determine whether a job analysis process is suitable for establishing evidence of validity includes the representativeness of the SMEs, the quality of the data collected and the accuracy of the retained duties and KSAOs. An explanation of these factors is included in the next section.

Data quality and integrity. The suitability factors of a job analysis process are some of the elements that may be scrutinized during a lawsuit. These factors determine if a job analysis process was representative of the job, which can be used to support evidence of validity. An important factor of any job analysis study is the quality of the data collected. Several variables can impact the quality of the data collected during a job analysis.

First, the individuals providing job analysis information and ratings should be highly knowledgeable about the job being studied. Best practices recommend that SMEs include current job incumbents and their immediate supervisors because these individuals are the most knowledgeable about the job. A second factor to consider when selecting SMEs is to ensure that the individuals participating in the job analysis study are representative of all incumbents working in the job. It is crucial that sample SMEs represent a subset of all job incumbents, specifically, SMEs should be of similar race, sex, job tenure, work shifts and represent the same departments as all current incumbents for the job. For example if there are 20 incumbents comprising 10 males, 10 females, 10 Blacks, and 10 Whites, and the sample that is needed is 8, the SMEs should include 4 males, 4 females, 4 Blacks and 4 Whites. That subset of the group is then representative of the entire group. Last, when differences are identified between SMEs within the same job, further investigation needs to take place to determine if the differences are related to true differences in the job or whether it is a function of a different shift or department. However, it might also be possible that poor quality data was initially obtained.

The integrity and quality of the data collected in a job analysis is critical to establish evidence of validity and the Federal government has developed guidelines that create uniform principles to establish structure for consistent, legal and valid employee selection procedures. These guidelines are called the *Uniform Guidelines on Employee Selection Procedures*.

Uniform Guidelines on Employee Selection Procedures requirements. The *Uniform Guidelines on Employee Selection Procedures* (hereinafter "*Uniform Guidelines*") were published in 1978 by the Equal Employment Opportunity Commission (EEOC, 1978). These *Uniform Guidelines* are a resource that outlines the government requirements employers must follow when testing and/or making other employee selection decisions in order to avoid potential discrimination. Specifically, the *Uniform Guidelines* are referenced in the enforcement of Title VII of the Civil Rights Act of 1964, as amended by the Equal Employment Opportunity Act of 1972. As clearly stated in the document, the *Uniform Guidelines* apply only if a selection procedure is used to make an employment decision (e.g., hiring, promotion, demotion, referral, licensing, etc.). The *Uniform Guidelines*, however, do not apply when there is a need for an agency to engage in targeted recruitment to increase the diversity of their applicant pool. The *Uniform Guidelines* also do not apply to the application of seniority systems.

As previously mentioned, a job analysis is an essential step in the validation process for any selection procedure. Whether you are establishing validity using criterion, construct or content validity, a thorough job analysis study is a crucial first step in the validation process. In order to provide the needed evidence to establish validity, it is also important to have documentation of the job analysis process. The *Uniform Guidelines* discusses the different forms of validity and also clearly outlines what information needs to be collected during the job analysis, as well as the documentation of the validation study. Regardless of the validation type, at minimum, a job analysis must be able to demonstrate that any selection procedure used to make an employment decision is related to important behaviors needed to perform the job at an acceptable level. In order to establish this evidence of validity, the *Uniform Guidelines* requires documentation of the work behaviors or duties related to the job, including how the data was collected and the criteria used for establishing each behavior's or duty's importance or criticality. Thorough documentation of the job analysis process, including individuals involved (SMEs) and the results, are essential components of the validity report. The *Uniform Guidelines* outline the specific content that must be included in all validity reports, as well as reports establishing evidence of each type of validity.

CONSIDERATIONS WHEN DEVELOPING A JOB ANALYSIS QUESTIONNAIRE (JAQ) PROCESS

The previous section has provided a general overview of different job analysis approaches, the critical aspects involved, and documentation requirements. It is now time to put that knowledge into practice and transition to the specific task of creating a Job Analysis Questionnaire (JAQ), including all necessary elements.

Content Decisions

There are many factors that need to be taken into consideration as one prepares a job analysis. There are also several steps involved in a job analysis process, but one of the most critical steps is the collection of data. The data is typically gathered using some form of questionnaire simply called a Job Analysis Questionnaire or JAQ. The main purpose of a JAQ is to collect data which will provide a thorough understanding of a job. This information is commonly used by agencies to develop selection procedures, as well as create job descriptions for classification purposes. Preparing to develop a JAQ requires extensive planning. At a global level, the steps include gathering and reviewing background material, identifying incumbents in the job and conducting site observations. From there, a preliminary list of work behaviors, tasks, knowledge, skills, abilities, physical abilities, and work conditions can be created. These lists will be later refined and finalized in task and KSAO focus groups that consist of incumbents and supervisors. Once the previous steps have been completed the JAQ is ready to be built.

Rating participants. One of the important decisions that need to be considered during development is determining who should complete the ratings on the JAQ. It is often recommended that job incumbents make decisions with regards to the importance of the each task performed as well as the frequency with which the task is performed. In addition, the incumbents will rate whether an individual needs to be able to perform the task on day one of the job without any training. Work behaviors, which are clusters of related tasks, are also rated on importance and the percentage of time spent performing those work behaviors. Tasks that require physical effort are rated on frequency and whether someone else can assist with those tasks. The thought is that the individuals doing the job are best suited to rate those aspects of the job.

Supervisors, on the other hand, are often used to rate the KSAOs needed to perform the job. Some examples of these decisions include KSAO importance, whether an individual is expected to already be proficient in that skill or ability on day one of the job, if individuals who are more competent to perform the KSAO are more effective at work and whether or not n item of knowledge needs to be memorized. Although it is common for job incumbents to provide some of these data, supervisors have a better understanding of the KSAOs that are necessary to perform a job successfully given they observe and make decisions regarding performance levels of multiple individuals in a position rather than only reporting first hand experiences as an incumbent would.

Elements of work behaviors, tasks, and KSAOs. When starting a job analysis process, it is important to determine what level of detail is desired for the job. It is a common practice for work behaviors, tasks, and KSAOs to be written specifically for each job that is studied. While this practice creates unique items and descriptors, it also creates a tedious process that has to be recreated every time a job needs to be studied and thus eliminates the potential for efficiency. Creating an automated, online system would allow for the development of a task and KSAO library. The libraries could be composed of generic work behaviors, tasks, and KSAOs that could be applied to a broader spectrum of jobs, but still capture the unique aspects of each job. For example, if an ability statement is written as the ability to read a water meter, the statement would then apply only to jobs that actually read water meters; however, if the statement is broadened to the ability to read a meter, it would then be applicable to jobs that read water, electric, and/or gas meters.

Creating less specific libraries also allows for an efficient JAQ development process. The core skills, abilities and other characteristics across most jobs are quite similar. For instance, interpersonal skills, conflict management, organization/prioritization skills, to name a few, apply to a wide variety of jobs, but the body of knowledge related to each is what distinguishes most jobs from one another. The creation of KSAO libraries would result in greater consistency and efficiency of JAQs. In addition, a KSAO library removes the individualistic style of how job analysts write task and KSAO statements. In order to maintain a level of detail consistency, as well as minimize stylistic differences in writing KSAOs for the library, it is important to establish a single reviewer of all KSAOs. This review process is important because new KSAOs will need to be added to the library, but the establishment of the review process must be vetted prior to submission to maintain standardization and consistency.

Review of Process

The traditional approach to completing a JAQ is to create a paper and pencil questionnaire and then schedule meeting times for the incumbents and supervisors to complete the questionnaire. Conducting a face-to-face meeting to complete a JAQ allows for a thorough explanation of the process and increases the SMEs' understanding of the job analysis approach. In addition, if the SME has questions, the job analyst is readily available to address any concerns.

Many JAQs are very lengthy, and contingent on the SMEs that are being surveyed, the level of understanding of the scales can vary. Depending on the criteria being assessed by the JAQ, the SMEs may have an overwhelming number of decisions to make in order to complete the rating process. For instance, some decisions SMEs will make include rating task importance, task frequency, work behavior importance, percentage of time spent performing the work behavior, KSAO and physical ability importance, and KSAO and physical ability needed at entry scales. Definitions of the rating scales could be confusing for SMEs that are not accustomed to evaluating a job in this manner. In these situations having a job analyst present that can explain the rating scales increases the understanding of the SMEs and should lead to a more accurate assessment of the job.

Length of Process

Completing a JAQ using the traditional paper and pencil is a very lengthy process. Depending on the number of tasks and KSAOs contained in the questionnaire, the SMEs may be required to make decisions regarding hundreds if not thousands of ratings. Oftentimes, requesting that SMEs complete this many ratings about any job is taxing and likely to lead to rater fatigue. This fatigue is compounded when SMEs are asked to complete the ratings at a single meeting so as to maximize their participation in the process. Unfortunately, once rater fatigue sets in, the quality of all ratings will deteriorate because the SMEs are no longer paying attention to what they are rating, but may be circling responses to simply "get it over with."

Once all of the SMEs have completed the JAQ, all the ratings provided by the SMEs need to be compiled in order to analyze the ratings. Unless a scannable form (e.g., Scantron) is used to collect the ratings, a job analyst would be required to manually enter the ratings provided by the SMEs into a spreadsheet for subsequent analysis. In order to ensure accuracy of the data entry, it is recommended that the data be entered twice and then data matching formulas be used to ensure accuracy and resolve any discrepancies that are identified. Once the data is entered and cleaned, any calculations required as part of the job analysis process will need to be completed.

Interpretation of Results

The traditional paper and pencil JAQ process relies on the use of software such as Excel where basic formulas and conditional formatting can be used to perform data analysis. The criterion for which job analysis items are retained may vary depending on the overall sample size of the incumbents completing the JAQ. For jobs with a small number of participants one has to be mindful of the influence that one rater can have on the overall results of the JAQ. The main goal of a JAQ is to determine the content validity of a job. The summary of SMEs' ratings are pooled so the more they agree on the importance of a task, work behavior, or KSAO the more assured an individual can be that the item is content valid. In most circumstances where there are more than 30 SMEs completing a JAQ, the overall mean is determined for each item; however when there are 30 or fewer SMEs, an alternate method may be used. The reason an agency may want to use a different procedure when there are fewer SMEs is that, statistically, there is a greater potential for error when making decisions based on smaller numbers of ratings (Marascuilo & Serlin, 1988, pp. 562–591; Minium, Clarke, & Coladarci, 1999). Lawshe's (1975) technique corrects for the number of raters, which in turn reduces the likelihood of defining an item as content valid when it is not. Lawshe's (1975) Table for Level of Agreement may be used in order to ensure that the level of agreement among SMEs meets or exceeds the established values in the table which will minimize the potential for error when interpreting the results of smaller sample sizes.

There are obvious pros and cons to the traditional paper and pencil JAQ and organizations are constantly striving to find a better way. With the increasing accessibility of technology, the JAQ process can slowly be phased off of paper and placed online while still retaining established methodology.

INNOVATION AND EFFICIENCY— TRANSITIONING TO AN ONLINE QUESTIONNAIRE PROCESS

There are numerous details that can be incorporated into the most thorough of job analysis studies as detailed in previous sections. The *Uniform Guidelines* created data collection standards necessary to establish evidence of validity for a job, but agencies are likely to err on the side of caution and collect substantially more data than is minimally required. This thorough collection of data is not only time consuming, but can be incredibly cumbersome for many agencies to complete, thus emphasizing the importance that new innovations in this area should focus on streamlining the job analysis process. One innovation that would streamline the job analysis process is an efficient and user friendly Online Job Analysis Questionnaire (OJAQ) administered via the Internet.

Creating an Online Job Analysis Questionnaire (OJAQ)

Streamlining any process can be a huge undertaking for any agency, especially when it takes time, money and expertise that may not be readily available. There are several factors that should be discussed and decisions that need to be made before the creation of an online interface. Some agencies will merely want to automate the job analysis process they currently use, while others will want to improve upon the current process and plan for future developments. It is important to determine what the goal is for this innovative process. While establishing a goal to streamline the current process is a good place to start, a process that worked well on paper does not always translate well when technology is introduced.

As with all large scale projects, spending time during the planning phase can result in a better product with fewer issues or glitches. Never underestimate the importance of a well-thought-out plan. Anticipating modifications to the former paper and pencil process can save a tremendous amount of time in the future. Automating a process is never as easy as it seems and there are always hurdles that will impede it; however, extensive planning and researching will save time, frustration, and money down the road.

There are several decisions that will need to be made long before the programming starts. Thus, it is important to have a diverse group of people involved in the project conceptualization phase. While you will need someone knowledgeable about the job analysis process and experts regarding the uses of the data, you also need programming experts. Consider adding individuals to your team that are creative and good at evaluating and critiquing new processes. The project team members should bring a variety of perspectives to the table. Team members do not all have to understand the job analysis process but more so assist with the functionality and creation of a user friendly interface. Anticipating problems your SMEs may have in the conceptualization phase of the process will also be valuable information for programmers. This diverse group of people will need to work through a variety of considerations as the process is created. It is impossible to list all the things to consider in the planning, but some of the key considerations are detailed below.

Process Considerations

There are several aspects related to the job analysis process that the team needs to address. These considerations will ultimately define the direction of the project. The first consideration is to determine if the goal of the project is to simply automate the current job analysis process utilized by the agency or if this project will serve as a catalyst to modify and potentially improve the current process. If there is uncertainty regarding the goal of the automation project, strongly consider improving the current process. Once an automated procedure is established it may be difficult to make changes to the process without oppositions from users (e.g., job analysts and SMEs); however, if you utilize the automation project as a catalyst to modify and potentially improve the current JAQ process, then this transition period may be more acceptable to users of the new system. In fact, to users it may be more about becoming acclimated to the automated system and therefore less focused on any changes that were made to the ratings.

Define the job analysis process/approach. It is not uncommon for the most difficult stage of a new project to be defining the new process. Transitioning from the conceptual phase of the project to the step-by-step processes can be difficult, but when developing an automated JAQ, it is crucial that the project team determines the appropriate job analysis process for the agency. Specifically, determine what job analysis approach will meet the agency's goals.

As described in previous sections, there are two approaches to job analysis: task-oriented and worker-oriented. It is important to determine which approach will be utilized in order to define all the steps needed in the automation. While most job analysis processes fall into one of these two categories, the best approach in some cases may be a combination of the two. A combined approach clearly outlines the duties and tasks related to the target job, but also details and collects data regarding the KSAOs a person needs in order to perform the duties and tasks at an acceptable level.

At times it can be difficult to determine which job analysis approach is the best approach to use. When this is the case it is always best to consider the purpose of the job analysis process and how the results will be utilized. For instance, will the job analysis results be used to supply consultants with the information they need to develop selection tests or will the data be used as evidence of local validity for a published test being considered for purchase? Perhaps the results will be used to develop in-house employment tests designed to rank order candidates. Other potential uses that need to be considered include conducting the job analysis study for classification purposes or for establishing job-specific competencies for a performance appraisal system. There are many reasons that an agency requires a job analysis study, but each of these reasons may require a different set of ratings collected or a need to analyze the data provided by SMEs differently. Given these considerations, it is critical to discuss the possible future uses for the job analysis process to determine what data should be collected. The criteria used to determine the resulting work behaviors, tasks, and KSAOs for a job analysis that focuses on test development is very different from the job analysis criteria used when the results drive a performance appraisal.

Once the job analysis focus has been determined (i.e., task, worker or combination approach) and the uses for the job analysis data have been finalized (i.e., test development, job classification, performance appraisal, etc.), the next step is to define the specific steps in the job analysis process. Considerations regarding how the job analysis content will be added to the automated JAQ need to be discussed. For instance, will job analysts be typing the job content into a system that will then collect the ratings or will database libraries be established and only require minor edits to the content?

Regardless of the method chosen, mapping out the specific steps of the job analysis including the rating process and order of ratings selected are important considerations before programming starts. It is impossible to anticipate all possible ways that the system can be streamlined, but discussing the process and mapping it out will help programmers understand the desired outcomes required of the OJAQ, as well as allow individuals involved in the project to review and recommend additional areas for improvement and/or efficiency. Always be willing to adapt. It is possible for a great idea to bloom from what was initially perceived as a failed concept, but a good idea will never become great if it was never considered or tested in the first place. In other words, do not be afraid to mull over an idea that at first glance may not work, because small changes to an idea or concept may result in big benefits in innovation.

Creating and using a KSAO library. One of the job analysis areas that may easily produce the largest increase in efficiency concerns KSAOs. There are thousands upon thousands of KSAOs written for a variety of jobs. Many agencies have already moved toward creating databases or libraries filled with KSAOs, but other agencies are still in the initial stages of this process. The creation of a KSAO library can be difficult, especially if the KSAOs typically used are specific, highly detailed and tailored to each job. It is far more difficult to create a database or library of KSAOs if the chances of using that exact KSAO again is low. Recall the ability to read water meters example presented in a previous section of this chapter—if the ability was left specific to water meters a small subset of jobs would be able to use that ability. If the ability is written to be broader or more general to eliminate the water specificity, the ability is then applicable to a larger subset of jobs. Creating a database or library of KSAOs, or even work behaviors or tasks, is a time intensive process; however one way to save time and increase efficiency is to utilize existing KSAO libraries. A good place to start and an excellent source of information about a large variety of jobs is the Occupational Information Network (O*NET; see O*NET Online, n.d.).

After investigating potential resources to develop libraries, a consideration should be made regarding the creation of competencies or clusters. Competencies are groups of similar KSAOs that are given a name that reflects a larger generalization of the grouping. This decision to create competencies may be a reflection of the uses for the job analysis data. For instance, if the data will be used for test development, individual KSAOs may be the level of specificity desired, but if the job analysis process is used for performance evaluation or even career development, the establishment of competencies or clusters of similar KSAOs may be more informative for employees and supervisors that will use the system.

Finally, consider whether individual analysts will have the ability to add KSAOs to the library or if there will be limitations. One agency that created an online job analysis questionnaire had a very thorough database of KSAOs for analysts to use, but analysts had difficulty using the search function to find specific KSAOs that were needed for a job. This resulted in the addition of numerous KSAOs that were at a more detailed level than how the database was originally conceptualized. As a consequence a large number of duplicate KSAOs were added as knowledge, skills and abilities, thus resulting in statements from all three categories included in job analysis studies. A great example for this chapter is *basic mathematics*. After additions were made to the library in relation to basic mathematics, the library had the knowledge of basic mathematics, the ability to perform basic mathematics and the skill to perform basic mathematics. If this system initially had better searching capabilities of the current KSAO database this may not have happened. Therefore, another recommended consideration for the automated job analysis system is to determine the best way to create search functions for any included libraries as well as discussions regarding how permissions to add new KSAOs to the existing library will be handled to ensure poorly written and duplicate KSAOS are not added unnecessarily.

User Considerations: System Design

Once the content of the online job analysis system is finalized, there are several decisions that need to be made regarding how the SMEs will access the system, what they will see, and how they will work through it from start to finish. These are all important things to consider in ensuring the success of the new automated system. If the online system is difficult for SMEs to understand and use, then all those hours saved by streamlining the process will be spent encouraging SMEs to participate in the process or interpreting data that does not seem to meet expectations of the job. The ease of use of the SME/user interface is crucial. If users are not able to understand where they are, what they need to do, or worse, how to even access the system, they will be less likely to participate in the process.

Always keep in mind the varying levels of computer experience at an agency. There is an expectation that with social media, smart phones, and computers in most homes, everyone is computer literate and able to perform basic operations on a computer therefore would have little difficulty accessing or completing an online questionnaire. This may be true if all the jobs in the agency work at a computer for hours a day, but this is not always the case. Consider this when creating the interface—always be sure that someone with little or no computer experience will be able to easily move through the rating process. Making the system look nice and professional is an important goal, but be cautious of stressing appearance over function at the expense of the end-user. Always test the system with individuals that are not familiar with the job analysis process to make sure SMEs with varying computer experience will be able to easily complete the job analysis questionnaire.

Instructions are a critical part of the process, especially if SMEs will be completing the questionnaire without a job analyst present. While detailed instructions are important, keep in mind that very few people will fully read all of the instructions provided. In fact, you may want to consider shortening the instructions and/or utilizing bullet points when possible. In today's technology-driven world, it seems as though people spend less and less time reading provided information. Short and direct instructions written at a level no higher than an eighth grade comprehension will be the key to ensuring that SMEs complete the process successfully. Studies have indicated that most Americans read at a seventh or eighth grade level (on average) and anything written at a higher level will only confuse SMEs or force them to skip the instructions altogether (Kutner & Greenberg, 2005).

The same recommendations apply for any rating scale definitions. If SMEs are unable to comprehend the question, the rating scale, or more specifically the differentiations between two rating levels, then the data will be impacted and may even be useless. An online system may not lend itself to SMEs contacting a job analyst if they have a question, even if you provide them with the contact information. Taking the steps early on to ensure all written instructions and additional information is clear and easily under-standable will save headaches for users and SMEs as well as job analysts and should reduce SME confusion.

Data Considerations: Manipulation and Results

This chapter has provided options for how job content may be placed into a new online job analysis system, as well as considerations for what permissions or manipulation capabilities the job analysts will need to have in the online system. The next step is to discuss what calculations the job analysis system will perform, what job analysts will be able to export from the system and what job analysis results the system will generate. Several aspects that need to be considered from the analysts' perspective are related to putting the job analysis information (duties and KSAOs) into the system for the SMEs to rate. Some of the things to consider in relation to the duties and KSAOs were presented earlier in this chapter, now the discussion will focus on the data the analysts will export from the system.

The beauty of an automated system is that the SMEs will enter their ratings directly into the system, offering a great deal of efficiency over the traditional paper and pencil process, which would require data entry fol-lowing the completion of the JAQ. An automated system reduces errors in the data entry process and can be designed so that the system performs some calculations automatically. During the design phase of the system, the design team should also consider how the data entered by SMEs will be exported, what calculations will be automated and whether criteria established for the calculations can be manipulated by job analysts. All of these decisions may impact how the system will be designed and eventually created. Always consider talking to experienced job analysts to discuss the most common issues they deal with concerning data cleaning and the analysis process. It is highly recommended that focus groups be held with job analysts that will be using the system in your agency, but whenever possible also speak to individuals outside the agency. Both groups may offer unique insights with regards to common issues surrounding job analysis data and how they have been remedied.

BENEFITS OF AUTOMATION

As with many processes, automation would not have been developed or even considered if there were not a list of potential benefits to incorporating the process. An OJAQ is one process that greatly benefits from automation. The simplest way to outline the benefits of an automated job analysis process is to consider the benefits for the SMEs that complete the questionnaires and the benefits for the job analysts that administer the questionnaires.

SME Benefits

The most evident benefit to SMEs is that an automated system provides them with flexibility to complete the questionnaire. First, it allows for SMEs to complete the process in the comfort of their own workspace instead of completing a paper and pencil version during a specific block of time. This also allows the SMEs to complete the questionnaire at their own pace. If SMEs need additional time to process the decisions they are being asked to make, they can have it. Also, if the system is designed accordingly, SMEs can take frequent breaks during the rating process, decreasing the chances of rater fatigue. A system designed so that SMEs can stop and save their ratings at any point in the completion process will also allow busy SMEs to participate in the survey process even if they do it in several 15-minute increments of time.

Another feature that can be added to the design of the system to increase efficiency and reduce rater fatigue is to design the rating process to be adaptive. For instance, lower thresholds can be established that will exempt a SME from providing ratings on work behaviors, tasks or KSAOs that are not related to the job. For instance, if a SME indicates that a knowledge is not important to the job, any subsequent ratings for that knowledge can be eliminated from the SME's rating process. This same adaptive capability can be added to work behavior and task ratings as well.

Analyst Benefits

As already discussed, an automated job analysis questionnaire system offers several benefits for the SMEs providing the ratings, but there are also benefits for the job analysts using the automated system. One of the first benefits for a job analyst using the new system is related to document creation and reproduction. During the job analysis study, once a job analyst has finalized the job content, the ratings related to the content need to be collected. This data collection is typically completed using some form of job analysis questionnaire. Prior to the use of an online job analysis system, analysts would have to manually create the needed questionnaire. Whether a template is available or not, this step can require an extensive time commitment to create the document, review it for editing and resolve any formatting issues. Once this is completed, an analyst would then need to create photocopies of the questionnaire, likely creating more copies than will actually be used, thus wasting paper. The benefit of an automated system is that the job analyst will not waste valuable time formatting and creating photocopies or repeating the entire formatting and copying process if a change needs to be made or the process needs to be updated. Also, if a KSAO database is created as part of the new system, less time will be spent writing KSAOs and job analysts will instead select from the existing lists available.

Another benefit for the analyst is that there will be less time spent contacting and scheduling questionnaire administration sessions with SMEs. Depending on how many incumbents and SMEs an analyst needs to participate in the job analysis questionnaire, this could take a few hours to set up administration sessions and to schedule SMEs to attend one of the sessions. With an automated system that allows SMEs to complete the questionnaire from their own work areas, the job analyst will save time scheduling meetings and instead can generate a mass e-mail that contains all the information needed to get the SMEs logged into the system and to start completing the questionnaire.

Another benefit of an automated system is the reduction of errors at several points in the process. First, as presented in a previous section, the design of the system will allow SMEs to provide their ratings directly in the system, hence removing the likelihood of data entry errors inadvertently created by job analysts. This also decreases the amount of time spent cleaning and researching the source of data entry errors. Furthermore, in the development of the system, checks and balances can be added for another layer of error reduction.

Another noticeable benefit to job analysts is the decrease in time spent performing the calculations required to determine the results of the job analysis study. The use of the automated system also allows for the automation of calculations thus reducing the amount of time spent by analysts performing these calculations, and also reducing the potential for errors in the calculation process.

CHALLENGES TO CONSIDER WHEN INCORPORATING AUTOMATION

SME Challenges

When making the decision to go to a fully automated system it is important to consider how the data will be used now and in the future. That will allow a structure that is versatile to be designed from the beginning. One of the major challenges that should be considered is the computer literacy level of the individuals that will be completing the JAQ. In many government agencies there is a wide variety of jobs ranging from very high level positions (e.g., directors, managers, engineers, etc.) in which a majority of the work is performed on a computer to basic laborer positions in which there is minimal computer work, if any at all. Completion of a paper and pencil JAQ is a complex process in itself, but now there is the challenge of completing an OJAQ which requires the use of a computer. Automating the process also removes the face-to-face interaction between the job analyst and the SMEs. The rating scales can be confusing for any SMEs that are not familiar with the job analysis process and it can be a challenge assessing a SMEs level of understanding of the rating scales. Although an analyst may be available to answer questions via email or phone calls, there is no immediate interaction and depending on the comfort level of the SMEs, they may not contact job analysts for assistance but instead will continue to muddle through the OJAQ.

The automation of the JAQ will also allow SMEs to complete sections of the OJAQ at different times rather than having to complete the entire questionnaire at one sitting, but this may lead to a loss of concentration or the SMEs may have trouble recalling where they were in the process and the purpose of the section. In other words, if a SME devotes multiple smaller chunks of time to complete the questionnaire, it is less likely the SME will suffer from rater fatigue, however, if the SME does not review the ratings they already provided when they return to the system at another time, there is an increased chance for the SME to create a disconnect between related ratings from a previous section of the job analysis; this could possibly affect the validity of the job analysis process, thus should be avoided if possible.

Analyst Challenges

The automated OJAQ presents another set of challenges from the analyst perspective. As stated earlier there has to be an assumption made that the SMEs have a thorough understanding of the process and that quality ratings are provided in the OJAQ. At this point, it can be difficult to ensure that the ratings provided by SMEs are valid and not just "garbage." Basically, if you have poor data entered by a SME, the integrity of the data is compromised and should not be used to establish content validity regarding the job. There is also the challenge of making sure that the SMEs understand the rating scales. For example, occasionally data will result in a KSAO that is rated as not important; however, it is subsequently rated as needed at entry or required on day one of the job. This rating pattern typically does not make sense for any job, so it is still important for job analysts to review the data even though the process is automated. There should never be an assumption that the data generated is 100% accurate. Human beings are entering data therefore there is always a chance of error.

Another challenging area is related to instructions provided in the system. Although instructions are provided at every step in the process, many times individuals do not read all of the instructions but rather jump in and start rating. When situations like this arise, errors can occur on the part of the SMEs that require time of the programmer to go into the system and fix or reset an OJAQ. While it is not as much time as the traditional calling and scheduling of meetings, a considerable amount of time may be spent on ensuring that all required SMEs have completed the process. This may result in job analysts spending time later in the process contacting desirable SMEs or their supervisors and encouraging them to complete the OJAQ.

Job analysts may also need to develop creative methods of encouraging SMEs to complete the OJAQ by desirable deadlines. This is because for some SMEs, the benefit of not requiring them to attend a meeting to complete a paper and pencil questionnaire makes it easier for them to procrastinate and prioritize their own workload instead of participating in the job analysis study. This online, automated system creates a disconnect in responsibility for the SMEs, whereas with an in-house meeting there is a captive audience that is required to complete the questionnaire before they can leave, so analysts know who exactly participated in the meeting.

The automation of the system can also make it easier for analysts to become disconnected from the entire process hence losing focus of the important content related to the jobs. In other words, there is too much focus on each individual step in the job analysis process and a loss of the "big picture." This loss of the "big picture" stems largely from the automation of the calculations and data analysis processes. As stated earlier, all data still has to be analyzed and evaluated to some extent. As a result of the automation of the data analysis process, job analysts may not have a full understanding of the formulas that are used to make the determinations related to work behaviors, tasks, and KSAOs that are retained as part of the job content or are dropped for failure to meet appropriate criteria. Job analysts may become "blind" to the automated analysis and therefore may allow critical information to be omitted because the OJAQ automatically designated an item as one that should be dropped from the job content, when in fact, it was the result of a rating error or the ratings of one SME that eliminates important job content because it did not meet the criteria threshold.

System Challenges

One of the major challenges with creating an automated OJAQ is ensuring that all communication is understood between the programmers and the job analysts developing the system. There are two different languages spoken by each profession and ensuring a mutual understanding for both groups can be difficult. For example most programmers may not feel that they need to understand the process as long as they know what the final outcome should be; however, a results driven outlook of making sure formulas run correctly will likely create problems for job analysts. Job analysts see more than just numbers—as mentioned above, the data presents a picture of the job providing the analyst with information regarding the intent of the data, purpose, and criteria that are being used to determine the job content to establish evidence of validity. Although the skeletal structure of a job analysis process is the same, there may be a need within an agency to do things differently or establish different criteria for results. These considerations will also need to be incorporated into the system where possible, but maintaining a standardized process by not overly customizing.

Once the system is built there should be a standardized training of all users where possible to ensure everyone has an understanding of the intent of the system, what data it will generate and how that data will be used. Given this, there also need to be controls established for the system. For example, who will be allowed to add and edit KSAOs, whether data can be deleted and who will have the permission or authority to make these edits. Be cautious when determining who will have the authority to manipulate data and the content of JAQs.

Another challenge associated with an automated OJAQ is that at times the standard criteria after the administration of the questionnaire may change. Depending on how the system is developed, it can be difficult to document these changes given that these types of changes are performed after the data has been exported. These changes in data can be related to an outlier SME or a SME that simply did not understand the rating scales or the job analysis process. This information should always be documented in a job analysis and validity report, but some of those changes may not be captured in the main database and future uses of the data may not necessarily be reflective of the data used. Another challenge with an automated system is determining which Internet browser works most effectively and efficiently for the system and then ensuring that is communicated to all SMEs. Most SMEs will be completing the OJAQ using their work computer or an agency computer, but if the appropriate browser is not available on the computers SMEs are using, they may not be able to complete the survey or may require assistance from an IT specialist. This wastes time and creates frustration for both the job analysts and SMEs, especially if the issue is not identified immediately.

It is also crucial that once the system is finished, there should be an extensive pilot and validation of the system to ensure everything is functioning properly. Because all of the formulas are in the background, it can be difficult to determine if everything is functioning appropriately without real data. In the pilot phase, and while the system is active, it may be more productive to keep a list of desired changes that are not critical to the function of the system and then present them to the programmer. Making programming changes takes time and to have a list to make several adjustments at once will be helpful, rather than making piecemeal changes. Also, it helps programmers to keep track of which changes they made and which will require more work in the future.

RECOMMENDATIONS FOR
IMPROVING ANY ONLINE SYSTEM

This chapter has presented several considerations in developing an automated OJAQ as well as presented the benefits and difficulties associated with its creation. Below is a summary of the important points to consider when developing the automated system, in addition to recommendations for potential improvements for agencies that already have an automated JAQ process.

Be Creative

The great thing about building a system that is custom to your agency is that you can do anything you want with it. Spend the time planning and designing, but do not be afraid to think outside of the box. Many agencies get tied down in the minutia of how things have always been done and have a difficult time thinking about new ways in which old processes can be changed, improved, or even eliminated. Be sure to consider potential future uses for the system other than just job analysis. For instance, manipulating the calculations performed by the system to provide information regarding job classification or using the data to determine competencies important for a performance appraisal system. The opportunities are endless as long as you have the idea and the talent to create it.

Knowledgeable Development Team

When starting the preparation for creating the team that will build the online system, make sure that key individuals are included that are well versed and knowledgeable about the process. There also needs to be a mix of "big picture" and "detail focused" thinkers to make sure that all aspects of the analytic processes are captured. Of course a well versed and competent programmer (or two) must be included, but chose someone who is also open-minded and willing to recommend new ideas to streamline the process. A great development team will also include individuals that are the "doers" as well as the supervisors. This will increase the potential for new ideas and perspectives to be brought to the table for consideration. Finally, remember to include agency employees that will be using the system (e.g., job analysts). They should be given a voice and opportunity to add input; this also creates buy-in when the system is ready to be fully incorporated into the job analysis process.

Adapting the System for New Uses

One thing to keep in mind is that an OJAQ system will never be static; it will be an animal that is dynamic and ever changing, especially since this is new territory for many agencies. The online system will never be perfect; however, there is a fine line between overly customizing a system to meet every single need and making the system work for the masses. Regardless, a system such as this will generate and provide substantial amounts of data which will need to be stored. This may also require the system to have a means of exporting the data to allow analysts the flexibility to customize the data to their own specific needs using other software such as Excel or SPSS. Also, continue thinking about what other uses there may be for job data. For instance, job analysis data can be used for job analysis, performance appraisals, classification surveys, job descriptions, and job announcements.

The information collected using the system can have multiple purposes, as well as a wide variety of users accessing the system. Another recommendation is to consider all the potential users that may have access to the system and then establish a consistent method for identifying each user. An employee identification number or other similar form of identification rather than just a SME's name will allow for there to be a unique, constant identifier so an individual's data can be pulled and used for multiple purposes and systems. New systems also require training for the customer that will be utilizing it, so consider using online tutorials to show SMEs what the OJAQ will look like before they start the process and a review of the rating scales in order to help ensure the SMEs have a better understanding of the system before they have to complete a questionnaire.

CONCLUSION

The lists of recommendations are endless and may vary drastically depending on the automated system. When developing an automated job analysis system remember first to establish a project development team that includes job analysis experts, programmers, analysts interpreting the data as well as individuals that do not understand the job analysis process. Second, be sure to place a large amount of effort in the planning stages to consider all potential goals of the system and keep options open for future uses. Third, it is highly recommended to be creative with the system to allow fresh ideas to be considered that may not have been possible with traditional paper and pencil versions. Finally and most importantly, remain flexible and willing to continuously update and improve the system. While you do not want to constantly be changing the system, as changes in your processes or issues/ concerns are addressed, changes will need to be made. The best automated systems are ever-changing to continue to improve usability and efficiency.

REFERENCES

Equal Employment Opportunity Commission, Civil Service Commission, Department of Labor, & Department of Justice. (1978). Adoption by four agencies of uniform guidelines on employee selection procedures. *Federal Register, 43*, 38290-38315.

Fleishman, E. A. (1992). *Fleishman—Job Analysis Survey (F-JAS)*. Potomac, MD: Management Research Institute.

Kutner, M., & Greenberg, E. (2005). *National Assessment of Adult Literacy (NAAL) a first look at the literacy of America's adults in the 21st century*. Washington, DC: National Center for Education Statistics, U.S. Dept. of Education, Institute of Education Sciences.

Lawshe, C. H. (1975). A quantitative approach to content validity. *Personnel Psychology, 28*, 563–575.

Levine, E. L. (1983). *Everything you always wanted to know about job analysis: And more!—a job analysis primer*. Tampa, Fl: Mariner.

Marascuilo, L. A., & Serlin, R. C. (1988). *Statistical methods for the social and behavioral sciences*. New York, NY: W. H. Freeman and Company.

Minium, E. W., Clarke, R. B., & Coladarci, T. (1999). *Elements of statistical reasoning*. New York, NY: Wiley.

O*NET OnLine. (n.d.). Retrieved from http://www.onetonline.org/

Schmitt, N., & Fine, S. A. (1983). Inter-rater reliability of judgments of functional levels and skill requirements of jobs based on written task statements. *Journal of Occupational Psychology, 56*(2), 121–127.

Taylor, F. W. (1911). *The principles of scientific management*. New York, NY: Harper & Brothers.

Viteles, M. S. (1923). Job specifications and diagnostic tests of job competency designed for the auditing division of a street railway company. *Psychological Clinic, 14*, 83–105.

CHAPTER 9

MAINTAINING AN ETHICAL CULTURE IN MUNICIPAL GOVERNMENT THROUGH THE USE OF A PROFESSIONAL ETHICS WORKSHOP FOR ALL CITY EMPLOYEES

William I. Sauser, Jr. and Steven A. Reeves

INTRODUCTION

The City of Auburn, Alabama—home to Auburn University—is a thriving community of approximately 60,000 residents. It is located along Interstate 85 in east central Alabama. The city employs 465 regular employees in 13 departments who seek to provide a high level of professional service in a variety of areas to the city's residents and visitors. Among the core values adopted by the employees of the city are respect, integrity, fairness, reliability, and professional excellence. Regarding professional ethics, the city's statement of core values asserts, "Unquestionable integrity must be at the heart of our efforts to provide citizens with the best public services

Transforming Government Organizations:
Fresh Ideas and Examples From the Field, pp. 265–289
Copyright © 2016 by Information Age Publishing

possible." These are not hollow words. For many years the elected and professional leaders of the city have sought to maintain this ideal, and annual citizen surveys have documented the high level of effectiveness of the delivery of city services.

Over a decade ago, in an effort to demonstrate the importance of maintaining the city's excellent reputation for quality service to its citizens, a decision was reached to provide professional ethics training to all employees of the city as a planned, proactive organizational intervention. To date—since February, 2003—more than 650 employees at all levels of the organization have undergone ethics training in the form of a 2-hour "hands-on" workshop designed to explore issues city employees face in the everyday performance of their duties. Cases and examples were developed by the workshop presenter (Sauser) from critical incidents supplied by a group of city employees who oversaw the development of the workshop.

Steve Reeves, the Director of Human Resources for the City of Auburn, originally conceived the idea and engaged William Sauser, Professor of Management at Auburn University, to prepare and facilitate the workshop. Over the years since 2003 the mandatory workshop has been offered to all employees of the city in multiple small group settings. While the workshop has been modified slightly each year (due to changes in the regulatory environment and the needs of the citizens) its basic structure has remained the same. There has now been enough experience with the workshop to draw some conclusions with respect to its practical significance.

What does the workshop look like, how has it been received, and what has been the effectiveness of the workshop with respect to the expectations of the city leaders and employees? These are the key questions addressed in this chapter, which draws on and expands upon ideas earlier published by Sauser (2010, 2011, 2013).

The chapter includes a brief review of the theoretical basis of the workshop plus a description of its structure, the materials used, and how the workshop has been offered over the years. The chapter also contains a discussion of the origins and impact of the program. This discussion includes empirical results from a survey completed by 304 employees who have participated in and/or are familiar with the program. The authors conclude the chapter by presenting "lessons learned" and suggestions for other organizations considering developing and offering their own professional ethics program for public sector employees.

ETHICS IN LOCAL GOVERNMENT

Ethics in local government has to do with the behavior—specifically the moral behavior—of the elected officials, public employees, and professional administrators who work to carry out the operations of the government. The extent to which a local government's organizational behavior measures up to society's standards is typically used to gauge its ethicality—and this is true for the individuals representing the government as well as the organization itself. There are a variety of societal standards for behavior, of course, so ethical behavior is often characterized with respect to such standards as the law, organizational policies, professional and trade association codes, popular expectations regarding fairness and rightness, plus one's own (and the surrounding society's) internalized moral standards—"the way we expect things to be done around here."

Consider for a moment the public's expectations of an ethical local government. Business is conducted "in the sunshine" by elected officials, appointed administrators, and government employees in a manner that serves the needs of all the citizenry in an effective and efficient manner (Veal, Sauser, Tamblyn, Sauser, & Sims, 2015). Priorities deemed important by the electorate are accomplished in a manner such that public assets—time, money, equipment, land, human resources, buildings, and the like—are not wasted but rather are employed to their maximum public benefit (Sauser, Sauser, & Sumners, 2005). The government is transparent, meaning that its meetings and records are open for observation, its budget is posted for public inspection—and is followed, its financial statements are audited by external reviewers and pronounced accurate, its motives are understood, and the well-being of the citizenry is clearly paramount (Veal, Sauser, & Folmar, 2010). Its policies are fair to all concerned and are administered even-handedly. All citizens are provided excellent service and the day-to-day operations of the government run smoothly. Though there may be differences of opinion among elected officials, they all strive to work together for the common good. No one places his or her self-interests above those of the populace, and no member of the government seeks to use his or her public position for private gain.

Contrast this blissful circumstance to that of an unethical local government. In an unethical government, self-interest is placed above the general welfare, and elected officials, appointed administrators, and government employees substitute their own agendas for that of the populace at large. There may be corruption in the form of bribery and graft, falsification of records, theft or misuse of public property, and blatant favoritism toward one segment of the population at the expense of another. Government resources are wasted and government policies are biased or selectively applied (or even patently ignored or misapplied). Decisions are made in secret, records are "missing" or difficult to access, financial shenanigans are suspected, and "cover-ups" are the order of the day. Factions in the government actively work against one another, debates are acrimonious and fruitless, priorities are ignored, and the public's business is handled poorly if at all.

Why are there such contrasts in the way local governments operate? Why are some local governments respected as ethical, while others fall far short of the public's expectations for moral behavior? One important reason—in the present authors' opinion—is the organizational culture of the local government itself. The government's organizational culture sets the tone for its operations, and is a major factor in how the government conducts the public's business. If this is true, then how can government officials create an ethical culture for the local government in which they serve? How can the public's expectations with respect to moral government be met?

Today's more sophisticated citizens clearly are demanding more of their local governments in terms of moral behavior. They desire government organizations that are proactive in gaining and maintaining a reputation for ethicality, transparency, and trust. They desire a local government that exhibits a *culture of character* (Sauser, 2008a), one that displays moral firmness, self-control, and integrity. What can local government leaders do to transform the culture of local government such that it exhibits transparency with respect to motives and actions and trustworthiness in its dealings with stakeholders? Each member of the local government's leadership team must understand and carry out his or her prescribed role in an ethical manner if the local government is to succeed in accomplishing this mission.

ROLES OF ELECTED AND APPOINTED LOCAL GOVERNMENT LEADERS

It is the responsibility of every elected official, appointed administrator, and supervisor—yea, every employee—to act as a guardian of the ethical integrity of the local government. Since they set the tone for the organization, it is especially important that the local government's elected and appointed leaders understand, accept, and manifest their leadership role with respect to character, morality, and ethicality. As do the leaders, typically so do the rank and file, so it is imperative that every member of the government's leadership team "walk the talk" by exhibiting high ethical standards through behavior that is beyond reproach.

Each member of the local government's leadership team also has particular ethical responsibilities. For example, there are important symbolic responsibilities for the elected officials in local government, since they hold overall responsibility for the local government and its ethical culture. Local governments have varied forms of structure: Some cities and towns are led by a mayor or a council president, others charge a professional city manager with overall executive responsibility. Similarly, some counties are led by the probate judge or commission chair, while others employ a professional county manager. No matter his or her title, it is essential that the *chief executive officer* (CEO) serve as the touchstone, chief proponent, and spokesperson for ethicality and character within the local government. The most visible leader needs to be the most visible example of "walking the talk." She or he must not only rally the organization around character, but must daily demonstrate the ethical tone of the local government by making high-minded decisions, asking tough questions about ethical implications of the local government's operations and community relations strategy, and appointing persons of good character to leadership roles within the local government. The CEO must communicate and ensure commitment to the local government's ethical code, act with due diligence, and balance the needs and rights of all stakeholder groups. The CEO should be a leading proponent of governmental responsibility. When there are multiple elected officials holding leadership positions within a jurisdiction, they all must accept this responsibility. Undermining one another's work through "end runs" and backbiting is not acceptable in an ethical and well run local government (Sauser, Palmer, & Evans, 1981, p. 53). Differences of opinion and partisanship should never outweigh the interests of the citizenry.

Whoever is serving in the role of CEO of the local government may wish to appoint and support—through a direct reporting line—an *ethics compliance officer* (ECO) for the local government. It is the responsibility of the ECO to ensure that the organization implements the best practices listed above. He or she is responsible to see that the local government's ethical code is well written and understood, disseminated widely throughout the organization, and updated as circumstances warrant. It is the ECO who should set up a hotline or similar mechanism for reporting ethical violations, and it is the ECO who must protect whistle blowers, investigate potential ethical violations while maintaining a sense of fairness, and advise the CEO on appropriate corrective action. The ECO should design and participate in ongoing ethics training for elected officials, appointed administrators, and employees of the local government. The ECO may also serve as mentor and ethical guide to other members of the leadership team when they are weighing the impact and ethicality of decisions they must make within their own spheres of influence.

The *chief operating officer* (COO)—typically the city or county manager when the local government's CEO is an elected official—must take responsibility for the safety and integrity of the government's operations, programs, and services. He or she must make certain that all operations are environmentally responsible and do not endanger the health or welfare of the citizenry. Harming the environment through the government's operations must be anathema to the COO. Likewise, the local government's *chief public affairs officer* (CPAO) must ensure that the local government's programs and services are meeting the various needs of the citizenry, that public statements are accurate and nondeceptive, and that good public relations are maintained through rapid follow-through on all commitments.

The *chief financial officer* (CFO)—typically titled comptroller, finance director, or budget officer in a local government—must make certain that all financial decisions and financial reports adhere to applicable laws and standards, and that due diligence is taken as the government makes decisions about investments and capital expenditures. Credit and billing policies must be examined for fairness, and the integrity of all funds and accounts must be maintained. Likewise, the chief information technology officer (CITO) must maintain the security and integrity of the local government's information technology (IT) and assets. It is the CITO's responsibility to ensure that sound IT usage policies are maintained, that information is accurate and—where applicable—kept confidential, and that all software is properly licensed and employed.

The *chief human resources officer* (CHRO) has a number of important responsibilities with respect to establishing and maintaining a culture of character for the local government. The CHRO is responsible for all programs of recruitment, selection, training, development, and discipline of employees, thus plays a major role in shaping the character of the local government's workforce. The CHRO also maintains systems of compensation and benefits, grievances and appeals, and security of confidential employee records, and must take careful action to maintain fairness in all these functions. Alongside the ethics compliance officer, the CHRO has an important role to play in establishing and disseminating the organization's ethical code and in conducting ongoing ethics training programs. It is the CHRO who is responsible for ensuring that all laws and regulations regarding equal employment opportunity and affirmative action are followed. With respect to drug testing, medical exams and information, and background checks, the CHRO is responsible for protecting confidentiality and human dignity while also ensuring fairness in implementation of all procedures. Sauser and Sims (2007, pp. 270–275) discuss the ethical choices CHROs face when dealing with such issues as workforce diversification, organizational downsizing, employee recruitment, compensation and benefits, privacy, and organizational exit.

Legal counsel clearly has a major role to play in maintaining a culture of character within local government. Legal counsel must maintain currency in all statutes, case law, and regulations relating to local government, and must provide competent, wise counsel to the leaders of the local government on all matters respecting legal and ethical responsibilities. Legal counsel should review all contracts, ordinances, and policy statements issued by the local government. There also may be an important role for legal counsel in the investigation of ethical complaints against the local government or its employees when they are acting within their specified government roles.

CONCEPTUAL FRAMEWORK

"Although it is clear that culture is not the sole determinant of what happens in organizations, it is an important influence on what they accomplish ... and how. The internal culture has the potential to shape attitudes, reinforce beliefs, direct behavior, and establish performance expectations and the motivation to fulfill them."

—Schermerhorn (2005, p. 96)

Organizational Cultures and Character

According to Trevino and Nelson (2004), "'Culture' has become a common way of thinking about and describing an organization's internal world—a way of differentiating one organization's 'personality' from another" (p. 225). Schermerhorn (2005) defines organizational culture as "the system of shared beliefs and values that develops within an organization and guides the behavior of its members" (p. G-12). "Whenever someone, for example, speaks of 'the way we do things around here,' they are talking about the culture," says Schermerhorn (p. 96). Using such important components of culture as core values, stories, heroes, symbols, rites, and rituals, ethical leaders must influence the organization and its members to incorporate and exhibit desirable virtues and behaviors.

Sauser (2008a) has distinguished among four types of organizational culture with respect to their stance toward ethical behavior in business. This classification scheme, modeled in part on Schermerhorn's (2005, pp. 75–76) typology of strategies for corporate responsibility, holds that there are four basic types of organizational culture with respect to moral thought and action in government and business. They are defiance, compliance, neglect, and character.

An organization displaying a *culture of defiance* would be expected to exhibit behaviors aligned with Schermerhorn's (2005, pp. 75–76) obstructionist strategy of corporate social responsibility. More bluntly, this organization would be likely to scorn the law and other ethical standards and seek to resist or defy them wherever possible. "Bending" the law, cutting ethical corners, breaking the law when the likelihood of detection is perceived to be low (or reward for breaking the law is gauged to be high enough to risk the consequences), and other such tactics would be rewarded and encouraged in this type of culture. Top management would model the way with questionable behaviors and messages indicating that defiance of the law is acceptable when necessary to meet or exceed economic or political goals. "Achieve success at any cost; just don't get caught" would be the theme of a public sector organization embracing a culture of defiance. Denial of guilt would be expected if illegal or unethical behaviors of members of such an organization were detected and made public.

The organization characterized by a *culture of compliance* would be expected to exhibit behaviors associated with the defensive and accommodative strategies of corporate social responsibility (Schermerhorn, 2005, pp. 75–76). Their leaders and members may not agree with the legal and ethical standards they are forced to operate within, but they would take actions designed to meet (at least minimally) their legal and ethical obligations. In fact, this is an important distinction between compliant organizations and those with character as defined below. In psychological terms, compliance means yielding to standards one does not necessarily accept (McGuire, 1969, p. 190). It is only when one internalizes (accepts and incorporates within one's value system) the principles underlying "the letter of the law" that character can be inferred as the underlying cause of behavior aligned with laws and ethical standards. In other words, compliance infers a grudging sort of acceptance of laws and ethics, not a true incorporation of the "spirit" of those standards within one's individual personality or corporate culture (Krech, Crutchfield, & Ballachey, 1962).

The *culture of neglect* is all too often a tragic case. The leaders of the organization may be seeking to follow Schermerhorn's (2005, pp. 75–76) strategy of accommodation or even proaction, but one or more flaws in the culture lead to a failure to achieve the goals of this strategy. Such shortcomings might include a failure to know or understand the laws and ethical codes regulating the business, a failure adequately to communicate those standards, a failure to detect and/or punish wrongdoers within the firm, or even a certain blindness within the culture that leads to unintentional moral failure. While leaders of cultures of character are constantly vigilant to detect and correct ethical shortcomings on the part of themselves or their employees, leaders of cultures of neglect fail in their responsibility of due diligence. The consequences of this failure of diligence can be as devastating as the consequences of the deliberate defiance of the law taken by organizations with cultures of the first type.

The final of the four types of organizational culture in Sauser's (2008a) taxonomy is the *culture of character*. This is the organizational culture whose leaders and members, according to Sims (2005),

> are truly committed to ethical conduct [and] make ethical behavior a fundamental component of their every action. They put a stake in the ground, explicitly stating what the organization intends and expects. Value statements and codes of ethical conduct are used as a benchmark for judging both organizational policies and every individual's conduct. They do not

forget that trust, integrity, and fairness do matter, and they are crucial to [everyone] in the organization. (p. 396)

Here is an important statement made by Carl Skoogland, the former ethics director of Texas Instruments, in a speech he made on October 16, 2003: "Ethical managers must *know* what's right, *value* what's right, and *do* what's right" (Skoogland, 2003, emphasis in original). These three key principles are essential in the practical and successful management of ethics at the organizational level. With respect to Skoogland's (2003) three key principles, leaders and members of cultures of *defiance* may (or may not) know what's right, but they certainly neither value what's right nor do what's right. Leaders of cultures of *compliance*, from this same perspective, know what's right and even do what's right, but do not really value what's right. Consequently, members of these organizations may be tempted to bend or break the rules when opportunities occur, and may even be surreptitiously rewarded by their supervisors and peers for doing so. In cultures of *neglect*, there may be a conscious effort to know what's right, value what's right, and do what's right, but—through some (often unconscious) flaw in the culture—this effort flags through lack of diligence, resulting in a breach of moral standards. Finally, in cultures of *character*, positive moral values are ingrained throughout the organization such that all of its members strive without fail to know what's right, value what's right, and do what's right.

Elements of a Culture of Character

A *culture of character* thus is the type of organizational culture in which positive ethical values are ingrained throughout the organization such that all its members strive without fail to know what's right, value what's right, and do what's right. Turknett and Turknett (2002) provide this definition of an organization with character: "Like people with character, they get results, but they do it with integrity and a respect for people. Like people with character, companies [and other organizations] with character are able to balance *accountability* and *courage* with *humility* and *respect*" (p. 2, emphasis in original).

Organizations with character not only comply with legal and ethical standards, they also internalize them from top to bottom such that every member of the firm becomes a guardian of integrity. In fact, this is the characteristic that distinguishes between the two cultures. In a culture of compliance, members of the organization seek to live by the "letter of the law," but do not take to heart the "spirit of the law." In a culture of character, what is right, what is legal, what is good, what is ethical is ingrained in the fabric of the organization. Ethicality is valued in the culture of character, and every member of the organization seeks to live by that key value.

How can its leaders establish an organizational culture of character? Many authors (e.g., Aguilar, 1994; Sauser, 2010; Sauser & Sims, 2007; Sims, 2005) have offered helpful guidance. However, Perkins and Van Valkenburg (2004) are insistent that the creation of values-based organizations must begin at the top. Cultures of character are built by leaders of character. Leaders of organizations with cultures of character should possess wisdom and knowledge, courage, humanity, justice, temperance, and transcendence (Peterson & Seligman, 2004). Furthermore, they should devote considerable time and effort to modeling these virtues through their day-to-day interactions with the organization's employees and other stakeholders. They must seek out subordinates who also have these values, then work to shape and reinforce them throughout the organization such that these virtues come to define the organization. When organizational character becomes self-sustaining such that it transcends the leader's term at the helm, then a culture of character is well on its way to institutionalization. Cultures of character are established by persons of character who pass their values on to succeeding generations of leaders and employees. This truly is the key—and the test—of character-building within the organization.

Crafting a Culture of Character

Leaders who wish to take proactive measures to establish and maintain an organizational culture of character are advised to take the following steps:

1. Adopt a code of ethics—one that everyone in the organization understands.
2. Provide ethics training—show how the code of ethics applies in everyday situations encountered by members of the organization.
3. Hire and promote ethical people—let all employees know that ethical behavior and decision making is an important criterion for advancement in the organization.
4. Correct unethical behavior—use progressive discipline immediately to correct any breach of the organization's code of ethics.
5. Take a proactive strategy—do not wait until an ethical breach occurs, instead, take preventive actions to avoid problems.
6. Conduct a social audit—invite external reviewers to examine the organization's policies and procedures, just like financial auditors examine the books.

7. Protect whistle blowers—do not allow them to be subjected to harassment or retaliation.
8. Empower the guardians of integrity—enable every member of the organization to take positive action to demonstrate a commitment to ethics.

The leader's chief task with respect to establishing a culture of character is to lead by example and to empower every member of the organization to take personal action that demonstrates the organization's commitment to ethics in its relationships with suppliers, customers, employees, citizens, and other stakeholders. The leader should serve as an ethical exemplar and mentor to others in the organization. The leader must take proactive steps to turn each employee of the organization, no matter what may be that individual's position in the organizational hierarchy, into a protector of the organization's integrity. When maliciousness and indifference are replaced with a culture of integrity, honesty, and ethicality, the organization will reap long-term benefits from all quarters. This is the culture of character.

Training Programs to Build a Culture of Character

As emphasized above, an important step in building an organizational culture of character is providing meaningful ethics training programs for all employees within the organization. While such programs can be led by a variety of professionals, this seems to be a natural role for business ethics professors. How should such programs be structured, and how can employees become meaningfully engaged in program development and delivery? What kinds of programs foster strong employee participation and lead to meaningful learning and implementation of ideas? This portion of the chapter is intended to stimulate further discussion of these important questions. Research relating to elements of an effective ethics training program is here reviewed before an important case example intended to extend this research is presented.

The idea that ethics training is an important component of any organizational effort to instill morality into the fabric of its being—and ethicality into its day-to-day operations—is not new, of course. In 1979, Purcell and Weber presented the concept of "institutionalizing ethics" straightforwardly as "getting ethics formally and explicitly into daily life" (p. 6). Sims (1991) counseled those who seek to institutionalize ethics into corporate culture to consider a number of actions, including: "Develop a systematic training program (with input from employees at all levels of the organization) for all employees explicitly concerned with ethical principles and with relevant cases" (p. 504). Research results on a national sample of

313 business professionals employed in the United States, summarized by Valentine and Fleischman (2004), "provide significant statistical support for the notion that businesspersons employed in organizations that have formalized ethics programs have more positive perceptions of their companies' ethical context than do individuals employed in organizations that do not" (p. 381). These results likely generalize to public sector organizations as well. In terms of economic incentive, LeClair and Ferrell (2000) credit—at least in part—the 'due diligence' standard of the 1991 United States Sentencing Guidelines for Organizations for turning the ethics training and consulting business into a billion dollar industry.

Providing ethics training is widely touted nowadays by experts as a key component in any effective organizational ethics program (Ferrell, Fraedrich, & Ferrell, 2011, pp. 228–230; Knapp, 2011; Trevino & Nelson, 2004, pp. 296–299). Sauser (2008b) found that conducting ongoing training and education programs with respect to ethics is a "best practice" recommended (or mandated) by key legal standards for organizations across the world, and Weber (2007) commented, "Formal … ethics training, often mandatory, is now common … around the globe" (p. 61).

While the number of ethics training programs being offered has increased exponentially over the past 30 years, research on the effectiveness of these programs is still in its infancy (Delaney & Sockell, 1992). The effectiveness of corporate ethics training has largely been inferred from studies of similar programs offered to business students in the classroom. Early reviews (e.g., Murphy & Boatwright, 1994; Weber, 1990) of the effectiveness of undergraduate and graduate classroom experiences in business ethics have been mixed, yet evidence is accruing that such educational experiences can raise students' ethical awareness and sensitivity (Balotsky & Steingard, 2006; Murphy & Boatwright, 1994) and level of ethical reasoning (Singer, Arora, & Roselli, 2004), if not their ethical attitudes (Jewe, 2008).

In an effort to determine if ethics training programs make a positive difference, Delaney and Sockell (1992) conducted a survey of over 1,000 Columbia University Graduate School of Business alumni from the classes of 1953 through 1987. Their conclusion:

> The results suggest that ethics training in firms has a positive effect. At a minimum, respondents exposed to ethics programs perceive that their firm treats moral dilemmas in a more sensitive way, and this may aid them in choosing what to do when they are faced with ethical dilemmas. (p. 719)

The results of a recent meta-analytic investigation of 25 business ethics instructional programs conducted by business schools and corporations are not as sanguine. "Overall, results indicate that business ethics instructional programs have a minimal impact on increasing outcomes related to ethical perceptions, behavior, or awareness" (Waples, Antes, Murphy, Connelly, & Mumford, 2009, p. 133). "However," Waples et al. (2009) continue, "specific criteria, content, and methodological moderators of effectiveness shed light on potential recommendations for improving business ethics instruction" (p. 133). Based on the results of their meta-analysis, Waples et al. provide the following suggestions for enhancing the effectiveness of organizational ethics training programs:

> Standardized programs are best—potentially workshops and seminars. Organizational support and a developmental focus may also enhance learning outcomes. Shorter instructional periods appear to produce the best results. Case-based learning is most effective, along with a variety of additional learning activities. (p. 146)

The ethics workshop described the next section of this chapter embraces the suggestions of Waples et al. It also builds on ideas drawn from the remaining sections of this literature review.

STRUCTURAL COMPONENTS OF EFFECTIVE ETHICS TRAINING PROGRAMS

Purposes

Knapp (2011, pp. 235–236) provides a comprehensive list of reasons often cited by employers as the primary purposes of ethics educational programs in business settings. He says the programs typically offered in industry are designed to:

- Comply with United States Sentencing Commission Guidelines and other compliance requirements
- Prevent illegal or undesirable conduct, thereby reducing risk
- Establish values and expectations of right conduct
- Familiarize employees with sources of guidance and relevant policies, such as a code of conduct
- Demonstrate the employer's commitment to its values and policies
- Sensitize employees to potential pitfalls before they encounter them in practice
- Heighten awareness of wrongdoing when it occurs in the workplace, thus making it more likely misconduct will be reported
- Develop critical thinking and moral reasoning skills

- Provide language and build competency for sustaining a workplace dialogue on conduct
- Establish clear performance standards for employee evaluation, rewards and disciplinary action
- Strengthen workplace trust and morale, as the best training is shown to reinforce shared values and equitable expectations
- Improve relationships with customers, suppliers, communities and other constituencies by ensuring that employees understand what contributes to, or detracts from, company reputation.

Goals

What should be the goals of an ethics training program for employees? LeClair and Ferrell (2000) provide a straightforward answer to this important question: "An effective program is organization-specific and takes advantage of self-regulatory incentives by developing ethical standards and appropriate communications, controls, and training to ensure employees and other agents understand and abide by these expectations" (p. 313). Kirrane (1990) argues that ethics training should (a) identify situations where ethical decision making is involved, (b) lead to a greater understanding of the culture and values of the organization, and (c) evaluate the impact of ethical decisions on the organization's well-being. Valentine and Fleischman (2004) suggest, "Such training should ideally teach individuals the ethical requirements of the organization, as well as how to recognize and react to common ethical problems experienced in the workplace" (p. 382).

Contents

What should an ethics program for employees contain? Contents should flow directly from the goals of the program, of course. Ferrell et al. (2011) provide a comprehensive menu from which to select relevant content:

> Training can educate employees about the [organization]'s policies and expectations, relevant laws and regulations, and general social standards. Training programs can make employees aware of available resources, support systems, and designated personnel who can assist them with ethical and legal advice. They can also empower employees to ask tough questions and make ethical decisions. (p. 228)

Weber (2007) conducted a thorough review of learning theory to glean some insights to guide designers of ethics training programs. His summary suggestions include: (1) Combine pedagogical approaches and use flexible physical settings to take into consideration various learning styles. (2) Leverage organizational influences, such as a statement of values and acceptable patterns of behavior within the organization. (3) Use group discussions, particularly among individuals at different levels of cognitive moral development. (4) Discuss real life situations, including business cases. (5) Integrate stakeholder analysis by considering viewpoints of stockholders, managers, peers, other employees, suppliers, customers, family, friends, industry groups, host communities, and other parties. (9) Assign participants an active role in designing the program. (10) Use inductive learning (learning by example).

Methods

With respect to training methods, LeClair and Ferrell (2000) provide a strong case for the perspective that experiential training—including behavioral simulation—is a highly effective approach to ethics training. Knapp (2011) comments favorably about the benefits of experiential training:

> Interactive training need not be dull conversation about law and regulation. After all, ethics encompasses some of the liveliest issues that live and breathe within organizations. The best approaches encourage spirited dialog and use creative methods, such as role-play, that can even be entertaining. (pp. 239–240)

From a pragmatic standpoint, Aguilar (1994) offers two important suggestions: (1) make certain any training materials and cases are clearly relevant to the audience, and (2) be sure all participants "are given ample opportunity to ask questions, challenge assertions, and generally to engage actively in the learning process" (p. 104).

Providers

Who is best suited to provide training in ethics? Answers to this question vary widely, and are dependent on the purposes of the program, its content, and the skills of the personnel available to provide the training. Possible trainers include moral philosophers, religious leaders, prominent citizens who have a stellar reputation for ethics, members of the organization's training staff, ethics officers, senior consultants, and company officers and senior executives. Lattal and Clark (2005) endorse the idea of using company managers as trainers, with the following caveat: "Depending on your role in the organization, it may be appropriate for you to conduct such workshops yourself after receiving training that would contribute to your own moral sensitivity and professional development" (p. 341).

No matter who is selected to lead the training, Weber (2007) believes—based on his review of relevant research in learning theory—there are some desirable traits that characterize effective trainers. He states, "Better facilitators" are effective at: (1) Encouraging participants to analyze and modify their views as a result of insights gained from others in group discussions; (2) Encouraging participant critical thinking and inquiry skills; (3) Supporting development of participant self-confidence by encouraging small participant groups to be independent in managing their discussions and in arriving at conclusions, while simultaneously encouraging individual creativity; and (4) Establishing a timetable and stages along the inductive learning process, including a planned close and logical wrap-up, where participants are encouraged to help evaluate their own progress toward learning goals (p. 66).

Business Ethics Faculty as Providers of Ethics Training

While meaningful ethics training programs for all employees within the organization can be led by a variety of professionals, this seems to be a natural role for business ethics professors, who typically possess the various skills described above by Weber (2007). Through the use of experiential and reflective learning (Sims & Sauser, 2011), business ethics professors can likely provide considerable value to employees and leaders alike as those audiences seek to learn more about ethical behavior in organizations. One of the present authors (Sauser) has been involved in the process of providing ethics training to organizations in the public, private, and voluntary sectors for more than two decades. The next section of this chapter describes the ethics workshop devised to train the employees of the City of Auburn, Alabama. This example illustrates the conceptual framework described above being put into action.

A PROFESSIONAL ETHICS PROGRAM FOR
MUNICIPAL EMPLOYEES

This ethics training program grew from a conversation between the two authors: a management professor (Sauser) and the city's human resources (HR) director (Reeves). The HR director wanted to establish a short (2-hour) workshop on professional ethics that would be suitable for all city employees. The city has a good reputation for ethics and professionalism; the workshop was designed to maintain this reputation and build on it, not because there were any ethical problems the city was facing. The HR director was aware of the professor's workshop facilitation skills and interest in professional ethics, and invited him to partner with the city to develop and lead a series of workshops that would enable as many as possible of the city's employees to participate.

Rationale for the Workshop

On a daily basis, we read and hear of questionable ethical behavior, not only in corporate America but also in the public sector. Unfortunately, we have sometimes seen or discovered ethical lapses in judgment among people in our own workforce. Because we are public servants, and because we must maintain the trust of our citizens, training and reinforcement in the area of ethical behavior is extremely important.

With this message, a new ethics training seminar was announced to the City of Auburn management team in February 2003.

The City of Auburn, Alabama, is a thriving university community of approximately 60,000 residents and many others that work in the community. More than 465 regular employees operating within the city's 13 departments provide a wide range of traditional municipal government services to a very diverse population. Many employees come from the private sector where behavior that would be perfectly acceptable, and perhaps even expected as social courtesies, would not be considered appropriate in the public sector. Conveying expectations and setting protective behavioral boundaries was, and continues to be, accomplished through recruitment, new-hire orientation, policies and procedures, effective supervisory practices and professional leadership. Although ethics training had previously been provided to supervisory personnel, missing in 2003 was a general program specifically focused on an examination of ethics and ethical guidelines within the context of employment with the City of Auburn.

A number of reasons support the decision to invest in ethics training. First and foremost, there is an obligation for all public servants to work in an ethical manner. This requires that they be able to recognize and address ethical dilemmas, that they understand guiding principles, and that they are aware of ethical guidelines and boundaries contained within the regulations and policies of the organization. Second, providing the training serves to convey to employees that this is an important subject. Together, these two reasons are important in actually guiding behavior which leads to a third reason, that of helping employees succeed in their jobs, avoiding performance and disciplinary issues.

Fourth, the training enables the City of Auburn to offer tangible evidence to citizens, judicial and quasi-judicial bodies, and others of the city's commitment to developing and maintaining an ethical workforce. Through the ethical behavior of employees and a documented commitment to providing this training, the city's service and reputation are enhanced and its potential liability reduced. Finally, this training supports other efforts to develop and maintain a strong corporate culture based on ethical conduct and service. While many activities are required to achieve such a culture, ethics training is one key component.

Structure and Contents of the Workshop

A steering committee for the workshop was appointed representing senior employees from throughout the city. The professor presented to this steering committee some introductory materials and sought their advice regarding relevant issues, examples, and methods that would appeal to the city's employees. Significantly, the members of the steering committee were asked to provide written examples of ethics issues they had faced, heard about, or observed during their career; these examples were then turned into a series of anonymous minicase materials used in the workshop. (All of the copyrighted training materials for this workshop may be found in Sauser, 2011). A 25-item City of Auburn "ethics quiz" was also prepared using items drawn directly from the city's personnel policy manual. To date over 650 City of Auburn employees have participated in this workshop, including the city manager and other senior managers. While there has been some turnover in employment within the city due to retirements, departures to pursue other opportunities, and deaths over the past decade, many of the employees trained in this program remain gainfully employed by the city.

Each workshop session includes approximately 30 participants widely representative of the city's workforce in terms of age, gender, racial-ethnic identity, and departmental assignment. The participants are seated at small tables in a city training room designed to maximize participant interaction. The HR director or a member of his staff introduces each workshop, explaining to the participants that the workshop was designed with input from a group of city employees. The professor begins the workshop by soliciting discussion using a series of questions regarding the nature of professional ethics. Is "ethics in public service" an oxymoron? Does "professional ethics" represent an (impossible?) ideal, or perhaps a manifestation of a person's value system, or even a way of life? Is ethics something one can learn? How does each person's life experience influence his or her approach to professional ethics? These questions are explored in a manner that encourages participant expression of multiple perspectives, thus setting a tone of openness for later discussion.

Attention then shifts to an examination of various guidelines for professional behavior, including moral codes; professional association standards; the law; city policy, rules and regulations; societal norms; and personal values and beliefs. Three key ideas are then presented; they are described as the major "takeaways" from the workshop: (1) Never use your public position for private gain. (2) Remember—the citizens are your employers, and they are always watching. (3) The perception of wrongdoing can be as damaging as actual wrongdoing. At this point the concept of "an ethical challenge" is presented: An ethical challenge is defined as "a situation with a potential course of action that, although offering potential personal benefit or gain, is also unethical in that it violates one or more of the standards for behavior we have just discussed." A list of examples of typical ethical challenges is then presented, and specific actions relevant to the jobs represented among the participants are discussed. (For example, mixing "dark water" with "clear water" would be an example of the provision of an unsafe service by employees in water resource management, as they readily recognize and point out.)

Attention then focuses on a brief discussion of unethical requests bosses sometimes make of subordinates—and how to handle them—followed by examples of rationalizations for unethical behavior—and how to identify and avoid them. After a short break the larger group is broken into small groups of five or six persons, and each group is assigned one of the mini-case scenarios mentioned above, with instructions to read and discuss the scenario, identify the ethical issues involved, and decide what action would be appropriate to take. The results of the small group discussions are then shared with the larger group, and all participants are encouraged to join into the discussion. Alternative solutions are examined and the group typically reaches a clear consensus on how to handle the situation. (This allows group norms to be solidified.) During the discussion the professor might change a fact or two about the scenario, and the participants are invited to describe how a change in facts might change the group-accepted normative response. Free discussion is encouraged during this portion of the workshop, and ideas flow readily from the group members.

When this discussion is concluded (and it typically takes a deliberate effort to close this lively discussion), a checklist for making ethical decisions, a list of double-check considerations, and suggestions for establishing a strong ethical culture are presented and discussed. The purpose of this discussion is to provide some tools to the workshop participants they can use when making their own ethical decisions. At this point in the workshop the City of Auburn ethics quiz is administered individually and discussed as a group. While the answers to many of the questions on this quiz are obvious (thus reinforcing city policy), several of them—different items among different groups—engender considerable discussion. Alternative responses are presented and defended, and city policies are read and interpreted for the group. This helps participants realize that not all cases are "black and white," and that standards of reasonable judgment must prevail. The workshop ends with a restatement of the "three key ideas" mentioned above, plus an admonition to "walk the talk" by exhibiting professionalism no matter what one's role within the city.

Evaluation of the Workshop

The authors firmly believe that the ethics training has been successful in meeting these objectives. Invariably, seminar participants struggle with some ethics scenarios and rules, and the discussions that follow help sensitize participants to ethical guidelines in the context of city employment. Brief evaluations following each offering of the workshop indicated that the participants enjoyed the workshop and found it helpful in identifying and considering solutions for ethical issues they encounter in their own day-to-day work.

To evaluate the longer-term impact of these workshops, current city employees were surveyed in December of 2014 to gauge their perceptions of the ethics training and its value. Because many current employees participated in the training years before and might not have had strong recollections of its content, the survey instrument began with a short review of the training (which in itself served as a brief reinforcement of the training they received). The following items were included on the survey:

1. When did you attend the seminar?
2. Do you believe that the ethics seminar has had a positive impact on promoting an ethical culture within the city workforce?
3. Did you get information from the seminar that helped you understand the importance of ethical conduct in your service to the public?
4. Did the ethics quiz serve as a helpful review of some employment related policies of the city?
5. Did you think the seminar was important for other employees to attend?
6. Did you think it is helpful for new employees to attend this training?
7. It makes me proud to be part of an organization that actively promotes an ethical culture.

Of the 450 surveys that were distributed, 304 were returned for a response rate of 68%. Thirty-eight respondents stated that they had not attended the seminar and answered the survey to varying degrees. Of those who had attended the seminar, the following observations are noted.

- 98% stated that it made them proud to work for an organization that actively promotes an ethical culture (2% said it did not).
- 70.2% believe that the seminar has a positive impact on the culture of the organization (8.3% did not think it did and 21.5% did not know).
- 78.4% indicated that the seminar helps employees understand the importance of ethical conduct in public service (8.7% said it did not and 12.9% could not remember).
- 72.2% responded that the seminar provided a helpful review of some employment related policies of the city (5.7% said it did not and 22.1% said they could not remember).
- 82.3% believe that it was important for other employees to attend (5.3% said it was not important and 12.5% did not know).
- 90.2% stated that it is helpful for new employees to attend the seminar (3.1% said it is not helpful and 6.6% did not know).
- Across the board, those respondents that could not remember when they attended the seminar had significantly higher "I can't remember" or "I don't know" response rates to the questions above, which, in itself, seems to suggest that honesty is valued.

LESSONS LEARNED

"All experience is an arch to build upon."

—Henry Brooks Adams (as cited in Knowles, 2004, p. 2)

Having offered versions of this ethics training program for most of the past decade, the authors have learned some lessons along the way that they now willingly share with others who desire to rise to the exciting challenge of training public sector employees to craft an organizational culture of character. These lessons are proffered in this concluding section of the chapter as an effort to extend the suggestions made above on the basis of the literature review. Developers and leaders of ethics workshops are urged to consider the following ideas and to test them in their own professionally-developed workshops:

- While face-to-face programs (like the example described above) may appear easy to deliver, it is very important to provide them in a highly professional manner. Mastering and using the facilitation skills described by Weber (2007) are essential when one is working with discerning professionals. Know how to manage time, foster meaningful group discussion that leads to shared insights, encourage critical thinking, and summarize important points gained through inductive learning. Be certain to explore multiple points of view, and allow positive group norms to become evident. Reinforce important organizational values (like customer service, professionalism, and honesty) whenever possible.

- To ensure relevance, use examples and materials that participants would encounter during the regular course of their work. Making use of an advisory committee of representative employees (as in the present example) is an excellent way to gather pertinent information and to test out ideas before they are brought up in the training environment.

- Minicases like those used in the example typically engender lively discussion and are often remembered by program participants and shared with their peers. It is important to select case examples carefully, edit them for anonymity, and make certain they are discussed thoroughly from multiple perspectives. When there is disagreement within the group on how best to handle a case example, discover the reasons for this disagreement, explore them for insights, and see if a group consensus emerges over time. This is when many seasoned group participants with high levels of moral reasoning have (and take!) the opportunity to provide leadership to the group, thus setting a good example for others to follow.

- The "ethics quiz" used in the example has proven over time to be an excellent tool for stimulating discussion and maintaining participant engagement. It takes time to review policies and create a meaningful ethics quiz, but the resulting inductive learning makes the effort worthwhile. Employees are able to "refresh their memory" about organizational policies (and, for some, to encounter them for the first time!) and see how the "black and white" language of many policies needs to be tempered by interpretation and judgment.

- Having a cross-section of employees from the various functional divisions of the organization participating in each workshop has proven very effective in this ethics training program. Employees get to see things from others' points of view, and to gain a better understanding of the ethical issues encountered across the organization. Having top and middle managers participating in these programs alongside the "rank and file" sets a good example, demonstrating that this material is important enough to be considered by persons at all levels of the organization. It has been the authors' experience that the presence of members of the organization's leadership team rarely stifles discussion; in fact, it often leads to a higher quality discussion of important ethical issues and provides an opportunity for leaders to set a high ethical tone for the organization.

Overall, it appears that the intervention program described herein has been an effective one that has met the objectives of the leaders of the City of Auburn. A culture of ethicality and character is being maintained across time. This continues to be borne out by findings from the citizens' survey, in which city services are given high marks for professionalism. The program evaluation conducted for this chapter provides specific evidence of the effectiveness of the provision of these ethics workshops.

We encourage other public sector leaders to consider developing and offering ethics training programs such the one described in this chapter in a proactive effort to transform the organizational culture to one of character (or to maintain that designation if it has already been achieved). Increasing the citizenry's confidence in the effectiveness and basic morality of its public work force will pay dividends for years to come.

ACKNOWLEDGMENT

The authors are indebted to Kristen D. Matthews who aided in the collection and analysis of the evaluative data presented in this chapter.

REFERENCES

Aguilar, F. J. (1994). *Managing corporate ethics: Learning from America's ethical companies how to supercharge business performance.* New York, NY: Oxford University Press.

Balotsky, E. R., & Steingard, D. S. (2006). How teaching business ethics makes a difference: Findings from an ethical learning model. *Journal of Business Ethics Education, 3,* 5–34.

Delaney, J. T., & Sockell, D. (1992). Do company ethics training programs make a difference? An empirical analysis. *Journal of Business Ethics, 11*(9), 719–727.

Ferrell, O. C., Fraedrich, J., & Ferrell, L. (2011). *Business ethics: Ethical decision making and cases* (8th ed.). Mason, OH: South-Western Cengage Learning.

Jewe, R. D. (2008). Do business ethics courses work? The effectiveness of business ethics education: An empirical study. *Journal of Global Business Issues,* Spring, 1–6.

Knapp, J. C. (2011). Rethinking ethics training: New approaches to enhance effectiveness. In R. R. Sims & W. I. Sauser, Jr. (Eds.), *Experiences in teaching business ethics* (pp. 231–245). Charlotte, NC: Information Age Publishing.

Kirrane, D. E. (1990). Managing values: A systematic approach to business ethics. *Training and Development Journal,* November, 53–60.

Knowles, E. (Ed.) (2004). *Oxford dictionary of quotations* (6th ed.). New York, NY: Oxford University Press.

Krech, D., Crutchfield, R. S., & Ballachey, E. L. (1962). Culture. In D. Krech, R. S. Crutchfield, & E. L. Ballachey, *Individual in society* (pp. 339–380). New York, NY: McGraw-Hill.

Lattal, A. D., & Clark, R. W. (2005). *Ethics at work.* Atlanta, GA: Performance Management Publications.

LeClair, D. T., & Ferrell, L. (2000). Innovation in experiential business ethics training. *Journal of Business Ethics, 23*(3 Part 1), 313–322.

McGuire, W. J. (1969). The nature of attitudes and attitude change. In G. Lindzey & E. Aronson (Eds.), *The handbook of social psychology: The individual in a social context* (Vol. 3., 2nd ed., pp. 136–314). Reading, MA: Addison-Wesley.

Murphy, P. R., & Boatright, J. R. (1994). Assessing the effectiveness of instruction in business ethics: A longitudinal analysis. *Journal of Education for Business, 69*(6), 326–339.

Peterson, C., & Seligman, M. E. P. (2004). *Character strengths and virtues: A handbook and classification.* New York, NY: American Psychological Association/Oxford University.

Perkins, R. D., & Van Valkenburg, D. (2004). Ethical leadership and the board of directors. *GoodBusiness, 3*(1), pages unnumbered.

Purcell, T. V., & Weber, J. (1979). *Institutionalizing corporate ethics: A case history* [Special Study No. 71]. New York, NY: The Presidents of the American Management Association.

Sauser, W. I., Jr. (2008a). Crafting a culture of character: The role of the executive suite. In S. Quatro & R. R. Sims (Eds.), *Executive ethics: Ethical dilemmas and challenges for the C-suite* (pp. 1–17). Charlotte, NC: Information Age Publishing.

Sauser, W. I., Jr. (2008b). Regulating ethics in business: Review and recommendations. *SAM Management in Practice, 12*(4), 1–7.

Sauser, W. I., Jr. (2010). Creating an ethical culture in local government. In R.R. Sims (Ed.), *Change (transformation) in government organizations* (pp. 53–70). Charlotte, NC: Information Age Publishing.

Sauser, W. I., Jr. (2011). Beyond the classroom: Business ethics training programs for professionals. In R. R. Sims & W. I. Sauser, Jr. (Eds.), *Experiences in teaching business ethics* (pp. 247–271). Charlotte, NC: Information Age Publishing.

Sauser, W. I., Jr. (2013). Empowering leaders to craft organizational cultures of character: Conceptual framework and examples. *Journal of Leadership, Accountability and Ethics, 10*(1), 14–27.

Sauser, W. I., Jr., Palmer, E. V., & Evans, K. L. (1981). *Labor relations in Alabama local government.* Auburn University, AL: Office of Public Service and Research.

Sauser, W. I., Jr., Sauser, L. D., & Sumners, J. A. (2005). Leadership challenges in local government: Economic development, financial management, and ethical leadership. In R. R. Sims & S. J. Quatro (Eds.), *Leadership challenges for management: Succeeding in today's competitive environment* (pp. 216–236). Armonk, NY: M.E. Sharpe.

Sauser, W. I., Jr., & Sims, R. R. (2007). Fostering an ethical culture for business: The role of HR managers. In R. R. Sims (Ed.), *Human resource management: Contemporary issues, challenges and opportunities* (pp. 253–285). Charlotte, NC: Information Age Publishing.

Schermerhorn, J. R., Jr. (2005). *Management* (8th ed.). New York, NY: Wiley.

Sims, R.R. (1991). The institutionalization of organizational ethics. *Journal of Business Ethics, 10*(7), 493–506.

Sims, R. R. (2005). Restoring ethics consciousness to organizations and the workplace: Every contemporary leader's challenge. In R. R. Sims & S. A. Quatro (Eds.), *Leadership: Succeeding in the private, public, and not-for-profit sectors* (pp. 386–407). Armonk, NY: M. E. Sharpe.

Sims, R. R., & Sauser, W. I., Jr. (2011). Reflection through debriefing in teaching business ethics: Completing the learning process in experiential learning exercises. In R. R. Sims & W. I. Sauser, Jr. (Eds.), *Experiences in teaching business ethics* (pp. 171–203). Charlotte, NC: Information Age Publishing.

Singer, J., Arora, R., & Roselli, M. (2004). Teaching ethical decision-making to students of small business. *Journal of Business and Entrepreneurship, 16*(1), 17–28.

Skoogland, C. (2003, October 16). *Establishing an ethical organization.* Plenary address presented at the Conference on Ethics and Social Responsibility in Engineering and Technology, New Orleans, LA.

Trevino, L. K., & Nelson, K. A. (2004). *Managing business ethics: Straight talk about how to do it right* (3rd ed.). New York, NY: Wiley.

Turknett, R., & Turknett, L. (2002). Three essentials for rebuilding trust: Code, character and conversation. *GoodBusiness, 1*(2), pages unnumbered.

Valentine, S., & Fleischman, G. (2004). Ethics training and businesspersons' perceptions of organizational ethics. *Journal of Business Ethics, 52*(4), 381–390.

Veal, D.-T., Sauser, W. I., Jr., & Folmar, M. T. (2010). The multiple dimensions of transparency in government. In R. R. Sims (Ed.), *Change (transformation) in government organizations* (pp. 255–274). Charlotte, NC: Information Age Publishing.

Veal, D.-T., Sauser, W. I., Jr., Tamblyn, M. B., Sauser, L. D., & Sims, R. R. (2015). Fostering transparency in local government. *Journal of Management Policy and Practice, 16*(1), 11–17.

Waples, E. P., Antes, A. L., Murphy, S. T., Connelly, S., & Mumford, M. D. (2009). A meta-analytic investigation of business ethics instruction. *Journal of Business Ethics, 87*, 133–151.

Weber, J. (1990). Measuring the impact of teaching ethics to future managers: A review, assessment, and recommendations. *Journal of Business Ethics, 9*, 23–42.

Weber, J. A. (2007). Business ethics training: Insights from learning theory. *Journal of Business Ethics, 70*(1), 61–85.

CHAPTER 10

CARING FOR THE POOR IN JEFFERSON COUNTY, ALABAMA

A Model of Change in Government-Run Healthcare

Roger McCullough

INTRODUCTION

> The moral test of government is how that government treats those who are in the dawn of life—the children; those who are in the twilight of life—the elderly; and those who are in the shadows of life—the sick, the needy, and the handicapped. (Humphrey, 1977)

Meeting the healthcare needs of citizens is increasingly a challenge for all levels of government, federal, state, and local and nowhere is this challenge greater than when it comes to providing healthcare to the indigent poor. The cost of healthcare in the United States continues to increase,

Transforming Government Organizations:
Fresh Ideas and Examples From the Field, pp. 291–312

placing added stress on already strained public-sector budgets. As a result, governments are pursuing models of healthcare delivery that maximize access to their underserved populations in as cost-effective and efficient ways as possible.

Modeling healthcare for the poor requires an understanding of both the economic and sociological aspects of healthcare delivery to this unique population. While the passage of the Patient Protection and Affordable Healthcare Act in 2010 represented perhaps the most significant regulatory overhaul of the U.S. healthcare system since Lyndon B. Johnson signed Medicare and Medicaid into law in 1965, it is important to note that lack of access to healthcare is multidimensional, particularly for low-income populations. Health insurance coverage alone does not guarantee access to healthcare.

The nation's experience with the implementation of Medicare and Medicaid in the 1960s is instructive. Charity medicine in theory would no longer be necessary since poor patients could obtain care in the private sector. However, as experience with public insurance has grown, it has become clear that poor people face barriers to obtaining healthcare beyond simply the inability to pay for it. There are many factors that contribute to lack of access, such as transportation, travel distance, availability of providers, and wait time for appointments. Importantly, there are also social conditions that influence access—education, literacy, language barriers, cultural barriers, trust in the healthcare system, employment flexibility, and lack of knowledge of symptoms important for early detection of diseases. As understanding of these barriers has increased, efforts to help low income people obtain healthcare have expanded to include more funding for community health centers, public health clinics, language translators, and educational programs specifically targeted at the poor (Swartz, 2009).

There is ample evidence that poverty has devastating and long-term consequences on health outcomes. According to calculations from the Longitudinal Mortality Survey, people whose family income in 1980 was in the top 5% had a life expectancy at all ages that was 25% longer than those at the lower 5%. Lower mortality and morbidity is associated with almost any positive indicator of socioeconomic status (Deaton, 2003).

According to the American Psychological Association (2015), living in poverty adversely affects both physical and mental health. The effects are linked to lower academic achievement, including concentration and ability to learn, to behavioral and emotional problems, including impulsive behavior, anxiety, aggression, depression, and low self-esteem, and to chronic health conditions such as asthma, anemia, and pneumonia, as well as to risky behaviors, such as smoking and early sexual activity.

Additionally, there is a growing body of evidence of a correlation between neighborhood conditions and health. A 2013 study by the Joint Center for Political and Economic Studies found that neighborhood conditions, such as the quality of public schools, the age, density, and size of housing, availability of medical care and healthy foods, availability of jobs, levels of exposure to environmental degradation, and availability of exercise options powerfully predict who is healthy, who is sick and who lives longer (Place Matters, 2013). This underscores that poverty and the effects of living in poverty act as social determinants of health; consequently, conversations about healthcare must necessarily include dialog around community infrastructure, community resources, and the physical environment (Peek, 2014).

> All Americans do not have the same opportunities to be healthy and to make healthy choices. Sometimes, barriers to health and to healthier decisions are too high for individuals to overcome, even with great motivation. (Braveman & Egerter, 2013)

Despite spending more on medical care than any other nation, the United States ranks below other wealthy nations on most health indicators, including: life expectancy; rates of mortality at all ages up to age 75; rates of low birthweight and premature birth; and rates of occurrence and mortality due to diabetes, intentional and unintentional injuries, heart disease, and respiratory and infectious diseases (Braveman & Egeter, 2013). Income, education, stress, race and ethnicity, and childhood experiences are all contributing factors to this conundrum. In *The Spirit Level: Why Greater Equality Leads to Stronger Societies*, Wilkinson and Pickett (2009) research the relationship between income inequality and how societies fare on eleven health and social metrics ranging from physical and mental health to violence and child well-being. Their research concludes that there is a high correlation between the equitable distribution of income and health and well-being on essentially every measure (Wilkinson & Pickett, 2009).

It is critically important that any models of healthcare for the indigent poor take into account underlying psychosocial influences that drive the behavior and attitudes in this population. Without taking these factors into account, simply providing insurance or otherwise providing financial access to healthcare may well not result in positive health outcomes.

INDIGENT HEALTHCARE: THE NATIONAL PERSPECTIVE

Healthcare for the poor is a significant problem in the United States. For a myriad of reasons, many poor individuals put off seeking medical help as long as possible and then rely on emergency rooms for their care, an extremely expensive alternative. Many of these patients feel they have no other place to go, and some have never gone anywhere else to receive healthcare. And, because emergency rooms in the U.S. are subject to the

Emergency Medical Treatment and Active Labor Act (EMTALA), they have no choice but to examine presenting patients and provide treatment, if medically indicated, regardless of ability to pay. As charity care costs increase and healthcare margins tighten, the willingness of providers to provide care to indigent patients is on the decline. In many states, even patients covered by Medicaid fare little better because of the fraction of incurred cost that Medicaid pays. Simply put, the poor are expensive to treat.

The following statistics indicate the scope of the problem (Caughlin, Holahan, Caswell, & McGrath, 2014). (See Figures 10.1 & 10.2):

- In 2013, the cost of "uncompensated care" provided to uninsured individuals was $84.9 billion. Uncompensated care includes health care services without a direct source of payment. In addition, people who are uninsured paid an additional $25.8 billion out-of-pocket for their care.
- The majority of uncompensated care (60%) is provided in hospitals. Community based providers (including clinics and health centers) and office-based physicians provide the rest, providing 26% and 14% of uncompensated care, respectively.
- In 2013, $53.3 billion was paid to help providers offset uncompensated care costs. Most of these funds ($32.8 billion) came from the federal government through a variety of programs including Medicaid and Medicare, the Veterans Health Administration, and other programs. States and localities provided $19.8 billion, and the private sector provided $0.7 billion.

JEFFERSON COUNTY, ALABAMA AND INDIGENT CARE

The previous paragraphs are important for broadly framing the discussion of indigent care, but healthcare is a local issue, particularly when it comes to providing care for vulnerable citizens. Assuring that adequate medical services are available to this population is the responsibility of local governments. There has been much debate, often along ideological lines, as to the role of government in providing healthcare for its citizens. While there may be disagreement as to the specific role that government should play and to the extent of government's involvement in providing healthcare, there is little disagreement that communities are collectively responsible for providing care to those who Hubert Humphrey (1977) described as in the "shadows of life."

In Jefferson County, Alabama indigent care is addressed through a county safety-net facility whose mission is to serve the healthcare needs of all residents of the county, regardless of their ability to pay. Safety-net

Sources of Funding for Uncompensated Care, 2013

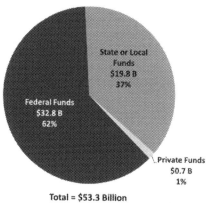

Total = $53.3 Billion

Source: Urban Institute estimates derived from provider and government data sources on spending for the uninsured.

Figure 10.1.   Sources of funding for uncompensated care, 2013.

Sources of Funding for Uncompensated Care, by Program, 2013

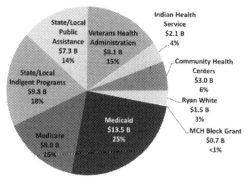

Total = $53.3 Billion

Source: Urban Institute estimates derived from provider and government data sources on spending for the uninsured.

Figure 10.2.   Sources of funding for uncompensated care, by program, 2013.

facilities provide a significant level of care to low-income, uninsured, and vulnerable populations and are committed to providing access to care for people with limited or no access to healthcare due to their financial circumstances, insurance status, or health condition. Health care safety-net providers include emergency departments, community health centers, public hospitals, charitable clinics, and in some communities, teaching and community hospitals—organizations that people turn to when faced with barriers to obtaining medical care elsewhere. While the county has a long history of providing healthcare to its poorest citizens, new economic realities and radical shifts in the national healthcare landscape caused the county's leaders to re-imagine its decades-old, government-sponsored approach. Jefferson is Alabama's largest county with a population exceeding 660,000. U.S. Census data from 2014 reflects that 42.9% of the county's residents are Black or African American, 54% Caucasian, and 3.8% Hispanic. The median annual income is $45,429. With 18.9% of its citizens below the federal poverty level, Jefferson County fares better economically than most other counties in the state. Alabama currently ranks as the sixth poorest state in the United States (Alabama Possible, 2015).

While the County's safety-net facility serves all County residents, its focus is clearly to provide care to the indigent poor, defined as residents who are uninsured and whose income is 200% of the federal poverty level or less. In Jefferson County, this would include some 60,000 residents. It is important to note that as of 2015, Alabama had not expanded Medicaid pursuant to the Patient Protection and Affordable Health Care Act. Should this expansion occur in the future, it would certainly have an impact on the provision of healthcare to the county's indigent poor. However, as pointed out earlier in this chapter, access to insurance in and of itself does not necessarily equate to access to healthcare. A more comprehensive and proactive approach to healthcare among this population would still be necessary to affect positive health outcomes.

A snapshot of the county's population by insured status and age (2014 estimates) reflected the demographic distribution shown in Tables 10.1 and 10.2.

HISTORY OF INDIGENT HEALTHCARE IN JEFFERSON COUNTY

Concern for indigent healthcare in the county dates to the late 1800s when a group of Protestant, Catholic, and Jewish women, wives of prominent Birmingham businessmen, created the Hospital of United Charity. The Hospital, renamed Hillman Hospital in 1896, was run by this "Board of Lady Managers" for the next 19 years and provided care for indigent

Table 10.1.   Insurance Status by Federal Poverty Level (FPL)

FPL	Direct	Employer	Govt.	Medicaid	Medicare	Dual	Uninsured	Total
<18%	717	7,082	448	23,657	1,636	4,750	12,118	50,407
19-100%	2,471	14,381	2,182	38,165	7,973	9,612	29,165	103,949
101-138%	1,778	15,325	550	12,561	9,967	4,465	10,066	54,712
139-200%	3,382	33,434	205	10,582	14,148	2,551	11,618	75,919
201-400%	8,051	107,932	3,275	9,117	30,057	2,697	17,293	178,422
>400%	6,829	157,685	1,521	4,317	20,198	737	6,162	197,449
TOTAL	23,228	335,839	8,181	98,398	83,979	24,812	86,423	660,859

Table 10.2: Population by Age and Federal Poverty Level (FPL)

FPL	<18	18-25	26-34	35-44	45-54	55-64	> 65	Total
<18%	1,761	2,395	2,139	2,951	812	1,868	192	12,118
19-100%	2,538	6,606	7,341	5,415	4,578	2,688	0	29,165
101-138%	750	1,430	2,296	2,617	1,149	1,646	179	10,066
139-200%	647	2,888	2,880	3,129	1,314	751	0	11,618
201-400%	1,691	4,200	3,183	4,003	2,409	1,692	116	17,293
>400%	871	314	1,954	1,232	1,032	759	0	6,162
TOTAL	8,258	17,833	19,800	19,347	11,294	9,404	487	86,423

patients, regardless of race or gender. In 1907, the facility was sold to Jefferson County. In 1944, the county gave the hospital to its new medical college that would later become one of the nation's leading academic health centers, the University of Alabama at Birmingham (UAB). Pursuant to this transfer, the county agreed to pay the University for the care of indigent patients, but funding woes that had plagued the effort to care for the poor in the county from the beginning continued as the number of indigent poor in the county grew and healthcare costs increased.

In 1949, Jefferson County faced a tax problem. $700,000 had been appropriated for indigent healthcare; however, patient per diem increased from $13.50 to $16.00 and the county paid the University only $9.50. By 1954, indigent patient cost had risen on a per bed basis to $16.17 and was rising at a rate of 8% per year. That year, the county had contracted to pay for 64,000 patient days per year at only $11.00 per diem (Jefferson County Health Authority, 2009). It was clear that another approach to indigent healthcare in the county was necessary and discussions began in 1962 about the need to establish a separate county hospital devoted to the indigent poor.

The following year, in January, 1963, Alabama Governor George C. Wallace, during his inaugural address, would make his infamous statement, "segregation now, segregation tomorrow, and segregation forever." Against this backdrop, Birmingham and Jefferson County would serve as the epicenter of the civil rights movement in the 1960s and healthcare equality would figure prominently in advancing the discussions about building the county hospital. Fueling the fire for reform were smoldering racial animosities and segregationist practices. In 1965, a group of Black plaintiffs filed for an injunction to enjoin the university from "discriminating against the plaintiffs in the use of the facilities of the Medical Center complex and maintaining the separate and segregated facilities for the plaintiffs because they are Negros" (Jefferson County Health Authority, 2009).

Figures 10.3–10.6 are stark reminders of the civil and human rights struggles that are part of Jefferson County's past (*Birmingham News* archives, Ed Jones, September 1963).

Figure 10.3.   Civil rights 1. Whites protesting the integration of Graymont Elementary School in Birmingham, Alabama (*Birmingham News* archives, Ed Jones, September 1963).

Figure 10.4.   Civil rights 2. Birmingham police use high pressure fire hoses during street demonstrations (Charles Moore/Black Star 1963) (*Birmingham News* archives, Ed Jones, September 1963).

Figure 10.5.   Civil Rights 3, Young civil rights protester attacked by police dogs in downtown Birmingham (Associated Press Bill Hudson May 3, 1963) (*Birmingham News* archives Ed Jones September 1963).

Figure 10.6.   Civil rights 4. 16th Street Baptist Church in Birmingham, Alabama, bombed on September 15, 1963. Killed from l to r Addie Mae Collins (14) Cynthia Wesley (14) Carol Robertson (14) Denise McNair (11) (*Birmingham News* archives, Ed Jones, September 1963).

A combination of factors finally led the State of Alabama to act. In an effort to address growing concerns over healthcare inequality, a shortage of beds in the county, and the growing cost of healthcare for the poor, the state legislature passed *Act 387, Section 125* of the Code of Alabama later

that year, mandating a tax of one half of one percent of all retail and liquor sales in the county to be used for indigent healthcare. The Jefferson County Commission would oversee this fund which provided over $48 million in 2015. The *Act,* applicable to all counties of 500,000 or more, reads, in part (State of Alabama, 2015):

> The Indigent Care Fund shall be used by the county for any or all of the following purposes: to acquire by construction, eminent domain or otherwise, a county hospital, hospitals and/or clinics, to operate, equip, and maintain the same for the medical care and treatment of indigent persons of the county suffering from injury, illness, disability or infirmity, including out-patients; and the furnishing of drugs and medications to such indigent persons, including out-patient care at the county hospital or at the clinic maintained by the county or under contract with the county, also the operation of an emergency clinic. In addition, the county shall be authorized to furnish part

of the cost of the medical care for those of the county able to pay for only part of their own medical care. (p. 2)

The fund paved the way for building the county's 319-bed indigent care hospital which opened its doors in October, 1972, as Mercy Hospital. The Hospital was renamed in 1975 as Cooper Green Mercy Hospital in honor the retiring President of the Jefferson County Commission and operated as a full-service acute care facility for the next 4 decades. At its height, the Hospital maintained three satellite clinics strategically located around the County, in addition to the main facility, and saw over one hundred thousand patient visits annually.

On November 9, 2011, Jefferson County, Alabama filed a voluntary petition for relief under Chapter 9 of the United States Bankruptcy Code. The $4.23B bankruptcy was the largest by a U.S. city or county until it was overtaken in July, 2013 by Detroit's $18 billion case. In a cost-cutting measure and after weeks of contentious debate, the county, which maintained that it had been subsidizing the operations of Cooper Green Mercy Hospital for years, voted on August 28, 2012, to close its inpatient beds.

> The Jefferson County Commission today voted 3–2 to close the inpatient care unit at Cooper Green Mercy Hospital, following weeks of debate and protests from community leaders who have begged the county to continue operating the facility for the sick poor. The decision was so quick that supporters of the hospital at first didn't realize what had happened.... The decision came after weeks of protests from hospital supporters, months of questions from county commissioners and years of debate on whether the county should be in the health-care business ... the vote came in a courthouse chamber packed with many of the same hospital supporters who had shut down the commission meeting two weeks ago when the majority tried to close the inpatient unit. (Wright, 2012a, p. 1)

On December 31, 2012, just after midnight, Cooper Green Mercy Hospital ceased operating as an inpatient facility and, under the name Cooper Green Mercy Health Services, began a difficult transition to a multispecialty outpatient facility that would provide primary, specialty, and urgent care. As outlined earlier in this chapter, UAB had been partners with the county in caring for the indigent poor since 1944. This relationship would now prove crucial to the success of the transition and to the continuing provision of high quality medical care to the poorest of Jefferson County citizens.

As a result of closing the inpatient beds, 233 employees lost their jobs as the facility right-sized to meet the needs of the new organization; 211 remained. Under County Civil Service rules, selection of those to remain was based entirely on seniority within job classification and did not take into account performance or skills needed to perform the jobs in the new clinic model.

The Safety-Net Unravels

For many, the safety-net on which they had long depended was broken. The quick decision on the part of the Commission to close the inpatient beds created a firestorm of controversy and criticism. The local press ran article after article covering the contentious fights between those who favored closure and those who vehemently opposed it. While the county commission maintained that the hospital was inefficient and should be downsized, members of the Jefferson County legislative delegation, principally along political and racial lines, accused the commission of mismanaging the finances of the hospital. So contentious was the fight that one long-time hospital patient and advocate stated, "They are vultures and they are picking the bones of the poor and needy and I hope they choke on them" (Wright, 2012b, p. 1).

The fight became national news when Al Sharpton took to the stage in a brief press conference outside the Birmingham Sixteenth Street Baptist Church, the site of a 1963 Ku Klux Klan bombing that killed four young girls and shocked the conscience of the nation. Sharpton said, "I had no idea of the gravity of this closing on the community and it is a national example of those who would put partisan politics over people's healthcare" (Wright, 2012b, p. 1).

On this same day, the *Birmingham Business Journal* carried an article by the Jefferson County Manager that read, in part,

> Jefferson County's commitment to the people who have historically been served by Cooper Green Mercy Hospital has not changed. The transition of Cooper Green Mercy Hospital is underway. It will result in a healthcare model that protects our historic commitment to provide access to quality healthcare. During this transition, healthcare services will go uninterrupted. (Petelos, 2012)

There was, however, a disconnect between the commitment and the execution of the transition. The county vastly underestimated its decision to close inpatient beds, not only on patients, but on other area healthcare facilities. Closing inpatient services necessarily included closing the hospital's emergency department. Area hospitals immediately expressed concern that they would be overrun with indigent patients who had previously used the Cooper Green Mercy ER, taxing emergency departments already facing capacity issues and tightening operating margins. In its last year of operation, the Cooper Green Mercy Emergency Department saw over 20,000 patient visits that now would have to be distributed to other area ERs.

As part of transitioning to an outpatient model, the commission promised to contract with the local hospitals under a fee-for-service arrangement as a means of offsetting costs incurred by the influx of indigent patients. This was widely publicized prior to closure as an integral part of the transition plan. Negotiating the contracts proved more difficult than expected and contracts were not put in place until May, 2014, some seventeen months after closure of the Cooper Green Mercy ER. With no mechanism to reimburse the local hospitals, both the patients and the hospitals were placed in a difficult position. Patients who were admitted pursuant to emergency room visits became charity patients of that hospital if they were unable to meet their financial obligations, and the county had no way of providing reimbursement for related hospital stays. This led the Jefferson County Medical Society to call the commission's plan "an abject failure" (Weld for Birmingham, 2013).

Attempts to mount a public relations campaign were insufficient to stem the tide of criticism and the community was unconvinced that the county was committed to continuing its legacy of providing healthcare services to the indigent poor. There was no plan forward and no unified vision for the future.

By 2014, Cooper Green Mercy Health Services had lost a majority of its primary care physicians. There was a widely held belief among the public that the facility had closed or was in the process of closing its doors altogether. Adding to the confusion were press references to Cooper Green Mercy Health Services as an urgent care clinic rather than as a multispecialty outpatient facility. Patient visits had fallen to their lowest levels in the history of the facility and the wait time to see a primary care physician had climbed to seventeen weeks. Morale among the remaining staff was low. The hospital CEO had been among those who were let go in December, 2012, and no administrator had been named, leaving a void of leadership at the top of the organization. While the management that remained was experienced and competent, with no defined leadership, the organization had begun to fracture, organizational communications broke down and coordination of services suffered.

Unrelated to these events, in October, 2013, a federal judge appointed a receiver to bring the county into compliance with a long-standing employment discrimination consent decree. The receiver was granted authority over all matters involving human resources in the county and, out of concern for the personnel, in April, 2014, he engaged a local consultant to study the issues and problems at Cooper Green Mercy. The report to the receiver contained eight key findings (McCullough, personal communication, 2014).

- The most significant problem facing the clinic was the perceived instability of the facility by the public. With no agreement on a plan forward, no communication strategy in place, and a county commission still divided as to the future of Cooper Green Mercy, public statements by the county's leadership conveyed inconsistent and mixed messages as to its future. This perception adversely affected the clinic's patient volume and was an impediment to recruiting physicians and staff necessary to provide patient care in a timely manner.

- The clinic was not making adequate use of midlevel providers, specifically, certified registered nurse practitioners (CRNPs) and physician assistants (PAs) to increase capacity to see patients. Because of availability, use of CRNPs and PAs is an increasingly common practice as hospitals and clinics struggle with a lack of primary care and family medicine physicians. Nurse practitioners and physician assistants can play an important role in expanding primary care capacity.

- The wait time to see a primary care provider was untenable. The clinic's indigent patients faced immediate health needs which forced them to either go without adequate care or to seek care through other charity programs, principally hospital emergency rooms.

- There was no strategic plan to serve as a roadmap during the transition and, consequently, no operating plan to achieve the clinic's mission, nor were there operating metrics against which to measure the success of the clinic or the quality of care being provided to patients.

- There was no nursing administrator in place to oversee clinical nursing standards or practices. Additionally, there was no medical director to implement and oversee an effective model of patient care or to assess the quality of medical care being provided.

- There was a lack of sociodemographic data on the indigent population in Jefferson County. The county did not know what percentage of the population was being served by the clinic, being served by other hospitals, or were falling through the safety-net.

- There was little recognition on the part of other county operations as to the unique nature of and greater sense of urgency surrounding healthcare compared to other county operations.

- There was a lack of competent executive leadership on site.

Mending the Broken Safety-Net

In May, 2014, the Receiver appointed the consultant as the Interim Director of Cooper Green Mercy Health Services with the mandate to address the issues and problems identified in the report.

The new administrator immediately faced challenges. One was to address the specific issues identified in the report. Another was to win over very skeptical and divided county leaders and to demonstrate that Cooper Green Mercy Health Services could be a financially viable and sustainable model for healthcare delivery to the poor. Neither an insignificant task— nor a task of lesser importance—was engendering a sense of trust and hope in an otherwise demoralized staff, many of whom feared further lay-offs and felt that the ultimate demise of the clinic was just a matter of time.

The University of Alabama at Birmingham (UAB), along with Cooper Green Mercy Hospital, had served as the safety-net medical providers in the county for decades; consequently, UAB had a vested interest in the continued existence and success of the clinic that geographically sits on the edge of its campus. In 2015, UAB provided over $56M in uncompensated care (American Hospital Directory, 2015), more than the uncompensated care provided by all other area hospitals combined (not including Cooper Green Mercy) and they recognized the potential impact on their bottom line if Cooper Green Mercy ceased providing healthcare to the county's indigent poor. As a large urban medical center, UAB had administrative resources and expertise that it could offer the struggling clinic and the two facilities shared a common mission. These synergies would result in a healthcare model that provided the poorest and most vulnerable in the county access to world-class healthcare through a system of managed primary care, advanced specialty care and inpatient services.

The initial steps in transforming Cooper Green Mercy Hospital were tactical and designed to stop the patient from bleeding further. The first step was to put key managerial personnel in place. A director of clinical nursing was appointed to be responsible for developing and monitoring clinical nursing standards and practices, to establish metrics for monitoring clinic operations, and to improve coordination and communication among the clinical units of the facility. Following closely behind was the appointment of a medical director responsible for developing the healthcare delivery model, for assisting in the recruitment of additional healthcare providers, and for assessing the quality of medical care provided in the clinic. The Medical Director held a faculty appointment at the University establishing an important link between the two organizations. These two appointments provided the leadership necessary to address immediate operational and clinical concerns. To assist further, the CEO of the university's health system designated a high-level administrator to serve as a liaison between the two organizations and to assure that resources were available to the clinic as needed.

The director of clinical nursing and the medical director together with the director of human resources, the finance director, and the ancillary service directors became the management team that would act as principal advisors to the new administrator. These appointments were also important because they provided a sense hope to the beleaguered staff that the last chapter had not been written in Cooper Green Mercy's history. Staff were encouraged, particularly as midlevel providers were added and the capacity to see patients increased. This also provided the administrator with a positive message to play in the local press which had continued to show intense interest in the future of the clinic and to a county commission that still had ideological and practical concerns about the county's role in and ability to provide charity healthcare efficiently and cost-effectively. Monthly reports were released to the commission and to the public reflecting the progress being made.

Addressing Staff Morale

Concern for the well-being of the staff was of critical consideration from the beginning. They previously had no input into the decisions that had been made about the closing of the hospital and no input in the ensuing months. They had witnessed their co-workers laid-off with no warning and had no way of knowing if they would be next. Some felt like victims, others like survivors.

To gain insight into their feelings and to begin to give a forum for the staff to provide input, a loaned executive from the University was engaged to conduct a series of focus groups with the employees. Participation was strictly voluntary. The groups provided staff an opportunity to express their feelings in a non-threatening setting, to share their thoughts and ideas about the path forward, and to begin to regain a sense of empowerment over their future as well as the future of the clinic. The loaned executive's report was insightful in that it reflected a continued deep sense of concern for the well-being of the patients. This commitment to mission was both surprising and encouraging in light of all the staff had been through (McCullough, personal commuication, 2014).

Clinic employees were then asked to develop the values by which the organization would operate going forward. These would become the values by which the organization would conduct itself in its interactions with each other, with patients, and with the public. Having the staff themselves define the corporate values helped assure buy-in and gave the employees a sense of ownership in securing the clinic's future. The corporate mission and vision were republished with the values statement added and together these would serve as the foundation upon which all future initiatives would be based. With the mission, vision, and values in place and the most immediate operational needs of the clinic addressed, the organization was ready to develop its strategic plan.

The Strategic Plan

Developing the strategic plan for the clinic was driven by its mission (see Figure 10.7). Disconnect between the strategic plan and the corporate mission and vision would risk wasting human capital, time, and money on efforts that would not further its core purpose.

> *Cooper Green Mercy Health Services is dedicated to serving Jefferson County residents with quality healthcare regardless of ability to pay.*
>
> *We are committed to the advancement of healthcare through education of our patients and their families, our staff, and the community we serve and to the pursuit of knowledge through educational and research activities that advance the field of medicine.*
>
> *We continuously seek to improve our services and to adapt to meet the changing health needs of the people we serve.*

Figure 10.7.   Mission Statement.

The strategic plan simply defined the short-term goals the organization wanted to achieve and set forth specific action plans and related success metrics. It served as a road map—an organized approach to accomplishing the defined goals and it helped the organization focus its resources.

The strategic plan would then need to address (1) the provision of quality care, (2) patient, staff, and community education, and (3) continuous improvement of health services to the community.

The first year strategic plan was necessarily ambitious given the dire circumstances in which the clinic found itself. Changes would need to occur quickly and be apparent to both the county commission and the community, so those things that could be accomplished quickly would need to take priority.

First and foremost was the development of a medical delivery model that would provide the highest quality of primary care based on the particular characteristics of the population served by the clinic. This was the job of the Medical Director. The decision was made to develop a patient-centric model, one that would be characterized by a comprehensive, multidisciplinary, team-based approach to primary care and one that would emphasize strong and trusting relationships with providers and staff. This model was selected for two reasons. First was because the clinic population presented with higher morbidity rates, often co-morbidities, and more chronic diseases than the larger population, making a multidisciplinary approach an appropriate and effective strategy for addressing these unique health needs. Second was that trust in the healthcare system by patients was valued as being a critical factor in maintaining patient involvement in their own healthcare.

In addition to general primary care, then, the model focused on chronic diseases that presented most frequently in the population. This included establishing a multidisciplinary diabetes clinic that incorporated weight management, nutrition education, and physical therapy. A pharmacy clinic was established to assure that patients were complying with medication protocols and that the medications prescribed were effectively managing their conditions. A pain clinic was established that addressed chronic pain through both medical and interventional strategies, such as injections, pain blocks, and physical therapy.

As the model was implemented, CRNPs were added to the staff to increase capacity to see patients in a timely manner. CRNPs are mid-level providers who deliver routine medical care and follow-up to patients under the general supervision of a licensed medical doctor and are increasingly being used in the U.S. where there is a shortage of physicians. The addition of CRNPs allowed the clinic to significantly reduce appointment wait time, a critical success metric and one that reflected the increasing stability of the organization.

Increased capacity to see patients allowed the clinic to become more proactive in community outreach. Marketing materials were created and widely distributed in strategic locations around the county and the clinic increased its presence at county and municipal civic events, educational forums, and community health fairs. The clinic routinely provided health screenings at nonprofits around the county that supported the indigent poor. Cooper Green Mercy appointment scheduling staff attended each event and appointments were scheduled on-site for participants who had no primary care provider in the community. This resulted in increased numbers of patients coming to the clinic for care. As this happened, the local press (that had not long before talked of the demise of Cooper Green Mercy Health Services) reported one commissioner as saying,

> I have heard nothing but success stories from some of the patients that go there. They're getting the proper medical care that they need. The atmosphere of the clinic is wholesome. The people are being taken care of. The wait time is not all day. (Wright, 2015, p. 1)

With the clinic stabilized and patient visits growing, attention could be focused on the future of the clinic, not just the present. A Corporate Compliance and Environmental Safety Program was created that addressed organizational integrity, the environment of care, and infection control and would become the clinic's guide for internal operations. The program was designed to assure the clinic's compliance with standards of both the Joint Commission on the Accreditation of Healthcare Organizations (JCAHO) and the Centers for Medicare and Medicaid (CMS). A learning management system was implemented that gave staff access to 24/7 online training and education opportunities, continuing medical education credits, and individualized curricula based on organizational role. Collaboration with UAB principal investigators on numerous grants targeting the clinic's patient population provided patients with opportunities to become involved in clinical research studies.

Cooper Green Mercy Health Services was now in a position to be a major player in helping shape how indigent care would be provided throughout Jefferson County, not just within its corridors. An idea that had been proposed many years earlier was to have Cooper Green Mercy serve as a central point of care, providing primary, specialty, and urgent care in one location, but to also have neighborhood-based clinics strategically placed around the county, particularly in those neighborhoods where the clinic's population was most concentrated. Increasing primary care points of access had been a part of the initial strategic plan and the clinic was now poised to move forward.

Rather than build free-standing clinics, the decision was made to partner with existing primary care providers in the county who shared the clinic's mission to care for the poor. Similar to the reimbursement contracts with the area hospitals discussed earlier in this chapter, participating primary care physicians would be reimbursed on a fee-for-service basis for seeing patients who met the clinic's income eligibility requirements. In turn, these patients would have access to specialty and ancillary services at Cooper Green Mercy, as well as access to advanced specialty and inpatient services through referral to UAB. This arrangement increased the capacity of county primary care physicians to see additional indigent patients and provided more convenient access to healthcare services to patients often challenged by transportation issues.

Another collaborative initiative involved the area hospitals. A clinical care coordinator was hired to work with the hospitals' case managers to proactively engage patients who routinely sought primary care through the hospitals' emergency rooms. The patients were provided information on the services available to them at Cooper Green Mercy and educated about the importance of being involved in a managed primary care program. Primary care appointments were made for immediate postdischarge follow-up.

Cooper Green Mercy Health Services Today

Cooper Green Mercy Health Services was successful in its turn-around efforts by focusing on its mission and through the strategic implementation of a plan to address the clinic's deficiencies. In fiscal year 2015, the clinic saw over 56,000 patient visits, up 11.6% over the previous fiscal year. Primary care visits, the single most important success metric, were up 35%. Services were expanded in the areas of diabetes, hypertension, and pain management, and new service lines, such as Women's Health and Wellness and Behavioral Health, were added.

Cooper Green Mercy Health Services now offers primary care, fourteen specialty clinics, physical therapy, occupational therapy, and speech therapy, urgent care and psychiatric services. The multispecialty clinics are staffed by UAB faculty who practice part-time in the facility. Patients are referred to the specialty clinics by the Cooper Green Mercy primary care providers or by participating primary care providers in the community. Pursuant to a contractual arrangement between the two organizations, comprehensive care for indigent patients is achieved through referrals to UAB for advanced specialty services not offered on-site and for in-patient services. UAB bills the Indigent Care Fund for clinical and hospital services based on annually negotiated reimbursement rates.

Through this collaborative approach, Cooper Green Mercy, in effect, becomes a portal to comprehensive, high quality medical services for the poorest citizens of the county. By making primary care accessible and by managing access to levels of specialty care and in-patient services through a primary care referral mechanism, unnecessary medical visits, including unnecessary emergency room visits, are curtailed and healthcare costs are controlled. This collaboration has proven to be an outstanding model for care of the county's indigent poor in terms of both mission and finances.

The comprehensive services offered at the clinic attract both insured and uninsured patients. Today, 60% of the clinic's patients are indigent, 10% have Medicaid, 23% have Medicare and 6% have some other form of commercial insurance. The remaining 1% is considered self-pay, meaning they are uninsured and fall just above 200% of the federal poverty level. Increasing the number of insured patients is an additional revenue stream that provides monies to further expand safety-net initiatives both in the clinic and throughout the community.

One initiative is the use of community health workers. Community health workers are typically nonmedical field personnel specially trained in activities such as community education, informal counseling, social support and advocacy. They may be trained around a particular disease or a particular population with the goal to improve health outcomes through interactive outreach in the population served. This proactive approach is a particularly important strategy for addressing the healthcare needs of a population that faces logistical, psychosocial and economic barriers and obstacles that often stand in the way of access.

Over the years, Cooper Green Mercy has been a beacon of hope for tens of thousands of poor county residents and remains a symbol of a long and hard-fought battle for healthcare equality and racial dignity in Jefferson County. While it still faces ideological challenges from those politically opposed to government-run healthcare, as it has since its beginning, there is no doubt that it has proven to be a financially viable and sustainable model for the delivery of healthcare to the indigent poor in Jefferson County, Alabama.

REFERENCES

Alabama Possible. (2015). *Alabama Possible 2015 data sheet*. Retrieved from http://alabamapossible.org/datasheet/

American Hospital Directory. (2015). *American Hospital Directory Medicare Cost Reports*. Retrieved from https://www.ahd.com/data_sources.html

American Psychological Association. (2015). Effects of poverty, hunger, and homelessness on children and youth. Retrieved from http://www.apa.org/families/poverty.aspx#

Braveman, P., & Egeter, S. (2013, June 19). Overcoming obstacles to health in 2013 and beyond. Robert Wood Johnson Foundation Commission to Build a Healthier America. Retrieved from http://www.rwjf.org/content/dam/farm/reports/reports/2013/rwjf406474

Caughlin, T. A., Holahan, J., Caswell, K., & McGrath, M. (2014, May 30). Uncompensated care for the uninsured in 2013: A detailed examination. The Henry J. Kaiser Family Foundation. Retrieved from http://kff.org/uninsured/report/uncompensated-care-for-the-uninsured-in-2013-a-detailed-examination/

Deaton, A. (2003, Spring). Health, income, and inequality. *NBER Reporter*: Research Summary. Retrieved from http://www.nber.org/reporter/spring03/health.html

Humphrey, H. H. (1977, November). Remarks at the dedication of the Hubert H. Humphrey Building, November 1, 1977. *Congressional Record, 123*, 37287.

Jefferson County Health Authority (2009). *A chronology of anecdotal references to events in the history of indigent care in Jefferson County Cooper Green Mercy Hospital our purpose and importance in Jefferson County*. Proposed for the Jefferson County Legislative Delegation. Retrieved from http://media.al.com/bn/other/Michael-Nowak-report-0902-12.pdf

Jones, E. (1963, September). *Birmingham News* archives Ed Jones. Retrieved from http://blog.al.com/spotnews/2013/08/post_979.html

Petelos, T. (2012, October 12). JeffCo's commitment to healthcare. Retrieved from http://www.bizjournals.com/birmingham/print-edition/2012/10/26/jeffcos-dedication-to-health-care.html

Peek, M. (2014, October 30). Poverty's association with poor health outcomes and health disparities. Retrieved from http://healthaffairs.org/blog/2014/10/30/povertys-association-with-poor-health-outcomes-and-health-disparities/

Place Matters for Health in Jefferson County, Alabama: A Special Report. (2013, September). Joint Center for Political and Economic Studies. Retrieved from http://jointcenter.org/docs/Jefferson%20Report.pdf

State of Alabama. (2011). *Act 387, Section 125* of the Code of Alabama. Retrieved from http://www.alnb.uscourts.gov/sites/default/files/natinterestcases/jca_0955_01.pdf

Swartz, K. (2009, Fall). Healthcare for the poor: For whom, what care, and whose responsibility? *Focus, 26.* Retrieved from http://www.irp.wisc.edu/publications/focus/pdfs/foc262l.pdf

Weld for Birmingham. (2013, May 22). Community forum on indigent care. Retrieved from http://weldbham.com/blog/2013/05/22/community-forum-on-indigent-care/

Wilkinson, R. G., & Pickett, K. (2009). *The spirit level: Why greater equality makes societies stronger.* New York, NY: Bloomsbury Press.

Wright, B. (2015, May 22). Turnaround at troubled Cooper Green Mercy Hospital: How the fix is being made. Retrieved from http://www.al.com/news/birmingham/index.ssf/2015/05/turnaround_at_troubled_cooper.html

Wright, B. (2012a. August 28). Jefferson county commission votes to close inpatient care at Cooper Green Mercy Hospital. Retrieved from http://blog.al.com/spotnews/2012/08/jefferson_county_commission_vo_19.html

Wright, B. (2012b). Rev. Al Sharpton says closing of unit at Cooper Green Hospital could spark changes nationwide. Retrieved from http://blog.al.com/spotnews/2012/10/rev_al_sharpton_says_cooper_gr.html

CHAPTER 11

BUILDING A BETTER DEPARTMENT OF REVENUE FOR THE PEOPLE OF ALABAMA

William I. Sauser, Jr., Julie P. Magee, Don-Terry Veal,
Julia B. Heflin, and Lisa P. Brantly

INTRODUCTION

The successful application of organizational change methodology (Cummings & Worley, 2009; Golembiewski, 1969; Huse & Cummings, 1985; Martins, 2011)—including the use of strategic planning as an organizational transformation (Bryson, 1995; DeKluyver & Pearce, 2012; Ketchen & Short, 2011) and management development (Bruner, Eaker, Freeman, Spekman, & Teisberg, 1998; Sauser, 1989) tool—has been documented in detail by Sims (2010b) and in the first chapter of the current volume. Furthermore, this book and its earlier companion volume (Sims, 2010a) include a number of case studies documenting the use of various organizational change methods to improve effectiveness of government organizations at the federal, state, and local level. This chapter extends this pioneering work by describing a case example of the application of organizational change and strategic planning principles to the transformation of an important state agency,

Transforming Government Organizations:
Fresh Ideas and Examples From the Field, pp. 313–331

the Alabama Department of Revenue (ADOR). Building the capacity of the organization's team to anticipate change (Sauser & Sauser, 2002) and to plan both strategically and operationally (Sauser, 1989) was the specific objective of the organizational intervention described in this chapter.

Alabama's newly-elected Governor Robert Bentley appointed Julie P. Magee, former vice-president of the Mobile, Alabama-based InsTrust Insurance group, to the post of State Revenue Commissioner effective January 18, 2011. Mrs. Magee's career, spanning over 20 years in the business community, largely focused on competitive sales and market expansion in the insurance industry. Upon her appointment Commissioner Magee sought to transform an already respected Department of Revenue into one that served the people of Alabama with imagination and a higher degree of effectiveness and energy. Based on advice from her senior management team, she contacted Auburn University's Center for Governmental Services (CGS), an outreach arm of the University with which the ADOR already had a successful relationship in training and continuing education efforts. She met with Dr. Don-Terry Veal and Ms. Julia Heflin to discuss ideas for a multi-day training and development program that would energize the ADOR leadership team, set a tone for collaborative leadership focused on results, and produce plans for specific projects that could be implemented by the ADOR over the next 12–18 months. This was the vision she wished to share and shape with her management team in an effort to better serve the people of Alabama: Collaborative leadership focused on results.

Veal and Heflin in turn invited to the team Dr. William Sauser, a colleague with whom they had produced a number of effective management training and organizational development projects over the years. Sauser, a Professor of Management at Auburn University, shared with the team five practices of exemplary leadership developed by Kouzes and Posner (2007), including "Model the Way," "Inspire a Shared Vision," "Challenge the Process," "Enable Others to Act," and "Encourage the Heart" (p. 26). Together this four-member team, aided by some of the Commissioner's staff members, designed a two-day management development and strategic planning work session for the leadership team of the ADOR. Dr. Lisa Brantly, a member of the CGS staff, then joined the team to assist in implementing these plans. The intensive work session was held on September 20 and 21 of 2011, with 41 ADOR managers participating.

The remaining sections of this chapter (a) describe the process and outcomes from the 2011 intensive work session, (b) discuss the effectiveness of the projects resulting from the 2011 session as reported by Governor Bentley to the people of Alabama at the end of his first term, (c) describe a second intensive work session conducted by Commissioner Magee and the CGS team on February 17 and 18 of 2015, and (d) present suggestions from the project team to leaders of other public sector organizations who may desire to use this approach to transform their own government agency.

THE 2011 INTENSIVE WORK SESSION

Commissioner Magee sent a letter to the members of her management team inviting them to attend an intensive work session with an agenda focused on four specific goals: (1) Recognize and discuss sources of pride and concern within the ADOR, (2) Establish SMART goals to address priority needs of the people of Alabama from their Department of Revenue; (3) Create a plan of action for each high-priority goal, and (4) Initiate an implementation process for accomplishing these goals within the next 12–18 months. The agenda included six 90-minute work sessions across 2 days, with breaks for meals, rest, and fellowship interspersed within. A set of questions to consider beforehand was provided to each participant. The program was carefully designed to encourage extensive and meaningful participation from all attendees and to establish and exemplify Commissioner Magee's vision for collaborative leadership within ADOR. A few invited managers were unable to attend due to unavoidable conflicting commitments, but overall the work session was robust, with 41 ADOR managers attending, including the Commissioner and her top management team. A comprehensive report of the results of the entire event was compiled by the CGS staff (Veal, 2011) and submitted to Commissioner Magee within a week of the conclusion of the intensive work session. Here are brief summaries of each 90-minute session.

1st Work Session—Who Are We and What Talents/Experience Do We Bring to ADOR?

After a brief word of welcome from Commissioner Magee, the first work session was facilitated by Sauser and recorded by Brantly. Attendees had been sent a series of questions to consider a week before the intensive work session. The first of these questions was "What knowledge, skills, abilities, ideas, experience, and wisdom do we bring to the ADOR? What human resource assets do we bring to the table?" Participants were asked to consider this question beforehand, but were not asked to bring any written responses to this (or any other) question with them to the intensive work session. The attendees were randomly assigned to eight small groups, and each group was asked to prepare a list of the talents the members of the group brought to the ADOR. One purpose of this exercise was to give the attendees an opportunity to get to know one another; even though they worked within the same department of state government many did not know one another very well. A second purpose was to construct an inspiring list of the many talents this group of managers shared among them.

After giving the small groups time to consider the assignment and to compile their lists, the groups were called on in turn to mention *one* talent from the list. This process continued for several rounds until a comprehensive list of unique talents was captured. Thirty talents comprised the final list, including "lots of experience," "analytical skills," "creativity," "mentorship ability," "not afraid of change," and "financial expertise." The full list included an impressive array of technical, human relations, and conceptual skills. The participants were surprised and impressed with the number and quality of talents available within the important human resources making up the ADOR's management team. They agreed that such a talented assembly of persons should be able to tackle the issues facing the ADOR if all contributed to the best of his or her ability. The group was highly energized at the conclusion of this first session. They were impressed to find that they had 979.5 years of experience among them with the ADOR.

2nd Work Session—Sources of Pride in Our Organization

The second work session, facilitated by Sauser and recorded by Brantly, was intended to begin engaging the participants in a "big picture" strategic view of the ADOR while further building their confidence and sense of team spirit. The entire group was redivided randomly into eight small groups in an effort to give members additional experience in working with and getting to know their fellow managers. The questions considered during this session were: "What are our particular sources of pride with respect to the Alabama Department of Revenue? What is the ADOR doing well? What is working, in our opinion?" As in the first session, teams were invited in turn to add to the comprehensive list being assembled *one* response at a time each, and rounds were continued until every small group had exhausted its list. This effort produced a list of 28 unique sources of pride. Examples include "good reputation," "right people in the right jobs," "consistent in fair treatment of taxpayers," "strong audit program," "integrity," and "open to feedback." Considering the entire list, the management team agreed that any change efforts within the ADOR that might compromise these areas of strength would need to be considered very carefully. The group did not want to take any action that might harm the reputation of the ADOR or adversely affect its ability to serve the people of Alabama fairly and responsively.

3rd Work Session—Sources of Concern in Our Organization

Now that the participants had begun to know and trust one another, and had made certain that the considerable strengths of the ADOR were understood and appreciated by all, they were ready to move on to the next work session (again facilitated by Sauser and recorded by Brantly). The questions to be considered during this crucial session were as follows: "What are our particular sources of concern with respect to the ADOR? What is ADOR *not* doing as well as it should? What is not working in our opinion?" If the ADOR was to be transformed into a more effective department of government, these issues must be brought to the surface and addressed. The participants understood the need for this and gave this question serious consideration. The process used was the same as in the first two work sessions: The participants were randomly assigned into eight small groups, each group discussed the question carefully and composed a list of concerns, and the overall list was assembled as each team contributed in turn *one* item. As before, as many rounds as needed were conducted until a comprehensive list of unique concerns was assembled.

This effort resulted in some general concerns about a lack of communication up, down, and throughout the organization; substandard facilities; a lack of resources stemming from a very tight budget; and employee apathy and lack of commitment. All agreed that these important concerns had existed for some time and needed to be addressed in a comprehensive multi-year effort. In all, 26 unique concerns were mentioned. Among them were such important issues as:

- Lack of cross-training
- Concern about work ethic of younger employees (generational differences)
- Lack of a call center to free up time for employees to complete upper level work
- Overuse of acronyms that the public may not understand
- Upper level management is out of touch occasionally with reality
- Concern about retention of younger employees
- Territorial turf battles
- Focus on our own issues within our unit: "Silo Vision"
- Need to strengthen our overall relationship with the legislature
- Inconsistent interpretation and application of the personnel laws
- Refund fraud.

4th Work Session—Priorities for Organizational Improvement and Growth

Now that important concerns had been identified, it was time to begin discussing what (specifically) needed to be done about them. The larger group was again randomly divided into eight small groups and asked to consider very carefully the following question: "What should the ADOR begin doing *right now* to become a better revenue department?" Each small group was tasked with identifying at least one specific action that the department as a whole should take to address the concerns identified in Session 3 without adversely affecting the sources of pride identified in Session 2. Following time for considerable small group discussion, a comprehensive list was constructed using the procedure described in earlier steps. This list was shorter, however, because several of the groups identified similar priorities for immediate action. In all, 10 key needs for action were identified.

Recognizing that it would be very difficult for the ADOR to address effectively all ten issues over the next 12–18 months, the group agreed that it was necessary to set some priorities. This was done by giving each participant two "votes," with the understanding that each vote represented a commitment on the participant's part to spend time working with others to address the chosen issue. All ten issues received votes, but five received votes in the "double digits" and thus were identified as the highest priorities for realistic action over the next 12–18 months. These were (alphabetically):

- Clarify personnel policies
- Create a Montgomery (Alabama) taxpayer service center
- Establish a central contact center for all taxpayers
- Establish a refund fraud task force
- Improve horizontal communication within ADOR.

5th Work Session—Developing SMART Goals

The focus of the next work session was developing a clear and concise SMART goal for each of the five priorities for action identified in Session Four. SMART is an acronym standing for Specific, Measureable, Attainable, Responsive, and Timely. Governor Bentley had challenged each state agency in Alabama to provide him with a set of SMART goals to be accomplished within his first 4-year term of office.

To accomplish this task, the larger group was again divided into six smaller groups, but this time the division was done in an intentional rather than randomized manner. The five priorities for action were posted on the wall, and participants were asked to stand next to the priority to which they wanted to devote effort over the next 12–18 months. Some participants were interested in two or more of the priorities; these were assigned voluntarily to the groups in a manner intended to result in 6–8 participants assigned to each small team. Five individuals volunteered to serve on a special *sixth* team designated by the facilitator as the "Devil's Advocate" team (with the comment from the facilitator that "The devil is in the details"). The members of the Devil's Advocate team were given special instructions by the facilitator to observe the work of the other five small groups and to ensure (by asking tough questions about details!) that each adopted goal was indeed a SMART goal. They took this responsibility very seriously, and contributed to the success of the other five teams in accomplishing their task.

The resulting outcome from this fifth working session was the following set of SMART goals (to be accomplished over the next 12–18 months):

1. Develop an attendance and punctuality policy that will be enforced uniformly across the Alabama Department of Revenue.
2. Create a centralized contact center for all Alabama taxpayers.
3. Establish a refund fraud task force.
4. Improve horizontal communication throughout the Alabama Department of Revenue.
5. Improve customer satisfaction with ADOR by creating a super Montgomery Taxpayer Service Center (TPSC).

At this point the participants had completed a very exhausting but productive day of work. They were dismissed by the commissioner to enjoy dinner and fellowship with the understanding that work would begin again "bright and early" on the second day.

6th Work Session—Create a Plan of Action for Each Priority

After a brief word of welcome by the commissioner, the five groups began working in earnest to develop a step-by-step plan to accomplish each of the five priority SMART goals. Each of the five teams established in Session 5 was given a free hand to organize itself and work its way through the process. The facilitator (Sauser) circulated among the groups to observe, answer questions, and provide advice when asked. Meanwhile the five members of the "Devil's Advocate" team also circulated among the five small groups, asking for specific responses to the following key questions which formed the assignment for Session 6: "How should we accomplish the SMART goal identified for each priority action? How should we proceed, step by step? Who should do what, where, when, how, and why?"

The recorder (Brantly) devised a matrix to help each team organize its response (see Figure 11.1). On the matrix the team was to write at the top its SMART goal, then, in each respective column, the team was to identify:

What—Each step to be done to meet the SMART goal.

Who—The name of the person who will be held responsible for each step.

When—The deadline for accomplishing each step.

The "status" column was devised as a control device. As the project proceeded toward completion this column was to be filled in with a green "smiley face" emoji if the step was proceeding "on track"; a red "frowny face" emoji if the step was proceeding "behind schedule"; and a gold "star" emoji if the step was "done!" This simple tool would be shared among the team members (and with the commissioner) to emphasize accountability for completing each task (and eventually each priority goal).

SMART GOAL:			
Who	What	When	Status
Jack	1.	Nov 3	
Jill	2.	Feb 6	
Toni	3.	May 2	
Max	4.	Aug 9	
Bruce	5.	Sept 4	

Figure 11.1.   Example planning matrix used in the ADOR intensive work sessions.

When all five teams had entered their data into the matrix, the results were shared by each respective team and critiqued by the entire assemblage. Revisions were made as necessary and the SMART goals and action plans were adopted by the group as a whole and accepted with pleasure by the commissioner. Commissioner Magee then pledged to provide a reasonable budget for accomplishing each of the five projects and charged the five groups to proceed (under the watchful eye of the "Devil's Advocates") to complete the tasks as assigned. Evaluation forms were then distributed for completion by each participant. The intensive work session was then adjourned and the work of completing the five priority projects was begun!

PROGRAM EVALUATION

The evaluation forms were tabulated by the CGS staff and results were included as part of a summary of the process and outcomes of each of the six work sessions. This summary report (Veal, 2011) was delivered to the commissioner within 1 week of the conclusion of the intensive work session and was made available electronically to each of the participants. The written report thus served as a record of the entire proceedings and provided a clear picture of each team's assignment. On a 5-point rating scale, the overall rating of 4.46 for the program's content indicated that the participants found the session to be stimulating and helpful.

While it is encouraging to know that the participants had a favorable *reaction* to the overall program, of even more importance is an indication of the *impact* of the program. Were the five projects completed within the 18-month time period and were they successful in terms of building a better Department of Revenue for the people of Alabama? Sufficient time has passed since the intensive workshop was completed to address the first question: Yes, all five projects were completed within the 18-month period. This is a matter of great pride for the entire ADOR. What about the second question, the qualitative question of whether the people of Alabama are now being better served by their Department of Revenue as a result of this process? This question is complex, of course, but a few excerpts from Governor Bentley's report to the people at the conclusion of his first term (Bentley, 2015, pp. 74–77) suggest that the overall program has indeed been a success. Consider the following bullet points quoted directly from Governor Bentley's report:

- For the fiscal year ending 2010, ADOR reported total revenue collections of $8.197 billion. For the fiscal year ending 2014, total collections were $9.402 billion, an increase of $1.205 billion or 14.7%.
- [The ADOR] created a Super Taxpayer Service Center in a new location on Taylor Road in Montgomery which allows a taxpayer to do business with ADOR, no matter the tax type or function. Every single type of process that we manage can be done in the Super Taxpayer Service Center making it easier to do business with ADOR.
- [The ADOR] created new processes for facilitating communications among divisions which improves the ability to share knowledge, actions and functions within the department.

- Over the past four years, ADOR had been dedicated to creating ways to stop identity theft and refund fraud, and as a result, created the Fraud Task Force. In 2013, we stopped 13,000 [fraudulent] refunds totaling $17,000,000 from leaving the state's coffers. We want to process legitimate returns quickly and concentrate on foiling criminals when they attempt to steal a citizen's personal information to file a fraudulent refund.

- A major revision of the personnel manual was completed, and decades old policies in almost all areas, including suspensions, terminations and nepotism, were rewritten. The new policies meet all of the required State Personnel guidelines.

- ADOR developed and implemented an in-house call center which is intended to improve our customer service by providing fast and knowledgeable answers to four basic taxpayer/customer call types:

  o Where's My Refund?
  o Where's My Title?
  o Mandatory Liability Insurance Questionnaire
  o Identity Confirmation Quiz (implemented to help prevent identity theft).

- The Discovery Module was integrated into ADOR's Tax Administration System. The Discovery Unit's purpose is to use the various external data ADOR receives along with data it already has in its system to identify additional revenue due to the state and to develop discoveries to aid in the collection of that revenue. The Discovery Unit collected over $15 million for fiscal year 2014.

- During FY 2013–2014, the Collection Services Division collected more than $78 million, which is $2 million more than the year before.

- As of September 30, 2014, ADOR collected $217,887,850 in delinquent taxes.

- Working with the Attorney General's office, we have conducted two very large tax evasion investigations, resulting in the arrests of three people accused of avoiding paying tobacco tax.

- ADOR was commended by State Auditor Samantha Shaw for achieving a perfect audit of personal property for the fifth consecutive year. The Department has 3,460 items on inventory.

- All divisions are now paperless and the documents in storage that we were required to keep are now scanned and stored on the network and then shredded.

These initiatives, and others like them, suggest that the ADOR is now more innovative, efficient, imaginative, and effective than it was before this organizational intervention took place. It would be inappropriate, of course, to credit exclusively the intensive work session described above with resulting in all of these improvements. It is likely, however, that the tone of collaboration, empowerment, and innovation Commissioner Magee deliberately fostered during this session and her subsequent support of the five priority projects discussed above was one of the keys to ADOR's success during Governor Bentley's first 4-year term.

THE 2015 INTENSIVE WORK SESSION

Governor Bentley was elected to a second 4-year term in November, 2014, and Commissioner Magee was retained in the role of Commissioner of Revenue. This gave her further opportunity to create a culture of prepared leaders within the ADOR. To set the tone for the ADOR's work during Governor Bentley's second term she again teamed with representatives of Auburn University's Center for Governmental Services (CGS) to conduct a second intensive 2-day work session. This session, conducted on February 17–18, 2015, was facilitated by Sauser and recorded by Heflin. It employed the same six-session format and process as used successfully in 2011; for the sake of brevity the six sessions will not be described herein in detail. There were, however, a few "tweaks" incorporated into the 2015 session based on lessons learned from the 2011 session. For example, the facilitator (Sauser) interspersed a few didactic comments—supported by illustrations—to help the participants understand the general "strategic planning" process they were following (see Figure 11.2) and how to operationalize strategy through more detailed project plans (see Figures 11.2 and 11.4).

Another important "tweak" was to include regional office as well as state office managers among the invitees. This led to a larger, though still manageable, number of attendees: 54 in 2015 as opposed to 41 in 2011. As a result, the small groups were also larger, but were still functional. Another result, of course, was a larger number of total years of experience with the ADOR: 1362 in 2015 as opposed to 979.5 in 2011. A third "tweak" was the inclusion of a review of the department's mission statement to provide a clear starting point for discussion. The existing mission statement, stated as follows, was endorsed by all in attendance: *"The Alabama Department of Revenue will efficiently and effectively administer the revenue laws in an equitable, courteous and professional manner to fund governmental services for the citizens of Alabama."*

Figure 11.2.   Conceptual outline of the strategic planning process.

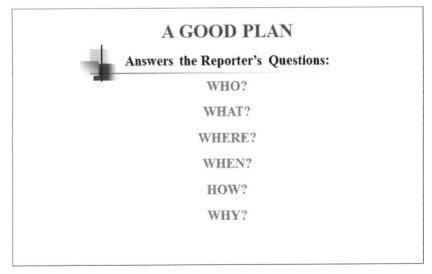

Figure 11.3.   Characteristics of a good plan.

Answering the questions

* WHO: a person's name
* WHAT: the objective to be accomplished
* WHERE: location and space requirements
* WHEN: deadlines and schedules
* HOW: budget, equipment, human resources,
            information resources and the like
* WHY: how does the objective relate to...
            the overall strategy?

Figure 11.4.   Answering the reporter's questions.

One important difference in tone between the two intensive work sessions was immediately apparent to the facilitator (Sauser). Whereas in 2011 there seemed to be some anxiety about the process on the part of some of the participants (as could be expected with a new program initiated by a new commissioner), the participants in the 2015 session appeared very comfortable with one another and with the process. A high level of participant enthusiasm was apparent throughout. This impression was borne out by the reactions of the participants on the evaluation form completed on the second day. An astounding 100% of the participants answered "yes" to two key questions: Did the program meet your personal needs? Do you think the program met the needs of the ADOR? Qualitative comments were also very supportive of the process used and results obtained during the six sessions. For example, one participant provided this very insightful comment:

> We know that we did not think of everything that has to happen to implement the projects that we've decided to tackle. However, this session forced us to discuss fully the critical tasks. We know that we have a plan of what has to initially occur to get started. We are then confident that whatever comes up after we start the implementation process, we will be able to discuss it with the team members to see what is the best course of action. (Veal, 2015, p. 30)

Another indication of increasing sophistication on the part of this group of leaders (and the organization as a whole) is the five priority SMART goals they identified and the more detailed planning processes they adopted.

The five priority areas and SMART goals adopted were as follows (Veal, 2015, pp. 9–10):

1. Online Registration Portal-Compliance Review

    Create a registration system that allows the Department to capture the necessary data at registration to properly establish the legal entity along with the proper accounts and to have in place procedures to manage the accounts over time for all tax types.

    - Identify weaknesses in the current registration process over the next 3 months.
    - Develop a plan to address the weaknesses (reach out to other parties) within 6 months.
    - Identify needs (resources) to reach the stated goal within 6 months.
    - Set timetable for all implementation.

2. W2 Match

    Require all W2s to be filed by January 31st in order to match the withholding claimed on individual returns against the W2s submitted by employers. Implement by January 2016.

3. Personnel Task Force

    Enhance recruitment for ADOR professional classifications by implementing a 4-phase project over the next 2 years.

    - Organize and have 2 career fairs.
    - District outreach to universities and colleges in their area.
    - Organize study of classifications within each division.
    - Track progress of project.

4. Sales Tax Suppression Compliance Task Force

    Combat sales tax suppression by taxpayers through:

    - Developing an audit program including policies and procedures.
    - Performing a pilot study.
    - Refining a training program.
    - Implementing by October 1, 2015.

5. Large Analytical Database

    Make ADOR's tax return data accessible to non-IT tax technical employees in a searchable sortable format by implementing a data analytics software platform to be fully functional by October 1, 2015.

- Prevendor presentation.
- Feasibility study.

    o Cost
    o IT Resources
    o Return on Investment

- Vendor selection.
- Testing.
- Go live (October 1, 2016).

These priority goals reflect and build upon the progress made by the ADOR during the first of Governor Bentley's terms, especially in the areas of information technology, data analysis, and cross-functional collaboration. The detailed plans of action, again using the matrix approach diagrammed in Figure 11.1, showed a similar level of sophistication. Objectives were clearly stated, accountability was firmly established, and deadlines were specific.

These five priority goals are lofty targets, but the commissioner again pledged budgetary support and the members of each small group demonstrated confidence that all five goals would be met. Time will tell, of course, if the impact of the 2015 intensive work session will match the apparent success of the 2011 intervention, but the enthusiasm and confidence expressed by all the participants during the 2015 session bodes well for the future. The participants expressed great satisfaction with their self-identified "marching orders" and confidence in themselves as leaders prepared to work effectively toward ADOR's continuing success.

LESSONS LEARNED

A number of important concepts were confirmed and lessons were learned during this case study. In this concluding section of the chapter we share some of the most important ones so others contemplating organizational change may include these ideas in interventions they may seek to implement in their own public-sector organizations.

1. This case study serves as yet one more piece of confirmatory evidence that sound organizational change and strategic planning processes can be effective in developing the capacity of a leadership

team and in focusing organizational energy on high-priority actions
for mission-directed success. Any effort to transform a public-sector
organization must, in our opinion, be informed and guided by
sound theory if success is to be obtained.

2. Election cycles are natural opportunities for organizational change.
    Newly elected or appointed leaders (or continuing leaders enjoy-
    ing public support through re-election) are expected to tailor their
    efforts to meet strategic priorities set during the electoral process.
    This mandate should be grasped as an opportunity for organi-
    zational renewal. A 4-year term is a reasonable period of time in
    which to effect significant positive change if strategic intent is iden-
    tified and sustained effort is focused on accomplishing well-planned
    priority goals for action.

3. Support from the top of the organization is an essential component
    for any successful organizational intervention. Without support
    from the commissioner (and by implication, from the governor who
    appointed her) this effort could not have taken place. An energetic
    champion for the effort will seek to sustain it throughout not only
    the planning process but the lengthy and difficult implementation
    process as well. By making budgetary resources available to support
    the priority plans developed by each small group, and by holding
    each group accountable for monitoring and reporting its own suc-
    cess—subject to independent verification, the commissioner showed
    strong visible support for the entire process. This certainly aided in
    energizing this particular organizational intervention.

4. Using the services of a professional facilitator and recorder enhanc-
    es the process and guides it toward success. Auburn University's
    Center for Governmental Services is a seasoned organization with
    respect to providing aid to government agencies, and the team it
    assembled to guide these interventions was experienced and dedi-
    cated to the success of the effort. While Commissioner Magee was
    recognized throughout the process as the leader of the effort, the
    use of a professional facilitator and recorder for each session en-
    abled her (and the other participants) to focus on the issues under
    discussion while the consulting team monitored the process, kept it
    on track, and ensured that detailed records were kept to document
    the entire process.

5. Participation in every step of the process enabled the assembled
    leaders of the organization to unleash their creativity and generate
    challenging but attainable goals that all agreed could be met within
    a reasonable time period. Participation in the planning process
    also generated commitment to and ownership of the goals, further

enhancing the possibilities for organizational teamwork that would lead to successful results.

6. The use of the "Devil's Advocate" teams in this organizational intervention process was guided by research reported by Sauser in 1988. Deliberately injecting contrast into the planning process by designating individuals to challenge assumptions, ask tough questions, and hold group members accountable for their collective decisions proved once again to be a valuable technique. Use of this technique is thus encouraged when any similar effort is contemplated.

7. This organizational development program was designed to increase the capacity of the ADOR's leadership team to think strategically and to design detailed implementation plans focused on real accomplishments. The ADOR's impressive accomplishments during Governor Bentley's first term suggest that these goals were met.

8. "Tweaks" made during the 2015 intensive work session appeared to enhance the process. The commissioner's decision to include regional as well as state-level organizational leaders sent a clear message to everyone that the regional offices are vital parts of the organization and are essential contributors to its overall success. It also served a second important purpose: To begin developing leaders at the regional level so they may be prepared to fill vital state-wide leadership roles in the future. One concern expressed in both the 2011 and the 2015 intensive work sessions was the recognition that senior leaders in the organization are rapidly reaching retirement eligibility and that succession planning must be viewed as a priority for the future.

9. The facilitator's framing of the 2-day intensive sessions through the use of didactic materials to convey the overall strategic and operational planning process seemed to enhance the participants' understanding of and acceptance for the interventions. Those who had participated in the 2011 session knew what to expect in 2015, but those who were new to the process expressed appreciation for creating a shared understanding among the group of the overall purpose and structure of the process and the expected results of this significant investment of their time.

10. A clear agenda for each of the two intensive work sessions, plus a set of questions for participants to consider and reflect upon prior to each session, also helped to reduce anxiety about the process and participation in it. Participants are more comfortable when they know what to expect.

Overall, this case study demonstrates once again the potential for effective application of behavioral science principles (organizational development theory) and sound management practices (strategic and operational planning) as the bases for organizational transformation in the public sector. This is, of course, the message of this entire volume. The authors of this chapter encourage leaders of other public sector organizations to effect organizational renewal in government through the use of the ideas presented in this and the other chapters of this volume.

REFERENCES

Bentley, R. (2015, January 14). *Administration accomplishments, 2011–2014.* Montgomery, AL: Office of the Governor.

Bruner, R. F., Eaker, M. R., Freeman, R. E., Spekman, R. E., & Teisberg, E. O. (1998). Strategy: Defining and developing competitive advantage. Ch. 13 in *The Portable MBA* (3rd ed., pp. 231–248). New York, NY: John Wiley & Sons.

Bryson, J. (1995). *Strategic planning for public and nonprofit organizations: A guide to strengthening and sustaining organizational achievement.* San Francisco, CA: Jossey-Bass.

Cummings, T. G., & Worley, C. G. (2009). *Organizational development and change* (9th ed.). Mason, OH: South-Western Cengage Learning.

DeKluyver, C. A., & Pearce, J. A., II. (2012). *Strategy: A view from the top* (4th ed.). Boston, MA: Prentice-Hall.

Golembiewski, R. T. (1969). Organization development in public agencies: Perspectives on theory and practice. *Public Administration Review, 29*(4), 367–377.

Huse, E. F., & Cummings, T. G. (1985). *Organizational development and change* (3rd ed.). St. Paul, MN: West Publishing.

Ketchen, D., & Short, J. (2011). *Mastering strategic management.* Irvington, NY: Flat World Knowledge.

Kouzes, J. M., & Posner, B. Z. (2007). *The leadership challenge* (4th ed.). San Francisco, CA: Jossey-Bass/Wiley.

Martins, L. L. (2011). Organizational change and development. In S. Zedeck (Ed.), *APA handbook of industrial and organizational psychology: Maintaining, expanding, and contracting the organization* (Vol. 3 pp. 691–728). Washington, DC: American Psychological Association.

Sauser, W. I., Jr. (1988). Injecting contrast: A key to quality decisions. *SAM Advanced Management Journal, 53*(4), 20–23.

Sauser, W. I., Jr. (1989). Strategic planning as a management development tool. *Journal of the Alabama Academy of Science, 60,* 29–38.

Sauser, W. I., Jr., & Sauser, L. D. (2002). Changing the way we manage change. *SAM Advanced Management Journal, 67*(4), 34–39.

Sims, R. R. (Ed.). (2010a). *Change (transformation) in government organizations.* Charlotte, NC: Information Age Publishing.

Sims, R. R. (2010b). Changing or transforming today's and tomorrow's public sector organizations. In R. R. Sims (Ed.), *Change (transformation) in government organizations* (pp. 1–29). Charlotte, NC: Information Age Publishing.

Veal, D.-T. (2011). *ADOR off-site work session: Building a better revenue department.* Technical report delivered to Julie Magee, Commissioner, Alabama Department of Revenue. Auburn University, AL: Center for Governmental Services.

Veal, D.-T. (2015). *ADOR intensive off-site work session: Creating a culture of prepared leaders.* Technical report delivered to Julie Magee, Commissioner, Alabama Department of Revenue. Auburn University, AL: Center for Governmental Services.

CHAPTER 12

INTERLOCAL DIFFUSION AND DIFFERENCE

How Networks Are Transforming Public Service

Kathleen Hale and Mitchell Brown

As perhaps the quintessential public service, election administration is primarily a function of local governments. Since the 2000 Presidential election, this area of public service has come under intense national scrutiny and become increasingly complex. Elections have also undergone radical transformation at the local level through local networks of election officials, other government officials, and nonprofit organizations that have changed the public administration of elections. Over the past 15 years, the interactions, collaborations, and innovations that have taken place in and between local networks of election administrators have generated a public service environment that possesses increased capacity to meet public needs and demands. These local networks and the information arrangements that define them are central to the development of innovation, and central to the spread of new ideas from one locality to another. In this chapter we examine these local networks and the information exchanged within

Transforming Government Organizations:
Fresh Ideas and Examples From the Field, pp. 333–353
Copyright © 2016 by Information Age Publishing

them, and demonstrate the ways in which local networks are central to innovation, key to the spread of new ideas from one locality to another, and fundamental to improving this area of public service across the country.

The stage for our analysis is set with the 2000 Presidential election, which focused attention across the nation on the specific processes that Americans use to conduct elections. In Palm Beach County, Florida, the use of a particular punch-card ballot layout known as a butterfly ballot sparked controversy about whether voters understood how to complete this ballot in the manner that would accurately express their intent to vote for President. A national firestorm ensued about variations in local election practices across counties in Florida and other states. Lawsuits were filed about when, where, and how to count and, in some cases, recount votes. The ultimate result was the United States Supreme Court case *Bush v. Gore* (2000), which resolved the election with a margin of victory of 537 votes cast for George W. Bush.

Since that election, the intergovernmental arrangements of public and other organizations that work to conduct American elections have changed dramatically. Always a function of local government and conducted primarily at the county level, the administration of elections gained national notoriety and exposed cleavages between state level officials such as the Secretaries of State and the local officials who serve as frontline public servants in interacting with voters. In the ensuing 15 years since 2000, the institutional landscape has consequently changed as well. Major federal reforms have been adopted that replaced punch card and lever machines with electronic voting systems across the country, and new methods of voting have been put in place for military voters and citizens overseas. States have spent in the neighborhood of $5 billion for voting systems, and have enacted hundreds of new voting rules that on the one hand expand opportunities for access and participation and on the other hand restrict the same. Courts have been busy interpreting new state rules and federal legislation. In 2013 the U.S. Supreme Court decision in *Shelby County v. Holder* significantly reorganized for some states and localities their interactions with federal agencies that oversee some aspects of election administration; states that had been required under the Voting Rights Act of 1965 to obtain prior federal review and approval of changes in election law and practice were no longer required to do so.

To navigate this newly complex and increasingly interdependent environment, local election officials must create and maintain information-based methods of demonstrating accountability as well as relationships with state officials, new national election officials, and countless other organizations. Efforts to demonstrate accountability and build relationships include best practices, model programs, templates, and methods of sharing information through working groups, conferences, and collaborations.

These efforts began informally but have now coalesced into a clear network that reaches across government offices and sectors and incorporate the activities of nonprofit organizations as well. What is important about this networked structure is that research demonstrates that such intersectoral networks are critical for the generation of new ideas, diffusion of new ideas, and the institutionalization of these ideas in ways that build capacity in public service (Brown, 2008, 2012; Hale, 2011; Hale & Brown, 2013; Hale, Montjoy, & Brown, 2015).

This concept of building capacity in public service is fundamental to our understanding of improving public service in the contemporary intergovernmental environment. Capacity, in the public administration context, is generally understood as the ability to do what is intended (Honadle, 1981). Over the past several decades the public service environment has expanded beyond government bureaucracy to include nonprofit organizations as service providers in myriad contracting relationships. These contracting relationships expanded significantly in both number and intricacy through devolution of responsibility for public services from the federal government to localities that began in the 1980s. New policy design, planning, and implementation relationships also evolved to inform government agencies and their nonprofit service partners about the latest developments in the field and to influence policy change. The result today is a complex and interdependent arrangement of government and nonprofit organizations charged with making good on the implementation of public policy decisions. One consequence of these complex and interdependent arrangements is that accountability and responsibility are distributed beyond the walls of any one organization, even as government is challenged to fulfill its essential functions. Institutional configurations and tools that improve capacity under these conditions bring value to public service; we show how that has happened in the case of election administration.

To illustrate and analyze the local election administration environment, we draw upon conversations with and data collected from numerous local elections officials around the country and present their descriptions of the ways in which the networked environment has shaped their work and how their work is different today than it was before the 2000 election.[1] Their experiences illustrate a clear departure in the practice of the public administration of elections and a clear departure for the work for local offices. These experiences also illustrate the attempts that local officials have made at transformation, both voluntary and as required by federal or state law. Their successes and failures, and the critical nature of networked support for design and implementation of solutions, demonstrate real challenges in the field today and how today's local public servants are paving the way for the government offices of the future.

HISTORY OF ELECTION ADMINISTRATION

Election administration in the United States is best described from a systems perspective (Hale et al., 2015). Otherwise put, election administration is characterized by interlocking systems, or separate units that must work together to form the whole, including people and organizations (or agents) and activities. There is a national election system, a series of state election systems, as well as local elections systems. The primary framework for timing and regulating the administration of elections happens at the state level, and the functions involved in the actual administration of elections occur at the local level. The federal government plays less of a role in this overall, but where involved it has a significant impact. The complex nature of electoral systems means that this particular function of government is ripe for collaboration and information sharing, as well as for potential problems. As a collection of interlocking systems at the local, state, and federal levels, the election administration environment typifies the complexities and interdependencies of public service. Accountability is diffuse and considerable coordination and collaboration occur both formally and informally, and within and across jurisdictions. As a consequence of this, many third party groups have formed around elections and election administration to exert different kinds of influence on the systems, from legislative monitoring and advocacy to training and technical assistance provision.

The landscape of local level election administration is heterogeneous, with differences both across and within states (Alvarez, Hall, & Llewellyn, 2008; Hale et al., 2015). In many counties, there is a local official who is elected through either a partisan or nonpartisan election who overseas elections for that county. In other cases, there is an appointed board of elections who themselves appoint a chief election administrator to oversee that county's elections. These boards may also have other functions with respect to the election process. Still in other places, the person who is in charge of the election may have their election functions as a part of a larger job (e.g., a county clerk or auditor). In almost all of these cases, there is a staff that works to support administration and implementation of elections. How we got here is in large part a function of path dependent processes.

Early Evolution of Elections

Election administration in the United States today is in part a function of decisions made more than two hundred years ago. Colonies conducted elections, usually as needed. There were differing rules and actors involved, and voting technology ranged from corn or beans to voice vote (Bensel,

2004; Bishop, 1893). Over time these practices evolved, political parties developed and took a more significant role in elections, concerns arose about corruption, and eventually regular rules developed through state legislative activity. The Australian ballot was widely adopted, the role of parties was minimized, and by the early twentieth century a profession began to arise around the administration of elections through the creation and adoption of state level legislation that created rules around registration, polling, polling places, and timing of elections.

As election rules evolved and were systematized, good government measures were developed to mitigate fraud (e.g., checking signatures on petitions, providing privacy in voting, maintaining the integrity of ballots cast, and counting and audit procedures). What makes the U.S. case remarkable is that these state laws were developed around original local practices, producing heterogeneity in the codification of these practices across the states. When the first major studies of election administration practices were conducted (see Harris, 1928, 1929, 1934), the result of this evolution of laws and practices across the states was illustrated as a series of states' systems characterized by lack of coordination or uniformity.

Contemporary Structure of Elections

In contemporary election systems, each state functions as its own election system under an umbrella of federal rules that impact operations. Each state has a chief election official, typically but not always the Secretary of State, who is directly elected but sometimes appointed by the governor or a state elections commission or board (Hale et al., 2015). Over time the authority of the state election offices have grown, largely in response to evolving federal oversight in multiple areas, including technology, registration, records keeping, and ensuring fair and equitable practices. Among the most recent and notable federal laws that influence states and localities in election administration are the Voting Rights Act of 1965 (VRA), which in essence provided for the oversight of another institutional actor, the Voting Rights Division of the U.S. Department of Justice (DOJ); the 1993 National Voter Registration Act (NVRA), which brought other state agencies into the process of registering voters; and the Help America Vote Act of 2002 (HAVA), which required the maintenance of statewide voter files, created the Election Assistance Commission (EAC), and provided funding and guidance about the voting system.

Despite the increasing role of states and chief election officials in election administration, local election officials still maintain significant influence. Local election officials are typically not appointed by the chief election officials and therefore operate quasi-independently, make important decisions about equipment, are usually in charge of decisions about how to maintain voter lists which are then shared with the state, and are largely autonomous when making decisions about the actual running of elections. Local election officials most typically supervise elections at the county level, but in some places with large cities there is a separate local election official, and in New England and a few other states local election officials typically oversee cities, towns, and townships. The burden of paying for elections is borne locally with some help from states and the federal government, and with this comes the responsibility of oversight of personnel, equipment, maintenance, and ballots under the local election official.

Today outside actors also have significant importance in election administration. These groups typically include political parties; the candidates themselves; the public where petitions are required for ballot access; the United States Postal Service (USPS) for vote-by-mail elections, registration forms, and absentee ballots that can be returned by mail; private companies which supply equipment and ballots; media outlets; national organizations like the National Institute of Standards and Technology (NIST) and the U.S. Election Assistance Commission; other labs where states require different testing and certification; and third party groups like the League of Women Voters (LWV) who help with voter information and registration (Hale & Brown, 2013; Hale et al., 2015).

In addition to those actors, there are a number of groups involved in information dissemination, training, and professional development related to election administration and in creating and improving election administration as a profession. Understanding election administration as a form of professional public service in the contemporary environment is important given the historic descriptions of election offices in the first half of the 20th century. In the seminal reports that catalogued the organization and operation of election offices of the late 1920s and early 1930s, Harris (1934) describes this aspect of public service as incompetent, unorganized, and a "dumping ground" for workers who could not find other work (p. 9). Today, election administration is increasingly understood as a profession, which means that the field has a defined set of skills and values and a path of education toward attaining those (Klinger & Nalbandian, 2003). Professionalism itself is important as it is generally understood to be an important component of successful performance in the public service arena (Berman, 2006; Berman & Wang, 2000; Rainey & Steinbauer, 1999). Networks are particularly important in the development of the concept of professionalism and are critical for creating organizational arrangements and relationships that first foster and then institutionalize professional culture and behavioral norms (Hale, 2011).

Calls for greater training and professionalization of election officials have been made over time to increase knowledge, standardize behavior, and improve systems through information sharing, particularly as the practice of administering elections becomes more complex (Fischer & Coleman, 2008; Presidential Commission on Election Administration, 2014). In response, many national associations have developed to support election administration efforts. Chief among these include the National Association of Secretaries of State (NASS), the National Association of County Recorders, Election Officials and Clerks (NACRC), the International Association of Clerks, Recorders, Election Officials and Treasurers (IACREOT), the Election Center, and the National Association of State Election Directors (NASED), among others. Universities, too, have begun education programs providing graduate certificates and graduate degrees in election administration specifically, most notably Auburn University and the University of Minnesota.

PUBLIC ADMINISTRATION, NETWORKS, AND TRANSFORMATION

The concept of a network is common and familiar: we understand networks generally as collections of individuals or organizations that coalesce around a common interest or that are interrelated in some way. In the study of public administration, the concept of a network is both more than, and different from, our common understanding. Here, networks are understood as interdependent interorganizational arrangements of all or parts of organizations in which the organizations or parts of an organization are not simply the subordinates of others in a formal hierarchy (O'Toole, 1988). Networks can be informal arrangements or more formally organized around a common goal or function.

Networks have consequences that can be seen as both negative and positive. At first impression, it may appear that networked arrangements are inherently inefficient, ineffective, or both. Networks combine multiple stakeholders, each with multiple, different, overlapping, and even competing goals. Stakeholders have different levels of commitment and resources at their disposal. Authority and accountability are diffuse, as is the ability to marshal resources across the network.

The broad distribution of resources, commitment, and the general lack of a unified mission, however, may more accurately mirror the same sort of broad understanding of public service that is shared by a broad range of constituents. Research demonstrates that information sharing through the process of information diffusion can result in goal alignment among network members and generate innovation where government offices are integrally associated with the network (Hale, 2011). Government offices realize performance gains when they affiliate with, or participate in, information exchanges with network members (Carman, 2007). These performance gains can occur through formally structured associations and information exchanges required by legislation or grant programs through meetings, peer-to-peer sharing, and training and technical assistance provision (Brown, 2008, 2012), as well as those that emerge informally and voluntarily (Hale et al., 2015).

Information Diffusion and Public Service Networks

Key to understanding networks in relation to public service is the concept of information diffusion within networks, which illuminates the power of networks to transform public service by transforming both policy and practice. Information exchanges between organizations—and between the people who lead and administer them—are central to the creation of new ideas. In this context, the term "information" is more than a collection of facts. Information has a particular meaning and refers to "specific knowledge or data that reflects the expertise and judgment of professionals engaged in a particular policy realm" (Hale, 2011, p. 1).

In the realm of election administration, for example, illustrations of information include the range and effects of different methods of voter identification at the polls, the variations across the states in the use of provisional ballots, the effects of different ballot styles and designs, the operability of various types of voting methods, and the implementation issues associated with new voting technologies. Information that is exchanged within networks thus extends far beyond raw data and carries with it value that comes from professional interpretation and from dialogue within the network about it.

The exchange of such information, known collectively as information diffusion, promotes policy innovation and policy diffusion from one organization to another (Rogers, 1995). Walker (1969) demonstrated that information diffusion actually affects the spread of policies from one state to another. Policy information and, subsequently, policy decisions diffuse from state to state in part through the efforts of networks of state officials and professional associations to share information about policies, problems, and solutions. This information sharing produces different results depending on conditions within a state; states may tend to emulate their neighbors or to adopt policies that reflect their own state needs, political conditions, citizen demands, ideologies, and available resources (e.g., Berry & Berry, 1990; Mintrom & Vergari, 1998; Mooney, 2001).

Within networks, public administrators tend to seek synthesized information that helps them interpret the multitude of data that they receive every day (Hale, 2011; Mossberger & Hale, 2002). Synthesized information is interpretive information that brings value to existing structures and data and to other forms of information such as grants and legal requirements. The diffusion of synthesized information (termed information software in earlier research by Mossberger & Hale, 2002) promotes a type of learning across jurisdictions, particularly when local jurisdictions seek to respond to new state or federal requirements. As one locality packages its responses and shares its ideas with other localities in the network, both entities gain additional information. The early responders learn what works; later responders can utilize the responses of earlier jurisdictions and tailor those to their own local conditions. Technical assistance and training are examples of synthesized information and valuable information exchanges in the networked context. These forms of synthesized information are among the types of information noted in the earliest discussions about public sector and public service capacity and the ability of local governments to implement public programs (Burgess, 1975; Honadle, 1981). Importantly, the concept of capacity in public offices is also linked to making connections with local preferences (Gargan, 1981).

Conceptually, we can imagine that information diffusion occurs horizontally, from locality to locality. County offices within the same state learn from one another as they attempt to innovate to address required challenges from federal and state mandates. They also learn from one another through voluntary innovation that occurs when offices resolve specific organizational and operational issues in their offices. Other offices learn from these innovations, and from the successes and failures that take place throughout the implementation process. Of course, these local learning experiences can occur between offices in different states. This horizontal diffusion also occurs between localities and local nonprofit organizations and third party groups. Information diffusion also occurs vertically, as states and federal offices pass information to local administrators about grant programs, training opportunities, and technical assistance in interpreting new laws and regulations in order to understand how to implement them and how their localities will be affected.

In addition to the horizontal and vertical movement of information, we can also consider information through the lens of the local election administrator and his/her election environment. This election context is an important factor in examining networks in this policy area, because election administration is constructed by local practice and rules, state law, and also by the interaction of state and federal law. Because election laws vary extensively across the states in the way that local elections are conducted, we conceptualize networks as *interlocal* (across states), and *intralocal* (within states). Interlocal networks reach from locality to locality across multiple states; intralocal networks are confined to one state and may revolve significantly around a state association of election officials.

Administrators gain advantage by participating in information networks and from the information diffusion process because the networked environment is actually central to the value of the information that flows within it. Information is ubiquitous; administrators continuously encounter multiple sources of information and competing views. Administrators face a real challenge in the contemporary, complex information environment in identifying accurate and trusted sources of information in a timely manner.

The collective synthesis of information that occurs within networks provides several distinct benefits. Ideas, policy preferences, and implementation strategies are not constrained; there is no requirement that organizations in a network agree with one another and frequently they do not. Instead, organizations interpret the information that they receive and then respond to it, often honing and refining the information as it is passed along. The information-sharing process is iterative; organizations continually refine the information that they generate and share within the network; some information may also be challenged, and opposing views are common. As a consequence, information that is diffused through the network has been subjected to numerous reviews and challenges as to factual accuracy and policy tone. Network information is also trusted by participants. Where the information represents a point of view, the interaction of network members tends to draw that point of view out into the open, and it is clarified through the iterative nature of the information exchanges in the network (Hale, 2011; Mossberger, 2000; Mossberger & Hale, 2002).

Another valuable dimension of information generated by, or disseminated in, a network is time. By interacting around information in networks, administrators can access multiple and competing views that highlight a broad range of questions and points on an issue. These interactions and exchanges of information, and particularly exchanges of synthesized information, are thought to represent a form of "bounded rationality" (Simon, 1986) in which administrators engage in networks as a rational method of reducing the costs of seeking information (Hale, 2011; Mossberger & Hale, 2002).

Transformational Approaches in Public Service

Several distinct types of synthesized information have been found to be valuable to public administrators in navigating policy changes and in creating innovations to address the challenges of a changing environment. Technical assistance and training were mentioned above as two of earliest forms of information exchange that benefited local governments in particular relationship to requirements imposed by new grant relationships with federal agencies. Four other forms of synthesized information deserve mention here, in relation to the election administration environment; these are best practices, model programs, research, and conferences.

Best practices and model programs are generally understood to be exemplars of "what works" in terms of effective strategies for program design, program implementation, and problem solving. Best practices can be considered to be innovations that reflect elements of successful performance in a given program area (Letts, Ryan, & Grossman, 1999). Best practices at times reflect the results of rigorous research; more commonly, they reflect the consensus of professional opinion in a field about how best to approach an issue. As a collection of best practices in a specific context, model programs illustrate a comprehensive strategy that blends program elements with resource constraints and political context. Best practice leaders are innovators whose views then become widely adopted in the practitioner community. Model programs may be somewhat less likely to be adopted by other localities if the comprehensive approach contains too many elements that are customized to fit unique local conditions; however, model programs are generally considered to contain aspirational characteristics of program design, strategy, and execution.

Research is a powerful tool for public administrators who seek information in networked arrangements. Evaluative research in particular presents a synthesis of program goals and program and office performance, and illustrates whether those goals are met, and also perhaps provides information about why that is the case. Research about what other offices are doing can also provide important comparative information about approaches, operating characteristics and requirements, and legal constraints. Research about the effectiveness of a new policy initiative can provide legitimacy for new approaches to solving problems, and can also highlight areas for improvement or disclose unintended consequences of policy decisions. Research relationships can also form within networked environments that are sustained over long periods of time and which generate iterative interpretations of the impacts of policy changes over time.

Perhaps the most common practice for sharing information occurs at regular, in person events. Meetings and conferences provide venues and structure for networks to exist and for information exchanges to occur; most meetings and conferences in public service networks are sponsored by membership organizations. Membership organizations exist for virtually every line of work pursued by government officials whether elected, appointed, or hired as civil servants. Leadership in these organizations has been linked to policy innovation in a wide range of public policy and public service arenas including criminal justice policy reform (Hale, 2011) and technological innovations in state government (Tolbert, Mossberger, & McNeal, 2008), among others. The meeting or conference venue typically consists of a series of presentations of synthesized information and numerous opportunities to interact personally with both the information presenters and with colleagues. Panels and presentations about best practices and research results are common, as are demonstrations of model programs. Some organizations highlight exemplary practices with awards. Some events also provide training and technical assistance for their members.

All of these methods of information exchange are tremendously important for election administrators and have been at the forefront of election administration transformation and innovation since 2000. Post-2000, election officials were inundated with changes to an already complex system. Some of the impetus for change came from the imposition of new, formal statutory requirements. These included changes in federal law in 2002 with the passage of the Help America Vote Act (HAVA), new requirements for voting systems, and the establishment of requirements for new forms of ballots to assist voters who appeared at the polls without state-specified forms of identification. Local officials began to meet in their states and around the country at meetings and conferences hosted by various professional organizations and membership associations. In open forums and special sessions, officials discussed their operational challenges and the ways in which they were marshaling limited resources to meet these. They also discussed the policy environment and how best to meet the changing demands of state and federal officials when elections replaced one ideological viewpoint with either its opposite or something very different.

More recently, states subject to certain provisions of the Voting Rights Act of 1965 (VRA) found themselves in relatively uncharted territory following the U.S. Supreme Court decision in *Shelby County v. Holder* (2013). From the inception of the VRA, certain localities as well as entire states (and the localities within them) were required to present any changes in election law and practice to the U.S. Department of Justice (USDOJ) or to a federal court for review and approval prior to implementation. Known as preclearance, this practice of prior review and approval generated a highly articulated set of formal and informal relationships between counties and USDOJ staff, and in some cases between state election offices and USDOJ. The *Shelby County* decision removed the preclearance requirement, however, the VRA general prohibition on discriminatory voting practices remains in effect and applies to all counties and states around the country. Election officials in jurisdictions previously subject to preclearance had to seek new sources of information about how to evaluate their election practices and the effects of contemplated changes against this new policy landscape.

It has also been the case that election officials have taken pro-active, voluntary approaches to resolving challenges in their increasingly complex environments. Local administrators have been at the forefront in developing new approaches to training the vast number of poll-workers required on election day; these include the implementation of online training, new methods for evaluating the efficacy of training programs, and developing new methods for recruiting and retaining pollworkers (Hale & Slaton, 2008). In some cases, local election officials have experimented with methods of organizing elections in various ways to reduce the number of poll workers needed; examples include the use of regional voting centers, increased use of absentee ballots, and all-mail voting systems that eliminate the traditional polling place (Hale et al., 2015). All of these innovations were fostered by the networked environment of election administration that we describe and analyze further in the following sections of the chapter.

THE EFFECTS OF NETWORKS: INFORMATION DIFFUSION & COLLABORATION

As discussed above, networks of election administrators provide opportunities for the exchange and vetting of information, and may also result in collaboration. We asked election administrators about their experiences with these networks and their effects, about how their work has changed, what challenges they face, the changing nature of administrative discretion, and how information and information sharing has changed. In our analysis, we parse these through an examination of major changes as well as consideration of intralocal and interlocal effects.

Major Changes

For the election administrators working both before and after the 2000 election,several important changes have happened in the profession. The 2000 election produced a national focus on ballots and equipment, making technical competence paramount, particularly with respect to information technology. But equipment and competence needs evolve. One election official noted that competence in this area is critical for ensuring that local election staff can respond to constantly changing state legislation. Another noted that they are "constantly responding to legislative changes. The rules of the game are never finalized it seems." Still another told us that

> the changes ... come fast and furious and constantly. Just when you get to know the laws and rules, they're changed and not always for the best.... [This is particularly] hard on poll workers. Every time they come for class, it's like learning everything from scratch instead of it being a refresher course as it was in the past.

The election administration work environment must respond to the rapidly evolving nature of court and legislative changes, making information sharing and capacity more important than ever in the field.

Rapid change has not been limited to legislative change or legal interpretation. Operational characteristics of election administration have become more complex and technically sophisticated. One election administrator noted that the "work is more technical now. [There is] more auditing involved and more training required for staff and poll workers. There are many more vendors in the election industry selling tabulation equipment, bags, and storage containers, software, etc."

All of these changes also mean that elections are increasingly expensive. They require more, and more skilled, staff members, shifting the nature of the workforce from what one administrator referred to as "clerical staff" to "younger people who are more interested in elections as a career." Elections require equipment that needs to be updated; however no federal HAVA funding remains to support this, and states and localities are assumed to be unable to bear the full cost of election technology (Hale & Brown, 2013).

Finally, one of the election administrators with whom we spoke called the attention brought to election administration post-2000 "a double-edged sword. Positive: the complexity of conducting an election was finally recognized. Negative: everything we do is now viewed under a microscope." To deal with these new challenges, election administrators increasingly come together in networks to share ideas, information, and best practices. The election administrators with whom we spoke noted their preferences. The most important are networks with peers in the same state (intralocal) and with national (interlocal) organizations, relationships with their state election offices (intralocal), collaboration with the news media (intralocal and interlocal), and working with vendors (interlocal). There was general agreement that the most useful peer-to-peer exchanges happened when they could coordinate and share with peers from similarly sized cities and counties.

Intralocal and Interlocal Effects

Intralocally, election administration has changed significantly since the 2000 election. The power of state chief election officers increased with the passage of HAVA. State chief election officers were charged with developing statewide plans to implement the federally-funded transition from mechanical voting machines to electronic voting systems. Chief election officials were also responsible for implementing electronic voter registration databases statewide, and for conducting outreach to voters. Every state has also had to develop provisional ballot systems and methods of voter identification. This new and increased power at the state level has produced more convergences across counties and localities. State associations provide consistent training and opportunities for exchanges of local level best practices. Because these occur within a homogeneous environment, these intralocal networks function as a rising tide which lifts all of the localities.

Election administration began changing interlocally prior to the 2000 election, but the pace of that change has hastened quickly since. There is specific federal oversight of election administration through HAVA's creation of the Election Assistance Commission, and there are more and more national organizations (also called third party groups) that work to promote interlocal exchanges. Table 12.1 lays out the external elements that election administrators believe influence, negatively or positively, their work. The biggest influence by far comes from government institutions, particularly Secretaries of State and state legislators (intralocal). Of the third party groups that were noted to directly influence their work, most discussed political parties followed by the convening organizations (interlocal).

Table 12.1.   External Factors That Influence Local Administration

Government/ Institutions	Nongovernmental Organizations	Public	Community Factors	Other
Federal gov't. (8.5%)	3rd party groups (8.5%)	Voter/opinion (12.8%)	Community (2.1%)	Ethics (2.1%)
Election rules (17%)	Political parties (21.3%)	Participation (2.1%)	Demographics (2.1%)	
State/SOS (29.8%)	Politics (6.7%)		Economy (2.1%)	
State/legislators (27.7%)	Candidates (6.4%)			
Courts (4.3%)	Press (2.1%)			
Election board (10.6%)				
Tax districts (2.1%)				
Local budget (10.6%)				
Post office (2.1%)				
Volunteers (2.1%)				

$n = 47$

However, election administrators do not always agree on the most appropriate roles of either the federal government or the third party organizations. When asked specifically about how these units could help enhance coordination and collaboration, one election administrator responded that the most appropriate role for the federal government is to coordinate the states, which would then coordinate localities within the states. Others noted that the most appropriate role for the federal government is education across states and localities. Alternatively, one election administrator stated that the only appropriate role for the federal government is to protect state sovereignty in the election administration process. Overall, though, less than 15% of the election administrators with whom we spoke or surveyed felt that there should be no role for the federal government in this process.

When asked specifically about the Election Assistance Commission, specifically, most election administrators surveyed allocated the most appropriate functions for the agency across four key areas: processes, information, advocacy, and coordination with states and localities (see Table 12.2). The most frequently desired role for the Election Assistance Commission was to ensure consistency in elections across the states, but only a small group felt that way. Other roles included providing training and technical assistance, coordinating with the states, lobbying, ensuring fairness, communicating best practices, educating the public, and providing funding for states and localities. Although there has been some talk about eliminating the agency, only one respondent felt that the agency should be eliminated.

Table 12.2.   Desired Roles of the Election Assistance Commission

Processes	Information	Advocacy	Coordination
Certify equipment (12%)	TTA (12%)	Ensure fairness (12%)	Coordination with states (12%)
	Best practices (8%)	Lobbying (12%)	Train LEOs (12%)
	Public education (8%)	Funding (8%)	Ensure consistency (16%)
	Data collection (4%)	Increase confidence (4%)	

n = 25

Calls for the national government to have a coordination and education role in election administration for states and local election officials either ignore or criticize the efforts of extant third party groups which already provide these services. Though some work in other areas that less directly

impact election administration (engaging in activities like public education, lobbying, providing legislative testimony, using legalism tactics to
promote reform, and engaging in voter registration and get-out-the-vote
drives), arguably their most significant influence on election administration practices, either inter- and/or intralocally, comes from coordination
through convenings, the provision of training and technical assistance, by
generating research, and through general information sharing.

Among the election administrators who responded to questions about
third party groups from our surveys, almost 70% felt that these groups are
important to election administration as compared with about 25% who felt
that they had no impact on election administration in their localities (see
Table 12.3). The groups they specifically mentioned include (in order from
the most frequently mentioned to the least): the League of Women Voters,
tribal groups, Abate, the Farm Bureau, the ACLU, PILF, Asian Alliance,
disability groups, the Tea Party, and the NAACP. However, none of the
election administrators who answered these open-ended survey questions
noted the importance of these third party groups in information sharing,
and instead focused on the impact of these groups on the day-to-day operations of election administration.[2]

Table 12.3. Roles of and Problems Generated by Third Party Groups in Election Administration

Roles	Problems
Public education (23.5%)	Incomplete registration (5.8%)
Outreach (11.8%)	Incorrect information (5.8%)
Registration (11.8%)	Do not follow rules (5.8%)
Advocacy (5.8%)	Register nonpeople (2.9%)
Monitoring (2.9%)	

$n = 34$

A critical result of the synergy between these changes in election administration practice and the increasing intralocal and interlocal exchanges
is innovation. Table 12.4 lays out responses from election administrators
about their ability to innovate, the areas in which it is most possible, and
the practices that enhance or challenge innovation at the local level. Of
those who answered, a plurality said that they can innovate, and that most
of the opportunity to do so comes in the information technology areas of
their work. Innovation was seen to be enhanced the most by support from
internal leadership but also by the support of third parties and vendors.
Active engagement in networks, though not mentioned as frequently, was

seen as another significant support for process improvements and innovation. Innovation was also seen as challenging for several reasons; most
typically these challenges revolve around cost, legal restrictions, staff, time,
and buy-in.

Table 12.4.   Local Innovation

Ability to Innovate	Types of Innovation	Constraints	Enhancements
Yes (46%)	Technology/IT (16%)	Cost (34%)	Internal leadership (12%)
Some (32%)		Laws (30%)	
Limited (10%)	Processes (6%)	Staffing (6%)	Third party groups (2%)
None (2%)		Buy-in (6%)	Outreach (2%)
		Time (6%)	Dillon's Rule (2%)
		Voter capacity (4%)	Odd years (2%)
		Leadership (4%)	Collaboration (2%)
		Personalities (4%)	Staff (2%)
		Legislature (2%)	
		Tradition (2%)	
		Parties (2%)	
		Security issues (2%)	

$n = 50$

IMPLICATIONS AND CONCLUSIONS

In the networked arrangements that characterize local government today,
and in the complex local environments of local election administration,
innovation is promoted through the process of information diffusion. As
has been shown in other substantive subfields of public administration and
public service (Hale, 2011; Mossberger, 2000; Mossberger & Hale, 2002),
information diffusion involves multiple actors and levels of government
that reach both horizontally and vertically within and across sectors, and
occurs in the various venues and forms outlined in this chapter. Through
the experiences of election administrators discussed in this chapter, we
illustrate both the processes and effects of information diffusion within
networks and the contributions of that process to creating innovations in
the field. By the process of information diffusion, local government officials are able to navigate the networked environments in which they must
operate. The networks themselves help address the conditions of complexity and interdependence that characterize public service activities. The
networks also help election officials assess the accuracy of the information
they receive, and the motives of those who generate and disseminate it.

It is important to consider the implications of our findings in the context of the persistent narrative that suggests that government is rendered inept by the complexities and interdependencies of modern public service. Our findings suggest that a much more optimistic view is warranted. The networks that engage local election officials with one another and with nonprofit organizations have generated a rich array of information interactions, and in turn, a rich array of innovations, best practices, model programs, and collaborations. Each of these has contributed to improving the capacity of public service in this area of public administration.

NOTES

1. These illustrations come from surveys collected from 105 election administrators in July 2014 and interviews with five hand-selected election administrators who have held their positions prior to and since the 2000 election as of August 2015. In both cases, the election administrators held local positions.
2. This is perhaps explained by whom we surveyed. While the interviews were done with more senior level local election administrators, the open-ended surveys were completed in most cases by less seasoned administrators whose jobs revolve primarily around day-to-day functions in local election offices.

REFERENCES

Alvarez, M., Hall, T., & Llewellyn, M. (2008). Are Americans confident that their ballots are counted? *Journal of Politics, 70*(3), 754–766.

Bensel, R. F. (2004). *The American ballot box in the mid-nineteenth century*. New York, NY: Cambridge University Press.

Berman, E. (2006). *Performance and productivity in public and nonprofit organizations* (2nd ed.). Armonk, NY: M. E. Sharpe.

Berman, E., & Wang, X. H. (2000). Performance measurement in U.S. counties: Capacity for reform. *Public Administration Review, 60*(5), 409–420.

Berry, F. S., & Berry, W. D. (1990). State lottery policy adoptions as innovation. *American Political Science Review, 84*(2), 395–415.

Bishop, C. E. (1893). *History of elections in the American colonies*. Franklin: Burt Publisher.

Brown, M. (2008). Improving organizational capacity among faith- and community-based domestic violence service providers. In P. Joshi, S. Hawkins, & J. Novey (Eds.), *Innovations in effective compassion* (pp. 39–60). Washington, DC: Department of Health and Human Services.

Brown, M. (2012). Enhancing and sustaining organizational capacity. *Public Administration Review, 72*, 506–515.

Burgess, P. M. (1975). Capacity building and the elements of public management. *Public Administration Review, 35*(6), 705–716.

Bush v. Gore, 531 U.S. 98 (2000).

Carman, J. (2007). Evaluation practice among community-based organizations. *American Journal of Evaluation, 28*(1), 60–75.

Fischer, E. A., & Coleman, K. J. (2008). *Election reform and local election officials: The results of two national surveys*. Washington, DC: CRS Report for Congress.

Gargan, J. J. (1981). Consideration of local government capacity. *Public Administration Review, 41*(6), 649–658.

Hale, K. (2011). *How information matters: Networks and public policy innovation*. Washington, DC: Georgetown University Press.

Hale, K., & Brown, M. (2013). Adopting, adapting, and opting out: State response to federal voting system guidelines. *Publius, 43*, 428–451.

Hale, K., Montjoy, R., & Brown. M. (2015). *Administering elections: How American elections work*. New York, NY: Palgrave MacMillan.

Hale, K., & Slaton, C. D. (2008). Building capacity in election administration: Local responses to complexity and interdependence. *Public Administration Review, 68*(5), 839–849.

Harris, J. P. (1928). Permanent registration of voters. *The American Political Science Review, 22*, 349–353.

Harris, J. P. (1929). The progress of permanent registration of voters. *The American Political Science Association, 23*, 908–914.

Harris, J. P. (1934). *Election administration in the United States*. Washington, DC: Brookings Institution Press.

Honadle, B. W. (1981). A capacity-building framework: A search for concept and purpose. *Public Administration Review, 41*(5), 575–580.

Klinger, D. E., & Nalbandian, J. (2003). *Public personnel management: Context and strategies* (5th ed.). Upper Saddle River, NJ: Prentice-Hall.

Letts, C., Ryan, W. P., & Grossman, A. (1999). *High-performance nonprofit organizations: Managing upstream for greater impact*. New York, NY: John Wiley & Sons.

Mintrom, M., & Vergari, S. (1998). Policy networks and innovation diffusion: The case of state education reform. *Journal of Politics, 60*(1), 126–148.

Mooney, C. Z. (2001). Modeling regional effects on state policy diffusion. *Political Research Quarterly, 54*(1), 103–124.

Mossberger, K., & Hale, K. (2002). Polydiffusion in intergovernmental programs: Information diffusion in school-to-work programs. *American Review of Public Administration, 32*(4), 398–422.

Mossberger, K. (2000). *The politics of ideas and the spread of the enterprise zones*. Washington, DC: Georgetown University Press.

O'Toole, L. J., Jr. (1988). Strategies for intergovernmental management: Implementing programs in intergovernmental management. *International Journal of Public Administration, 11*(4), 417–441.

Presidential Commission on Election Administration. (2014). *The American voting experience: Report and recommendations of the presidential commission on election administration*. Washington, DC: Author.

Rainey, H., & Steinbauer, P. (1999). Galloping elephants: Developing elements of a theory of effective government organizations. *Journal of Public Administration and Theory, 9*(1), 1–32.

Rogers, E. (1995). *The diffusion of innovation* (4th ed.). New York, NY: Free Press.

Shelby County v. Holder, 570 U.S. ___ (2013).

Simon, H. A. (1986). Theories of bounded rationality. In C. B. McGuire & R. Radner (Eds.). *Decision and organization* (2nd ed., pp. 161–176). Minneapolis, MN: University of Minnesota Free Press.

Tolbert, C., Mossberger, K., & McNeal, R. (2008). Institutions, policy innovations, and e-government in the American states. *Public Administration Review, 68*(3), 549–563.

Walker, J. (1969). The diffusion of innovation among the American states. *American Political Science Review, 63*(3), 880–899.

SECTION III

LESSONS LEARNED ON
TRANSFORMATION IN GOVERNMENT

CHAPTER 13

ARE PUBLIC AND PRIVATE SECTOR CHANGE EFFORTS DIFFERENT

Some Answers and Lessons Learned

Ronald R. Sims, William J. Mea, and John G. Veres, III

INTRODUCTION

Given the differences between public and private sector organizations discussed in the first chapter of this book one should also expect to find differences in their respective change or transformation efforts (see Sims, 2010). For example, Jack Miles, former Secretary for Florida's Department of Management Services, recently noted the difficulty in trying to bring about change in government procurement. In particular, Miles noted that the "rigid, procedure-heavy public-sector management makes it nearly impossible to run procurement as fluidly and efficiently as in the private sector (Miles, 2014, p. 2).

This chapter first compares and contrasts private and public sector forms of change by exploring salient issues and providing real-life examples as a focus for discussion. The discussion then turns to the challenges, barri-

Transforming Government Organizations:
Fresh Ideas and Examples From the Field, pp. 357–374
Copyright © 2016 by Information Age Publishing

357

ers to and drivers of public sector change. Next, a comparison of public and private sector change efforts is offered. Finally, best practices lessons learned for improving public sector change efforts are presented.

PRIVATE VERSUS PUBLIC CHANGE EFFORTS

In the private sector, procurement works with executive management and a board of directors, maybe 10 or 20 people who have hired the procurement chief for his or her expertise and delegated authority over the function to that person. And, such delegation allows for change and transformation as needed. In government, procurement has to deal with a legislative body made up of hundreds of people, all of whom have a say and believe they know how to do the job better. Thus, the legislative body can serve as a barrier to any efforts to transform procurement. Further, in the private sector, rules are in place governing what you can and cannot do—but some rules can be modified and exceptions can be made which is necessary for procurement to adapt, change or transform. In government, however, the rules are not just rules—they are laws, and bending them can land you behind bars. If you don't agree with the rules, you have to work with the legislature to get them changed, which Miles (2014) notes "is a crusade unto itself" (p. 1).

Jurisch Ikas, Wolf, and Krcmar (2013) have recently noted that the public sector is subject to constant changes and in an effort to tackle various financial, social, and political challenges, public sector organizations all over the world need to rethink, adapt, and change their underlying service processes. Prompted by these challenges public sector managers have turned to the private sector for transformation solutions like business process change (BPC) to facilitate resource efficiency and allow for a more straightforward way of service provision. Additionally, these researchers note that past research shows there are two more or less distinct approaches to public sector BPC research. One stream of research has been arguing that the public sector should learn from the experiences made in private BPC projects (Halachmi, 1995; Halachmi & Bovaird, 1997; Scholl, 2004). Another group of researchers has argued in favor of public-sector specific models and approaches (Becker, Algermissen, & Niehaves, 2004; Sharafi, Jurisch, Ikas, Wolf, & Krcmar, 2011; Stewart & Walsh, 1992). Jurisch et al. (2013) argue that the often oversimplifed private sector models disregard the distinctive purposes, conditions and tasks of the public sector. However, the situation is not that black and white. Both public and private organizations have accumulated considerable experiences with BPC in the last decades that the other sector could benefit from. This view is counter to the never ending call for "government to be run like business" and especially when one is referring to reform, change or transformation efforts (see, e.g., Bloomfield, 2013; Harvey, 2012; Rampell, 2015).

The work of Jurisch et al. (2013), like that of Sims (2010), shows that there are certain factors that public sector organizations appear to have more experience in, while there are others that private organizations are more accomplished in and propose that both public and private sector organizations may actually learn from one another's change (i.e., BPC projects) or transformation implementations (Sims, 2010). In reality, maybe as suggested by Jurisch et al. few organizations are purely public or private. Johnson and Scholes (2001) and Jurisch et al. (2013) suggest that (1) most organizations sit somewhere on a continuum between these two extremes, (2) numerous new mixed forms of collaboration have been created between private and public sector organizations (e.g., private-public partnerships), and (3) the increasing investment of private organizations into the public sector is likely to even increase this spectrum of private-public forms of cooperation Llewellyn and Tappin (2003) assert that "private sector sponsorship is, already, a significant phenomenon across the public sector" (p. 995). All of this has important implications as we continue to try to consider how best to transform public sector organizations in the field. Thus, it is important that those responsible for change and transformation in the public sector (and the private sector as well) understand why they might have been historically better in certain aspects of managing change and what they can learn from the other sector. Figure 13.1 summarizes the unique characteristics of BPC implementations for each sector (Jurisch et al., 2013).

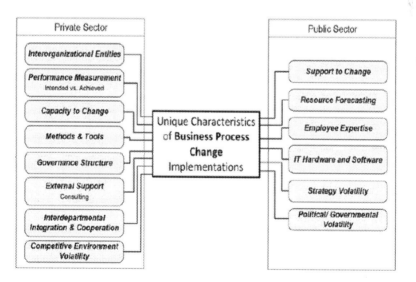

Figure 13.1.   Unique characteristics of private and public sector BPC implementations.

According to Mea, Sims, and Veres (2000) and Sims (2010) a number of issues provide important contrasts of private- and public-sector change efforts. While this list is not exhaustive, the issues presented below collectively illustrate fundamental differences in the world views of private and public sector organizations in the United States. Among them are:

Strategic Planning. Within the U.S. public sector there is often a desire on all parts for controlled change, when the need for change is acknowledged at all. The slow, evolutionary change that is often seen in public sector organizations provides the stability desired in the workforce. Within private-sector large-scale change efforts the organization's desire is more typically for fast-paced and radical change. Stability, in the sense of failure to scan the environment for better solutions, is viewed as the enemy of success. To illustrate this contrast, one might suppose that many constituencies would like to see dramatic change in the way the U.S. Postal Service conducts its business. Nonetheless, if one were to attempt truly radical design using competing business units that develop their own metrics and methods, the failure of any individual field effort would result in a public outcry. In private industry, on the other hand, competitors will enter the market niche and replace any organization that supports customer needs.

High-level Metrics. In private companies the targets can shift rapidly. Therefore, executives set high level metrics to serve as targets to maintain market leadership. Long, drawn out discussions of defining metrics would get in the way. They rely on innovation and commitment at every level. By contrast, as discussed earlier, the "market objective" of public sector organizations is fairly well defined and unchanging. While agendas may shift with political control within a public sector agency, there is always a push toward seeking stability. Public sector agencies or organizations are not free to choose their customers. While setting slowly shifting targets may undermine the nimbleness of the public sector organization, it does provide much-needed stability for the organization's understanding of direction, purpose, and capacity to measure. In private sector organizations, executives allow each cascading level of the organization to define how they will achieve their goals and are often given significant latitude for the process for achieving their goal metrics.

In publicly traded and privately held companies in the U.S. one metric dominates all management attention - profit. If there is a change in culture that changes the way business is being conducted, that is one that holds meaning to commercial U.S. interests. Change only matters in private sector organizations if it is translated into increased income, profitability or shareholder's dividends. Management must respond to the needs of stockholders, the stakeholders who matter in this value system. Stock price reflects the perceived underlying worth of the company and the culture's capacity to make required changes. In our experience, when executives are given summary figures or anecdotal evidence that reflects change in a culture, and at the same time they see changes in the bottom-line, they trust the figures. They are too busy to be bothered with the details that managers preview. Because the stakeholder picture is much more complex in the public sector, the measures are also more complex and subject to scrutiny. Sometimes the scrutiny of data in the public sector goes to extraordinary lengths.

Not all U.S. federal agencies use traditional outcome measures to drive improvement efforts to increase value to stakeholders. For example, one creative senior administrator at one federal sector hospital undergoing reengineering pared back the list of traditional outcome metrics, added several new customer satisfaction metrics, and directed the physicians and nurses to use any innovative process approach on which they could achieve some consensus. Each week the senior administrator reminded the leadership group of two metrics that mattered the most, long-term cost and customer satisfaction. Despite significant resistance from the university-based physicians who staffed the facility and threatening calls from Washington authorities, dramatic improvements were made in customer satisfaction and bottom-line costs. As a result, the hospital won several national awards for innovation.

Metric Philosophy. During the past decade some forward thinking organizations have used a combination of strategic planning and Balanced Business Scorecard approaches toward metrics. For example, one organization selected a limited number of high-level metrics (up to twenty at the high-end) to put the company in a strategically competitive position within the market. Then, rather than define how the work process must be done down to the individual level, they relied on the innovation of their managers and front-line staff. As each objective cascades downward through the organizational system, each department, team, and individual has an opportunity to define how they will contribute toward achieving the metrics in the areas of finance, organizational learning, operations, and customer service (Kaplan & Norton, 1996). Organizational success is created through an understanding of the goals, a commitment to overall and personal targets, and working cross-functionally to balance goals. In order to assure that success is achieved organizations must commit to training their workers. They must also provide an environment where learning and innovation are valued over strict conformance to defined process. In such environments, external and internal benchmarking of best practices, the use of quality tools, and systematic use of process improvement are encouraged at the lowest levels. People are also given rewards and recognition for their successful efforts.

One example provides a dramatic, although unusual contrast between public sector and private sector change projects. One federal agency would spend two days each month with senior managers and executives reviewing over 100 metrics. They held far ranging discussions about the driving forces for the metrics and labored to come to consensus about what actions to take. A competitor in the private sector held less than half day meetings each month to discuss three metrics. It is doubtless that there were some inaccuracies in data reporting in each case. Nonetheless, one organization's profit grew dramatically the other experienced only moderate recognition for its excellent service to the public.

In recent years, many public-sector reengineering efforts have historically spent a great deal of effort measuring the core process that is already in place. They sometimes fail to question which core processes are the right ones to serve their stakeholders. The method measuring the outcomes for customer service sometimes goes unquestioned. When other processes are suggested, they may be crushed under the weight of union pressure, lack of historical precedent for the measure, or the present skill sets drive forward the importance of the metric.

By contrast, in order to survive, private sector companies' approach to outcome metrics must be nimble and respond to market changes. Increased efficiency of the process is not as important as achieving the end product —customer satisfaction and repeat business. In the previously mentioned case above, a traditional cost metric got in the way of achieving customer satisfaction. Even though customers of the agency paid less for services in the short run, the long-term results of failure to implement new processes and metrics failed the customer.

Sponsorship of the Reform, Change or Transformation Initiative. Based on the discussion earlier, it is clear that U.S. public sector agencies' senior executives are often pushed from many directions. Historically, the dictates of various legislation over the years provide the moving force behind change rather than inspiring the organization's members. For example, at one public sector agency, field executives had only minimal interest in a project that provided dramatic improvements in customer satisfaction. Because it offered little in the way of improvement of agency profitability, external private-sector competitors complained of unfair advantage, and unions complained that it curtailed the traditional advantages older employees enjoyed. The project was nearly scrubbed as a concession to the union by the chief executive. When union personnel themselves complained that the union stemmed bonuses, the turnover of the chief executive provided the opportunity for the project to move forward.

However well-intentioned the change efforts of many U.S. public sector managers and executives, we have found that they are often bound by legislation or tradition to methods and processes they would rather discard.

Upward movement in public service organizations tends to be awarded to those who do their functional job well, and understand the process of their agency extremely well. They know how to measure outcomes based on their own functional processes, have culled senior sponsorship in the organization based on hard work, and demonstrated upward loyalty. They can be counted on to produce reliable and predictable results. In our experience, some of the strengths senior public sector managers possess would in the private sector create vulnerability for a culture that needs to change. Let us provide a few illustrations.

In one agency, there was a strong organization of regional field executives. Attaining a high level within the organization required a long history of functional expertise (and accompanying metrics), in-depth understanding of local conditions, and two-way allegiances built upon relationships. When changes were proposed during a change project to modify operations and metric calculations for operations, there was little support. The traditional rewards for these executives and their managers did not support the change. Each stage of the project required the personal intervention of an agency project executive as well as more senior executives from the central organization. While it was clearly understood that the changes would benefit customers in the long run, the legacy measurement (i.e., old measures that are out of date and may need conversion) and reward architecture did not support the change.

This contrasts with a similar, but private sector organization with which we came in touch whose core business was endangered. While the private sector manufacturer had similar semi-independent executives who were firmly rooted in old habits of measuring their operational success, they were more than willing to change metric collection and operations routines, and to adopt a centralized scheduling system. Small pilot projects had demonstrated the benefit of culture change. While there was no reward system to replace systems currently used, field operations executives were quick to adopt new systems because it would benefit the overall success of the firm and ensure survivability.

Involving the Whole System. When undertaking large-scale change with new accompanying metric systems, problems often begin when organizations fail to involve the people who understand the current system in the actual changes. If an executive group or task force dictates process changes, and it fails to at least consult the people who must implement them, the typical response during rollout is pushback or resistance. There are a number of reasons for this state of affairs. First, people typically are unwilling to get involved in implementing a new system, especially a new measurement system, into which they did not have some involvement and input. This involvement may be as in-depth as designing the new processes and helping to define the appropriate metrics, or be as simple as identifying the barriers to carrying out changes. One approach to overcome the problem is to include those groups in design of the new metric system who will be required to implement it. It may on the surface appear to slow down developing a new work and metric system, but over the long run leads to better solutions and ways to measure processes.

For example, in one public sector organization, a small alpha project was initiated to see if organizational improvements could be made by using teams of workers. The new teams used both professional and paraprofessional workers in an effort to overcome barriers that had interfered with customer satisfaction and cycle time reduction. At the beginning of the project there was a great deal of enthusiasm about making use of alternative processes and outcome metrics. Total cycle time reduction, customer satisfaction, and worker satisfaction were going to play a greater role in determining success. Within 6 months from startup the teams had developed an improved workflow, much improved customer satisfaction and worker camaraderie, an improved total product, and better total cycle time reduction. Some teams experimented with alternative processes to achieve these outcomes. However, a traditional agency metric had always used cost indices that pushed workers to increase the short-term throughput at the expense of quality and customer satisfaction. In the end, a system that had promised to serve the public better and make innovations to the traditional workflow was sacrificed to political pressures. Alternative outcome metrics, such as total product cycle time and customer satisfaction, could not gain the acceptance that short-term cost had always held.

A private sector example provides a contrast where political pressures forced adopting new methods and metrics. One international chemicals manufacturer had experienced failure of several of its initiatives due to slow implementation. However, when they initiated cross-site teams who devised an operations maintenance program they were able to involve people in developing their own programs. As a result, employment in the target positions stabilized, skills-bands increased, and learning transferred from one facility to others. Moreover, metrics were developed on which all facilities could agree and short-term as well as long-term costs decreased.

As one large public sector agency found, even a late start to involving frontline workers can benefit public service organizations. During the design phase of reengineering, frontline workers had minimal influence on design but potentially great impact on implementation. Higher echelon operations experts in this case designed both a metric and process control mechanisms to improve the primary process interface with customers. As a result, during the first two years resistance from the union, field executives, and frontline workers was significant. While their cooperation was required for achieving success on the project, those who carried out the new process could not provide information on barriers or improvements.

When union resistance became a severe barrier, the project leaders sent human relations experts to the 10 sites to identify sources of resistance and positive factors that could speed the implementation. As a result of the field studies, a recommendation was made to hold a series of information sharing and gathering conferences with frontline workers at a central location. At the conference frontline representatives met for focus groups to identify the best practices, barriers to carrying out the process, issues with the metrics, and alternative suggestions to improve the measurement of the process. Simultaneously, the leadership also solicited involvement from the union to increase its buy-in and identify sources of irritation with the metrics and the process. As a result, frontline workers carried back a greater desire to improve the process, identified new methods of measurement to ensure they got proper credit, and communicated to their peers that involvement in supporting the project was a benefit to them.

By contrast, another case example illustrates how the initial involvement that is stemmed can undermine success. One public sector agency set out to include participation and development of its workers from the very beginning in a reengineering pilot project. Workers from several job classifications were provided 2 weeks of orientation to a new process, training in group dynamics, review of up-to date technical methods, and an indoctrination into the higher-purpose of the project. During the first several months of the project employees were encouraged to focus first on long-term customer satisfaction and improved quality. Moreover, they were encouraged to develop alternative process paths to achieving the same end result. Many participants were suspicious that more traditional production metrics would eventually be applied to evaluate the project. Later in the project, when political pressures changed to apply traditional productivity measures, the experimental program appeared to be falling behind. A customer service metric and total cycle-time reduction focus was replaced by a focus on more traditional short-term cost metrics. The project participants had become so enamored of the new approach they redoubled their energies in the hope of surpassing goals based on legacy objectives. However, because the metrics were cumulative for the year, and because there had been a 2 month learning curve, there was never an opportunity to catch up. The project was scaled back dramatically and project staff was all the more disillusioned.

View of People's Capacity to Change. Public sector organizations in the U.S. often find it necessary not only to define overall objectives, but also to define methods for achieving results down to the lowest levels. Each important process is defined, often in minute detail. The purpose of the measurement system is to check for any deviations and correct them quickly. In smaller organizations with a mandate for dramatic change, process details are defined and developed at the business unit level in order to meet customer needs. Therefore, they can change as needed and harness creative input from front-line staff. The workers are self-motivated to ensure that the department level metrics they adopt are effective at achieving their high-level objectives. In U.S. public sector organizations, an external work group often defines the specific processes and metrics. Audits are often required in such systems because workers deviate from the top-down driven process and metrics. They often have other conflicting objectives and process requirements (with accompanying metrics). Input into the metric selection process is often absent because the selection is typically by expert panels. At times, because a new class of internal experts emerges, cynicism among frontline workers is the outcome. In large organizations, little effort is made to provide frontline workers the tools they need to refine the processes or ways of measuring them. By contrast private sector organizations with a mandate for change define targets for high-level metrics and leave it to the supporting functions to define how they will achieve the targets.

Developing the Business Case for Reform, Change and Transformation and Current Process Analysis. The authors' experience working with public sector agencies shows that reengineering projects, for example, typically begin with a lengthy period of data exploration. The first project phase often documents every twist and turn of process flows using input-output models. Sometimes the exploration takes up to a year to build a thorough process flow model. What typically emerges is a confusing morass of data that is bulky and requires an in-house operations expert to make sense of it. Many in-house staff will be assigned to the project and it will take on a political tone as agency personnel attempt to build alliances required to maintain both forward project momentum and individual career progression. As a result, building a concrete and logical business case for change becomes indistinguishable from the career interests of the in-house people who lead the project. For example, at one public sector agency, building the case for change took over 2 years. Ten consultants and 10 operations experts worked to define the processes and compare them to best practices in the private sector.

By contrast in some private sector organizations, developing the case for change and high-level current process analysis takes less than 3 months. Executives are disinterested in learning about the details of all related process flows. They already know that there is a need for change, a fact that may be reflected in decreased market share, lagging profits, or voter complaints. Unlike the situation for some public sector agency executives, the case for change is embedded in the nature of competition—change or die. Executives do not often need to convince stockholders, employees or local constituencies of the wisdom of change. Boards of directors will replace them if they do not. For example, in one company in the transportation industry, the desire to consolidate independent processes and functions led to a desire to look at changing the culture to one of teamwork and information sharing. A sudden change in market conditions soon afterwards led to the absolute necessity for change. Even employees who had been initially lukewarm toward reengineering soon saw it as the only avenue for survival of the business. Vice-presidents who rarely talked to each other began to hold meetings to ensure cross-functional integration of information flow. Employees who rarely ventured into each other's departments—much less provided mutual support—began to hold cross-functional team building events and selected shared leadership of quick hit teams.

Table 13.1 provides a summary and expanded list of a comparison of change issues in private and public sector organizations. While not all inclusive, the list does show that other issues (i.e., use of consultants, improvement tools at the point of change, and benchmarking) can also be used when contrasting public and private sector organizations.

Table 13.1.   A Comparison of Change Issues in Private and Public Sector Organizations

Issue/Area	Private	Public Sector Organizations
Strategic planning	• Focus on market share and speed of response • Imperative to survival, gaining market share • Project activities are bounded as platforms for whole strategy • Projects have clear scope at the outset	• Is a new experience • Executives seek input from outside consultants • Projects often have broad scope at first and can wander
Top level metrics	• Only what is needed for review and update	• Old processes are refined, specifics are measured further, and enforcement increases
Metric focus/ philosophy	• If the measure no longer has meaning, bypass and move on, do not linger	• Measurement Gnostics and aficionados wedded to their metric for their slice of the earth
Process Analysis	• Brief instructive study focuses on high level and issues that interfere with profit	• Overdependence on IDEF models are only good for instructional purposes

(Table continues on next page)

Table 13.1.   (Continued)

Issue/Area	Private	Public Sector Organizations
Role of second tier executives	• Given wide berth to make change; as long as results happen • Frontline workers can see benefits to change and risk if not	• Typically must seek approval to prevent upsetting a constituency
View of people's adaptive capacity	• People will change if it makes sense; give them the tools and the incentive	• People will resist; so make them change by measuring them
Involving the whole system	• If it makes sense, do it as soon as possible; history does not matter, profit does • Even unions must work together and see they have an interest in the profit outcome • People on the front lines are given the opportunity, the tools, and the expectation that they will contribute to the change	• Unions not typically interested up front and management not interested in involving them • Politicking to make it happen • Getting agreement from above first before making a move • People carry out the process directives and rarely have input into changing the process itself
Performance measurement	• If the measurement does not matter, throw it out • Letting the executive decision makers drive what will be done	• Constituencies have built up around a measurement • Letting the numbers drive decision making
Improvement tools at point of change	• Use of 7 Process tools by frontline operations people • Even unions must work together and see they have an interest in the profit outcome • People on the frontline are given the opportunity, the tools, and the expectation that they will contribute to the change	• Familiarity with quality tools at supervisor and manager levels • Quality history focus on incremental changes • Tracking a process until it is infinitesimally minute and refined • Building up a data base for narrow band of results and control of it by management • Removed specialists to develop the process flow tools and measures and control the changes made

(Table continues on next page)

Table 13.1.   (Continued)

Issue/Area	Private	Public Sector Organizations
Use of consultants	• Business advisors	• Contractors
Benchmarking	• Is actively used as a tool for strategic advantage • Provides ideas for competitive metrics	• Is used less frequently because executives feel comparisons are hard to draw

THE KEYS TO SUCCESS: LESSONS IN EFFECTIVE REFORM, CHANGE AND TRANSFORMATION

Radical change is very unusual in government organizations. Incremental change is much more common. Fortunately, there is growing awareness that positive change is simply necessary if government is to function effectively in the years to come. This awareness is more widespread at the upper levels than at the lower levels of the organization. One method of engaging the rank and file is to help employees "cope" with the change projects that are mandated by the executive level. "You have to do it, so here is how you can make it work for you" is one way to engage the interest of operational level employees. A better way would be to involve the employees in the design of the change projects at the very beginning, but this is rather unusual in public sector organizations. Typically, the driving forces for change originate in the public political arena, and often the nature of the "problem" as well as its solution are decided upon by parties outside of the organization. This can create feelings of dis-empowerment on the part of the rank and file employees.

Within the public sector, an important issue to bear in mind is the opportunities and challenges presented by the political nature of government, both the passion and the defensiveness that this generates. The opportunities include helping public service employees feel more connection to the value of their work and more control over the outcomes that they are able to produce. The challenges include a deep skepticism on the part of employees regarding both change as well as the commitment political leaders sincerely feel about effectively implementing it.

Nevertheless, there is growing awareness at all levels of public sector organizations that change is necessary if government is to meet the challenges of the future. Change in the public sector is both a frustrating as well as a highly rewarding enterprise. It is primarily an enterprise that is about strengthening a spirit of public service. As former California Governor Pete

Wilson (1991) said "We will not passively experience change. We will make change. But to shape our future, we need a new vision of government."

The greatest challenge public sector organizations will face in the years to come is to achieve their mission and do so while adapting swiftly to change. Flexibility will be needed in a number of areas, from the expansion of service delivery channels, to changes in internal working practices based on technological developments, to partnerships with private-sector organizations. Changing *how* public sector organizations are run will be as, if not more, important than *what* they do. In some instances, new business models may be more necessary in public sector organizations than the addition of new services.

So, what should the reader take away from this chapter on implementing public sector change? The list of "lessons" that follows provides a brief review of best practices from both private and public sector firms that can be adapted to public service applications. The list is illustrative rather than exhaustive, but we hope it offers some limited practical advice to those responsible for planning, implementing and evaluating change efforts to improve public service organizations.

Lesson 1—Focus on a Few Metrics for the Reform, Change or Transformation: Many U.S. public service organizations have a rich history and catalogue of metrics. However, when trying to introduce change, it is far better to follow the private industry example and have leaders focus managers on a few well-chosen metrics. That way the organization begins to develop a common language, focus, and purpose.

Lesson 2—Have a Real Reform, Change or Transformation Strategy: Over the last decade or so a number of public sector organizations began major reengineering projects without having gone through the strategic planning process. Some had only cursory plans that were drawn up by the senior administrator within a week, while some others had not even identified their core business. While a few industries may grow regardless of their planning mechanisms, effective change can only take place when there is a unified and agreed upon business plan for the future. A thorough evaluation of future customer and market demands, evaluation of weaknesses and threats, and selection of the right business objectives, mechanisms, and measurement systems are critical to creating distinctive "market" advantage.

Lesson 3—Simple Ad-Hoc Reform, Change or Transformation Methods Often Work Best: Because U.S. public sector organizations have a history of being closely scrutinized, they often create burdensome processes during change efforts. They spend a great deal of time developing and defining how a process must be performed down to its most minutet detail, expect no deviations, and develop new policies and auditing systems to cope with variations. Private sector organizations set targets for its leaders and managers, provide high-level metrics, and give them the tools to be able to create and improvise. Public sector organizations would do well to give their executives, managers, and frontline personnel the discretion, the tools, and the rewards needed to improvise quickly.

Lesson 4—Organizational Learning must Become Second Nature: Many public service organizations pull experienced operations people to lengthy "details." While working on a change project these people develop a core skill set specific to the project. Oftentimes however the project does not take the time to provide thorough training for the frontline staff in the field who must actually implement a new process change. After the project, the detail-staff often stay on because it has been institutionalized. Private industry on the other hand relies on and rewards its field staff. It involves them in the training, development of the new changes, and ownership of the program once the project is on line. U.S. public sector organizations could adopt the model of training and keeping their best people on the front lines rather than "on detail."

Lesson 5—Involve a Lateral Slice of Agency / Organization Stakeholders in the Reform, Change or Transformation Planning: Both public sector and private sector organizations frequently forget to include frontline staff in planning during a major change. They often rely on consultants or internal experts to design the change and then seek executive approval. A more foolproof design is to involve as many representative people as the new process will affect, and get their buy-in by involving them in some aspect of the development of the new process. This ensures that the new process will have greater acceptance because the factors that could potentially undermine the process are discovered beforehand. Seeking out the involvement and trust of people throughout the organization can be potent mechanisms for overcoming resistance and communicating with employees as suggested in lesson nine.

Lesson 6—People Matter—Before, During and After Reform, Change or Transformation: Related to lesson five is the concept that putting people first makes for success. For many public sector organizations, people historically were seen as obstacles to change rather than avenues to success. For example, rather than focusing on downsizing, such agencies might consider following America's best manufacturers by focusing on communication, training, financial rewards, and empowering teams.

Lesson 7—Change Speed and Control Mechanisms: Related to lesson three, large public sector organizations are often more concerned about controlling reform, change or transformation than the speed of these efforts. Private sector organizations have learned that mistakes come with rapid change. However disorderly it may seem, public sector organizations can speed up the total delivery of change if they are less concerned about missteps than making innovation and rewarding people for progress toward strategic goals.

Lesson 8—Knowledge Management: Do not create a new sub-organization of Gnostics or acolytes, spread the knowledge. All too often, efforts to improve organizations spawn "high priests," gurus of the new order who inadvertently revert to a hierarchical structure based on information rather than position. These Gnostics, as keepers of special knowledge, begin to act in many of the same ways as the pre-change management hierarchy— recreating the conditions the change effort was designed to prevent. Public sector organizations should consider developing rewards / incentives that institutionalize broad sharing of new knowledge instead.

Lesson 9—Communicate, Communicate and Communicate: Build a network of people who take a stand for a better organization. Widely disseminating information on the ultimate goals and objectives of any change effort is more likely to surface champions of the change than limiting information flow. Real change must be felt at all levels of the organization. The lowest paid employee in the organization may offer a suggestion that dramatically improves organizational performance. Ongoing communication and full disclosure by those responsible for reform, change and transformation in public sector organizations can be potent mechanisms for overcoming resistance and giving employees a personal stake in the outcome of the organizational transformation.

Lesson 10—Unpredictability. There is no lesson 10, despite a long history of enumeration that insists the numbers 3, 7, and 10 are the only potential quantities of axioms, theories, factors or lessons. However, it is clear from our experiences that the unexpected always has a way of emerging in organizational interventions. It appears that there is a lesson to be learned from unpredictability after all.

CONCLUSION

A continuous emphasis on and attention to reform, change and transformation is central to the success of today's and tomorrow's local, state, and federal public sector organizations. In short, like their private sector counterparts, public sector organizations must aggressively pursue change or reform and transformation efforts. This means, for example, that effective government requires a first-rate workforce. Civil servants must be able to identify the opportunities and risks associated with both old and new challenges and develop the necessary change or responsive solutions that enhance their public sector entities' efficiency and effectiveness. Public sector organizations also need individuals who understand the concepts of partnership and stewardship, who are committed to transformation for the greater good, who strive for continuous improvement, and who are able to show others the way forward. Stewardship means building on past accomplishments and leaving things not just better off but better positioned for the future. With a focus on reform, change and transformation public sector organizations at the forefront, employees at all levels will be better able to design, implement and evaluate much-needed change efforts.

Effective stewardship of reform, change and transformation initiatives in the public sector requires at a minimum an understanding of the forces that drive change in the public sector to include those responsible for the change efforts having requisite skills in analyzing internal capacity and external constraints. And, as referenced in this chapter, public-sector organizations in the U.S. historically have (and continue to be) known for their hierarchical structure and bureaucratic modes of operation. In such centralized, top-down bureaucracies initiatives are threatening to employees who must implement and attempt to institutionalize change but are frequently overlooked by top management. Despite the reality of the structural and other differences one finds in comparing public and private sector organizations those who work in local, state, county and federal entities will need to use whatever best practices exist, be they from the private or public sector, if they are going to successfully reform, change and transform

REFERENCES

Becker, J., Algermissen, L., & Niehaves, B. (2004). Organizational engineering in public administrations. In H. M. Haddad (Ed.), *Proceedings of the 2004 ACM Symposium on Applied Computing* (pp. 1385–1389). New York, NY: ACM Press.

Bloomfield, A. (2013, March 12). Bill Gates says government should be run more like a business: Why that's a bad idea. http://mic.com/articles/29749/bill-gates-says-government-should-be-run-more-like-a-business-why-that-s-a-bad-idea

Halachmi, A. (1995). Re-engineering and public management: Some issues and considerations. *International Review of Administrative Sciences, 61*(3), 329–341.

Halachmi, A., & Bovaird, T. (1997). Process reengineering in the public sector: Learning some private sector lessons. *Technovation. 17*(5), 227–235.

Harvey, J.T. (2012). Why government should not be run like a business. *Forbes.* Retrieved from http://www.forbes.com/sites/johntharvey/2012/10/05/government-vs-business/

Johnson, G., & Scholes, K. (2001). *Exploring corporate strategy.* Upper Saddle, NJ: Prentice-Hall.

Jurisch, M. C., Ikas, C., Wolf, P., & Krcmar, H. (2013). Key differences of private and public sector business process change. *e-Service Journal, 9*(1), 3–27.

Kaplan, R. S., & Norton, D. P. (1996). *The balanced scorecard: Translating strategy into action.* Boston, MA: Harvard Business School Press.

Llewellyn, S., & Tappin, E. (2003). Strategy in the public sector: Management in the wilderness. *Journal of Management Studies, 40*(4), 955–981.

Mea, W., Sims, R., & Veres, J. (2000). Efforts in organization transformation: Getting your money's worth. *International Review of Administrative Sciences, 66,* 479–493.

Miles, J. (2014). Government vs. private-sector procurement: An unfair comparison. Retrieved from http://www.govtech.com/state/Government-vs-Private-Sector-Procurement-An-Unfair-Comparison.html

Rampell, C. (2015, May 11). What it would really take to run the government like a business. *Washington Post.* Retrieved from https://www.washingtonpost.com/opinions/not-all-spending-is-created-equal/2015/05/11/db47bc96-f7fb-11e4-9030-b4732caefe81_story.html

Scholl, H. J. (2004). Current practices in e-government-induced business process change (BPC). *Proceedings of the 2004 annual national conference on digital government research* (p. 10). Digital Government Society of North America.

Sharafi, A., Jurisch, M. C., Ikas, C., Wolf, P., & Krcmar, H. (2011). Bundling processes between private and public organizations: A qualitative study. *Information Resources Management Journal (IRMJ), 24*(2), 28–45.

Sims, R. R. (2010). *Change (transformation) in government organizations.* Charlotte, NC: Information Age Publishing.

Stewart, J., & Walsh, K. (1992). Change in the management of public services. *Public Administration, 70*(4), 499–518.

Wilson, P. (1991). Inaugural address: "A path to prevention: Expanding horizons, changing young lives." Retrieved from http://governors.library.ca.gov/addresses/36-Wilson01.htm

CHAPTER 14

LEADERSHIP

The Common Thread in Successful
Government Transformation

Barry Hoy

Even the most casual review of the pages between the covers of this book will reveal that government transformation manifests itself in many ways. In every instance, the transformation involves some form of change to, addition to, or deletion from the status quo. The text is replete with examples in wide variety. Some forms of transformation find their origin in concepts such as changes to organizational structure. Others involve quasi-tangible things, an exemplar of which would be new software tools or a website as was the case in the advent of the Affordable Care Act. Still others rely on revisions to an organization's operational or strategic approach. Researchers suggest the focus for transformation. They develop a plan by which the critical elements of the transformation will be achieved. They provide guidance on the critical path. They review successes and challenges.

One commonality in every aspect of organizational transformation is the human component. That means that without regard to the nature of the transformation, the behavior of the humans who inhabit the system must support the transformation. The reaction of the people who are involved

Transforming Government Organizations:
Fresh Ideas and Examples From the Field, pp. 375–404
Copyright © 2016 by Information Age Publishing
All rights of reproduction in any form reserved.

with or who are impacted by the transformation must be understood and mitigated. It also means that every transformation initiative must possess a component which targets the human behavior aspect. This chapter will address the application of systems theory in understanding the process of transformation and specifically the human component of the transformation. It will then explore the manner in which good *leadership* as separate from good *management* is particularly, and perhaps even singularly essential, in bringing about the transformations of which we speak. The chapter proceeds from the premise that a goal of leadership is to set the stage for transformation initiative completion with minimal investment of management effort.

A Note on Semantics

The present text addresses government transformation. This *transformation* will be variously referred to as *transformation, change*, or *transition*. Where one of the terms is used to identify a concept other than government transformation, the distinction will be contextually clear. Similarly, the term *organization* even when used alone, can normally be assumed to be referring to a government organization and likely a government organization which is undergoing transformation. Those persons who are tasked with implementing a transformation initiative are given the name "manager" or "leader," however in the context of this chapter, which addresses management and leadership, it should not be assumed that the use of the word leader automatically implies the application of the skills of leadership exclusively nor that the individual who in our discussion is referred to as a manager is employing only the management skill set.

Systems Theory

In the beginning, there was *systems theory*. This concept was originally described by Ludvig von Bertalanffy in 1950. We are informed by this scholar and reminded by others that system performance is influenced by (a) the internal behavior of entities within each component of the system and (b) the nature of the interaction between and among the components of the system (Pouvreau & Drack, 2007). Hence, to change system performance, either the internal behavior, or the nature of the interactions must change (Lemak, Henderson, & Wenger, 2004). The noted scholar of systems theory, Talcott Parsons, demonstrated the usefulness of systems theory in understanding transformation in organizations (Strauss, 2002). This includes sociopolitical systems (Deutsch, 1985).

Resistance to Change, Opposition to the Transformation Initiative and Friction

The bulk of the discussion engaged in this chapter will address resistance to change or opposition to the transformation initiative. While the importance of the *source* of the resistance will become obvious once the discussion turns to the application of leadership, at this point the *source* of the resistance may be less significant than the *impact* of the resistance upon system performance and hence upon system transformation. Since human systems are somewhat complex, it might be useful to consider a more comprehensible model. That model is available to us in the form of a mechanical system such as a machine.

Mechanical or physical systems bear some important similarities to human systems. This fact contributes to the usefulness of mechanical systems as a tool to understand human systems. Primarily, we are attempting to build good comprehension of the impact of human resistance to the change initiative. The mechanical system parallel to human resistance is the friction between the running parts. The impact of friction is to slow operation of the mechanical system or to require more force (effort). Hence, when parameters within the mechanical system are manipulated to cause a change, the effect of the friction is to attenuate the change. In order to restore the mechanical system back to proper operation, additional mechanical force must be invested.

Let's explore an example, imagine a mechanical system that involves turning a shaft at 1,000 revolutions per minute. Engineers may calculate that it will require 700 watts (roughly one horse power) to cause rotation at that speed. They may further calculate that friction resists shaft rotation such that the system requires an additional 300 watts. Hence the power required to turn the shaft at 1,000 RPMs is not 700 watts, it is 1,000 watts. Taking the friction model to its extreme, when mechanical systems present too much friction, they either stop or even fail catastrophically. Finally, applying the friction model, we acknowledge that there are two ways to counteract the effects of the friction and restore a mechanical system to proper operation. The first option, previously mentioned, is to simply expend additional energy in a way that overcomes the friction. Recall that our imaginary 700 watt system requires 1,000 watts of power, because the 300 watts which is dissipated in the friction adds to the 700 watts required to turn the shaft. The second way to counteract the effects of friction is to reduce its impact by improving the interaction of mechanical parts through lubrication or smoothing of running surfaces, thereby reducing the friction. So if engineers are able to reduce the friction in such a way that only 100 watts of power is required to overcome its effects, the system which once required 1,000 watts will now operate at full speed with the investment of only 800 watts (700 watts to turn the shaft and 100 watts dissipated in the friction). It is easy to see why the quest for mechanical system efficiency seeks *friction reduction* as opposed to *investment of more power*.

While this chapter is not intended to be a lesson in physics, this mechanical example is far too enticing to ignore. The mechanical model is analogous to human or social systems where the counterpart of mechanical friction is human resistance to change. Management effort is applied to move the transformation initiative forward. When there is opposition to the initiative (resistance to change), additional management effort must be invested. The mechanical parallel to this additional management effort is the 300 additional watts of physical effort.

Two Areas in Which Effort Must Be Expended

Isaac Newton (third law of motion) would tell us that effort is expended against an opposing force. This is true not only in physical or mechanical systems but also true of management effort in human systems. Organizations undergoing transformation present two resistive forces to which effort is applied. Primarily, and inescapably, all managers who embark upon a transformation initiative are well aware of the effort that is associated with each of the tasks that comprise the initiative. That effort is quantifiable and is very likely reflected in the implementation plan. For this discussion, the opposing or resisting force shall be referred to as *process induced resistance* (PIR). We shall refer to the effort which is applied against PIR as *anticipated management effort* (AME). As an example, in an imaginary transformation initiative involving installation of new equipment, management effort must be applied to the tasks involving choosing, acquiring, installing and testing the equipment and to training persons to use the equipment. For clarity, it must be understood that the effort, referred to is not the effort in choosing, acquiring, and so forth. It is the effort that managers expend to manage those tasks. Every operational task associated with the transformation initiative requires the expenditure of time but here we are speaking only of the management time. At the beginning of a well-planned project, the effort required is relatively easy to quantify. Examine the outline of an IT installation process in Table 14.1. In this example, effort is quantified in time and measured in hours. Obviously, there are other measurement systems but that model will suffice for this simple example. The total management hours required for the project is the sum of the hours applied to each of the six phases (530 management hours). The actual activities the manager will engage during these hours are covered later. But for now, assume that if this transformation project proceeds optimally with no unexpected delays, the management team which is in charge of the initiative will spend 530

Table 14.1. Notional Outline of an Imaginary IT Implementation involving Equipment Installation

Phase	Title	Primary Task	Management Hours
1	Strategic Development	Select equipment and contractor	50
2	Acquisition	Select vendor, purchase equipment	30
3	Staging	Receive and store equipment	200
4	Installation	Install equipment	50
5	Testing	Test installation	100
6	Training	Train all effected personnel	100

hours. It is because this time is anticipated and hence included in the plan, that it is called, *anticipated management effort* (AME). This AME is known before the project starts and the AME is relatively fixed. Little can be done to reduce it and little will happen short of catastrophe that will substantially extend it.

The second area in which management effort must be expended involves that effort which must be applied to overcome *member induced resistance* (MIR) to the transformation. While MIR will be more comprehensively explored later in the chapter, for now it can be generally quantified as the various things that the members of the organization do, or fail to do, that slows the project or requires additional management effort to overcome. MIR always adds to the effort required to complete the transformation initiative because it requires the investment of *unanticipated management effort* (UME) to overcome. Since the MIR to the initiative is difficult to predict, the effort to overcome it is similarly difficult to plan. For this reason, this effort cannot be anticipated, which is why it is termed, *unanticipated management effort*.

Just as this chapter is not intended to be a dissertation in mechanical physics, it is neither a lesson in mathematics. The reader's indulgence is requested as the author takes a temporary, but very necessary, excursion to the realm of sums and remainders. Thankfully, the excursion is not embarked to teach math, only to prompt the reader to recall what is already known. The time model and therefore the effort model for the example project is expressed as an arithmetic problem involving sums. In essence, it states that the total effort that managers will expend (*total management effort or* TME) to complete the project is the sum of *anticipated management effort* (AME) plus *unanticipated management effort* (UME).

So:

$$AME + UME = TME$$

That wasn't so bad, right?

As previously stated, the AME is relatively fixed. It can be viewed as a constant in our algorithm, since nothing that the manager does apart from consistently and conscientiously applied management has much effect on it. On the other hand, the UME is difficult to quantify. At the beginning of the initiative, it is hard to know how much MIR should be expected and hence how much UME will need to be expended. It should also be noted that since UME is difficult to quantify, it is wise to avoid underestimating the percentage of the TME that the UME will contribute. We may deduce from these observations that a primary goal of organizational transformation initiative leaders is to understand and minimize the MIR such that UME is similarly reduced.

Quantifying the Member Induced Resistance

To the extent that managers need to have a good up-front understanding of UME, the MIR must be understood. Member induced resistance (MIR) is the antecedent to unanticipated management effort (UME). Since the member induced resistance is manifested in human behavior, in order to predict the member induced resistance, the manager must be able to predict future human behavior. He or she must be able to predict the various ways in which the members of the organization will resist the initiative. The best way to predict future behavior is to examine past behavior. In this way, it is possible to have at least a general idea of the cause and magnitude of the MIR.

It is important for managers to have a good idea of the source and magnitude of the member induced resistance. There are two reasons for this. In the first place, nearly every manifestation of MIR will require some UME. In the second place, a good understanding of the source of the member induced resistance will inform the manager as to the appropriate management and leadership techniques that will be most helpful. The effect of MIR is to impede the change in the human system in question. These impediments reveal themselves in two functional categories. The first functional category includes those impediments which the member engages *consciously*. The complimentary category includes impediments that are *subconscious*.

THREE TYPES OF CONSCIOUS IMPEDIMENTS TO CHANGE IN THE HUMAN SYSTEM

The reader is encouraged to recall that the human system parallel to mechanical friction is resistance to change. According to Kotter and Schlesinger (1979), the primary progenitors of the resistance to change in social systems exist in the humans who inhabit the system under consideration. That is to say that resistance to change in a social system starts in the minds and is manifested in the behavior of the persons who are members of the system. This may sound somewhat dogmatic, but just for a moment allow us to proceed on the premise that we are breaking new ground. The aforementioned researchers conclude that three aspects of human reaction to change impede transformation. These human reactions are found in impediment types as follows:

   a.   Parties to the system who react in a manner that is predicated on their belief that there are *shortcomings in the implementation of the transformation*. They believe the process that has been selected to achieve change will not produce the desired change. They may see change as necessary but believe the chosen method will not produce it.

   b.   Parties to the system who react in a manner that is predicated on their belief that there is *doubt that the desired outcomes will be forthcoming*. They may think that things are fine, that the system is performing adequately as it is. Hence, they believe that change is unnecessary.

   c.   Parties to the system who react in a manner that is predicated on their belief that the process of change will *require more investment of resources and effort than should be economically applied* given the value of the anticipated result.

Managers, in their effort to affect change in a human system, must expend energy in moving the system forward in the transformation process. Here we are speaking of the things a manager does which are strictly within the management skill domain. Consulting Table 14.1 may inform the reader regarding this effort investment. For clarity, a review of the management skill set (Greenwood & Hoy, 2015) is useful. These skills have been compiled and proposed as the "Big Ten of Management." An exhaustive review of scholarly and practical sources has produced this list which represents a substantially complete inventory of management skills. Those managers who possess the skills and who apply them consistently may be said to be skillful managers. The skills include:

1. Comprehension of strategy
2. Comprehension of financial issues
3. Comprehension of social and public policy issues
4. Assignment and stewardship of resources including time
5. Ability to communicate
6. Ability to collaborate
7. Self confidence
8. Ability to think critically
9. Ability to conceptualize programs
10. Conducting effective meetings

There can be no doubt that a manager who employs these skills will be more successful than one who does not. A cursory review of the Management Big Ten permits us to clearly imagine the activities of the manager as he or she goes about the workday. The manager is holding meetings, assigning resources, thinking about the process and activities, communicating to persons in the system and so forth. Impediments to the transformation described in the three human reactions compel managers to expend additional effort. Moreover, this additional effort must be expended as long as the impediment exists. The situation comes to life in the following vignette: Sally is a manager in a government organization which is embarked on a transformation project that implements a technology solution to data management in the organization. Her assistant, Rudi, comes to her with a situation report.

Rudi: "We are moving forward but the going is slow."
Sally: "Oh, how so?"
Rudi: "Well Jane, our IT Department Head, thinks we have selected the wrong software."
Sally: "We have been through this, and we know that the software we chose is the right platform given all of the considerations. Why don't you explain the rationale to Jane."
Rudi: "I did that at the beginning of the project but I guess I'll do it again." Rudi continues, "Anyway, Bill, in Client Relations, questions the wisdom of the entire project. He thinks that the present system is working and doesn't want to disrupt operations to make the change."
Sally: "But the entire initiative to implement this new technology was predicated upon client complaints! Doesn't Bill know that?!"
Rudi: "Maybe I should show him the data. Maybe that will convince him."

Sally: "Go ahead and talk to him. Anything else?"

Rudi: "Yes Mark, over in Accounting thinks the improvement in client satisfaction is hard to measure accurately and considering the expense of the new software he is not sure how to prove to the 'bean counters' that the project makes sense."

Sally: "Sounds like we need to come up with a way to accurately measure client satisfaction."

Rudi: "Right, but that is not Mark's expertise. Maybe someone in his department can build a Client Satisfaction Survey or something."

Sally: "Good idea. Figure out who should do it and let's set up a meeting."

It should be relatively obvious that the impediment types illustrated by the reactions of Jane, Bill, and Mark are: a, b, and c, respectively. It should also be obvious that to address the impediments, many of the members of the system will be required to do more work (expend more management effort) to counteract the effect of the impediments. Sally has to do more critical thinking (8) more communication (5), and hold more meetings (10). Rudi has done and will need to do more collaborating (6) and communicating (5) and so forth. The numbers in parentheses refer to the number on the Management Big Ten list. All of these efforts are included in the Management Big Ten. That means they are all included in management effort and all are in response to MIR. Thus, they may be referred to as UME. The parties to this system will be expending more energy to bring the transformation process up to speed just as a truck with a heavy load requires more fuel to move at the same rate as an empty one. Thus, we are enlightened as to the impact of resistance to change in a human system. We are also beginning to seek a more progressive approach which employs leadership (as a way to reduce the resistance) rather than management (as a way to overcome it).

The previous example explored the first of two ways to react to the friction. Recall that the physical friction present in a mechanical system is functionally paralleled by resistance to change in a human system. Sally and Rudi were reacting to mechanical friction's approximate human counterpart, resistance to change. By now, the reader should be comfortable referring to that resistance as MIR. Their reaction in the example was to overcome the resistance which will certainly require the investment of additional UME. We shall see after close examination and comparison of the management skill set to the leadership skill set that management skills may be employed to overcome the resistance, while leadership skills may be more useful at reducing or eliminating the resistance. To repeat, the action of management is to expend additional effort to overcome resistance. The effect of leadership is to reduce resistance in the first place.

Two Categories of Subconscious Impediments to Change in the Human System

Resistance to change may be generated instinctively. Some persons in an organization will resist change subconsciously because their instinct tells them that change is bad. This means that the resistance to change is not connected with a viable rationale. In fact they may not even be consciously aware that they are resisting the change (Reardon, Reardon, & Rowe, 1998). In other cases members of the system may take the change as a personal affront. They may associate themselves with the status quo. They may see the change initiative as an attack on the status quo and, by extension, on them personally. Consequently, they internalize their reaction to the change. To ease the task of comparison of the two different categories, the first type of resistance is hereinafter referred to as *intrinsic resistance* while the second is referred to as *internalized resistance*. While both styles of resistance present challenges to the leader, internalized resistance may be more difficult to eradicate than intrinsic resistance (Reardon et al., 1998).

These two resistance types possess one commonality. That commonality lays in the fact that the two subconscious impediment types have no reasoned approach as a progenitor of the opposition to change. While organizational parties who may be placed in Kotter and Schlesinger's (1979) three categories of conscious resistance base their opposition upon their perceived cognition of the transformation initiative, adherents of Reardon's two categories do not employ similar logic. Indeed, they may apply no logic at all. Consequently, while we may confront Kotter and Schlesinger's opposers with a logical argument, in Reardon's groups there is no logical argument to attack. Their response would be, "Don't confuse me with the facts. My mind is made up."

What is the Difference Between "Conscious" and "Subconscious" Resistance?

In the previous paragraphs, the concepts of conscious and subconscious resistance were introduced. The distinction between the two may seem obscure; nonetheless, the distinction is present. Predicated upon the premise that the two forms of resistance compel two different leadership approaches, an examination of that distinction is mandatory at this point. *Conscious resistance* springs from a reasoned approach applied by persons who belong to one or more of the three impediment categories described previously. The persons in those categories have, at least to a minimal extent, examined their perception of the facts surrounding the transformation initiative. They have used their ideation of those facts to form a belief system which opposes or resists the change. *Subconscious resistance* employs a less reasoned approach. Persons who exhibit subconscious resistance do so, not because of a careful examination of facts, but because of an innate instinctive hostility toward the change simply because it is change. The innate hostility is internalized in the individual as a rationale for the opposition to change.

The distinction may seem unimportant. Consider, though, that our leadership style will be chosen based upon its appropriateness to appease the rationale for the resistance. The source and nature of that resistance must be ascertained and understood to inform our choice of leadership style. The source of the resistance is a determinant of the style to be used. In the case of conscious resistance, the leader can apply a reasoned approach to attack a reasoned resistance. If the resistance is truly based, in the individual's mind, upon an understanding of the facts, then all that is required of the leader is to ensure that the facts are clearly and accurately presented to the individual. Thus provided with the truth the individual will "see the light," modify their behavior and cease resisting the transformation.

In the case of the individual who subconsciously opposes the change, the challenge for the leader becomes a bit more arduous, the solution more elusive. Since the individual is not employing a rationale for opposing the transformation initiative, the option to attack that rationale is absent. The recalcitrant members are not basing their opposition on facts so providing them with the facts is not the solution. These are the people who resolutely declare, "If it ain't broke, don't fix it" or "We have always done it that way."

Back to Systems Theory

When considering transformation in social systems, Forrester (1971) refers to human or social systems as "multi-loop nonlinear feedback systems" (p. 1). He demonstrated that the effect of transformation is often delayed in comparison with the effects in physical systems. He also showed that in some cases comprehension of the system including the predictability of the outcomes of changes in the system is a complex undertaking. Forrester's findings support Kotter and Schlesinger (1979) in their proposal of the three categories of resistance to change previously discussed. Parenthetically, Forrester made little distinction between corporate systems and government systems since their operation as a system is largely identical. Those things that work in government system transformation also work in corporate system transformation and vice versa. The effect of these scholarly conclusions is that transformation in a human system is more difficult than transformation in purely mechanical systems. It must also be inferred from the research that the modification in behaviors that oppose the change is more challenging than management's implementation of the transformation.

As has been said, the origin of the resistance to change may be less important than the manifestation of that resistance in behaviors that attenuate the change. However, as has also been stated, the source of the opposition is a determinant of the leadership style to be applied. The origin cannot be completely discounted since there is a linkage between the behaviors and the attitude which generated the behavior. Kurt Lewin (1951) initially described the change process as involving the three stages; "Unfreeze," "Change," "Refreeze." That basic premise has endured as a jumping off point for later researchers. While Elizabeth Kubler-Ross' (1969) work was associated with a field that is relatively unrelated to organizational transition, her elaboration of the grieving process is useful in triangulation of Lewin's theory because of the striking similarity in the progression of the thought process. Her five phases have been repeatedly matched to Lewin's three stages. The comparison is codified in Table 14.2.

Table 14.2.   A Comparison of Lewin's and Kubler-Ross' Theories

Lewin's Three Stages	Kubler-Ross' Five Phases
Unfreeze	Shock and Denial
	Anger and Frustration
Change	Bargaining and Experimentation
	Depression and Decision
Refreeze	Acceptance and Integration

Kubler-Ross' (1969) change curve is included as Figure 14.1. She uses the change curve to depict the progression of the emotional reaction to grieving over time. It should be noted that grieving is an individual's emotional reaction to a traumatic personal event. The primary source of the reaction is the individual's realization that there will be a change in one's life. A grief stricken surviving daughter might declare, "My life will be different now that my father is no longer with me." The parallel declaration when considering transformation in government is, "My life will be different now that I have to master another software system." Change causes stress and stress impacts behavior (Begley, 1998; Kocalevent, Mierke, & Klapp, 2014; Silva & Navarro, 2012;). Note that in the Kubler-Ross curve, the vertical axis relates the emotional reaction to morale and competence.

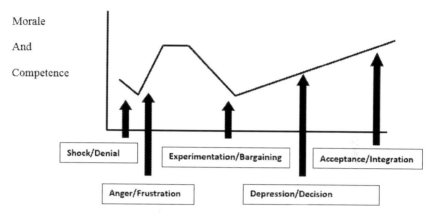

Figure 14.1. Kubler-Ross' change curve depicting the progression of the emotional reaction to grieving over time.

Weick and Quinn (1999) used Lewin's theory to explain the factors which impact the rate of change in organizations under transformation. Behaviors which are indicative of a resistance to change may be slow to manifest themselves. Further, these behaviors may resist efforts that are intended to eradicate the behaviors. Finally behaviors may persist in spite of all efforts at eradication. Luthans (2002) described a linkage in perception of the facts associated with the transformation initiative and the resistive behaviors which slow the process. He described this linkage as a progression from knowledge to action stating that the linkage exhibits three components:

- Informational—The personally held beliefs and interpretation of information about the idea.
- Emotional—The internal feelings be they positive, neutral or negative, about the idea.
- Behavioral—The tendency to behave in a particular way toward the idea.

Finally, Elrod and Tippett (2002) validated Luthans' linkage and demonstrated that the linkage manifested itself in decreased performance of the organization while the transformation process was in its early stages. Given that Kubler-Ross (1969) held that there is a relationship between the phase of the emotional reaction and the morale and competence of the individual, Elrod and Tippett's observations are not surprising. This paragraph began with the word *finally*, but that is not to imply that no further literature was found that substantiated the progression of research embarked upon by Lewin decades ago. The use of the word *finally* is intended to imply that the observations of Elrod and Tippett occur at the point in the scholarly progression at which the case is proven: A behavioral component associated with the organizational transition is predictable, observable, and perhaps to a lesser extent, measurable. Hence, consultation of additional scholars is unnecessary.

By observing the behavior of the members of the organization and matching it against the emotional state on the change curve, the curve can be used to assess the point at which members of the group are with respect to the transformation initiative. Thus informed, the person who is managing the change will be able to adapt his leadership style to match the needs of the members of the group.

Returning to Figure 14.1 it should be noted that resistive behaviors will be observed in the early part of the transition process. Considering Lewin's three stages, resistive behaviors will be observed in the first stage and to a lesser extent in the second stage. A similar decline in resistive behaviors can be predicted in Kubler-Ross' (1969) model, such that by the time the members of the group reach the final phase, "integration and acceptance," negative behaviors have all but disappeared.

Manifestation of Behaviors That Indicate Resistance to, or Acceptance of Change

Ultimately, transformation initiative leaders must be prepared to understand the interworking of two characteristic classes of member behaviors. These behaviors are observable. They are indicative of an individual's acceptance of or resistance to the change. The first class of behaviors may be referred to as negative behaviors. Negative behavior incidence is high in persons who are resistant to the transformation initiative. The spectrum of behaviors which may be observed that indicate that an individual or group in an organization is resisting transformation initiatives is relatively easy to quantify. They may be organized into categories. These categories include:

a. Verbalizations—Criticizing the initiative, sarcastic remarks, plotting against the initiative
b. Inward passive behaviors—Failure to perform as directed, slow performance, partial completion or poor quality completion of tasks
c. Outward active behaviors—Sabotage, continuing to employ the "status quo" process.

The second class of behaviors includes the positive behaviors. Just as there are resistive behaviors as described above, there are also supportive behaviors that are similarly observable and which may be organized using the previous three categories:

a. Verbalizations—Speaking positively, planning outwardly with peers to promote the transformation, contradicting criticism from others
b. Inward passive behaviors—Using the transformation initiative, maintaining workflow in spite of disruption, maintaining quality
c. Outward active behaviors—Assisting others in the process, suggesting and implementing enhancements to the transformation.

The individual member's acceptance of the transformation initiative may be ascertained through observation of the incidence of negative and positive behaviors. As negative behaviors decline and as positive behaviors increase, the member may be assumed to be moving from resistance to acceptance. Consult Figure 14.2 for a graphic representation of this phenomenon. It represents that, as observed incidence of negative behaviors declines and positive behaviors increases, the member or members pass from resistance through neutrality to acceptance. The red line refers to negative behavior occurrence. The green line is conversely a graph of positive behavior occurrence. The arrow at the bottom of the figure indicates that the desired trajectory is from resistance to acceptance.

Transformation initiative managers can get a sense of the state of acceptance by carefully observing the positive and negative behaviors. When negative behaviors outnumber positive behaviors (Point A) the group or member may be said to be resistant to the change. The reverse situation (Point B) is true as well.

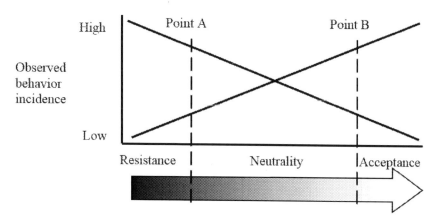

Figure 14.2.   A graphical representation of observed positive and negative behaviors as an indication of acceptance of the transformation initiative.

The fact that a member of the organization may be included in the groups that exhibit negative behaviors mentioned previously does not compel us to conclude that the member cannot be prevailed upon to behave in ways that support the transition. Indeed, the goal of both management and leadership is to mitigate negative behaviors, increase positive behaviors and move the member to the right on the graph in Figure 14.2. This is true without regard to the source of impediment be it *conscious* or *subconscious*. Both categories are reasonably subject to appeals to modify their behavior. To counteract the stated impediments, persons in the system must be convinced to support the transition in spite of the fact that they may be consciously or subconsciously opposing the change. Indeed one of the purposes of the application of leadership skills is to bring members of the organization into harmony with the transition, to prepare the culture of the organization for change.

The previously mentioned scholars give us three concepts as follows:

- Lewin and Kubler Ross assist us in identifying the member's place in the transformation resistance process. They also confirm that there is a positive end to the process in the last phase.
- Luthans and Weick and Quinn postulate that the application of leadership skills in reducing the resistance may be a slow and arduous process.
- Elrod and Tippett confirm that there are observable behaviors which can indicate the appropriate leadership reaction including whether or not a reaction is even needed.

Leadership

In human systems, leadership is a primary component of change (Folta, Seguin, Ackerman, & Nelson, 2012). The human aspect of organizational transformation embodies a modification of behavior. Where the management skill set is used to promote behavior modification through directions, coercion and discipline, leadership skills achieve it through motivation, inspiration, and empathy. Latham (2013a) established the value of employment of solid leadership skills as a precursor to success in organizational transformation. Latham (2013b) measured the effect of nine leadership behaviors which closely mirror the "Leadership Big Ten" discussed later. Leadership skills are applied universally. That is to say that the skills can be applied to the transformation process without regard to the nature of the transformation. Zomorrodian (2009) declares that of the various styles of leadership, "transformational leadership" is particularly appropriate in instances of organizations in change. Specifically he states that the transformational leader's ability to create vision, elicit commitment, empower members of the organization, and instill a culture that is ready for change are particularly important. Other scholars have validated these findings, stating that "Creating a change ready climate within the organization is the leader's job" (Baesu & Bejinaru, 2013, p. 1) and that, "Leaders make use of their power to influence and motivate others" (Reardon et al., 1998, p. 130). The behavior modification that must precede success in government transformation is squarely in the leader's domain.

Examine below a revision of the previous vignette. This is how it could go when managers step out of the management skill set and into the leadership skill set.

Rudi: "We are moving forward and it is going a little better."

Sally: "Oh, how so?"

Rudi: "Well Jane, our IT Department Head, trusts in spite of her original misgivings that the software that was chosen will do what it is supposed to do. She has begun to train her people on its use."

Sally: "That is great! Tell Jane how pleased we are with her support."

Rudi: "I will." Rudi continues, "And Bill, in Client Relations, sees the enthusiasm that everyone has for the project. He is working up some communication to the clients telling them the value they will gain and the problems that will be eliminated."

Sally: "Is he doing this on his own?"

Rudi: "No. He is leading the effort but the graphic arts people are actually making up the fliers."

Sally: "How is Mark doing?"

Rudi: "I was able to make him understand that the strategic significance is far reaching. He knows what to say to the 'bean counters.'"

Sally: "Well, we had planned to bring everyone together for an emergency meeting to get their support. It sounds like that might not be needed, right?"

Rudi: "Correct."

Sally: "So, instead of the meeting, why don't we get some pizza on Friday to show the people our appreciation?"

Where is Leadership?

In their important work on government transformation, Osborne and Plastrik, (2000) refer to the need for vision and a comprehension of grand strategy, two components in leadership. Their "Fieldbook" provides specific recommendations and practical applications. Infusion of leadership in the transformation process is assumed. A recent trend in organizational transformation, prompted by well publicized government missteps, has been the advent of the concept of open data, the concept that information should be available for dissemination without restrictions. This is especially true when the organization under consideration is affiliated with a government entity (Arzberger et al., 2004; Surowiecki, 2004). However, Jannsen, Charalbidis, and Zuiderwijk, (2012) observed that open data alone does not necessarily lead to open government. Thus, where government transformation embodies a movement to open data, there is good reason to suspect that resistance to the transformation will be logically based and hence will defy, at least momentarily, efforts to suppress the resistance on logical grounds.

Can Change be Managed or Must It Be Led?

People resist change. To resist change is to resist a modification of behavior. Scholars are specific in their pronouncements, "Resistance to change inhibits successful organizational transformation" (Appelbaum, Degbe, MacDonald, & Nguyen-Quang, 2015, p. 73). People must be motivated to modify their behavior (Summerfield, 2014). Summerfield (2014) reduced eight definitions of leadership spanning three decades, revealing the following three features:

- Good leaders inspire organizations toward common goal attainment.
- Good leaders influence rather than dictate.
- Good leaders instill a desire for improvement in the organization.

"Leadership acts as an input at multiple levels influencing organizational outcomes both directly—by continuously shaping employee attitude throughout change—and indirectly—by regulating the antecedents and moderators of their predisposition to change" (Appelbaum et al., 2015, p. 135). Another researcher demonstrated the need for sustained and continuous application of good leadership. This sustained leadership helps to overcome the gravitational pull of the status quo (Jackson, 2005). If we accept these commonalities, it is clear that while the logistical and practical considerations of organizational change can be managed, the modification of the sociopolitical component of transformation must be led.

What is Good Leadership? The Leadership Skill Set

During a recent inquiry, scholars (Greenwood & Hoy, 2015) were able to compile a notional inventory of ten specific skills that combine to comprise the substance of leadership. Being a good leader is predicated upon possession and employment in a substantial way of the leadership skill set. In the way of amplification, one commonality in the various definitions of the word *leadership* is the inclusion the word "inspire" or the concept of "inspiring" (Eager-Sirkis, 2011). This triangulates Summerfield (2014) above. Pashke (2004) conjectures that leaders must be good communicators. They must possess self-confidence and self-awareness. Other authors (Jackson, 2011; Pace & Easter, 2005) advise frequent self-analysis. Leaders must be able to conceptualize at a strategic level. They must be critical thinkers. Finally they must be able to identify with others, a second manifestation of empathy. An additional trait in a high quality leader is the ability to create a motivating environment (Hulme, 2006; Kuttner, 2011). Research in Great Britain (Pace & Easter, 2005) revealed that good leaders are humble. A domestic study (Bret, Gulliya, & Crispo, 2012) adds the group of skills contributing to emotional intelligence (EQ). In a tabular format the skills may be expressed as the Leadership Big Ten:

1. Communication skills
2. Self confidence
3. Self awareness
4. Self analysis
5. Strategic thinking
6. Critical thinking
7. Empathy
8. Ability to motivate
9. Humility
10. Emotional intelligence

While the elements of the Leadership Big Ten are referred to as skills, they could just as easily be called traits, or features of mindset. They are not behaviors per se. But their employment leads to behaviors. Moreover, when the skills in the set are applied conscientiously, their application engenders productive leadership behaviors.

It is pointless to encourage managers to promote leadership skills in their organizations without answering the manager's question, "Where do the skills come from?" In a team in which leaderships skills, or any skills, for that matter, are lacking or absent, the decision makers of the team have two options. The skills may be taught to those persons who are already members of the team. Alternately, skills may be acquired through the staffing process by identifying employee candidates who can demonstrate that they possess and employ the skills, hire only those who do and avoid those who don't.

Development of Skills Through the Training Learning Process

Examination of the leadership skill set leads the author to the belief that leadership skills can be taught to those who do not already possess them and enhanced in persons who do. Review of scholarly literature on the topic provides support (Bret et al., 2012; and Kuttner, 2011). The proliferation of leadership training and programs, beginning roughly in the middle of the 20th century, are testament to the idea that leadership skills are academically transferable. It is worthwhile to note that all training is intended to engender a modification of behavior. Thus, while training leadership skills, the ultimate goal is to instill in the learner an appreciation for employment of the skills manifested in enlightened leadership behaviors.

Acquisition of Skills Through the Recruiting and Staffing Process

As an alternative to training or personnel development as a means of acquiring leadership skills, organizations can access these skills by hiring persons who can demonstrate that they possess and employ them competently. Ironically, a review of the Fortune 100 Companies "manager," "director," or "leader" (MDL) job postings provides a stark revelation. In the job listings reviewed, nearly 90 in total (While 100 firms were reviewed, only 90 had MDL positions listed.) very few of the listings included leadership skills as requisite in viable candidates for the position. Of the ninety MDL listings reviewed, less than 10 stated that possession of any of the skills on the Leadership Big Ten should be present in candidates who apply. In those few postings that included Leadership Big Ten skills, the most frequently mentioned were "critical thinking" and "communication skills." A few of the listings did state in the job qualification or job requirement section that the candidate needed "leadership" skills. Given the present discussion, this "leadership" requirement is overly vague. In all cases the applicant was left to define "leadership" for himself or herself.

Not surprisingly, nearly all of the listings named Management Big Ten skills as essential in successful candidates. One may be compelled to conclude that acquisition of leadership skills by these major employers is not part of the hiring process. Departing from Fortune 100 firms, a review of numerous MDL jobs listed on O*NET[1] reveals that the skills and abilities which are requirements as an entering qualification of the candidates for the listed positions are nearly identical. That is to say that the listings bear a striking similarity, one to another. This similarity emanates from the method by which the listings are formatted and presented. Essentially, it is a menu driven process with qualification requirements chosen from a pre-existing list. With only very minor variations, all job listings recommend that the successful candidate must possess and employ (O*Net Online, 2015):

Critical Thinking—Using logic and reasoning to identify the strengths and weaknesses of alternative solutions, conclusions or approaches to problems.

Judgment and Decision Making—Considering the relative costs and benefits of potential actions to choose the most appropriate one.

Reading Comprehension—Understanding written sentences and paragraphs in work related documents.

Speaking—Talking to others to convey information effectively.

Active Learning—Understanding the implications of new information for both current and future problem-solving and decision-making.

Active Listening—Giving full attention to what other people are saying, taking time to understand the points being made, asking questions as appropriate, and not interrupting at inappropriate times.

- Coordination—Adjusting actions in relation to others' actions.
- Management of Personnel Resources—Motivating, developing, and directing people as they work, identifying the best people for the job.
- Time Management—Managing one's own time and the time of others.
- Complex Problem Solving—Identifying complex problems and reviewing related information to develop and evaluate options and implement solutions.

The above position requirements were excerpted from representative examples of job postings on O*NET in February of 2015. Only those positions which were listed as seeking a manager, director, or leader were examined. While there were numerous positions listed, all of them included requirements which were identical to the above inventory. With only minor variation the MDL position requirements in O*NET are literally identical.

It is noteworthy that, of the skills that were included as requirements in a viable candidate in the O*NET listings, *critical thinking* alone is on the Leadership Big Ten. In addition a subset of "Management of Personnel Resources" includes *motivating* which may be practically applied as a leadership skill. Most of the remaining skills are included on the Management Big Ten. It is little surprise that organizations seeking managers would want their candidates to be strong in the Management Big Ten skill set. The listings bear this out. However, it appears that the organizations sampled do not rely upon the staffing function to acquire leaders. They are not seeking leaders, they are seeking managers. The approach of organizations listing their openings on O*NET appears to match the *Fortune Magazine* 100 firms.

One is left to guess the intentions of the directors of these organizations with regard to leadership skills. On one hand, the decision not to include leadership skills in the job listing may reflect the fact that hiring managers believe that persons who are already employed by the organization or who will join as a result of the recruiting process can be assumed to possess good leadership skills. The assumption is that leadership is an important ability which exists in all managers. A simple comparison of the Management Big Ten to the Leadership Big Ten reveals that this should not be assumed. For those organizations in which the hierarchy does not make this assumption, three remaining options present themselves. First of all, it is entirely possible that organization staffers intend to impart leadership skills in their organization by use of the training function. In the second place, the identification of requisite leadership abilities in the successful candidates may occur at a later point in the hiring process, such as during the interview phase. Such intentions would not be detected through a review of the listings as described. Finally, organization leaders may feel that leadership skills are unimportant. This may seem dangerous given the present discussion, however, it must be acknowledged that there are management positions which embody the management of things rather than people. As leadership skills apply only to people, leadership may be less important in such positions.

Leadership Behaviors That Facilitate Success in Government Transformation

There are two points to this chapter. Initially the reader is encouraged to fully understand the part that leadership plays in furthering the interest of a given transformation initiative. Essentially, the goal is to build in the manager who reads this book, a Krathwohlian style, affective domain devotion to the idea that leadership, properly employed, is essential to all transformation initiatives. The second point is to suggest that leadership behaviors may be chosen which are appropriate and effective in a given phase of the transformation process. Indeed the determinant of the choice of behaviors has much less to do with the point in the process and much more to do with where the members of the group are in their acceptance of the initiative. Here for clarity purposes refer to Figure 14.2. To the leader who employs the Leadership Big Ten, the chosen leadership behavior is more likely to be productive when it is tailored to appeal to the people who are part of the transformation and considering where they are in their acceptance.

Scholarly inquiry assists in placing leadership behaviors in their proper context. Higgs and Rowland (2005) identified three distinct groupings of change leadership behaviors. These were:

1. Shaping Behavior: the communication and actions of leaders related directly to the change; "making others accountable"; "thinking about change"; and "using an individual focus."
2. Framing Change: establishing starting points for change; "designing and managing the journey"; and "communicating guiding principles in the organization."
3. Creating Capacity: "creating individual and organizational capabilities"; and "communication and making connections" (Higgs & Rowland, 2005).

Kubler-Ross (1969) and Lewin assisted us in understanding that persons who are involved in a transformation initiative go through a process of acceptance of the initiative. It may be true that everyone who is involved in the initiative begins with skepticism and resistance. The members of the team of stakeholders move from resistance to acceptance at varying rates. Some members of the team quickly accept the change. They "get onboard" and look forward to the positive outcomes. On the other hand, some others move from resistance to acceptance at a slower rate. Transformation initiative managers will note an increased incidence of positive behaviors or a decline in the incidence of negative behaviors as persons move from resistance to acceptance.

Figure 14.3 demonstrates this emergence from resistance to acceptance. It plots the tone of the behavior of the member over time. On the left vertical axis, the tone of behaviors is characterized as either negative or positive at the extremes. Tone is directly proportional to the incidence of positive behaviors and inversely proportional to the incidence of negative behaviors. The green line represents an organizational member who quickly accepts the initiative. Negative behaviors disappear and are replaced by positive ones at a rapid pace. The red line indicates an individual who is more devoted to the status quo at the expense of the transformation initiative. It should be noted that tone can be observed both in the individual and in the group as a whole.

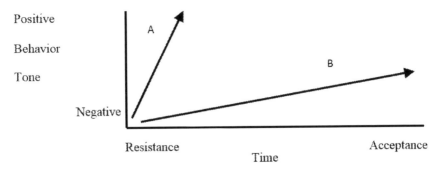

Figure 14.3.   A plot of the tone of the behaviors of individuals or groups involved with or impacted by the transformation initiative over time.

It is obvious that Figure 14.4 does not provide all of the answers. Specific leadership behaviors have not yet been established. Indeed, the suggestions given are intended to be general. The actual manifestation of leadership behaviors chosen by the leader, is a matter of his or her ability to employ enlightened leadership. The ability to choose wisely is what the leadership philosophers are referring to when they declare that leadership is an "art." Table 14.3 provides an amalgamation and amplification of the rationale for the aspiration of leadership behavior associated with the individual's Lewin stage and/or Kubler-Ross phase. However, even Table 14.3 cannot tell the leader exactly what to say or do. It assists only in answering the first of the two questions that the leader must have answers to in order to be truly effective.

At this point it might be useful to review the Leadership Big Ten with an eye toward choosing the skill which might be an appropriate behavior guide in specific Kubler-Ross phases. Check the skill and imagine its applicability in resolving the conflict, for example, in the "Shock and Denial" phase. Certainly numbers 1, 2, 7, 8, and 10 could be useful. Understand, though, that as stated previously, the choice of leadership approach is a matter of personal preference. Two different leaders might choose two different approaches and both could be completely effective.

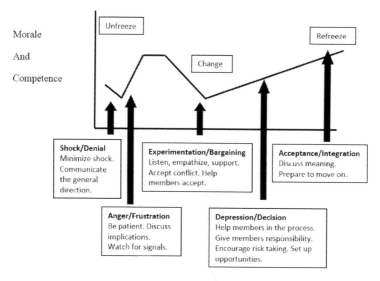

Figure 14.4. Suggestion of leadership behavior associated with the individual's Kubler-Ross Phase and corresponding Lewin Stage.

Table 14.3. An Association of the Higgs-Rowland Group, Kubler-Ross Phase, and Lewin Stage with Leadership Behavior

Lewin	Kubler-Ross	HR Group	Behavior
Unfreeze	Shock and Denial Anger and Frustration	1 & 2 1, 2, & 3	Minimize shock. Give full and early communication of intentions, possibilities and direction. Be patient. Discuss implications of change with individuals. Notice and pay attention to small signals. Listen and empathize. Help members weather the storm. Don't take resistance personally.
Change	Bargaining and experimentation	1 & 3	Help members to complete. Encourage members to take responsibility. Create goals. Encourage risk taking. Exchange feedback. Set up development opportunities.
	Depression and decision	3	Discuss meaning, overview, and reflection. Overview of experience.
Refreeze	Acceptance and integration.	3	Celebrate success.

Leadership Big Ten

1. Communication skills
2. Self confidence
3. Self awareness
4. Self analysis
5. Strategic thinking
6. Critical thinking
7. Empathy
8. Ability to motivate
9. Humility
10. Emotional intelligence

Challenge: Answering the Second Question

Here is the second question: What specific leadership behavior(s) should I use? The chapter has brought the reader nearly all of the way to the answer to the second question. But it is beyond the scope of the chapter to go all of the way. As has been said, the leadership approach and hence the specific leadership technique are a meter of personal choice. What is right for one leader might be wrong for another.

In the interest of not leaving the reader feeling as though he or she is only half way home, there is herein provided a set of guidelines. It may be helpful at this point to codify some of the present work in a set of rules. While these rules should not be assumed to be universally applicable, they are at least generally correct. The rules assist the reader in forming an understanding of the problem at hand. Thus informed the reader will be better able to approach the leadership challenge.

SOME RULES AND PARTING SHOTS

1. Process induced resistance (PIR) is defined as that opposition to progress in a transformation initiative which is created by known, accepted, and anticipated tasks or events that are part of the initiative. This resistance does not impede the initiative since it was planned for at the outset.
2. Member induced resistance (MIR) is defined as the unanticipated and undesirable action or inaction of the members of the organization which is undergoing the transformation or of stakeholder groups that are impacted by the transformation. This resistance serves to impede the initiative.

3. Anticipated management effort (AME) is that effort or work which is done to meet the needs of the process induced resistance (PIR).

4. Unanticipated management effort is that effort or work which must be applied to overcome member induced resistance (MIR)

5. PIR is relatively easy to quantify and predict. It is generally part of the implementation plan.

6. PIR is relatively fixed and hence management effort will have little effect in reducing PIR.

7. MIR is more difficult to quantify and predict than PIR.

8. MIR can be quite variable.

9. Total management effort (TME) is the sum of anticipated management effort (AME) and unanticipated management effort (UME).

10. Management effort is specifically expended to address PIR and overcome MIR.

11. Leadership effort is specifically expended to *reduce* MIR.

12. Reducing MIR is desirable in comparison to overcoming MIR.

13. The resistance phase of the individual or group can be generally determined by observing the incidence of negative and positive behaviors.

14. The resistance phase, once identified, can be a determinant in the choice of leadership skill application.

15. Choice of leadership technique is informed by application of rules 1 through 14. The specific leadership behaviors are up to the leader.

We are left with a minor dilemma. It appears that in spite of repeated encouragement from the academic community, the present trend in efforts to remake government does not include acquisition or development of leadership skills in the persons who are responsible for the transformation. While these skills certainly are present and certainly are applied, the phenomenon appears largely to be the result of happenstance rather than deliberate action. In order for meaningful government transformation to occur, good leaders must be an integral part of the organization. Such leaders can be included in the organization by recognizing the following three concepts:

1. There is an quasi-complete set of leadership skills.

2. These skills can be identified in persons who are employed by or who are seeking to be employed by the organization.

3. The skills can, for the most part be taught and once taught their employment can be encouraged.

Acknowledging that the skills can be taught, we must simultaneously admit that teaching of the actual behaviors cannot and should not be attempted. What is right for one leader may be wrong for another. What is right for one member may be wrong for another. What is right today may be wrong tomorrow. The key to successful leadership of government transformation efforts, admittedly an art—appears to be acknowledging that leadership is necessary. This may be guided by the leader's choice of a subset of the Leadership Big Ten skills as seem to be appropriate for him or her, for the members of the team and the situation they are facing.

NOTE

1. O*Net is a free online database that contains hundreds of occupational definitions to help students, job seekers, businesses and workforce development professionals to understand today's world of work in the United States. It was developed under the sponsorship of the US Department of Labor/Employment and Training Administration (USDOL/ETA) through a grant to the North Carolina Employment Security Commission (now part of the NC Commerce Department) during the 1990s.

REFERENCES

Appelbaum, S. H., Degbe, M. C., MacDonald, O., & Nguyen-Quang, T. (2015). Organizational outcomes of leadership style and resistance to change. *Industrial & Commercial Training, 47*(2), 73–80.

Arzberger, P., Schroeder, P., Beaulieu, A., Bowker, G., Casey, K., Laaksonen, L., Wouters, P. (2004). An international framework to promote access to data. *Science, 303*(5665), 1777–1778.

Baesu, C., & Bejinaru, R. (2013). Leadership approaches regarding the organizational change. *USV Annals of Economics & Public Administration, 13*(2), 146–152.

Begley, T. M. (1998). Coping strategies as predictors of employee distress and turnover after an organizational consolidation: A longitudinal analysis. *Journal of Occupational and Organizational Psychology, 71*(4), 305–330.

Bret, B, Gulliya, T., & Crispo, A. W. (2012). Emotional Intelligence. *Insights to a Changing World Journal, 1*, 52–64.

Deutsch, K. W. (1985). The systems theory approach as a basis for comparative research. *International Social Science Journal, 37*(103), 5–19.

Eager-Sirkis, J. (2011). Developing leadership in community college managers. *Community College Enterprise, 17*(2), 46–61.

Elrod, P. D., II, & Tippett, D. D. (2002). The death valley of change. *Journal of Organizational Change Management, 15*(3), 273–292.

Folta, S. C., Seguin, R. A., Ackerman, J., & Nelson, M. E. (2012). A qualitative study of leadership characteristics among women who catalyze positive community change. *Biomedical Central Public Health*, *12*(1), 383–394.

Forrester, J. (1971). Counterintuitive behavior of social systems. *Technology Review*, *73*(3), 52–68.

Greenwood, V., & Hoy, B. A. (2015). An examination of the intersection of leadership skills and management skills: Why some excellent managers are such poor leaders. *Proceedings of the Fourth Annual International Business Conference*. Saint Leo, FL.

Higgs, M., & Rowland, D. (2005). All changes great and small: Exploring approaches to change and its leadership. *Journal of Change Management*, *5*(2) 121–151.

Hulme, V. A. (2006). What makes a good leader? *China Business Review*, *33*(2), 24–25.

Jackson, D. V. (2011). Perception is reality. *Journal of Leadership Education*, *10*(1), 115–122.

Jackson, R. (2005). Achieving strategic change in government. *Public Manager*, *34*(1), 40–50.

Jannsen, M., Charalbidis, Y., & Zuiderwijk, A. (2012). Benefits, adoption barriers, and myths of open data and open government. *Information Systems Management*, *29*(4), 258–268.

Kocalevent, R., Mierke, A., Klapp, B. F. (2014). Adjustment disorders as a stress-related disorder: A longitudinal study of association among stress, resources, and mental health. *PLoS ONE*. *9*(5), 1–8.

Kotter, J. P., & Schlesinger, L. (1979). Choosing strategies for change. *Harvard Business Review*, *57*(2), 57–70.

Kubler-Ross, (1969). *On death and dying*. New York, NY: Touchstone.

Kuttner, R. (2011). Conflict specialists as leaders: Revisiting the role of the conflict specialist from a leadership perspective. *Conflict Resolution Quarterly*, *29*(2), 103–126.

Latham, J. R. (2013a). A framework for leading the transformation to performance excellence, Part I: Perspectives on forces, facilitators, and strategic leadership systems. *Quality Management Journal*, *20*(2), 12–33.

Latham, J. R. (2013b). A framework for leading the transformation to performance excellence, Part II: CEO perspectives of forces, facilitators, and strategic leadership systems. *Quality Management Journal*, *20*(3), 19–40.

Lemak, D. J., Henderson, P. W., & Wenger, M. S. (2004). A new look at organizational transformation using systems theory: An application to federal contractors. *Journal of Business and Management*, *9*(4), 407–423.

Lewin K. (1951). *Field theory in social science*. New York: Harper & Row.

Luthans, F. (2002). *Organizational behavior*. New York, NY: McGraw-Hill

O*Net Online. (2015). Skills search. Retrieved from https://www.onetonline.org/skills/

Osborne, D., & Plastrik, P. (2000). *The reinventor's fieldbook: Tools for transforming your government*. San Francisco, C: Jossey-Bass.

Pace, R. W., & Easter, P. (2005). Defining leadership skills. *Manager: British Journal of Administrative Management*, *49*, 18–19.

Pashke, G. F. (2004). Bring back the generalist. *Strategic Finance*, *86*(4), 33–36.

Pouvreau, D., & Drack, M. (2007). On the history of Ludvig von Bertalanffy's general systemology and its relationship to cybernetics. *International Journal of General Systems, 36*(3), 281–337.

Reardon, K. K., Reardon, K. J., & Rowe, A. J. (1998). Leadership styles for five stages of radical change inventory. *Acquisition Review Quarterly, 19*(2), 129–146.

Silva, J. L., & Navarro, V. L. (2012). Work organization and the health of bank employees. *Revista Latino-Americana de Enfermagem, 20*(2), 226–234.

Strauss, D. F. M. (2002). The scope and limitation of von Bertalanffy's systems theory. *South African Journal of Philosphy, 21*(3), 163–180.

Summerfield, M. R. (2014). Leadership: A simple definition. *American Journal of Health System Pharmacy, 71*, 251–253.

Surowiecki, J. (2004). *The wisdom of crowds: Why the many are smarter than the few and how collective wisdom shapes business economies, societies and nations.* New York, NY: Doubleday.

Weick, K. E., & Quinn, R. E. (1999). Organizational change and development. *Annual Review of Psychology, 50*(1), 361–386.

Zomorrodian, A. (2009). Transformation innovation or patchwork juxtaposition of public policy process and the role of leadership in a chaotic environment. *Theoretical & Applied Economics, 163*, 20.

ABOUT THE AUTHORS

Martinique "Marty" Alber is a test administration and assessment coordinator with the Personnel Board of Jefferson County in Birmingham, Alabama. She received her PhD in industrial and organizational psychology from Auburn University. Marty's experience and expertise lies in personnel selection, assessment, and psychometrics. She has served as a consultant for the State of Alabama, State of Mississippi, and DeKalb County, Georgia. Marty has presented research to multiple professional associations including the Society of Industrial Organizational Psychology and the International Personnel Assessment Council. She serves as a frequent guest lecturer to graduate programs in industrial/organization psychology in the area of assessment centers and employee selection.

Marcia A. Beck received her PhD in comparative politics from the University of Notre Dame and pursued field work in civil society development in the former Soviet Union and postcommunist Russia. She is the author of *Russia's Liberal Project: State-Society Relations in the Transition from Communism* (Pennsylvania State University Press, 2000) and co-author with James S. Bowman and Jonathan P. West of *Achieving Competencies in Public Service: The Professional Edge*, 2nd edition (M.E. Sharpe, 2010). Beck has contributed articles and reviews to the journals *Comparative Politics*, *The Review of Politics*, *The Russian Review*, and *Public Integrity*, among others. She has taught courses in comparative politics and international relations at Bowdoin College, the University of Notre Dame, and the University of Miami, where she most recently developed an online course on Organizational Dynamics and Management for the Masters of Public Administration program.

Sheri Bias, PhD, MBA, SPHR is an Assistant Professor of human resources administration at Saint Leo University and has been teaching at Saint Leo since 1997. Dr. Bias has worked for NASA, Anheuser Busch, Philip Morris, and Pricewaterhouse Coopers in various HR positions. In addition to her PhD, Dr. Bias possesses the credentials for senior professional in human resources (SPHR) and the Society for Human Resources—senior certified professional (SHRM-SCP). Her specialties include ERP implementations such as SAP and PeopleSoft, as well as integral pieces of the HR infrastructure such as strategic staffing, employee development, and total rewards. Dr. Bias's research interests include generations in the workplace and the implications on HR, as well as corporate social responsibility and HR.

James S. Bowman is professor of public administration at the Askew School of Public Administration and Policy, Florida State University. Noted for his work in ethics and human resource management, Dr. Bowman is author of over 100 journal articles and book chapters, as well as editor of 6 anthologies. Bowman is co-author of *Human Resource Management in Public Service: Paradoxes, Processes and Problems* (5th ed., 2016) and *Achieving Competencies in Public Service: The Professional Edge* (2nd ed., Sharpe, 2010). His most recent book with Jonathan P. West is *Public Service Ethics: Individual and Institutional Responsibilities* (Sage, 2015). He served for 17 years as editor-in-chief of *Public Integrity*. A past National Association of Public Affairs and Administration Fellow, as well as a Kellogg Foundation Fellow, he has experience in the military, civil service, and business.

Lisa Brantly, EdD, has been with Auburn University Outreach since 2002. Her focus is workforce development and entrepreneurship training. Previously she has worked as a software trainer in private industry and has taught public speaking and business communication since 1990. She currently works with the Global Leadership Initiative at Auburn University's Office of Professional and Continuing Education to provide supervisory skill training for automobile manufacturers in Alabama.

Mitchell Brown, PhD, is an associate professor in the Department of Political Science at Auburn University and is the director of their PhD program in Public Administration and Public Policy. Dr. Brown is the author of numerous books, research articles, and reports, including her two most recent, *Administering Elections: How American Elections Work* with Kathleen Hale and Robert Montjoy, and *Applied Research Methods in Public and Non-Profit Organizations*, also with Kathleen Hale.

Kathy Cabler, BSW, MPA, DSL '17 is an organization development consultant and senior facilitator with NASA *Langley Research Center, Hampton, VA.* In this role, Kathy serves as a strategic business partner and change agent, collaborating with senior leaders to plan and execute strategic initiatives in support of organization vision, mission, values, and goals. Kathy has partnered with management in local governments, professional services, academia, media and retail and has extensive experience with complex, matrix, and diverse environments. Additionally, Kathy is the founder and President of Cabler Consulting Group (CCG), a leadership development organization providing organization development consultation, change management and human capital learning & performance solutions. CCG helps leaders generate a professional environment—where people work together toward better solutions; where change is not only accepted, but encouraged; and where high performance is achieved by building trust, valuing teamwork and fostering employee development.

Kathleen Hale, JD, PhD, is MPA director and associate professor at Auburn University. Her research examines information exchanges in intergovernmental and cross-sectoral relationships. She is the author of *Applied Research Methods in Public and Nonprofit Organizations* (Wiley, 2104) and *How Information Matters: Networks and Public Policy Innovation* (Georgetown University Press, 2011), which was named Best Book by the Academy of Management Public and Nonprofit Section (2012). She has been recognized for teaching by the American Political Science Association and with Auburn's Award for Excellence in Community and Civic Engagement. She was named an Auburn Engaged Scholar from 2012–2015 for her research with community organizations and national professional associations. Her most recent book is *Administering Elections: How American Elections Work* (Palgrave, 2015). Kathleen was Chair of NASPAA's nonprofit section from 2013–2015, and served on the Section Executive Council from 2010–2015. She is also a former member of ARNOVA's Teaching Section Board.

Julia B. Heflin has worked with Auburn University's Center for Governmental Services (CGS) since November 1999. She has served as the training program manager for 13 years. As manager of the training unit for CGS and with the assistance of a staff of 5, she has oversight of approximately 60 to 100 training projects per fiscal year; development of new programs and projects yearly; and the maintenance of curriculum, processes for certification records, marketing, accounts receivables and accounts payables. She has a master's of education in adult education and a bachelor's degree in public relations, both from Auburn University. In her current position, she serves on several advisory boards and works with many state agencies and associations to develop, plan, organize and maintain education programs throughout the State of Alabama.

Stacey Lange is an industrial organizational psychologist with the Personnel Board of Jefferson County in Birmingham, Alabama. She received her PhD in industrial and organizational psychology from Central Michigan University. Stacey's experience and expertise is primarily in job analysis, personnel selection, and assessment. She also has extensive experience in training, personality testing and survey development. She has served as a consultant for the Human Resources Research Organization (HumRRO) and has assisted on committees for the Society of Industrial Organizational Psychology. Stacey has presented research to multiple professional associations including the Society of Industrial Organizational Psychology, the International Personnel Assessment Council, and the National Collegiate Honors Council.

Julie Prendergast Magee was appointed Alabama Revenue Commissioner by Gov. Robert Bentley in January 2011. During her tenure as commissioner, Magee has had the distinction of serving in leadership roles in the Federation of Tax Administrators, the Multistate Tax Commission, and the Southeastern Association of Tax Administrators. Magee's service to taxpayers and the business community also includes her work with several significant commissions, task forces, and advisory councils, and she provided expert testimony to the U.S. House Judiciary Committee's Subcommittee on Regulatory Reform, Commercial and Antitrust Law in June 2015. She is also an active participant on the Authentication and the Financial Services workgroups that were formed at the IRS Security Summit, working with the IRS and industry partners to prevent ID theft and tax fraud. Prior to her appointment, Magee was vice president of the Mobile-based InsTrust Insurance Group. Her 20-year career in the business community focused largely on competitive sales and market expansion in the insurance industry. Magee received her bachelor of arts from the University of South Alabama.

William (Billy) Mea has worked at the Office of Management and Budget since 2006. He earned a PhD at Auburn University, specializing in clinical and industrial-organizational psychology. Billy retired from the Navy reserve in 2015. He recently attended the Dwight D. Eisenhower School at National Defense University where he focused on China strategy.

Roger Scott McCullough, BA, MA, has over 30 years of management experience in public, private, and government sector industries. Mr. McCullough is retired from the University of Alabama in Birmingham where he served in a number of roles, including assistant vice president for human resource management. He joined the Personnel Board of Jefferson County, Alabama, as an HR consultant in 2002 and as manager of information and technology services in 2004. He currently serves as director of Cooper Green *Mercy* Health Services, a multispecialty ambulatory facility that provides comprehensive healthcare to indigent residents of Jefferson County.

Donna L. Phillips, MA, is currently the talent development officer at NASA Langley Research Center in Hampton, VA. She has 33 years of federal government experience with more than 20 of those years in learning and development. Ms. Phillips holds a bachelor of science degree in business administration with an emphasis in management from Christopher Newport University and a master of arts degree in education and human development from George Washington University. She also possesses a leadership coaching certification from Georgetown University and an organization development certificate at the National Training Laboratory (NTL) Institute. In her role Ms. Phillips provides expert knowledge to Langley leaders on human capital management issues with regard to training, development, academic programs, organization development, and leadership coaching. She assists management in identifying the developmental needs of Langley Research Center and designs and develops programs such as leadership development, technician apprenticeship, distance learning, project management, workforce retraining, creativity and innovation and leadership coaching to address them. Some of her most recent achievements include: reestablishing the organization development services at NASA Langley Research Center; developing and implementing an on-boarding orientation program for new employees; envisioning an outside-the-box mentoring program and supporting its successful implementation. In addition as an internal coach for NASA, Ms. Phillips works with early career professionals to transform themselves into perceptive leaders.

William I. Sauser, Jr., PhD, is professor emeritus of management in the Harbert College of Business at Auburn University. Dr. Sauser earned his BS in management and MS and PhD in industrial/organizational psychology at the Georgia Institute of Technology and an MA in business ethics from the University of Wales. He is licensed to practice psychology in Alabama and holds two specialty diplomas from the American Board of Professional Psychology. Dr. Sauser's interests include organizational development and change, strategic planning, human relations in the workplace, business ethics, and continuing professional education. He is a frequent consultant to public, private, and voluntary-sector organizations and has been awarded the 2003 Frederick W. Taylor Key by the Society for Advancement of Management, the 2012 Harbert College of Business Excellence in Outreach Award, and the 2013 External Consulting Award and 2014 Algernon Sydney Sullivan Award by Auburn University. He also received Auburn Author Awards in 2012, 2014, and 2015.

Ronald R. Sims is the Floyd Dewey Gottwald Senior Professor in the Raymond A. Mason School of Business at the College of William and Mary where he teaches leadership and change management and human resources management in the executive, residential and flex-masters in business administration programs, and organizational transformation/change management, organizational behavior and business ethics in the BBA program. He received his PhD in organizational behavior from Case Western Reserve University. His research focuses on a variety of topics to include leadership and change management, HRM, business ethics, employee training, and management and leadership development (i.e., human resource development), learning styles, and experiential learning. Dr. Sims is the author or co-author of 34 books, 74 chapters and more than 80 articles that have appeared in a wide variety of scholarly and practitioner journals.

Don-Terry Veal is the chief of staff for the president at Morgan State University. Previously he served as director of the Center for Governmental Services at Auburn University. Veal earned a bachelor's from Southern University at New Orleans, a master's from The University of Mississippi and a doctorate from Northern Illinois University.

Dr. John G. Veres III became the first alumnus appointed chancellor of Auburn University at Montgomery in 2006. A Montgomery native, he graduated from Montgomery Catholic High School in 1972 and earned bachelor's and master's degrees in psychology from AUM in 1976 and 1978, respectively. He was awarded a PhD in industrial/organizational psychology from Auburn University in 1983. First hired by AUM in 1976 as a Research and Training Assistant, Veres was promoted over the next 37 years to positions of increasing responsibility, including director of the AUM Center for Business and Economic Development (October 1982–March 2000) and executive director of University Outreach (March 2000–June 2006) until the Auburn University Board of Trustees named him Chancellor. Veres has more than 35 years of experience as an organizational consultant. He has published some 50 articles and book chapters, two edited volumes and one book on human resources management topics. He has consulted in over 80 employment discrimination lawsuits, primarily on issues of adverse impact and test validation, and currently serves as special master for the United

States District Court for the Northern District of Alabama. In the community, Veres currently serves on the boards of the Alabama-Korea Education and Economic Partnership, Alabama World Affairs Council, AUM Confucius Institute, Auburn University Foundation, Committee of 100, Helicity, and the Montgomery Area Chamber of Commerce. Veres also serves on the Air Education and Training Command Commander's civilian advisory group. He has served on the boards of the Alabama Technology Foundation, Catholic Housing Authority of Montgomery, Montgomery Area YMCA, and the River Region United Way. He was appointed to the Alabama Governor's College and Career Ready Task Force and the Governor's Commission for Action in Alabama's Black Belt, and served as a technical advisor to the Alabama Commission on Government Accountability. He is a recipient of the H. Roe Bartle Presidential Leadership Award from the Nonprofit Leadership Alliance. Veres and his wife of 37 years, Beth Sullivan Veres, have three children—Erin, Johnny and Olivia—and two grandchildren, Cole and Lena.

Jonathan P. West is professor and chair of political science and director of the MPA program at the University of Miami. His research interests include human resource management, productivity, local government, and ethics. Professor West has published nine books and over 100 articles and book chapters. His most recent books are *Human Resource Management in Public Service* (5th ed., Sage, 2016) with Berman, Bowman, and Van Wart and *Public Service Ethics: Individual and Institutional Responsibilities* (CQ Press, 2015) with Bowman. Other recent books are co-edited with Bowman, *American Public Service: Radical Reform and the Merit System* (Taylor & Francis, 2007) and with Bowman and Beck, *Achieving Competencies in Public Service: The Professional Edge* (2nd ed., Sharpe, 2010). He also co-edited, *The Ethics Edge* (2nd ed., ICMA, 2006) with Berman. His forthcoming co-authored book with Daynes and Sussman, *American Politics and the Environment*, is scheduled for publication by SUNY Press (2nd ed., 2016). He was managing editor of *Public Integrity* for 16 years. He taught previously at the University of Houston and University of Arizona and served as a management analyst in the U.S. Surgeon General's Office, Department of the Army, Washington, D.C.

William J. Woska has been a faculty member at several colleges and universities including the University of California, Berkeley, Saint Mary's College, Moraga, Golden Gate University, San Francisco, and San Diego State University. He is presently on the faculty at Cabrillo College in Aptos, California. He has more than 30 years of experience representing employers in employment and labor law matters. His research interests include labor and employment law, human resource management, and issues addressing local government. His research has been published in a number of publications including *Public Personnel Management, Police Chief, Labor Law Journal, Public Administration Review, Lincoln Law Review, Labor Relations News, HR News, Public Personnel Review,* and *Legal and Regulatory Issues in Human Resources Management.* He is a member of the labor and employment law section of The State Bar of California.

INDEX

Printed in the United States
By Bookmasters